The Believer's Guidebook

LARRY RICHARDS

ZONDERVAN PUBLISHING HOUSE
OF THE ZONDERVAN CORPORATION
GRAND RAPIDS, MICHIGAN 49506

THE BELIEVER'S GUIDEBOOK: The Christian Life From Aspirin to Zoos
Copyright © 1983 by The Zondervan Corporation
Grand Rapids, Michigan

Library of Congress Cataloging in Publication Data

Richards, Larry, 1931-
    The believer's guidebook.
    1. Christian life—Dictionaries.   I. Title.
BV4501.2.R5118   1983   248.4'03'21   83-3482
ISBN 0-310-43470-X

Designed by Louise Bauer
Edited by Edward Viening

Printed in the United States of America

83   84   85   86   87   88 89   /   10   9   8   7   6   5   4   3   2   1

Preface

Puzzling our way in a world cluttered with conflicting opinions on just about everything isn't easy. Even words are sometimes twisted in our society, so that their meaning is hidden rather than unveiled. Just how to look at words, and the issues of life they deal with, is important if life is to be in focus.

In dealing with life, Christians have a great advantage. We have the Word of God and the Holy Spirit within each of us to point the way we should go. We need not be blinded by the bright illusions that captivate the lost.

Even so, making our way through life safely doesn't happen automatically. A Christian also needs to sort out the distortions in the notions or ideas awash around him. Christians need to make sure that what they *think* is a biblical viewpoint really does reflect the teachings of God's Word. Because we Christians need both information and a biblical orientation to the issues of our lives, this *Believer's Guidebook* can help. Oh, you won't find the kind of advice here that's given by the people who are sure they know just what everyone else ought to do. You will find information, and insights from Scripture, that will help you think and pray your way through to a personal understanding of what God wants you to do.

All sorts of topics are covered in the *Guidebook*. Some are serious, and some aren't. After all, abortion and aging and adoption and even boredom are things that make a serious difference in life. We want some serious help to think through these issues. But baldness and beastly behavior touch us a little more lightly. So the *Guidebook* touches on them a little more lightly too.

Actually, Christian faith brings a fresh and different perspective to everything in life; to the little things as well as to the big ones. So relax and enjoy browsing through the *Guidebook's* light articles. Or, when you do have a problem, find that problem cataloged here, and gain information and a biblical perspective that will help you through.

ABANDONED. The dictionary tells us that abandoned means "utterly forsaken; left finally and completely alone." What a contrast to the total faithfulness of God. The psalmist was sure that "though my father and mother forsake me, the LORD will receive me" (Ps. 27:10). He knew God as a faithful person. Because he realized how totally committed God is to His loved ones, the psalmist wrote words that still comfort you and me today. "I am still confident of this: I will see the goodness of the LORD in the land of the living. Wait for the LORD; be strong and take heart and wait for the LORD" (Ps. 27:13–14).

ABNORMAL. What do we mean when we say someone isn't normal? The word abnormal means "not average or typical." It means "deviating from a standard."

Modern psychology and the biblical languages recognize an abnormality that involves a distressed or diseased mental condition. While most people in Jesus' day drew back helplessly from such sickness, Christ reached out with His healing touch. → MENTAL ILLNESS

But the New Testament also recognizes the tyranny of the normal; of pressure placed on individuals because they do not conform. This pressure isn't experienced only by exceptional individuals, like the Old Testament prophets or the apostle Paul. Peter writes of the pagan world's reaction to the early Christians, who in a most abnormal way settled down to quiet lives of doing good. The standard these believers adopted was contradictory to the standard of the world: a believer would "not live the rest of his earthly life for evil human desires, but rather for the will of God." Peter goes on. "They think it strange that you do not plunge with them into the same flood of dissipation, and they heap abuse on you" (see 1 Peter 4:1–6).

Relying on the tyranny of the normal, the world around us keeps pushing to squeeze Christians into its mold. But for us there is God's call to an abnormal life. That life is marked out in Peter's words: "be clear minded and self-controlled so that you can pray . . . love each other deeply. . . . offer hospitality to one another without grumbling. Each one should use whatever gift he has received to serve others . . . doing it with the strength God provides, so that in all things God may be praised through Jesus Christ'' (1 Peter 4:7–11).

When we as members of Jesus' special community commit ourselves to the abnormality of selfless love, we experience that peculiar and wonderful thing—the normal Christian life.

ABORTION. "But I just *can't* be having a baby!" Sometimes this anguished cry is a reaction to inconvenience. A baby would spoil a vacation, or a baby simply wouldn't fit into a couple's plans for at least two years. Sometimes the reaction is panic, as when a teen-ager discovers the high price of relaxed standards. At times the cry represents tragedy, the outcome of forcible rape. Increasingly today, this cry is a prelude to abortion, the voluntary termination of a pregnancy. In 1979 some 1.2 million fetuses were aborted, about one for every three live births in the United States. For anyone in our society faced today with the inconvenience or the tragedy of an unwanted pregnancy, abortion is an open option.

To those who identify themselves as "pro choice," abortion is a woman's right; a matter of freedom to do what she chooses with her own body. To those who identify themselves as "pro life," abortion is murder; the killing of an unborn child. Both the legal and moral issues hinge on our definition of the fetus. Is a fetus a person, or merely tissue that later will become a person?

Legally. At this writing an unborn child is not recognized as a true human being, and thus is not given the protection of law. In January of 1973 the Supreme Court established guidelines for state abortion laws that clearly withhold this recognition. The court's ruling insists that states leave abortion decisions during the first three months of pregnancy up to the woman and her physician. During the second three months the state may determine qualifications for those doing abortions, but may not enact laws that make abortion illegal. During the last two or three months of pregnancy, state laws may forbid an abortion, unless it is necessary for the mother, to "preserve her health or life." Since this court decision, millions of legal abortions have been performed in the United States with more than 1.4 million of them paid for by federal tax money. As of 1981, however, the legislature of forty states had acted to prevent the use of tax money to pay for abortions.

Currently a strong effort is being mounted by pro-life groups to extend the protection of the Constitution to the unborn by winning legal recognition of the fetus as a person. These groups point out that an 1857 Supreme Court decision (Dred Scott) ruled that blacks were not legal persons under the Constitution. This discrimination was corrected after the Civil War by the Thirteenth and Fourteenth Amendments, which extended legal and constitutional protection to all living human beings. Pro-life groups now argue that further definition is needed in order to include an unborn child in the category of "living human beings."

Medically. At this point the issue shifts from the legal to the medical arena. Is a fetus really tissue of the woman's body, over which she has unquestioned rights? Or is the fetus a separate, distinct individual? When does a fetus become a distinct individual? At quickening (about the 26th week)? At birth?

Medically speaking there is no doubt that the argument "a woman has the right to do what she wants with her own body" is an outright distortion. Each cell in our body bears the distinctive genetic stamp, the pattern of our personal genes and chromosomes. Whether a living cell is taken from our tongue or toe, our skin or an internal organ, that cell bears the stamp of our identity. A fetus, from conception, carries its own genetic code, distinct and different from its mother's. Whatever a fetus may be, it is *not* a part of the woman's "own body."

Joseph Fletcher, the Protestant minister recognized as the father of "situation ethics," argues that even so a fetus "is not a moral or personal being, since it lacks freedom, self-determination, rationality, ability to choose either means or ends, and knowledge of its circumstances.'' Accepting this argument, pro-choice advocates insist that while a fetus has the potential to *become* a human being, the unborn are not yet persons in a meaningful sense. Thus abortion is a morally neutral act, not a killing.

The problem with Fletcher's definition is that it is far too broad. After all, a two-month child also lacks freedom, rationality, self-determination, ability to choose either means or ends, and knowledge of its circumstances. Yet babies are considered persons the day they are born.

The fact is that human life involves a continuous process; a stream flowing unbroken from conception on through many stages of development until death. In that process each human being goes through many changes in form. But the process is unbroken: the adult is just as present in the fetus as he or she is in the child. And there is no clear medical point at which one ''becomes'' a person, unless we accept conception—the beginning of the process—as that point. Medically speaking, the individual is distinctively himself or herself, a separate entity, from conception until death.

Biblically. The Christian is particularly concerned about biblical evidence for a position on abortion. So what does the Bible teach?

The biblical evidence is difficult to develop, for Scripture does not speak plainly on the issue. We do know that abortion was known in the ancient world. In fact, Assyrian law (1450–1250 B.C.) prescribed death by torture for abortion, but no parallel law is found in the Mosaic Code.

What we do find in the Old Testament is a constant affirmation that conception is a direct gift from God (cf. Gen. 4:1; 16:2; 17:19; 29:31; 30:22; Ruth 4:13). This is important, in that not every act of sexual intercourse issues in conception. God is viewed in the Bible as directly supervising the creative act.

It is also significant that while Arab and Greek peoples practiced exposure of newborn infants (cf. Ezek.

16:5), the Old Testament protects young children (cf. Lev. 18:21; 20:2). The practice of exposure in the ancient world is parallel to abortion today, for each practice seeks to control unwanted pregnancies. In many ancient cultures a newborn was not recognized as a person until it was acknowledged by its father. Unwanted children, especially girls, were simply placed outdoors in some garbage heap and left to die. Because the infants were not viewed as persons in that culture, no evil was thought to have been committed.

There is one Old Testament passage, however, that deals directly with the life of the fetus. This passage is Exodus 21:22–23 and reads:

> If men who are fighting hit a pregnant woman and she gives birth prematurely but there is no serious injury, the offender must be fined whatever the woman's husband demands and the court allows. But if there is serious injury, you are to take life for life. . . .

Long before the modern abortion debate, the great Hebrew scholars C. F. Keil and Franz Delitzsch explained this passage. "If men strove and thrust against a woman with child, who had come near or between them for the purpose of making peace, so that her children come out into the world, and no injury was done either to the woman or to the child that was born, a pecuniary compensation was to be paid. A fine is imposed, because even if no injury had been done to the woman or the fruit of her womb, such a blow might have endangered life." The fact that the life for a life principle of Old Testament law is applied here to both the woman and unborn child indicates that, biblically, the fetus is considered to be a true human person.

Another passage often cited in support of this view is Psalm 51:5, which reads "from the time my mother conceived me." The point is made that from conception the psalmist identifies the fetus as "me"—not "it."

Conclusions. Today abortions are readily available, and are socially acceptable. In our society Christians are likely to be called on to answer three specific questions.

(1) What about an abortion for me? This question can only be answered by facing squarely the central issue: "Is my unborn child a person, with a God-given life of his or her own?" If your answer to this question is yes, then abortion for convenience is clearly wrong. Only in those infrequent cases where a real and imminent threat to the mother's life exists will serious and prayerful consideration be given to the possibility of an abortion.

(2) What should my attitude be toward those who are considering abortion? This is a particularly difficult question for many to deal with. We live in a pluralistic society; one in which a fetus is not legally a person. In this society many may honestly believe a fetus is not an "unborn child." In addition, many who consider abortion are under great pressures and suffer real inner anguish. In such a society Christians can seek to persuade others of what they believe is a biblical view. But we must also freely give the supportive love and understanding others need so desperately in times of stress.

But Christians cannot demand. Ultimately, each individual must take responsibility for his or her own actions, and one day each will give account to the Lord.

When you relate to others struggling with the question of abortion you can pray, give loving emotional support, and seek to persuade by sharing in love medical and biblical evidence.

(3) What should I do about national public policy? Today the legal and constitutional issues have been drawn and two groups formed to influence public policy. One group sees the "right to life" drive for constitutional protection for the unborn as an attempt to force their morality on an unwilling minority. The other group insists that the drive is not to legislate morality, but to extend the protection of law to the unborn, who are today murdered by the millions.

In our free society, each individual has both the right and the obligation to influence the making of laws on those issues he or she believes are important. Christians who are concerned, and who sense a moral obligation to take a stand on one side or the other, can participate in the efforts of the Right to Life or Pro-Choice committees now organized in every state and in many localities.

ABSENCE
ABSENTMINDED
ABSOLUTES

ABSENCE. For years, every time I got on a plane to take another of my all-too-frequent trips, I felt an aching emptiness. Absence from home was something more than that "state of being away" the dictionary dispassionately describes. Absence was a state of hurt: a compound of fear and helplessness mixed with anxiety. I wouldn't be at home to help if anything went wrong. Worse, absence seemed a taste of what might be if something terrible happened to my wife or children.

What helps the hurt of absence? Paul wrote to brothers and sisters he missed, "though I am absent from you in body, I am present with you in spirit and delight to see how orderly you are and how firm your faith in Christ is" (Col. 2:5). When I was away from the family I would call home every night (running up terrible phone bills) to experience the apostle's delight. Most importantly, I reminded myself that however far I might be from my loved ones, God was always present. "God is our refuge and strength," the psalmist affirms, "an ever present help in trouble" (Ps. 46:1). The best prescription for absence may well be remembrance of God's presence (cf. Ps. 139).

ABSENTMINDED. Now, what was I going to put in here?

ABSOLUTES. People today are wary of absolutes. We all know how complex our world is: how many different beliefs and values compete for allegiance. To even suggest that absolutes exist in such a world wins ridicule from the wise. Why, people are so absolutely sure everything is relative they're even willing to admit that Christian faith might be "true" for you, though not of course for everyone.

We needn't surrender absolutes so easily. One meaning of absolute is "a thing which must be viewed independently, not comparatively." Christianity can't be evaluated as just another of mankind's religious inventions. Christian faith is rooted in revelation. The God behind the visible universe stepped through the veil, and has shown us Himself. He has boldly spoken out in Scripture and in His Son. His revelation is absolute in the sense of its independence: none of it depends on our imagination.

Another aspect of absolute is "freedom from restriction or limitation." Scripture points up one terrible limitation on everything in the material universe: "What is seen is temporary" (2 Cor. 4:18). The one certain thing in this world is uncertainty. We ourselves, and all around us, are trapped by onrushing time, carried along in a flood of change. In this shifting, aging universe, the Bible tells of an unseen that is solid and eternal.

Actually, the notion of absolutes is basic to our faith. We believe God has spoken, and has revealed unshakable truths. We believe that beyond this world of flux lies an unshakable reality. We know that a day is coming for the "removal of what can be shaken—that is, created things—so that what cannot be shaken may remain" (Heb. 12:27). Measuring the fleeting against the changeless, we conclude with Paul that our "light and momentary troubles are achieving for us an eternal glory that far outweighs them all" (2 Cor. 4:17).

With a faith like ours, we're not easily enticed to try building our lives on the drifting sands of the ever-changing opinions of society.

ABSOLUTION. Mark this one religious, not biblical. "Absolution" is somewhat similar to forgiveness, but it implies release from the consequences of wrongdoing.

We should always be eager to forgive. But not necessarily quick to absolve. We forgive a teen who wrecks a car by driving too fast, but it's probably a good thing that his broken leg will spend months in a cast. The consequences of his actions will help him be more careful in the future.

Sometimes parents try to insulate their children from the consequences of their actions. Usually that's a mistake. Don't give your son cookies when he misses a meal. Don't pay for a window he broke: have him use his own money or work off the debt. Absolution as a release from consequences seldom helps anyone grow up.

ABUNDANT LIFE. The new barns were built, grander than the old, and were filled with riches. The wealthy farmer settled down at last, looking forward to an easy life of abundance. But that night, according to Luke's report of Jesus' story, God called the rich man a fool, for his life on earth was ended (Luke 12:16–21).

What do people today look to when asked to envision an abundant life? Asked to imagine the most important things in life as percentages of a pie, respondents to one poll ranked life's important elements this way: love relationships won 30% of the pie, work 19%, money 15%, parenthood 14%, social life 13%, fun 9%, and religion 8%. Deep down, most agreed with Jesus' observation: "a man's life does not consist in the abundance of his possessions" (Luke 12:15).

But it's one thing to agree on life's good things, and another to agree on the nature of an "abundant life." That phrase is taken from John 10:10, "I have come that they may have life, and have it to the full." A life that can be lived to the full is uniquely offered to us in Jesus Christ.

This is because Jesus brings us a new life: a life that links us with God. The New Testament explains. "You have been born again, not of perishable seed, but of imperishable" (1 Peter 1:23). One modern paraphrase explains by saying we have been given God's own indestructible heredity.

The new life within us must grow, blossoming into that character of love and peace, of patience and joy, of kindness and faithfulness and simple goodness that are the unmistakable mark of God within us (Gal. 5:22, 23). For you and me, "abundant life" isn't to be measured by what we have, but by what we are becoming. The abundant life, which brings us fulfillment, is a life lived in intimate relationship with the Lord, through which we reach our full potential as His own children.

As long as attaining Jesus' likeness is our goal, we can never fall into the trap of the rich fool, who tried to measure the meaning of life by counting up his possessions.

ACCEPTANCE. There's really only one issue here. It's not, "Who needs to be accepted by others?" We all do. The question that counts is, "What is the price of acceptance?"

The question is overwhelmingly important during the teen years, when self-concept is fragile and self-doubts surge. Then teens try to find a group of others they can identify with; a group to which they can belong. No wonder it's so important to wear what the other kids wear, to like the same music, and to do whatever others do. By acting like the others in their group teens win acceptance and feel that they belong.

It's the same with most adults. We dress the same for work. When asked out to dinner the first question is, "What should we wear?" Underneath the obvious patterns of dress are more subtle rules. To fit in one crowd you need to play tennis and belong to the club; to belong to another you need to become involved in a common cause.

In every human society there's a price to pay for acceptance: conformity. Conformity in dress, or activities, or values and lifestyle. If we're like others, we'll be accepted by them, and will finally feel that we too belong.

Christians have also adopted this system and have set up their own standards for belonging. We too put a price tag on acceptance. For some the price tag is doctrinal: to be accepted you must believe in an inerrant Bible, or Jesus' return before the millennium. There can be other price tags too. You mustn't smoke or drink. You must meet in church, or you must meet in home Bible studies. You must be a political conservative, or a liberal: be for or against the moral majority. You must take a strong stand on abortion. If you fail the test you may be tolerated, but you won't be accepted. In subtle ways you'll be informed that you don't really belong. We may not advertise our prices, but they are there, and people read them.

Biblically. When we understand acceptance as something that the world offers in return for conformity, we can understand how jolting the Bible's teaching is. Paul writes extensively on acceptance in Romans (14:1–15:7), and begins his instruction with these words: "Accept him whose faith is weak, without passing judgment on disputable matters" (14:1).

The passage goes on to explain. As in Christian communities today, believers in Paul's day had begun to put the price tag of conformity on belonging. One group accepted only vegetarian Christians. Another accepted only those Christians who agreed with them on which day of the week is most sacred. A person would be truly accepted only if he believed in Jesus *and* conformed to the splinter group's distinctives.

But Paul speaks out boldly for the freedom of the Christian. He reminds the Romans that each individual belongs to the Lord now, and that "Christ died and returned to life so that he might be the Lord of both the dead and the living" (14:9). We are not then to judge or look down on our brothers, for Jesus alone is qualified to pass judgment (14:10–12). Released from our self-imposed responsibility to live others' lives, we are free simply to love them. Paul puts it this way: since God has accepted our fellow Christian, who are we to set up additional tests for fellowship (14:3, 4)?

This is a wonderful freedom that we have in Christ. In the world, human beings may fearfully insist on setting up tests others must meet. In Christ, we can open our hearts to others warmly, welcoming even those whose faith is weak. Paul concludes his explanation with these wonderful words: "Accept one another, then, just as Christ accepted you, in order to bring praise to God" (15:7).

How did Jesus accept you and me? He welcomed us in our imperfection. He welcomed us in our ignorance. He welcomed us while old habits and practices still clung to us like the linen wrappings of the grave clung to a raised Lazarus (John 11:44). Jesus welcomed us to a transforming experience of love, confident that the power of God's forgiveness would cleanse and purify us.

17

It is the privilege of Christians to reach out, with this same loving welcome, to everyone who confesses Jesus as Savior.

Accepting others doesn't mean that we must agree with all they believe just now. It doesn't mean we approve of all they do. In the world, acceptance means there must be conformity. In Christ, acceptance means that, in the company of Jesus' people, there is welcome and warmth and a love that tells brothers and sisters that, at last, they have found the people to whom they belong.

ACCIDENTS. Some accidents are just irritating, like catsup splattering a clean shirt. But accidents aren't funny. In home accidents 40,000 people are killed and 6,250,000 are injured annually, and we all know the tragic toll taken by automobile accidents. What we may not know is that in one study of auto accidents, 84% were judged to have psychological causes. The driver was either tired, or upset, or angry, or feeling guilty.

Some people are accident prone: they seem to attract accidents. In fact, anyone who has had two auto accidents is four times more likely to have a third than a person with one accident. And one in every five who has had three accidents will have a fourth.

How can we avoid accidents? If we're accident prone, the best way is to stop driving and stay away from dangerous places. For most of us, the most important thing is to avoid driving or dangerous activities when we're under emotional stress. Hostility, worry, grief, or guilt can be hazardous to your health! Realizing that inner turmoil causes accidents, there may be more than one application of the affirmation that Christ can "cleanse our consciences from acts that lead to death, so we may serve the living God" (Heb. 9:14).

ACCOUNTABILITY. We hear a lot about accountability these days. We want the government to be accountable and to stop wasting our money. We want schools to be accountable and to really educate our children. In our drive for accountability we try to fix responsibility: we want to clearly define "Here is what is to be done," and we want to measure how each individual performs. But what about accountability in the Christian life?

Browsing through the Bible we're struck by the fact that giving account is between God and the individual, and is delayed. God does not encourage us to run hurriedly about, setting up standards by which to measure each other. Paul even dismissed one irrelevant little self-constituted jury of critical Corinthians: "I care very little if I am judged by you or any human court." He went on, "I do not even judge myself. My conscience is clear, but that does not make me innocent. It is the Lord who judges me. Therefore judge nothing before the appointed time; wait till the Lord comes" (1 Cor. 4:3–5). When we give account it will be to God (Rom. 14:12; Heb. 4:13), so that accounting will have to wait for Jesus to personally appear.

This notion of delayed accountability bothers many people. For non-Christians who scoff, the Bible makes it clear that delay on God's part is no evidence of weakness. Instead, delay is a demonstration of His kindness and patience and His eagerness for the lost to respond to grace. But the Book of Romans warns, "Because of your stubbornness and unrepentant heart, you are storing up wrath against yourself for the day of God's wrath, when his righteous judgment will be revealed" (Rom. 2:5, 6). Even for Christians, the passages that deal with accountability are tinged with somberness, to remind us that giving account to God is a serious thing.

But underneath it all, the Bible sings with the message that the fact that we are accountable means that our life is important after all. The fact that God watches and waits is solid evidence that your life and mine has a significance of which we may have lost sight. But the real bubbling up of joy comes when we realize *what* is important: just what we are to give account of.

We make that discovery in some of Jesus' last words to His disciples before the crucifixion, when He talked about the unnumbered years that would stretch out from His resurrection to His return. In Matthew 24–25 we read four stories about that time. Three of the stories are for Jesus' followers, and one for the rest of mankind. The three for us include a story about servants, another about attendants waiting for a bridegroom, and a third about employees with investments to make for an absent master. Each story has a common element. We are to watch, for when our Master returns unexpectedly, we will be held accountable. In addition, each story spells out one of the standards by which we will be judged.

The first story emphasizes relationships between servants in the household of the absent Lord (Matt. 24:42–51). We are to love and care for, not mistreat, one another. The second story emphasizes faithfulness (Matt. 25:1–13). We are to prepare to wait as long as necessary for Jesus to return. The third story emphasizes ministering (Matt. 25:14–30). We are to use whatever gifts God has given us in His service.

How exciting to read these stories and to realize that each of us can easily meet God's clear standards. They require no special training, no great wealth or intellect. You can love your brothers and sisters in Christ. You can remain faithful. You can use whatever gifts you have in Christ's service. God asks no more from us than we have to give.

In the deepest sense, the Bible's teaching on accountability is rich in promise, and is no threat at all. We're shown clearly what is important to God and how we can please Him. What we are accountable for is this: the simplicity of our love, the quiet faithfulness of our waiting, the humble use of our talents in His service. No wonder Paul says confidently, "Wait till the Lord comes." He then goes on to give us this wonderful promise. "He will bring to light what is hidden in darkness and will expose the motives of men's hearts. At that time each will receive his praise from God" (1 Cor. 4:5).

ACCUSATIONS. The fact that Satan is called an "accuser of our brothers" (Rev. 12:10) alerts us. We're sure of this when we realize that Paul describes the natural mind as busily at work, conjuring up accusations and excuses (Rom. 2:15). Both Testaments warn against false accusations (Ps. 35:20; Hos. 4:4; Luke 3:14; 2 Peter 2:11). But they say even more. "One witness is not enough to convict a man accused of any crime or offense he may have committed. A matter must be established by the testimony of two or three witnesses" (Deut. 19:15). The New Testament follows the same principle in a passage on leaders. "Do not entertain an accusation against an elder unless it is brought by two or three witnesses" (1 Tim. 5:19). So if we hear entertaining gossip about a brother or sister, and we do not personally *know* whether it is true, we must never repeat it. After all, Satan makes enough trouble without us to help.

ACHIEVEMENT.   Psychologists have come to believe that achievement is a basic motivation in human beings. We have a drive to accomplish by the exercise of our own ability and efforts. Some dislike this notion. It seems to them to smack of self-effort; something they identify as a basic sin. But God seems to approve of achievement. The Bible even suggests that ability to achieve is one of God's gifts to us.

Deuteronomy puts the tension in perspective. Israel is about to enter the Promised Land, and Moses warns of the coming prosperity. God's people are not to look around them and puff with pride, saying "My power and the strength of my hands have produced this wealth for me." Instead Israel is to remember the Lord, "For it is he who gives you the ability to produce wealth" (Deut. 8:17, 18).

God did not simply hand Israel wealth.

God gave His people ability to produce wealth.

God wants you to have the same joy of accomplishment He provided for Israel. He values the satisfaction that comes when you taste the fruits of your own efforts. He only asks that when you do achieve, you remember that He is the One who gave you your ability.

ACTIVISM.   A seminary friend of mine was an activist. How could he sit in classes, with a world to be won, and Jesus to return momentarily? He felt a compelling urge to throw himself vigorously into life; only furious action could give meaning. I'm not sure he was wise. But I prefer him to those of us who settle down in the comfortable pew, who are satisfied to watch our world rush toward moral destruction, just waiting, because only Jesus' return offers hope.

The New Testament peers at the complacent and, in the words of J. B. Phillips' paraphrase, shouts that "the present time is of utmost importance" (Rom. 13:11). Urging us to awake, the passage calls for an active life of love and purity (Rom. 13:8–14).

My class graduated from seminary twenty years ago. By now my friend, a long-term missionary in France, has probably realized that the years of study weren't wasted. But even then I think that the Lord appreciated his desire. He was the best kind of activist. One who really cared.

ADDICTION.   Addiction simply means to give yourself over or apply yourself to a particular practice. Generally we view addiction as dangerous. → **ALCOHOLICS** → **DRUG ABUSE** Actually, God wants His people to be addicted . . . to good works (Titus 3:8).

ADJUSTMENT.   For most of us this word conjures up an image of the mythical "well adjusted" individual: that stable paragon, happy, free from anxiety and problems, able to get along famously with everyone. But adjustment doesn't mean being at rest. It actually implies constant struggle. Peter speaks about successful adjustment when he writes, "make every effort to add to your faith goodness; and to goodness, knowledge; and to knowledge, self-control; and to self-control, perseverance; and to perseverance, godliness; and to godliness, brotherly kindness; and to brotherly kindness, love. For if you possess these qualities in increasing measure," he promises, "they will keep you from being ineffective and unproductive in your knowledge of our Lord Jesus Christ" (2 Peter 1:5–8). It is in the dynamic process of our struggle to adjust *ourselves* that we grow.

ADOLESCENCE. My first inclination was to dismiss adolescence with a light remark. Like; adolescence is that wonderful time when teens wish they were adults— and adults wish they were teens. But on second thought adolescence seemed too serious to joke about.

Part of our problem with adolescence is that even psychologists and sociologists aren't sure how to define it. We do know that adolescence is in many ways an artificial time: a later invention of complex societies. In simpler times and simpler lands, a child became an adult when sexually mature and immediately took on adult tasks. But our world is too complex. Young people must spend years in school, and more years getting established in occupations. They live at home without any real work to do when in other cultures they'd be on their own.

Special characteristics. Much research these days makes it clear that teens are really not yet adult. While mental growth enables even a young teen to think in ways that are significantly different from the ways they thought in childhood, full mental powers do not develop till they are in the mid or late twenties. Research on moral reasoning indicates that principled, abstract moral thought is unlikely until the late twenties or early thirties.

Some researchers suggest that youth face certain "developmental tasks" during adolescence. By this they mean that in the years between 13 and 23 or so, growth in several specific areas is critical. Most would agree that during these years a young person growing toward a healthy maturity needs to: build a strong sense of personal identity (self-concept), develop healthy interpersonal relationship skills, begin to establish personal values and goals, and learn to relate well with the opposite sex. Christians might add that these years are also important for developing awareness of the importance of experiencing God's presence in daily life.

It helps us to view adolescence as a time of transition, as years during which a young person takes steps that prepare him or her for independence, before he or she is really ready for independence. For many these are years of stress. Some fail to cope and turn to drugs or other practices that enable them to avoid rather than face the real issues of life.

What can parents do?   It's impossible in a brief article to outline all the "how tos." But we can list several basics, which focus on the pattern of the relationship between parent and adolescent. Each basic expresses a way in which a parent treats a teen with respect, for respect is the key. Teens are no longer little kids and resent being treated like little ones—even though they sometimes still act that way. Following these guidelines they can be helped to feel that you've given them the freedom they need in order to grow.

● Listen without automatically giving advice. You can give advice if asked for it. But unasked-for advice is a put down and a sure way to keep your kids from sharing with you. Instead, ask questions that help your teens talk about their experiences and feelings. Listen, and try not to tell them what they ought to do.

● Increase responsibilities. A key here is to involve your teens when working out family ground rules. They should have a say in what they think are reasonable limitations and reasonable consequences for failures.

Don't give teens total freedom. They don't even want that. But kids need to feel they are respected and that you trust their judgment. As your youth grow more responsible, the areas of personal freedom and responsibility can be extended.

● Build a truly Christian interpersonal relationship with your teens. Many aspects of such a relationship are outlined in the Bible. These are particularly significant: Express your love in open, positive, affirming ways. Share your own feelings when you are upset, without blaming or attacking. Overlook the little faults, which all human beings have, and always be ready to forgive. →
COMMUNICATING → FORGETTING

This is of course to be a mutual relationship, so you need to give your teen the right to express his or her feelings, to express love, and to forgive you for your failings.

Biblical insights.   There is little in the Bible that helps us with adolescence, but Jesus' story of the prodigal son does suggest insights. There we see a youth eager to be on his own, but still not wise. His father gives him the freedom he must have, and when he makes the tragic mistakes that finally bring him to himself, the father is there to welcome him home again.

This story is a comfort to parents whose children have made their own tragic mistakes in life, for it points out that God can use the results of sin to bring individuals to Him.

But the story is also a pattern for smaller things. It is a reminder that children will step out and make mistakes, but they may learn from them. And it is a reminder that every young person needs a home rich in unconditional love, a home he or she can return to and find the support that helps him or her try again.

ADOPTION.   The decision to adopt is a difficult one these days. It's particularly hard when a person looks around and discovers there are few babies available for adoption. Contraception and more than one million abortions a year means that there are few infants, and especially few white boys and girls. In fact, child adoptions have dropped from about 175,000 in 1970 to less than 105,000 a year. About half of those are children adopted by relatives.

A number of other factors also make couples hesitate to adopt. Children are costly investments. Some fix the cost of raising a child through the college years at hundreds of thousands of dollars. And there is fear. It's one thing to adopt a cute little baby, but it's something else again to take a two- or a four- or even a seven-year-old child. Most people believe that if a child has been deprived of parents those first two critical years, he or she will be warped for life!

But studies have shown that older children adopted into stable, loving homes are generally well adjusted. They do well in school, and are particularly responsive to their adoptive parents. In fact, many who do adopt these days do so out of a desire to care for a child who, without them, will grow up never knowing family love. Because there are far more black and hispanic children who need homes, many are adopting across racial lines.

If you should feel led to share your family with an unwanted child, how would you go about adopting?

Steps toward adoption.   About 75% of all adoptions in our country are handled through agencies. In most states these must be licensed. So a good first step is to locate the appropriate department of your state welfare or social services division and obtain a list of licensed agencies. Then write those in your area for information. You particularly want to find out what children they have available for adoption (age, etc.). Their replies will probably lead you to phone or visit some of them.

You can expect a licensed agency to want to know about you. When you show you are serious, they will need to find out about your age, marriage, finances, health, religious faith, and other factors related to the stability of your home.

The adoption process is unlikely to proceed quickly, but there are thousands of children in our country who need homes, as well as children available for adoption through international agencies. Agency fees vary widely, but average less than $1000. You will also need to hire a lawyer to handle the necessary legal papers.

In biblical perspective.   One question that seems to trouble adoptive parents is, Shall we tell her that she's adopted? For Christians there's a special wonder added to the warmth of adoption that makes it easier to explain. The New Testament uses the word adoption just as we do: as a technical, legal term that means accepting a child as one's own. When we look in Ephesians 1 we find that term applied to all believers. More, we're taken back, before the Creation, and shown the wonder of God's love. Even then He chose us "to be adopted as his sons through Jesus Christ" (1:5).

We were not God's natural children. Ephesians pictures us as strangers, gratifying cravings of a sinful nature, blindly following wrong desires and thoughts (2:1–5). But God loved us anyway. He determined to take us into His family, and by His one great redemptive act in Christ He adopted us as His own.

It's like this with our adopted children. They are chosen. Freely chosen, they are family now, just as assured of our love as you and I are of the love of God.

There's one more fascinating thing about spiritual adoption. Even though something of the old heredity remains when we come to Christ, being part of God's family means there's beauty ahead. The power of relationship with God overcomes the remnants of the old within, and means that one day He will display in us the incomparable riches of His grace (Eph. 2:5–10). As members of God's family, His Spirit works within, shaping the good and pure.

Sometimes couples are concerned about the impact of heredity on the boys or girls they may adopt. It's true that some things will be shaped by heredity. For instance, an active or placid temperament will be linked to the nervous system a child inherits. But his character—ah, that is something God will use you, and your family, to mold.

ADULT. The other day I bought a tooth brush. But for a time I stood there, puzzled by the array of options labeled stiff, medium, and soft. Finally I saw a box labeled "adult." I took it. I knew that must be for me.

Satan also knows the power of verbal suggestion. Like advertisers, he too has a way with words. So he busily pastes an "adult" label on childish approaches to sex, suggesting R- and X-rated films are "for adults only."

Even governments are confused about adulthood. Is it 21—the old voting age? Or 19? Or maybe 16, when driver's licenses are passed out? Or 18, when you can join the army?

It's good to learn that the Bible isn't confused. It doesn't connect adulthood with any specific age, and it certainly doesn't connect maturity with society's headlong dash into silly sins. The Bible views adulthood as ethical maturity. In fact, the idea is related to a Greek word that means reaching a goal, and in that sense being perfected. John uses the same word in speaking of love: maturity is seen in a love expressed as obedience to God (1 John 2:5) and in a deep caring for others (4:5). Disdaining the foolishness of those who confuse adulthood with ethical immaturity, the Bible says "In regard to evil be infants." And goes on, "but in *your* thinking, be adults" (1 Cor. 14:20).

ADVICE. There are several very practical rules for advice giving and receiving. ● Never give advice unless asked. ● Never ask for advice unless you want it. ● Never insist anyone follow the advice you give. ● Never follow another person's advice without first checking with God (cf. Josh. 9:14). Oh, yes. One more. Seldom listen to advice from anyone who says "never."

AFFAIRS. Words have a flavor, a taste, and today society is busily trying to sugar-coat infidelity. A host of researchers contend that more than 50% of Americans succumb to the promise of sweet extramarital experiences. But Proverbs warns about what happens when the sugar coating wears off. "The lips of an adulteress drip honey," the writer admits, "and her speech is smoother than oil; but in the end she is bitter as gall, sharp as a double-edged sword. . . . Do not lust in your heart after her beauty or let her captivate you with her eyes, for the prostitute reduces you to a loaf of bread, and the adulteress preys upon your very life. Can a man scoop fire into his lap without his clothes being burned? Can a man walk on hot coals without his feet being scorched? So is he who sleeps with another man's wife; no one who touches her will go unpunished" (Prov. 5:3, 4; 6:25–29).

AFFLUENCE. The dictionary describes affluence as

an abundance of money and other material goods. The problem is that abundance is seldom enough. Habakkuk describes those who are driven by a desire for more. Such a person will never find rest, the prophet says, "Because he is greedy as the grave and like death is never satisfied" (Hab. 2:5). When plenty really is plenty, it's a blessing. When plenty still isn't enough, it's a curse.

AGING. On a recent trip to California I met Enid Forsberg again. Enid, a missionary in Africa for four decades, had been my secretary at Wheaton College one furlough year. Now she and her husband are retired. Enid talked about some of the differences old age makes. "Life narrows in," she explained. "We can't drive at night. The challenge of our work is gone. There's not much chance for contact with others our age." But Enid didn't reflect the yearning of Job, "How I long for the months gone by" (29:1).

Today some 25 million Americans (11% of our population) are over 65. By the year 2,000 that number will rise to 50 million, and 18%. Many of those millions look ahead to old age with a sense of panic. They need not. There's abundant evidence that most of the stereotypes we have of aging are false, and the golden years are more satisfying than we imagine.

For instance, older people generally maintain their intelligence and their ability to learn. Most are far from miserable. In fact, a higher percentage of those over 65 claim to be happy than of those under 65! Most older Americans are relatively healthy, most are not lonely, and, in addition to the public programs designed to meet the needs of the aged, 75% of our older population own their homes and 65% own automobiles. Retirement hasn't meant an automatic loss of health, and only about 5% of the elderly are in nursing homes or other care facilities.

Yes, things are different for Enid and Malcomb. There are adjustments to make. But their next years can still be active and full.

Volunteering. One exciting feature of the retirement

years is that a person over 65 may have more free time available than ever before. Age may slow us down some, but it also enriches with wisdom and experiences that enable us to contribute to others. A number of organizations encourage older persons to volunteer their free time and the benefit of their experience. (For instance, *Administration on Aging,* HEW, Washington, DC 20201; *National Council of Senior Citizens,* 1511 K Street NW, Washington, DC 20005; *National Center for Voluntary Action,* 1785 Massachusetts Ave. NW, Washington, DC 20036.) But we hardly need to look beyond our church or local community for ways to serve others. Here are just a few ways older volunteers can minister.

- Activities of day care centers, for elderly/for children
- Aides in state hospitals
- Aiding Red Cross safety programs
- Aiding unwed mothers
- Assisting in physical or occupational therapy programs
- Big Brother or Big Sister programs/foster grandparents
- Bookkeeping assistance/clerical tasks
- Canvassing for voters/for candidates
- Carpentry/plumbing/home repairs and maintenance
- Committee work on community programs
- Emergency room or hospital aide
- Library assistance
- Meal sites/meals on wheels
- Musical activities/teaching/instruments/leading choirs
- Police-community relations/probation or parole programs
- Providing transportation/driving community service vehicles
- Raising money for the needy
- Social security aides
- Suicide prevention center services

- Teacher's aide/tutoring
- Technical and financial advice to small businesses
- Telephone answering for information/referral/ counseling
- Working with handicapped/sheltered workshop for retarded

These, and many other avenues of service, are open to an older person who, perhaps for the first time, has time to give of himself or herself.

Biblically. No less than four times in the Old Testament do we read the phrase, "a good old age" (Gen. 15:15; 25:8; Judg. 8:32; 1 Chron. 29:28). Yes, there are infirmities that come with age, but old age can be good. Moses, so eager at 40 to rescue his people from slavery, was put aside until he was 80. Only then did he launch the ministry that occupied his final, productive, 40 years.

In the world of the Bible the aged received respect and often authority on the grounds that their experience had led to wisdom. The selection of the term "elder" to identify the key leaders of the local church reflects this cultural pattern. More important, it stresses the necessity of Christian maturity as a prerequisite for leadership. We see the value of age in 1 Timothy as well, where he describes a special role for a woman "over sixty" who "has been faithful to her husband, and is well-known for her good deeds, such as bringing up children, showing hospitality, washing the feet of the saints, helping those in trouble, and devoting herself to all kinds of good deeds" (5:9, 10). In Titus we catch a glimpse of the supportive, counseling kind of ministry such older women enjoyed (cf. 2:3–5).

Essentially, then, the Bible's outlook on age is positive. A person who has grown in godliness and matured through the years is more ready than ever for a more productive life!

In our culture, we lack this healthy appreciation for aging. But no older person should settle back sourly, sulking because church or society fail to recognize his or her potential. Instead today, just as in Bible times, there are people in our world who need to be loved and served. Perhaps for the first time some older men and women have the time to give themselves.

Certainly the aging have something more to give as well. Testimony: "I was young and now I am old," the psalmist says, "yet I have never seen the righteous forsaken or their children begging bread" (Ps. 37:25). From the perspective of years we see even more clearly the faithfulness of God.

There is even a special word of testimony *to* the older. It comes through Isaiah, directed to Israel, but surely for you and me today.

> Even to your old age and gray hairs
> I am he, I am he who will sustain you.
> I have made you and I will carry you;
> I will sustain you and I will rescue you
> (46:4).

AGGRESSIVENESS. Like many words, this one carries a mixed message. Sometimes it seems to mean only a healthy self-assertiveness; a drive to accomplishment. Other times it means an unprovoked, hostile attack. We like the person who aggressively looks for a job. But how about the Christian who aggressively witnesses?

Perhaps the best way to distinguish unhealthy from healthy aggressiveness is to examine how we're treating other persons. When we stay within the bounds of respect, zeal is healthy. The New Testament in 2 Timothy 2:25 reflects the respect with which we should approach others. "Those who oppose [the Lord's servant] he must gently instruct, in the hope that God will grant them repentance leading them to a knowledge of the truth." It's gentle aggressiveness that wins.

ALCOHOL. The frustration we feel dealing with this topic can be summed up in several quotes from the Psalms; quotes that reflect an ambivalent attitude. Psalm 4:7 speaks of joy when "grain and new wine abound." But Psalm 60:3 describes desperate times as a "wine that

makes us stagger." Psalm 75:8 holds up "foaming wine
mixed with spices" as a symbol of divine judgment. But
Psalm 104:15 affirms God as the giver of "wine that glad-
dens the heart of man." What are alcoholic beverages? A
blessing? Or a curse?

Biblically. The vine was an important part of the Old
Testament economy, and wines were often included in
lists of produce (cf. Deut. 7:13; 11:14; 2 Kings 18:32; Jer.
31:12). Wine was drunk at feasts, given as a gift (1 Sam.
25:18; 2 Sam. 16:1), and praised by the psalmists. Wine
was also used in offering to God (Exod. 29:40; Lev.
23:13; Num. 15:7), although priests were not to drink
when serving at the altar (Lev. 10:9). In the Old Testament the vineyard portrayed Israel (Isa. 5:1–7), and in the
New Testament Jesus is the vine from whom believers
draw strength to produce fruit (John 15:1–11; Gal. 5:22,
23). For those celebrating the wedding at Cana (John
2:1–11), wine was a blessing, heightening the pleasure of
a joyous social occasion.

Balancing this happy picture, both testaments speak
out against drunkenness, and disapprove love for alcoholic
beverages (cf. Prov. 20:1; 21:17; 23:20). Drunkenness is
characteristic of a pagan, not Christian, lifestyle (1 Peter
4:3), and there is no excuse for excessive drinking (cf.
Eph. 5:18). While Timothy is urged to use wine medici-
nally (1 Tim. 5:23), Christians are also encouraged to give
up the practice if it causes other believers in the community to stumble (Rom. 14:21). It's helpful for us to realize
that the wine drunk with meals in Bible times was charac-
teristically diluted with between three and seven times as
much water.

Medically. The principle effect of alcohol is on the
brain. Significantly, alcohol is accumulated in the blood
and is not transferred to other tissues, and a single drink
will leave traces in the blood for about four hours.

The initial effect of alcohol is a sense of release and
well-being. As alcohol content increases, internal checks
on impulsive behavior are removed. Skills deteriorate.

Accuracy as well as speed of response are impaired, along with judgment. It's not surprising that a major factor in more than half the automobile accidents in the United States resulting in death or serious injury is the alcohol or drug impairment of one of the drivers.

Conclusions. In some Christians' minds there simply is no question. In a society like ours, in which so many evils are associated with drinking, Christians should not drink. Ever. Other believers are not so persuaded. Drunkenness, no. But a glass of wine with dinner?

Where there are honest differences, and where Scripture does not speak bluntly with unmistakable prohibition, Paul's words to the Romans are important. "Each one should be fully convinced in his own mind" (Rom. 14:5). Whatever conviction you arrive at, you need to give others the freedom for responsible decision-making you exercised in arriving at your conclusion. And it's good to remember this as well: "the kingdom of God is not a matter of eating and drinking, but of righteousness, peace and joy in the Holy Spirit" (Rom. 14:17).

ALCOHOLICS. An alcoholic is not a person who drinks, but a person who has become physically or psychologically dependent on alcohol. Four patterns have been suggested: the problem drinker, who could stop if he so chose. The periodic drinker, who is psychologically dependent and may stop for a time, but once started cannot control how much he drinks. The constant drinker, who must always have a significant level of alcohol in his blood, and suffers withdrawal symptoms when he tries to stop. The interrupted drinker, who may maintain long periods of abstinence, but then returns to drinking.

Alcoholics Anonymous gives the following list of Thirteen Steps to Alcoholism to help an individual diagnose himself or herself. 1. You have begun to drink. 2. You start having blackouts. 3. You find liquor means more to you than to others. 4. You consistently drink more than you meant to. 5. You start excusing yourself for drinking. 6. You start taking eye-openers in the morning. 7. You begin to drink alone. 8. You become hostile when you drink. 9. You start going on benders. 10. You know deep remorse—and deeper resentment. 11. You feel deep, nameless anxiety. 12. You realize drinking has you licked. 13. You get help, or go under. These steps are arranged in progression. Typically, it is only when a person reaches the twelfth step that he or she is willing to get outside help.

Help is also needed for an alcoholic's family. Drinking distorts relationships with spouse and children, and loved ones may unknowingly react in ways that make it more difficult to solve the problem.

Most communities and some churches have programs to help alcoholics and their families, the best known being Alcoholics Anonymous. But, as with other addictions that enslave, self-help provides no reliable solution. "Don't you know that when you offer yourselves to someone to obey him as slaves, you are slaves to the one whom you obey—whether you are slaves to sin, which leads to death, or to obedience, which leads to righteousness?" This query, posed in Romans 6:16, focuses on the basic issue. Any sin enslaves, and alcoholism masters millions in our society. The Romans passage goes on, "What benefit did you reap at that time from the things you are now ashamed of?" (6:21). Only in turning to God, and committing ourselves to obey Him, can we find true freedom: then "the benefit you reap leads to holiness" (6:22).

It would be wrong to suggest that salvation, or commitment, brings automatic release from addiction. The process of release is often long. Release also takes the understanding and support of loved ones and friends. But in Christ we do have an alternative to alcholism: a slavery to Jesus that frees us for a new life we can begin to live now.

ALIENATION. Some social scientists have called our age the age of alienation. Ours is a time when many feel isolated and cut off. We become indifferent to or suspicious of others and tend to turn away in order to create our own private space. Even here we can become

lost, for alienation only deepens when we are alone. Soon
life itself can seem unreal and vague. If you've ever felt
the loneliness and uncertainty of alienation, you know
how important it is to find your way back. Back to reality.
And back to relationships.

The New Testament speaks about three different
kinds of alienation to which we are prone. ● The first is
alienation from God. Remember the days when you
weren't a Christian? Here's how Colossians describes
them: "Once you were alienated from God and were enemies in your minds because of your evil behavior" (1:21).

This kind of alienation takes the form of suspicion
and hostility. There's a nagging sense of guilt associated
with sin that makes humanity look hesitantly over one
shoulder, sure that God can't be there, but always afraid
that He is. God doesn't seem real. But the very idea that
He might be is uncomfortable and impels us to turn away.

God has dealt decisively with this kind of alienation
in Christ. Colossians 1:22 continues, "Now he has reconciled you by Christ's physical body through death to present you holy in his sight, without blemish and free from
accusation." The good news of the gospel comes, and we
discover we have nothing to fear. God is not our accuser!
Jesus has dealt with our sin and offers us the bright robes
of His holiness. We're free to turn back to the God from
whom we fled, amazed to learn He's followed us all these
years only that He might be our Friend.

● The second kind of alienation the New Testament
speaks of is from other human beings. Even in the early
church there were people eager to create splinter groups,
to sow suspicion and fear. "These people are jealous to
win you over," Paul warns the Galatians, "but for no
good. What they want is to alienate you from us, so that
you may be zealous for them" (Gal. 4:17).

Alienation is a great danger for us, for when we build
our barriers and plug our ears, we cut ourselves off from
that vital, living body of which the New Testament says
we are a part. The more we are cut off, the more lonely
and isolated we feel. Even more serious, it is within the
warm network of intimate personal relationships that God

intends us to grow. "Joined and held together by every supporting ligament," the whole body "grows and builds itself up in love, as each part does its work" (Eph. 4:16). When we are alienated from our brothers and sisters we're cut off from that context in which we can grow.

There are some very practical steps we can take to break out of our isolation and gradually rebuild the links of trust and love with other believers.

(1) Consciously identify with God's people. There will be differences you'll notice. But remember, as a Christian you are a child of God. Others who confess Christ as God's children are your brothers and sisters. Consciously identifying yourself and others as family is a first basic step.

(2) Listen to others and try to understand how they think and feel. Don't be judgmental, but accepting. Remind yourself that you don't have to agree with others to care about them.

(3) Take the risk of communicating. Let others know what you think and how you feel. Wearing a false face offers no security. It only cuts us off, deepening our alienation. When we are ourselves with others and find they accept us, we come to realize we're not alone.

For a person who feels alienated, steps like these aren't easy. But they needn't be rushed. You can join a group of believers and sit quietly among them as long as you wish. You can listen to others and develop a habit of praying for them as you sense their needs and concerns. You can begin, gradually, to share your own thoughts and feelings and needs, even waiting for encouragement if you want, before you go on.

The wonderful truth is that just as Jesus brings us back to God, so in Jesus we discover we're no longer alone, but are part of a wonderful family of others who will grow to love us as we learn to love them.

● The third kind of alienation in the New Testament might be called alienation from the source of power. The verse that mentions it is probably one of the most misunderstood in the Scripture. "You who are trying to be justified by law have been alienated from Christ," Paul warns the Galatians. "You have fallen away from grace" (Gal. 5:4). In this great letter Paul is writing of a dilemma experienced by many Christians even today. Having come to Christ, we're eager to please Him, and are desperate to find our way out of the barrenness of an empty life into the rich fullness of a life filled with significance. Some Christians in Paul's day tried to find that new life by adopting the strict pattern of regulations laid down in the Old Testament. But they found the dos and don'ts a cold comfort. In turning back to look at Law they lost sight of Jesus and became indifferent to Him. Somehow they failed to realize that "the only thing that counts is faith expressing itself through love" (Gal. 5:6).

Emptiness invades a Christian's life whenever his or her focus shifts from Jesus. Even a good thing like the Law can never replace the dynamic found in love for the Lord.

Wherever we turn in Scripture we make a common discovery about alienation. It is emptiness: a loneliness that exists as an aching void within. That emptiness can be filled only with intimate personal relationships.

For the lost of mankind, the promise of Scripture is that Jesus will fill the void. For us, the Bible is filled with promise too. We can reach out to others now, for they are no longer strangers but family. Living close to Jesus, we can experience a fulfilling life of faith, which expresses itself as love.

ALLOWANCES. We give allowances, and make them. Children need allowances when they're young to get the feel of responsibility. But everyone needs to make allowances for others. God provides the model. "The LORD is compassionate and gracious," the Bible says. "He does not treat us as our sins deserve, or repay us according to our iniquities . . . for he knows how we are formed, he remembers we are dust" (Ps. 103:8, 10, 14). It's wise to follow God's example in our relationships with others. And it helps if we remember how often God has had to make allowances for us.

ALTERNATIVES. Christians seem particularly prone to dichotomistic thinking: that approach to life that forces every issue into two opposing alternatives. A thing is right, or it's wrong. Something must be done this way, or that way. The solution involves doing it my way, or your way.

How tragic that it never seems to dawn on many of us that timing and circumstances have something to do with right and wrong . . . for instance, it might be wrong to marry your fiancé now, but right three months from now. It's hard for many to imagine there might be a dozen ways to get something done, and that if we explored possibilities together we might discover an "our way" that's better than either "my way" or "your way."

People who keep their minds closed to alternatives also tend to confuse means and ends. For instance, most Christians feel that praying with others is a desirable goal. But to some, praying in church on Wednesday nights is the way to do it, and the idea of praying in small groups in homes another time is viewed with suspicion. The means (getting together to pray on Wednesdays at the church building) has been confused with the end (praying together), and has been frozen in sacred form by God's people.

Alternative thinking frees us from such traps and from the suspicion dichotomistic thinking generates. And alternative thinking is appropriate to what we know of the nature of God. God, who is so creative that no two snowflakes are alike, places no premium on slavish conformity to the practices of the past. How exciting for us to realize that our security does not depend on maintaining traditions. We can freely examine all the alternatives, for our security is found in our personal relationship with a God who has promised to guide the humble in what is right and to teach them His way (Ps. 25:9).

AMBIGUITY. Doubt and uncertainty aren't popular in the Christian community, so you'll hear few sermons on the glory of an ambiguous life. Perhaps that's too bad. After all, even prophecy is ambiguous until it has been fulfilled. Who in Isaiah's day could have explained these words about the Messiah: "he was assigned a grave with the wicked, and with the rich in his death" (Isa. 53:9). Looking back now, remembering the crucifixion of Jesus between two thieves and the deposit of His body in the tomb of Joseph of Arimathea, we see how unambiguous God's plan really was (Matt. 27:45–60).

Whenever we're uncertain about the direction of our own life, we can be sure of a wonderful truth: God has built in the ambiguities purposely. And they need not detract from a positive approach to life. "We are always confident," Paul says, "and know that as long as we are at home in the body we are away from the Lord. We live by faith, not by sight" (2 Cor. 5:6, 7). It is the ambiguity of life that gives us the opportunity to exercise faith.

Someday we'll look back on our life, and then everything will be clear. The ambiguities will be resolved. Until then we'll live in an uncertain world, by faith.

AMBIVALENCE. Have you ever felt affection for your two-year-old at the same time you are struggling with an impulse to strangle him when he shouts "No!"? Then you understand ambivalence. It's the simultaneous experience of positive and negative feelings toward the same person: pleasure at an unexpected gift momentarily spoiled by the suspicion, "What did he do *now?*"

Ambivalence is one of the facts of life we must learn to put up with. It reflects our own nature as saintly sinner and our loved one's nature as sinning saint. But the moral issue raised by ambivalent feelings has little to do with our emotions. The moral issue is much simpler. Which feelings do we express? Does the two-year-old's "No" earn an angry frown and a slap, or do we win beyond our flaring irritation to act with loving firmness?

I know I'll keep on having ambivalent feelings about the people I love. But I know too I can decide which feelings I'll act on, and which I will not.

AMUSEMENTS. By definition, an amusement is a pastime: a pleasant diversion. At various times in history most things have been on some Christian list of proscribed behavior. Laughing on Sunday. Card playing. Mixed bathing (too diverting?). Bowling. I suppose someone has even been critical of that sport of wise kings and not too wise ex-presidents, fishing. But I doubt that the real problem has been with particular practices. I suspect that what the critics find disturbing is the frivolity of people who take time to indulge in fun. How strange. When God Himself is the One who gave us "everything for our enjoyment" (1 Tim. 6:17).

ANGELS. God seldom satisfies anyone's curiosity about angels. Once, when a hostile army surrounded a prophet and servant, the terrified aide was permitted to see these veiled realities. His eyes opened, he saw the hills filled with horses and chariots of fire, between the enemy and the lone pair (2 Kings 6:17). That veil is seldom lifted. Yet the New Testament tells us that angelic beings, directly created by God to do His bidding, are "all . . . ministering spirits sent to serve those who will inherit salvation" (Heb. 1:14).

The Old Testament gives angels a number of descriptive names. They are called "holy ones," and "strong ones" and also "heavenly beings" [as "sons of God" is best understood]. Angels witnessed our world's creation (Job 38:7) and served as mediators of God's Old Testament revelation (cf. Zech. 1:9, 11; Heb. 2:2). Today they watch nations (cf. Dan. 10) as well as individuals.

Even though angels are spoken of some 175 times in the New Testament, they are most often connected with the return of Christ. Paul insists in Colossians that we not be distracted from our relationship with Christ to focus on angels, as though they were now mediators between us and God (2:16–23).

The Bible pictures angels as personal beings: self-aware individuals with personal identity, and with knowledge and powers beyond our own. At least some angels have personal names (Gabriel being known best). There are several different types of angelic beings. Many appear in the Old Testament in human form. There is no instance of a female angel appearing despite the feminine representations in much Christian art. Other angelic beings have distinctly different forms (cf. Ezek. 1:5–11; 10:19–22; Isa. 6:2). Many believe that it is fallen angels, who once followed Satan in his rebellion against God, which are called demons in the New Testament.

However curious we may be about angels, there's little in the Bible to satisfy us. Perhaps the most significant passage dealing with angels is Hebrews 2:5–18. It points out that God created humanity lower than angels (2:6, 7). Yet God's Son stepped into the world of men, and took on our nature. He shared our humanity so that through death He might free us from Satan's power, and lift us to stand by His side, crowned with glory and honor. The angels may intrigue us. But, as Hebrews points out, "Surely it is not angels he [Jesus] helps, but Abraham's descendants" (2:16). The focus of God's attention is not angels, but you and me. Surely in return we can focus our attention on Him.

ANGER. At first the red-hot fury seems overpowering. You want to strike out; to hurt the person or thing that hurt you. But what can you do? If you swallow hard and suppress your anger, won't others keep on taking advantage of you? If you do strike out, others will react by becoming angry at you! How nice it would be if believers were simply immune to anger.

David, the Old Testament hero, was a passionate man. When wealthy Nabal, whose herds David's men had guarded, contemptuously refused to acknowledge his help or express appreciation, the enraged David swore to kill every man in his household. Marching to take grim revenge, David was met by Nabal's wife, who had learned of the situation from upset servants, and who brought appropriate gifts. Rushing to David she righted the wrong and implored him to forgive. David thanked God. Abigail's quick action had prevented a wrong, "keeping me from bloodshed this day and from avenging myself with my own hands" (1 Sam. 25:33). The "staggering burden" to his conscience (v. 31) of acts impelled by anger was avoided. When Nabal heard about it, he suffered a heart attack and died.

Anger had surged. But further sin had been avoided. Restitution was made, forgiveness extended, and justice had been meted out by God. The whole story is filled with insights that help us understand anger and how to deal with it.

Biblical view of anger. Scripture gives little support to those of us who try to justify anger. The Old Testament views an irritable temperament as well as outbursts of anger as wrong and foolish. According to Proverbs, anger is cruel (27:4), generates quarrels (30:33), and is so unwise (29:8) that it is a mark of fools (29:11).

While we might try to distinguish between justified and unjustified anger, Jesus insists that anger simply is no way to treat other human beings (Matt. 5:22). In fact, anger is found in the most prominent New Testament lists of sins (Gal. 5:20; Eph. 4:31; Col. 3:8; Titus 1:7). While Scripture recognizes that anyone's anger may flare, it insists we not permit anger to control our actions and lead us into sin (Eph. 4:26).

Several verses help us understand the New Testament's view of anger. James writes, "Everyone should be quick to listen, slow to speak and slow to become angry, for man's anger does not bring about the righteous life that God desires" (1:19, 20). "In your anger do not sin," Ephesians reflects on Psalm 4:4. "Do not let the sun go down while you are still angry" (Eph. 4:26). The emotion may flare in anyone, but it is not to be permitted to control.

God's anger. In view of warnings against anger in both Testaments, it's something of a surprise to find God described as being angry. It's no surprise to learn that Greek and Roman deities were thought to be vindictive, and their outbursts of senseless anger needed to be turned aside by gifts and offerings. But our God?

Yet the Old Testament pictures an angry God, furious at times with humanity and with individuals (cf. Exod.

4:14; Num. 25:3; Deut. 29:20; 2 Chron. 19:2; Ps. 78:21). The New Testament also speaks of a wrath of God, "being revealed from heaven against all the godlessness and wickedness of men who suppress the truth by their wickedness" (Rom. 1:18). Both Testaments picture a dark day of anger approaching, when a vengeful God will be "revealed from heaven in blazing fire with his powerful angels" to punish those who have resisted His grace (2 Thess. 1:7, 8). Revelation, the book unveiling that day, is filled with expressions of God's wrath.

Yet God's anger is different from ours. First, God's anger is a reaction to sin: to actions that harm the sinner as well as other persons. God's truly is a righteous anger, aroused for the right reasons. However we may justify ourselves, we do tend to become angry—as David did—at personal affronts. "He shouldn't have done that to *me!*" is usually what triggers our anger.

Second, God's anger does not forget love. In history we see that God's anger has been designed to restore (cf. Isa. 42:25; Jer. 4:4), and even the angry times are "momentary" against the backdrop of God's endless love (Ps. 30:5; Isa. 26:20). In our anger we tend to lose control and forget love. God does not.

Third, God is wise enough to accomplish good through His anger. We lack that wisdom, as well as the love that keeps good in mind even when we are angry. So God's anger is clearly different from ours—in its cause, in its control, and in the concern with which it is linked.

What to do about anger. Scripture traces the origin of our anger to the sin that lurks in our personalities. Ultimately release from our anger can be found only in the renewal that comes through personal relationship with Christ (cf. Col. 3:5–10). Our inner life, and the way we respond to others, will experience a transformation as we grow in faith.

Yet there are several basic concepts that, as we remember and apply them, can stimulate personal growth. The Old Testament story of David and Nabal can help us see the concepts clearly.

• The real problem lies within. David's fury was a response to a specific situation, but it was not the only possible response. He might, for instance, have been sad that Nabal was so insensitive. Instead David got angry.

The first step in dealing with anger is to realize that the problem is with our response, and is not necessitated by the situation. Anger alerts us to look within.

• The moral issue is in actions. Abigail was right. If David had acted in anger to kill Nabal and his servants, a staggering burden would have been added to his conscience. Our first impulse when angry is to strike out at others. But it is only when we let such hostile emotions control us and issue in sinful acts that anger becomes a moral issue (cf. Eph. 4:26).

One of the greatest moral victories a person can have is a victory over his or her own emotions. Feelings need not control. We can choose to do good rather than evil.

• Refusing to act out anger does not imply passivity. Abigail's quick action shows that angry retaliation is not the only way to get redress. When we've dealt with our own feelings, there will be some positive way to deal with the situation.

• Make a distinction between the problem and the person. Abigail was right when she asked David to forgive Nabal, and she prefigured Jesus' own teaching by some thousand years. Other persons—like you and me—are imperfect. Either willfully or unwittingly we all do wrong. The Christian has the wonderful privilege of loving everyone, even enemies (Matt. 5:43–48).

• Let God judge. David was freed from the temptation of acting as judge when God took Nabal's life. We can remember that it's unnecessary for us to take vengeance, or even to judge another person's motives. God is judge, and righteous as well as loving. If wrong has been done, He will repay.

We don't gain our victory over anger easily, any more than we develop other Christlike qualities of life overnight. But God is at work in us, to make us loving. If we pause when we feel anger aroused, and remember to apply the principles Scripture teaches us for dealing with anger, we *will* grow beyond this problem that may torment us now.

ANTICIPATION. Have you ever noticed that only human beings are not captives to the present? Unlike animals, we can remember. And we can look ahead. That ability to anticipate, to taste now something pleasant that we expect in the future, enriches our lives. Surrounded by winter snow, we can plan a garden, or lose ourselves in the maps and guidebooks of some colorful vacationland.

Some misuse the gift of anticipation, and dismally think of everything that can go wrong. As Christians we're freed from that trap. We look ahead to times filled with promise, for "I know the plans I have for you," declares the Lord, "plans to prosper you and not to harm you, plans to give you hope and a future" (Jer. 29:11).

ANXIETY. Picture yourself applying for a new job. Or taking a test that might affect the rest of your life. Or waiting, for the first time in your life, in an unemployment line. Or going to the dentist for an abscessed tooth. Or waiting in a doctor's office for a diagnosis. We all know the feelings that can come at times like these. We all experience anxiety.

Psychologists have defined anxiety as a feeling of apprehension, cued by a threat to something we hold essential. Normal anxiety is (1) an appropriate reaction (2) to an objective threat (3) which is relieved when the objective situation changes. The way to handle normal anxiety is to cope: to admit our feelings and then face the situation and seek to deal with it. As David pointed out in one of his psalms, "When I am afraid, I will trust in you" (56:3). Trust did not drive out fear. Fear gave an opportunity to exercise trust. When we face our anxieties with trust in God, we will be able to cope.

At times people respond to anxiety in destructive rather than constructive ways. They run out of the dentist's office when the nurse says, "You're next." Their mind goes blank when the test is handed out, no matter how thoroughly they've studied. Trust won't remove our fears, but confidence in God's presence will enable us to meet rather than flee from or repress our fears.

For some persons anxiety is a constant companion. Their anxiety isn't linked to a specific objective threat, but has become a constant unease. We've all known anxious persons, always tense and afraid even when there seems to be no cause. There are anxious Christians too. But the believer has a tremendous advantage. Even when a believer cannot locate an objective cause for his anxieties, there is something he or she can do. And that is to consciously relate himself to a God who holds us securely in His hand.

The psalmist shared a personal experience in these words from Psalm 94:18, 19. "When I said 'My foot is slipping,' your love, O Lord, supported me. When anxiety was great within me, your consolation brought joy to my soul." Despite feelings of helplessness, as if his feet were slipping out from under him, this man anchored himself in the supportive love of God.

The New Testament gives this same prescription for dealing with both normal and neurotic anxiety. We are to recognize and express our feelings of anxiety to God, consciously linking our lives and the circumstances to Him. "Cast all your anxiety on him," Peter says, "because he cares for you" (1 Peter 5:7). Paul expands on Peter's words, and adds a promise. "Do not be anxious about anything, but in everything, by prayer and petition, with thanksgiving, present your requests to God. And the peace of God, which transcends all understanding, will guard your heart and your minds in Christ Jesus" (Phil. 4:6, 7).

APOLOGIES. It's hard to own up to a fault, gulp, and blurt out "I'm sorry." But what's really hard is to accept apologies. Especially when they have to be repeated.

Jesus once spoke of repeated apologies. He told how members of God's family were to rebuke a brother who sinned against them and, if he repents, forgive him. Then Jesus added this. "If he sins against you seven times a day, and seven times comes back to you and says, 'I repent,' forgive him'' (Luke 17:4).

What's hard is that the second or third apology, whether given by one of our children or our spouse or a friend, begins to create suspicion. By the fourth and fifth we're sure: the other person couldn't really mean it! And then we begin to feel responsibility. I mean, forgiveness is OK, but isn't he just getting away with it? Shouldn't we make sure he *pays?*

In giving that "seven times" instruction (a phrase the disciples rightly understood to call for unlimited forgiveness), Jesus gave two gifts. One gift was to the person who made the apologies, and the other gift to the person who received them. The gift to the receiver is this: You are not obligated to judge your brother. You are freed to love him and forgive him without hesitation.

Just think what a burden it would be if we Christians were made responsible for others' actions; if we constantly had to be suspicious of their motives or sincerity. Just think if we weren't allowed to forgive until a brother "proved" he meant it.

The gift to the one who keeps failing is even more wonderful. You see, constant failure robs anyone of hope. If we try, and fail, and try again and fail, we soon become afraid to try anymore. We feel captive to our past, bound forever by our proven inability to change.

And then forgiveness comes. We find others who care so much about us, and believe in us enough not to become discouraged by our repeated faults. This is the same principle that operates in our relationship with God. "If we confess our sins," John promises, "he is faithful and just and will forgive us our sins and [keep on] purify[ing] us from all unrighteousness" (1 John 1:9). God tells us ahead of time that His forgiveness is ours, in endless supply. When we are sure of forgiveness, we can risk trying again and again, until we break out of the trap of our past, and learn to live Jesus' new kind of life.

So next time you're frustrated and angry when your child disobeys you again, or your spouse falls short, or a friend disappoints, remember God's gifts that accompany every apology. You are freed to forgive. And your forgiveness gives the one who has failed God's gift of hope. → BECOMING

APPEARANCES. The word appears just once in our NIV translation of the Bible. It was spoken by Jesus, to a crowd who had scrutinized His miracles and listened to His words and decided He just didn't measure up to their high standards. "Stop judging by mere appearances, and make a right judgment" is what Jesus said (John 7:24).

If people could be mistaken about Jesus, just think how easy it must be for *us* to make mistakes when we judge by mere appearance.

ARGUMENTS. A good, loud argument has great value. For one thing, it lets others know you really care.

Sometimes we argue over things that aren't important. "He did so throw five touchdown passes in one game!" You can settle that argument by finding an NFL record book and looking up the facts. That argument isn't very important, because the only thing at issue is who is right. And in significant relationships, winning and losing don't really count.

It's when we argue over important things that we discover the value of healthy argument. "Shall we buy a new car?" "Can we go to mother's this Saturday?" "Let's both go on a diet, 'cause I can't while you eat." These are good, juicy topics for argument. In fact, it would be *unhealthy* if we didn't express ourselves on things about which we really care. It's unhealthy to sulk in silence, or to "submit" with a martyred air. A good argument is important because it is a positive, creative way to enrich important personal relationships.

What makes for a good argument, and how do we conduct one? Well, the first thing to remember is that an argument isn't a competition: it is not focused on persons, so that one "wins" while the other "loses." Argument is a form of communication, and its focus is on issues and how we feel about them. We're not to use arguments as arenas in which to take personal pot shots at someone else.

49

To keep an argument healthy and productive, you need to give and to receive several kinds of information. (1) You need facts that help define what you're arguing about. It's not unusual for one person to think he's arguing about missing a big TV game on Saturday, while the other person thinks she's arguing about neglecting mother! (2) You need to express what you think is important about the issue. Once you agree what you're arguing about, it helps if you can each say why that issue seems important to you. (3) You need to say how you feel about the issue. It's never enough to just know what others think. We need to understand feelings as well. Suppose he discovers she's feeling guilty because she hasn't called Mom in three weeks, and that feeling is what makes Saturday so important. (The chances are the argument has helped *her* discover those feelings too!) If those feelings come out, we've taken a big step toward resolving the issue or finding alternatives. (4) You need to express what you would like the other person to do to help resolve the problem. It may be enough if he reassures her that her feelings are more important to him than some old game!

A good argument is one that gets all this hidden information out in the open. When we understand our own feelings and those of each other, we've got a good chance to resolve the problem in a fair, mutually acceptable way. It is when our thoughts and feelings are bottled up inside that relationships wither and people discover they just can't get along.

This is what is meant in the New Testament when the Bible speaks of Christian interpersonal relationships and mentions ''speaking the truth in love'' (Eph. 4:15). This is not ''truth'' in contrast to lies. This is expressing what's inside instead of keeping it masked. It's then, when we speak this truth, that ''we will in all things grow up into him who is the Head, that is, Christ'' (4:15). So if you want to grow as a Christian, and grow in your relationship with others, go ahead. Argue. → **CONFLICT AND RESOLUTION**

ASPIRIN. My father was two years old in 1899 when

they compounded acetytlsalicytic acid, that anti-fever and -pain drug we call aspirin. Today, whatever is wrong with him or anyone else, Dad has one prescription: take aspirin and drink a lot of water.

It seems most people follow his advice. The U.S. consumes some 27 million pounds of aspirin yearly— enough for about 17 billion headaches. And though aspirin won't dull severe pain, everything from arthritis to muscle aches surrenders to the little white tablets.

Like most things in this world, even the good can be misused. Large doses can cause ringing in the ears and a temporary decrease in hearing. Ten to 30 grams can be fatal to children (each tablet has about 1/3 gram). And aspirin makes some of us sick to our stomach. Still I suspect that aspirin is a greater blessing to us than the fabled balm of Gilead, or the olive oil used so liberally for healing in Bible times. I wonder. If the psalmists had had aspirin, would they have praised God for it?

ASTROLOGY.   Yesterday my horoscope read, "Put those creative ideas to work with the aid of persons who are business experts and get excellent results." Too late! I read it today. And I neither have creative ideas, nor friends who are business experts. Ah, well.

Actually, millions of Americans consult astrological columns in newspapers, buy astrological magazines, or visit the more than 5,000 working astrologers in our country, paying from $5 to many hundreds for a personal casting.

Astrology is based on the notion that the position of the moon and planets in relation to the stars, linked with a person's day of birth, controls his life and personality. To know what is likely to happen, to be warned of what to avoid, or be guided in what actions to take, a person need only consult an astrologer who will consult the charts and provide as much detailed advice as one is willing to pay for.

The belief that the stars control human destiny is an old one, and can be documented as early as 2,400 years B.C. The Zodiac (the division of the heavens into twelve segments, each ascribed a special name and qualities) is traced back to the Babylonians. Astrology was popular in pre-Christian Greece, suffered a decline during the early days of the church, and revived in the 10th and 11th centuries A.D. It declined again in the 17th century when society was enamored with the scientific method. Hitler, like many others in our modern world, returned to astrology for guidance. Modern man is anxious and uncertain about the future. Neither faith nor science are trusted by millions, and so in a search for reassurance they turn again to the stars. Perhaps there really are cosmic forces represented in the points of light that provide a stable framework for our unstable world. Perhaps then they can offer guidance and security.

Astrology and the Bible. When the people of Israel were about to enter the Promised Land, God gave specific instructions about seeking guidance. "Let no one be found among you who sacrifices his son or daughter in the fire, who practices divination or sorcery, interprets omens, engages in witchcraft, or casts spells, or who is a medium or spiritist or who consults the dead" (Deut. 18:10, 11). Such practices encompass astrology, are called "detestable," and were not permitted by God's people.

The passage continues with a promise. "The LORD your God will raise up for you a prophet . . . from among your own brothers" (18:15). God does not leave His own without guidance. Instead, He promises to provide that guidance Himself! Through the prophets and the Scriptures they produced, God gave Israel the instruction they needed to live secure lives.

God maintains that same commitment to you and me. When we struggle with anxiety and uncertainty, we have no need to turn to the ambiguous advice of the plotters of horoscopes, or look for comfort to distant, impersonal stars. We can turn to the personal, living God, who is with us always.

"Since you are my rock and my fortress, for the sake of your name lead and guide me" (Ps. 31:3).

ATHEISM.

Atheism is the belief that there is no God. It's hard to imagine people who are so confident. Agnostics at least admit they don't know. But atheists insist, "We're sure."

The Bible makes a few comments about atheists. Twice the Book of Psalms repeats, "The fool says in his heart, 'There is no God'" (Pss. 14:1; 53:1). The Hebrew word for "fool" doesn't imply that such people are lacking intellectually. Instead the Hebrew word for "fool" is a moral term. It affirms that the atheist is morally lacking.

The New Testament picks up and explains this thought. "This is the verdict:" John quotes Jesus. "Light has come into the world, but men loved darkness instead of light, because their deeds were evil. Everyone who does evil hates the light, and will not come into the light for fear that his deeds will be exposed" (John 3:19, 20). The root of atheism is not planted in a man's intellect but in his heart.

Proof. When we look at the evidence, it's hard to understand how a person could be an atheist. Psalm 19 speaks of the created universe, with its order and beauty, as giving wordless testimony to its Creator. It's as reasonable to imagine our orderly universe coming into being through the random action of atoms as it is to believe a tornado blowing through a junk yard could produce a computer (cf. Rom. 1:19, 20).

But the evidence isn't just found in nature. It's found within us. Romans speaks of persons who have never known a written revelation doing "by nature" things required by law (Rom. 2:12–16). The point is that humanity possesses a moral sense. Every society sets up its own rules to govern behavior, and the rules invariably cover the same moral issues as those dealt with in God's Word. What's more, all are aware of the gap between what they agree is right and how people behave. Conscience itself, marking each individual's struggle to accuse others while excusing himself, demonstrates the reality of the moral universe. God and judgment to come are understood through the moral sensibilities within.

But neither the internal witness of conscience nor the external witness of Creation convinces the lost to admit the existence of a God they fear. It seems safer to deny He exists than to face Him in their sin.

When we understand the moral roots of atheism, we understand better how to relate to a person eager to argue the existence of God. Objectively, a Christian has far more reasonable evidence for his belief than an atheist does for disbelief. But winning such arguments won't win the atheist. As the Bible says, it is "by faith we understand that the universe was formed at God's command, so that what is seen was not made out of what was visible" (Heb. 11:3). The basic issue is, how do we help someone toward faith? → EVANGELISM

The answer to that question is a wonderful one. Oh, we can calmly share the reasons why we're convinced Christianity is intellectually respectable. But in our sharing we need to keep the focus on Jesus. In our relationship we need to communicate a warmth and caring that show Christ's attitude toward all the lost. And in our relationships with others in the Christian community we need to love, for it's love in the family of God, Jesus said, that will convince our lost and watching world that He lives, and that we are His disciples (John 13:35).

AUTHORITY. There's hardly a more dangerous word in our vocabulary. In the world it implies the right to control. In Christ "authority" must be understood as the right to influence.

The reason for the difference is that authority has a different purpose in each setting. The world is concerned about how others behave, and so authority is shaped to control behavior. Christ is concerned about inner transformation and maturity, so authority is shaped to help others grow.

Jesus describes the secular approach in Matthew 20:24–25. He pictures an authority that rests on position ("over" them) and on power; an authority that forces others to conform to the demands of the one with authority. While such authority wins compliance, it tends to create resentment. Position and power are ineffective when it comes to winning an eager and willing response.

So when Jesus had described the secular approach to authority, he told his disciples bluntly, "Not so with you" (Matt. 20:26). And He went on to hold up a strange model of authority: a servant. "Whoever wants to become great among you must be your servant," Jesus said. In the servant we discover an authority unknown in the world of mere men.

Several passages in Scripture fill in the picture of authority sketched by Jesus in Matthew. We see that it is not exercised from a position above others, but "among" them (20:26, cf. 23:8–11). Rather than demanding that others act, this authority calls for providing an example. Rather than relying on force to win conformity, this authority trusts a working of God within. When Paul wrote about this spiritual authority to the Corinthians, he pointed out that its goal is to build others up (2 Cor. 10:8). The authority is effective because God is at work in believers to create the willingness to respond (2 Cor. 13:3). In this context the one with authority can teach and urge, but will not demand (cf. 2 Cor. 8:8, 9; 9:7).

Living in our society, it's difficult to visualize how servant authority works. We live in a world where those in authority tell, require, direct, praise, reward, or fire. The idea of servant authority seems weak in comparison. But because it is a spiritual authority, with power to transform others from within, the servant authority is the most potent of all.

What are basic principles for exercising spiritual authority? (1) Build a close personal relationship with others. Do not try to lead or to relate from an "above" position over them. (2) Be a good model or example. Demonstrate your own personal commitment to what you encourage others to do. (3) Teach. Communicate as clearly as possible the beliefs and values that guide your own actions. (4) Continue to relate, to model, and to teach faithfully, even when response seems to come slowly. Trust God to work in others' lives, and pray that He will motivate and discipline them.

There is a place for secular power and position authority in the world of mankind. We would hardly try to replace the military chain-of-command authority with the family kind of authority called for in the church. In fact, it is only because of the presence and power of the Holy Spirit in believers that servant authority has such power. But within the body of Christ, God's authority is exercised through servanthood, and God's people *are* transformed.

When our children are little there will be times when we need to punish them, to help them to obey. But even when they are young and as they grow our basic approach to helping them grow will call for an exercise of biblical authority. And within the church, in every situation we will heed Jesus' warning about the authority of the world: "Not so with you." For us God has a far better, and more powerful, way.

AVERAGE. A 1979 study confirms it! Average people see themselves as "better than average." In God's sight no one is average. Each of us is special, and important to Him.

† † †

BABY TALK. It's embarrassing, hearing adults talk baby talk. At least, it embarrassed the translators of our Bible whenever they came to Romans 8:15. They all seemed to blush, and then wrote down the Aramaic word "Abba" instead of translating it into English.

You see, "Abba" is baby talk. It's one of the first words a Palestinian child learned. It means "dada," and it calls to mind a toddler, arms outstretched, reaching for daddy to pick him or her up. The Romans passage teaches us about our relationship with God in Christ, and says we have "received the Spirit of sonship." Now we address God in the most intimate of terms: "by him we cry, 'Abba, Father'" as "the Spirit himself testifies with our spirit that we are God's children" (cf. Rom. 8:14–17).

We sophisticates may sneer at baby talk. And the
Bible translators may blush. But God doesn't mind. So the
next time you're hurting or lonely, look up to God and call
out for Daddy. He'll take you in His arms, and comfort
you. You're His child. Your cry of "dada" will never
embarrass Him.

BABYSITTERS. Worry about the kids back home
spoils many a night out. Especially if we're not used to
leaving precious with a babysitter. But there are some
things parents can do to reduce the worry. 1. Check with
friends, and choose a known, reliable sitter. 2. Leave
phone numbers: where you can be reached, a neighbor,
police, medical emergency. 3. Write out instructions:
what your child can eat, bedtime, any routines to follow.
4. Have PJs, diapers, etc. in one location. 5. Have an
emergency box, with flashlight, fire extinguisher, fuses,
map to fuse box. Then have the sitter come early to go
over the lists. It may seem like a lot of fuss, but it illustrates a pretty basic principle. Trusting the Lord about the
things we neglect isn't being spiritual, it's being pre-
sumptuous. Prepare as carefully as you can. Then you can
trust in good conscience.

BACKSEAT DRIVING. Now and then my teen
does it to me. "The light's yellow, Dad." "You're too
close to the curb." I confess it irritates me. I know he'd be
upset if I did it when he's at the wheel, but I resist,
because backseat driving shows a lack of trust, and erodes
self-respect. We just are not to treat others in degrading
ways, and backseat driving is a putdown of those we love.
If you doubt that backseat driving shows a lack of respect,
just consider this: We wouldn't do it to a stranger!

I think of backseat driving when I run into people
who want God to speak to them about every little decision
in life. I've concluded that this just is not spirituality. It's
more likely an indication that a person has less respect for
himself than God does.

You see, God gives us intelligence, and a love for
Him and others, and assures us that He is always by our

side. Then most of the time He settles down comfortably beside us and lets us drive. Oh, He'll let us know if we get way off the track. But He doesn't nag, or shout out in a panic when a possible danger nears. God trusts us more than some of us trust ourselves. And He always treats us loved ones with respect.

BACKSLAPPING. The dictionary identifies it as making a loud, effusive display of friendliness. Proverbs dryly observes, ''The kisses of an enemy may be profuse, but faithful are the wounds of a friend'' (27:6).

BALDNESS. Despite all those ads in the Sunday supplements, my research indicates there's little anyone can do about baldness. Even those expensive hair transplants aren't likely to work. But the Bible doesn't have a good word to say about baldness: all eight references indicate a preference for well-dressed hair (cf. Isa. 3:24). Of course, well-dressed hair isn't preferred to good character. Still, I don't suppose a comfortable wig would destroy a good character, and it might improve a person's looks. → **BEAUTY**

BANKRUPTCY. Each year more than 200,000 citizens go legally broke. They go to court, surrender most assets to their creditors, and walk out of the court debt free. It is quite simple to file for bankruptcy, and few today struggle with the question of whether or not it's right.

The legal process. You can walk into your local bookstore or stationery store and buy forms for filing bankruptcy: a lawyer isn't even necessary. In most states, laws exempt your home, furniture, clothing, and a car from surrender when your assets are turned over to your creditors. Some states even exempt a certain amount of savings. Generally, both husband and wife should file for bankruptcy.

After filing and paying a small fee, you'll appear in court to be questioned about your situation. Certain debts cannot be wiped out in bankruptcy court: taxes, alimony, child support, certain court judgments against you, and any debts you incurred by deceit, such as lying on a credit application.

The court then appoints a trustee to collect and sell your unprotected assets. When this is done, the judge closes your case. You no longer have any legal obligation to pay the debts covered in the bankruptcy decree.

Reasons for filing. The obvious reason for filing for bankruptcy is crushing debt. You fall behind on your payments. You're harassed by bill collectors and repossessors, and some creditors file to garnishee [take part of] your wages direct from your employer. Under this kind of strain some marriages fail, and some individuals suffer physical or mental health problems.

Mountainous debt may build with the loss of a job or with a massive medical bill. But in most cases, those who file for bankruptcy simply misused credit. They bought more and more on time, until they were unable to make monthly payments and still pay for food and housing. One of the best ways of avoiding bankruptcy is simply this: control your credit buying. → BUYING ON CREDIT

An alternative. An alternative to bankruptcy is consolidation of debt under a wage-earner plan. The court works with you to develop a budget for paying off your debts, often over a three-year period. This may involve only partial payment (say, 80¢ on the dollar), and may mean reduced interest. Each month you turn over the amount agreed on to the court, which then makes your payments to creditors. About half who try this approach are able to complete the pay-off plan.

The moral issues. There seems to be no clear-cut biblical perspective on bankruptcy. On the one hand, each of us should feel a natural obligation to fulfill promises, and debts are promises to pay. Yet bankruptcy is normally considered when a person *can't* repay, not because he does not want to. The issue is further complicated by the discovery that the Old Testament actually provided a system much like bankruptcy for the needy in Israel. → **BORROWING AND LENDING** There is thus in Scripture the implicit recognition that at times a person simply is unable to repay debts, and that mounting debt is oppressive. In compassion for the oppressed, God Himself acted to provide a way of release.

When pressed by unmanageable debt, we should seek God's personal leading. We do have several options:

(1) Continue the struggle to make payments. Perhaps negotiate extended payments with creditors.

(2) File for bankruptcy, and accept the release provided for in our system as well as in Old Testament law.

(3) File for court help through a wage-earner plan, to consolidate and perhaps reduce your debts while you make regular payments.

(4) File for bankruptcy with the intention of paying your creditors anyway when you get on your feet. If you do take this route, do *not* begin making small payments: you immediately become liable for the entire debt again. Wait till you can pay a former creditor off in full.

Perhaps the most important commitment we can make is to maintain control of our spending. It's one thing when an illness or loss of work brings unmanageable debt. It's another if greed is the cause. God is in control of the disasters that may strike us. But we are to control our regular expenditures. → **BUDGETING**

BAPTISM. Christians become enthused and confused about baptism. What is it? Who should be baptized: babies, or only adult believers? How should a person be baptized, and is baptism necessary for church membership? There are many more questions: enough to fill a small book without ever getting to answers. Different Christian traditions draw different conclusions about baptism, and I won't even try to suggest who is most right. But here is an overview of the basics.

Historically. Baptism was not practiced in the Old Testament. By the time of Jesus a ritual bath was part of the rite by which a Gentile converted to Judaism. When John came baptizing (Matt. 3:1–6), he introduced both a new term and a new symbol. The individual who came down to the river to be publically baptized thus promised to turn away from sin, and associated himself with the coming kingdom of God.

Different traditions have linked the practice of Christian baptism with one of two sources. To some water baptism is a rite that replaces the circumcision of the Old Testament. To them baptism of a newborn child identifies him with the people of God, and the rite expresses his parents' commitment to bring him up in the faith.

In other traditions water baptism is modeled after John's baptism and requires that an individual be old enough to make a public profession of faith.

Generally the first group tends to sprinkle or pour the baptismal waters, and the second stresses immersion as the mode.

Biblical distinctives. It's important to realize that water baptism isn't necessarily in view when we read ''baptize'' in the New Testament. The two most common baptisms are:

• Water baptism, which Jesus commanded us to practice (cf. Matt. 28:19).

• Spirit baptism, which is a supernatural work of the Holy Spirit, by which all believers are linked to Jesus and one another in one body (1 Cor. 12:13) → **BODY** Romans 6:1–7 explains this linkage as union with Jesus. We are so intimately united with Jesus that His death is considered ours, and His resurrection ours as well. Because the Spirit has baptized us into this relationship with Jesus, we can break the inner grip of sin and live godly lives.

One of the strongest arguments for immersion as a mode of baptism is that it expresses what has happened within us: we have gone down into death with Jesus, and been raised up in Him to life.

We must of course follow Jesus' instructions and practice water baptism in our churches. And come to our own conclusion about how to best obey God's command.

But we must never forget that our true heritage is the reality the rite reflects. We are united to Jesus and to one another. We died His death and have been raised in His resurrection.

Now we can follow Him.

BARGAINS. I got it while I was in the Navy: a slick, twenty-dollar suit. It looked so good on the racks. But the first time I wore it it crumpled into permanent wrinkles. I've been suspicious of bargains ever since. What to do? I'm not an expert, and not even as frugal as my good friend Norm Wakefield. So I can only offer a few observations, without even a proof text to back them up. However . . . ● Never buy from a person who comes to your home and says he can't give you today's low price tomorrow. ● When something is on sale "30% off the regular price" visit some other stores and find out their regular price. ● Look up products in a consumer's guide or report before buying any large ticket item. ● If you don't need it, or have not wanted it for a long time, don't buy it whatever the price. It's no bargain.

BARGAINING WITH GOD. Researchers on dying → DEATH → LIFE-THREATENING ILLNESS have discovered that nearly everyone with a life-threatening illness comes to a time of bargaining with God. After an attempt at denial ("this can't be happening to *me!*"), most try promises: "Lord, if only You'll do this for me now, I'll. . . ."

We bargain in far less serious situations, too. "Lord, if only Joey will ask me out, I promise I'll . . . ." Chances are that if you try, you'll be able to identify a bargaining thought or two of your own from the last month.

Well, what about bargaining? Is it right? Certainly it's very human. And there are biblical precedents. Hannah, hurting and depressed because she was unable to give her husband a son, wept and promised God that if He would give her a son she would give him back to the Lord (1 Sam. 1:3–12). God answered Hannah's prayer. Her son, Samuel, served as judge and prophet during some of the most critical decades in the history of God's Old Testament people.

But some passages we might assume involve bargaining really do not. For instance, David, in the grip of guilt, cried out

> Create in me a pure heart, O God. . . .
> Restore to me the joy of your salvation and
>   grant me a willing spirit, to sustain me. . . .
> Then I will teach transgressors your ways,
>   and sinners will turn back to you (Ps. 51:10, 12, 13).

Despite the "if/then" form of David's prayer, it is not bargaining. Instead, David expresses his understanding of a basic truth. Only when cleansed and in close relationship with God can we have a ministry to others.

In fact, most of the Bible's "if/then" expressions need to be understood in just this way. They are not bargains. They express facts we must grasp if we are to understand reality. When God promises blessing if we obey, He is not bargaining. He simply tells us that we need to walk close if we are to experience blessing. When God promises problems if we disobey, He is not threatening. He simply tells us that the further we turn from Him, the more tragic life becomes.

So what about our attempts to bargain with God? We can gain an important insight by looking at the experience of Hezekiah. This godly king was ill, and the prophet Isaiah had the painful task of telling him he was going to die. In 2 Kings 20 we learn that Hezekiah wept bitterly and reminded God of His past devotion. God responded to Hezekiah's anguished plea as He had to Hannah's, and Isaiah returned to announce to the king that he would live another fifteen years.

But the next chapter introduces the most evil of Judah's kings, Manasseh, and begins, "Manasseh was twelve years old when he became king" (21:1). How much better it would have been for Judah if Hezekiah had died, and Manasseh never been born to inflict his fifty-five years of idolatrous terror on God's people.

This is the real problem with our bargaining. We

experience our hurts. And we know what we think we want. But we can't know whether granting our request will issue in a Samuel or a Manasseh result. God does care when we hurt: He wants us to come to Him with our tears and to express our desires. But instead of bargaining, wouldn't it be better to follow the example of Jesus in Gethsemane and simply say, "May your will be done" (Matt. 26:42)?

BEASTLY BEHAVIOR. Some animal lovers resent this phrase. They argue that animals behave better than a lot of people. At least we don't see armies of dogs and cats marching out to do battle. But they miss an important point the Bible makes. For instance, in describing arrogant false teachers Peter writes, "They are like brute beasts, creatures of instinct" (2 Peter 2:12; cf. Ps. 73:22).

One argument for relaxed sexual standards insists that sex is such a normal instinct it must be all right. Well, what sets humanity apart is the ability to judge and control instincts. We don't have to live as brute beasts, controlled by our instincts.

BEAUTY. Have you ever yearned to be really beautiful? Then think about this. As a 19th-century woman you would have struggled to display overly plump breasts and buttocks; as a man nothing less than an imposingly big belly would have done. Of course, today men struggle to keep athletically trim, and women starve themselves in vain attempts to imitate the emaciated models and undernourished waifs our society so admires. Depending on your era and nationality, you might have scarred your face, enlarged your lips and ear lobes, squeezed into an hour-glass corset, or even balanced a head bound in infancy so your profiled skull would resemble a tilted watermelon. And of course you would have added, depending on the age, mud or paints or powders and scents galore. What a strange thing, this search for beauty. And how deceptive.

Centuries ago the Roman poet Martial wrote to a woman of his day,

Galla, you are but a composition of lies. Whilst you were in
Rome your hair was growing on the banks of the Rhine; at
night, when you lay aside your silken robes, you lay aside
your teeth as well; and two thirds of your person are locked
up in boxes for the night; the eyebrows with which you
make such insinuating motions are the work of your slaves.
Thus no man can say, 'I love you,' for you are not what he
loves and no one loves what you are.

Martial's wry humor provides little comfort for the
young, or for anyone who wants to be noticed and appreciated and loved. But the Bible reflect's Martial's observation, though in a more positive tone. "Your
beauty," Peter writes to believers, "should not come from
outward adornment, such as braided hair and the wearing
of gold jewelry and fine clothes. Instead, it should be that
of your inner self, the unfading beauty of a gentle and
quiet spirit, which is of great worth in God's sight. For
this is the way the holy women of the past who put their
hope in God used to make themselves beautiful" (1 Peter
3:3–5).

It's not wrong for a Christian to be in style. But we
must realize that true beauty is inner, in character and
personality, not in appearance. If "beauty" becomes such
a big thing in our circle that we're constantly competing,
then we need to follow the advice Paul gave to some who
saw going to church as just another dress-up affair: "I also
want women to dress modestly, with decency and propri-
ety, not with braided hair or gold or pearls or expensive
clothes, but with good deeds, appropriate for women who
profess to worship God" (1 Tim. 2:9, 10).

Real beauty is more than skin deep. When someone
says, "I love you," you want to be sure that what's loved
is what you are, not what you lock up in boxes for the
night.

BECOMING.   I leaned against the kitchen counter,
looking out into the back yard. I was ready to give up. The
kids and I had been playing basketball, and our youngest
had ridiculed a clumsy neighbor—again. I'd snapped at
him, and I know he sensed my frustration and disgust. I
didn't mind when he forgot to make the bed. But putting

others down; that really hurt. And no matter what I tried I couldn't seem to help him break the pattern.

I expressed those frustrations, and then my wife remarked casually, "Well, Paul was like that when he was his age." What? I just couldn't believe it! Our oldest, who never knowingly hurt anyone? "Yes, just like that. Don't you remember?" I didn't remember. But my wife's remark led me to explore one of the most important concepts in the Bible: becoming.

It's important, because there are times when all of us feel as I did that afternoon: discouraged, and ready to give up. Our kids talk back, or they won't take responsibility. Our spouse apologizes for the 8,012th time, for the same thoughtless act. We promise ourselves we'll break that old habit, and five minutes later do it again. The people at church seem unresponsive to spiritual things. A friend gossips something we shared in confidence. Such experiences are so discouraging. Repeated over and over again, they make us feel like giving up. No wonder we all need to grasp and hold on to the truth about "becoming"!

Seen, and unseen. To understand, we need to learn an unusual rule of evidence. The Bible suggests that only one kind of evidence be permitted in court when we evaluate others.

Paul is the one who teaches us the principle, because he had the same problem with a group of young believers at Corinth that I had with my youngest. He had spent years teaching the young church there. But when he looked at their lives all he saw was arguments over doctrine, parties formed around favorite teachers, fussing over spiritual gifts, ignoring of sexual immorality, and court cases in which believers accused each other of fraud. No wonder he calls these people worldly, "acting like mere men" (1 Cor. 3:3). Becoming Christians hadn't seemed to make much difference in their lives.

It would have been easy for Paul to give up on them, or to let them know how hopeless they were. But he didn't. He remained optimistic, and even told them "I have great confidence in you" (2 Cor. 7:4). He could do this because he considered one kind of evidence, and he disregarded another kind of evidence as irrelevant.

"We fix our eyes not on what is seen, but on what is unseen," Paul explains. "What is seen is temporary, but what is unseen is eternal" (2 Cor. 4:18). The things he *sees* in the Corinthians can and will change, so they do not count. It is what is unseen that shapes Paul's attitude toward these immature brethren.

What Paul is concerned about is "what is in the heart" (2 Cor. 5:12). He is convinced that the motivating force that can bring about transformation is the compelling love of Christ (5:14). With Jesus present, a new future opens up for anyone!

Paul is certain about the impact of the unseen reality of Jesus in a person's life. He argues that Jesus died and rose so believers might live for the Lord (2 Cor. 5:15). Was Christ's sacrifice for nothing? Never! What Jesus died for will come to pass. And so we have to evaluate our fellow believers and ourselves in a new way. In Christ we are each a "new creation; the old has gone, the new has come" (2 Cor. 5:17). Renewed within, we can count on God's own incomparable power, and we can know that we will "become the righteousness of God" (2 Cor. 5:21).

The evidence that counts is not what we see *now*. The evidence that counts is hidden from our view. But the reality of Jesus in the heart of the believer is the abiding, eternal proof that His people will not be trapped in present sins.

Confidence. The New Testament describes the impact of Jesus in our lives in these words: we "are being transformed into his likeness with ever-increasing glory, which comes from the Lord, who is the Spirit" (2 Cor. 3:18). God is at work. The process is taking place. We are not what we are. We are what we are becoming.

Understanding becoming gives a great surge of confidence. I can look at my youngest without despair. I can correct in a positive way, sure that he will change.

This confidence is important as we relate to other Christians, and even as we look at our own hard-to-shake habits. When you or I expect another person to fail, those expectations are communicated. And they have a significant influence on the other person. → **EXPECTATIONS** My youngest had come to be discouraged by his own behavior because he sensed that I had no confidence he could change! When that happens, we trap ourselves by refusing to try and failing to trust God to help us change.

But "becoming" says that God is at work committed to helping us become more and more like Jesus. We're not to overestimate the importance of present behavior, or become discouraged. Instead we can count on the hidden presence of God Himself in a human life, and confidently expect growth and change.

I've found that seeing the importance of "becoming" is one of the most important principles in Christian life. I can now relate to my children and other believers in a positive, encouraging way. I don't have to evaluate others by their failings or their weaknesses. I don't have to be critical. Instead I can honestly express my confidence in them, for I know that God is at work in their lives.

Expressing such confidence may be one of the greatest gifts one person can give to another. When another person who feels trapped in the habits of his life realizes that you or I believe he can and will change, he too may begin to trust God and open up his life to Jesus, and thus begin to become.

BEGINNING. The bearded old leader leaned on his staff and made one demand of God's people: "choose for yourselves this day whom you will serve" (Josh. 24:15). It's like this with every beginning. Choose. Today. Whenever we decide that we'll begin tomorrow, what really has happened is that we chose not to begin!

Like good intentions, decisions to begin later make ideal paving stones. But not for roads to anyplace you and I want to go.

BELIEFS. Beliefs are important to Christians. After all, our beliefs have been revealed by God. They're far better than those guesses and wishful thinking others grope after. No wonder we sometimes feel pleased about what we believe.

The trouble is, those beliefs we're so sure of can lull us into complacency. When we're so sure, we tend to evaluate beliefs only by their truth or falsity. We ignore other important questions that go beyond whether a belief is right or wrong.

For instance, when we want to pass on our beliefs we set up schools ("Sunday" and others). Are schools the way God intends Christian beliefs to be shared from generation to generation? Well, we never ask. And if someone else asks about our education, we defend ourselves by saying that what we teach is true. We just assume that since *what* we teach is true, the *way* we teach it must be all right.

Actually, whether a belief is true is not the only issue. Oh, truth is important. Of course it is. → **TRUTH** But truth isn't *enough*. We need, for instance, to ask another question about our beliefs. What are we to *do* with them?

Some people answer that by simply "holding" their beliefs. They pull them out on Sunday, like pictures of their grandchildren, and proudly show them off. But holding beliefs, even true ones, is often irrelevant!

When Israeli spies crept into Jericho, they questioned a woman there named Rahab. Rahab shared that her whole city was completely demoralized. The citizens had heard reports of the children of Israel, and were sure that "the LORD your God is God in heaven above and on the earth below" (Josh. 2:11). They held on to that belief a week later as the tumbling walls of Jericho crushed out their lives. Only Rahab had acted on her belief and asked God to accept her.

One night a man named Nicodemus came to see Jesus secretly to interview Him. He was one of the inner circle of religious leaders, and that night he admitted the whole council knew "you are a teacher who has come from God. For no one could perform the miraculous signs you are doing if God were not with him" (John 3:2). They were right. Yet within a few years these same men spearheaded the movement to crucify Jesus.

The apostle James goes a little further. He pulls back the veil and lets us peek for a moment into the hidden world of supernatural beings. Pointing into the crowded darkness, James looks over at us and asks, "You believe that there is one God. Good! Even the demons believe that—and shudder" (James 2:19). Their beliefs were absolutely true. And the truth terrified them.

Being right in our beliefs may not be as all-important as we make it. We can hold a true belief and have it be of absolutely no value to us. So we're back to that point I tried to make earlier. What we *do* with our beliefs, not just whether they are true or false, is important.

Scripture stresses this over and over. You're convinced that Jesus died and rose again? Then act on your belief and receive Him as Savior (John 1:12). You're positive that God loves even the sinners of this world? Then love your enemies (Matt. 5:43–48). You confidently expect the world to end at God's command? Then check out your values and concentrate on living a holy, godly life (2 Peter 3:10, 11). Every truth of Scripture can make a difference in the way we live our lives. Christian beliefs aren't just to be held, but are realities meant to reshape our lives. Jesus put it this way:

> Therefore everyone who hears these words of mine and puts them into practice is like a wise man who built his house on the rock. The rain came down, the streams rose, and the winds blew and beat against that house; yet it did not fall, because it had its foundation on the rock. But everyone who hears these words of mine and does not put them into practice is like a foolish man who built his house on sand. The rain came down, the streams rose, and the winds blew and beat against that house, and it fell with a great crash (Matt. 7:24–27).

Yes, Christian beliefs are a firm foundation for life. But they are also a foundation we have to build on—by putting our beliefs into practice every day.

BELIEVING IN. The people of the first century were familiar with believing "that." But believing "in"? This phrase, so common today, was new enough that the writers of our New Testament actually invented a grammatical construction to express their thought. It's called the "mystical dative," because it connects "believe" and "in" with "God."

In the first century belief focused on facts. "Sure," a person might say, "I believe that." But when it comes to truths revealed by God, the Lord isn't primarily concerned with our nodding agreement. God is no cosmic quizmaster. He doesn't run a supernatural game show, or pass out salvation as a prize for right answers. God is a Person who loves, and who wants a personal relationship.

And that's what "believing in" was all about. Belief "that" agrees with the facts. Belief "in" reaches out to trust the Person the facts reveal. → **FAITH/FAITHFULNESS**

BIG. It's a little disconcerting when we Americans, so impressed by bigness, see the rather cavalier way the Bible dismisses the subject. In fact, all we get in Scripture is the mention of ten big toes and one (each) big pit, big price, big branch, big stone, and big talk.

Actually, the Bible seems more impressed with small. Saul, a good head taller than any other Israelite of his generation, was a total failure as king. It took an average-sized David to make it as monarch. And Zechariah encouraged the few discouraged thousands who reestablished a colony in the Promised Land after the Babylonian captivity by telling them not to "despise the day of small things." From that struggling community, Messiah Himself one day emerged.

Personally I like Jesus' parable of the talents. He told of a man who left his servants money to invest while he went on a journey. When he came back, the servants reported how they had invested the few thousand dollars he'd left them. Each one who had put his resources to work heard the same words of praise: "Well done, good and faithful servant! You have been faithful with a few things; I will put you in charge of many things."

Do you suppose it's not the big things we yearn for that are important after all? It may be that faithfulness in little things is what counts with God.

BIRTH CONTROL. Historically there are two forms of birth control: the prevention of conception and the termination of pregnancy (abortion, exposure). The Roman Catholic church has traditionally condemned both, holding that sexual relations in marriage are justified only if children may be conceived. Protestants have generally held that sex in marriage is an expression of love and commitment and is good whether or not a child might be produced. So Protestants have been more open to contraception, although the typical American Catholic practices birth control despite official church disapproval.

Today a number of birth-control methods are available. These range from surgical sterilization of husband or wife, to chemical (the pill) and mechanical (condoms, IUD) means to prevent conception. Any couple considering birth control should consult a physician, and particularly ask about possible harmful side effects of the pill.

Few Christians argue that sexual relations in marriage are valid only when there is the possibility of producing a child. But some do feel uncomfortable with the idea of an artificial prevention of conception. Isn't practicing birth control or family planning an attempt to avoid what might be the will of God? Wouldn't it be better to leave it in His hands? Others point out that God has given humanity dominion over nature (Ps. 8:5, 6). This dominion carries with it responsibility and the necessity of consciously discerning God's will. Shouldn't we then accept responsibility for family planning? Shouldn't Christians expect the Holy Spirit to guide them in the timing of conception as in the other decisions a married couple must make?

Biblical. There's little specific biblical material to help a couple decide which approach they should take. The Old Testament of course prohibits the killing of infants once conceived → **ABORTION** and also seems to discourage sterilization (cf. Deut. 7:14; 23:1, but see also Matt. 19:12). Continence (refraining from sexual relations) is never suggested in Scripture as a means of birth control. Instead, regular sexual relations are considered to be the right of both husband and wife (cf. Exod. 21:10; 1 Cor. 7:3–5).

It is clear that modern methods for prevention of conception were not available to believers in Bible times. However, one form of contraception was available and was practiced. This form is male withdrawal (coitus interruptus), and is mentioned in Assyrian and Babylonian records, in the Talmud (writings of Jewish rabbis), and in Genesis 38:8–10. This form of birth control is not prohibited, or discussed, in either Testament.

One reason for the lack of discussion of birth control may well be the strong positive attitude toward large families reflected in the Old Testament (Ps. 127:3–5; Deut. 28:15–18). In a rural society large families were important, and thus a blessing. In addition, underpopulation was a persistent problem in many periods of Israel's history, when fewer children survived to become adults. It is not at all clear that large families are as desirable today, when overpopulation and depletion of world's resources are constant threats.

Conclusions. What if a couple does determine that, as Christians, they should take responsibility to be personally guided by God as to when (or if) they will have children? What factors might they consider? One consideration surely is their ability to provide for children (1 Tim. 5:8). Another consideration is the impact of a child on the emotional or physical well-being of mother or father. There is reason to believe that a common calling to a special ministry that might be hindered by children is an important consideration (cf. 1 Cor. 7:32–35). Certainly the decision to bring children into the world calls for serious commitment to their upbringing (Prov. 22:6).

Each couple which uses—or chooses not to use— birth-control means needs to remain sensitive to their changing situation and remain open to fresh leading from the Lord. God has a way that is best for each of us; He will teach us to walk in it.

BITTERNESS. It's strange. Most bitter people argue

that they've got a "right." It's almost as if the Constitution guarantees us the right to "life, liberty, and the pursuit of bitterness." Still, I suppose it's understandable. From the earliest use of "bitter" to describe a person rather than a taste, bitterness has been associated with disappointments, grief, hatred, and anger.

• He got the promotion I deserve. Don't I have a right to be bitter?

• She was so young, and the kids still needed her. Don't I have a right to be bitter?

• They always preferred my younger brother. Don't I have a right to be bitter?

Maybe. But do you enjoy the surging animosity and resentment? Do you like the hard and harsh edge that bitterness gives to your personality, and to life itself? Even the person most sure he has a right to be bitter hardly enjoys the impact of bitterness in his life. It's cold and empty comfort, this strident conviction that at least *my* bitterness is justified.

The Bible shows us how to deal with bitterness, in two New Testament passages. Each challenges the notion that bitterness is justified. Hebrews 12:15 says, "See to it that no one misses the grace of God and that no bitter root grows up to cause trouble and defile many." James 3:14, 15 teaches, "But if you harbor bitter envy and selfish ambition in your hearts, do not boast about it or deny the truth. Such 'wisdom' does not come down from heaven but is earthly, unspiritual, of the devil." Bitterness is not a right. It's a sin.

How then do we deal with this particular sin and break the grip of bitterness? The context in Hebrews and James shows us.

(1) *Stop blaming.* Bitterness is a person's response to a situation. It is not caused by someone else. Getting victory over bitterness begins when we admit that our reaction is wrong, and we "do not boast about it or deny the truth."

(2) *Recognize God's grace.* The context in Hebrews stresses discipline (cf. 12:1–13). God the loving Father brings difficult experiences into every life, "for our good,

that we may share in his holiness." Such experiences are not pleasant, but are painful. Yet they are intended to produce "a harvest of righteousness and peace."

Bitterness takes root when we look at our painful experiences and see only injustice. God invites us to look again. Behind each we can see the hand of our loving God, committed to use even what hurts us for our good. No wonder the writer says, "See to it that no one misses the grace of God" (12:15). Only by losing sight of God's gracious love could a person imagine he has a "right" to be bitter.

(3) *Keep on loving.* How do we react to people who hurt us? Hebrews simply tells us to "make every effort to live at peace with all men and to be holy" (12:14). James develops this theme more fully. He contrasts the envious and angry reaction bitterness stimulates with a response made possible by applying God's wisdom in our personal relationships. Heaven's way, James says, "is first of all pure; then peace loving, considerate, submissive, full of mercy and good fruit, impartial and sincere. Peacemakers who sow in peace raise a harvest of righteousness" (3:17, 18). Put simply, we respond to others with love, not antagonism.

For anyone who has cultivated bitterness, God's uprooting prescription seems terribly hard. Despite all the inner turmoil bitterness brings, the right to be bitter seems too precious to surrender. But the life bitterness spoils is not the life of the person we're angry at. It's our own! And God loves us too much to want us to spend our days wandering in a garden in which the fruit of every tree sets our teeth on edge.

Try God's way. Reject bitterness, and taste the satisfying sweetness of His harvest of righteousness.

BLAME. "He made me angry!" Or, "She starts every fight!" It's so comforting to blame and to deny responsibility. The trouble is that anger is my reaction, not his. He didn't "make" me. I got angry on my own. And that fight . . . well, I joined in, no matter who started it. You and I can try, but when it comes to reality, we

BLESSED
BLOOD
TRANSFUSIONS

really cannot blame others for what we feel or do.

How about blaming them for what *they* feel or do? Sorry, God's got a different way to deal with that. It's called forgiveness.

When you come right down to it, we might as well cross "blame" and "blaming" out of our dictionaries. It's a word you and I just can't use.

BLESSED.   We don't use this word much anymore. But anyone who realizes that this old-fashioned, King James term means "fortunate" and "happy" is likely to want to be blessed! At least, he will until he comes across a list of people Jesus considers blessed, and hears about being poor in spirit, about mourning and being meek and merciful, and about hungering for righteousness. And of course about the blessedness of being persecuted.

Somehow being humble or mourning doesn't sound much like being "fortunate" or "happy" to us! Where are all those new cars and fun vacations and success and health and the loving family life we think of as the real blessings in life?

But as usual, Jesus has a better idea. He shares that idea with us in the Beatitudes (Matt. 5:1–10). He contrasts present with future (mourn now, be comforted then), and He focuses our attention on the inner character of a follower of God (humble and pure in heart) rather than on the material things human beings immediately imagine when they think of blessings.

Why is Jesus' approach better? Because His approach recognizes the fact that this world is rapidly decaying, and is about to be replaced by the shining glory of God's eternal kingdom. When the material universe is shrugged off like an outworn suit of clothes, and we step into the gloriously new, all we will bring with us are those inner qualities our present journey forms. Then the real root of happiness will be clearly seen, and all will realize that the truly fortunate are not the rich, but the righteous.

BLOOD TRANSFUSIONS.   Those ten pints of blood in the average adult are literally life fluid. Blood carries oxygen and proteins that feed the body, transports waste products, regulates chemical balance and temperature, and has components that defend against invading bacteria. Today many lives are saved and many kinds of surgery are possible only because millions of pints of blood are collected and distributed for transfusion.

Blood transfusions are carefully regulated. Individuals have different factors in their blood, and are classified by different types (A, B, O, etc.). The different types cannot be mixed without danger. In 1951 it was discovered that red blood cells could be frozen, kept for up to five years, and then thawed and transfused.

As the blood system has been understood for only a few hundred years, it's not surprising that a number of strange notions have been associated with transfusion. For instance, some used to think that the characteristics of the donor could be transferred with their blood: a speculation that gave Samuel Pepys "occasion to many pretty wishes, as of the blood of a Quaker to be let into an Archbishop." In fact, blood is no carrier of character. Nor are racial differences reflected in the blood. Under the skin, a human being is a human being.

It's the religious significance of blood that has led some to hesitate over transfusions. The Old Testament's announcement that "the life of a creature is in the blood" (Lev. 17:11), and God's gift of blood on the altar to make atonement for sin, gave an early significance to blood that has only been understood later. But the significance of the blood shed on Old Testament altars was symbolic: it prefigured the coming sacrifice of Jesus and the cleansing of all things by His blood (cf. Heb. 9:15–28). The blood that is the focus of our Christian faith is that of Jesus. No spiritual significance carries over to the fluid that courses in our veins and sustains our life on earth.

Christians have no reason to hesitate about accepting transfusions. And have every reason to serve as donors. As Jesus explained once to Pharisees who tried to put obstacles in the way of an act of healing, it is always lawful to do good (cf. Matt. 12:9–14).

BODY. I understand that the chemicals in the human body, which used to be valued at a little more than $2, are now worth more than $41, and going up. Of course, that price is without you being present. With you there, your body's priceless.

BOREDOM. Boredom once was known as the "royal disease." Only kings had time to spare to become bored. In today's democratic society, even the average person can afford the luxury of ennui. With no need to struggle constantly for necessities, we suddenly discover that extra time and extra possessions can't keep life interesting. The extras we've worked for simply litter our lives. We're left standing, looking around at emptiness. How boring it all seems.

Some people suggest a simple remedy for boredom. Get excited about something. The trouble is, when we're really bored, there's nothing that seems exciting.

Solomon was a victim of boredom when he wrote the Old Testament Book of Ecclesiastes. As the wealthiest of Old Testament kings, Solomon had been able to gratify every whim. Blessed with a vast intelligence, he had cataloged plants and animals, recorded a thousand philosophical sayings, carried off diplomatic coups that kept his nation out of war, designed and built beautiful buildings, reorganized the administration of his kingdom, and still found time as a sociologist to carefully observe the way others lived. But ultimately Solomon lost his bearings. His accomplishments seemed meaningless, and his despairing conclusion was simply: "Utterly meaningless! Everything is meaningless" (Eccl. 1:2).

Solomon's conclusion about life was wrong. But as boredom edges over into despair, that's how life looks. And boredom is likely to strike anyone. On one quiz of personal problems, the item most often checked by college students was "boredom." The mid-life crisis we hear so much about, that dulls the life of so many between 35 and 40, is likely to be a chronic form of boredom.

So what can we do about boredom? That depends on the kind of boredom a person experiences. There are at least three perspectives on boredom that should help us think through these types and how to deal with them.

Boredom as a blessing. Some psychologists believe that deep chronic boredom—those long-term blahs that threaten to become depression—may be a doorway to self-discovery and growth. They note that every ten years or so most adults draw near the end of one stage of life and need to stretch out to grow into another. Boredom often marks the end/beginning of our life stages. A time of boredom may be a natural hesitation; a pause, warning us to break out of the pattern of our normal activities and wait.

Many suggest that waiting quietly isn't enough. They say we need to look inward at such times, and need to reexamine our feelings and values and goals. The reexamination may be the key to breaking the grip of boredom. Breaking out into new growth is the unexpected blessing of this kind of boredom.

Boredom with our lifestyle. Boredom need not be a warning light on the dashboard of life, telling us we need an inner overhaul. Boredom may be a sign of exhaustion: a symptom of a hectic, active life that has been overburdened by busyness. Or it may be the product of routine: of a bland diet of repetitions, day after day after day.

The cure of lifestyle boredom is relatively simple. Break the bland patterns. Eat out and order foods you've never had. Plan five unusual vacations, imagining yourself in strange situations. Take a different route each evening when you drive home from work. Take a course in a local evening school. Volunteer as a Big Brother or Big Sister. Put yourself purposefully in situations in which you feel some stress. When boredom is rooted in hectic rush or in dull, comfortable routine, breaking out of the pattern can make a real difference.

One point here, however. Just imagining and planning something new won't break the grip of boredom. Acting is the key. Decide to do something different—and do it. Feelings of boredom are unlikely to change immediately, and it may take an effort to dredge up enough energy to act. But that change in behavior will have an impact. A change in feelings will follow.

Boredom from purposelessness. The boredom Solomon experienced as a deepening despair was spiritual. The Old Testament historical books tell us that in his later life Solomon turned away from God. The Book of Ecclesiastes tells us that he determined to search out the meaning of life on his own, using only his own intelligence and reasoning from evidence his senses could gather in our world of time and space. Purposely ignoring revelation, Solomon searched for some human experience or achievement around which to build a satisfying life. Exploring intellectually, and personally trying each avenue that seemed to promise purpose, the discouraged monarch ultimately surrendered to boredom and reached the conclusion that life is meaningless after all.

Sometimes the look within our personality, and the look around at our pattern of life, fail to provide the answer to boredom. It's then we need to go back to the basics that Solomon deserted and ask what is it that God says provides a sense of purpose. Linking life to God, and committing ourselves to those things that God says makes life significant is the ultimate answer to boredom.

BORROWING AND LENDING. We live in an age of institutionalized lending. Banks and loan companies, and even department stores, are in the business of lending money or merchandise. For a healthy rate of return, of course. After all, business is business.

It's rather startling then to look in the Bible and discover individualized lending. There borrowing is viewed as an interpersonal transaction, not as a business deal. "If there is a poor man among your brothers in any of the towns of the land that the Lord your God is giving you, do not be hardhearted or tightfisted toward your poor brother," the Old Testament instructs. "Rather be openhanded and freely lend him whatever he needs"

(Deut. 15:7, 8). Later writers pick up this theme. David describes the righteous man in Psalm 15 as one who "lends his money without usury." Proverbs is convinced that "he who is kind to the poor lends to the LORD, and he will reward him for what he has done" (19:17).

This encouragement to openhandedness is most striking when we realize that under Old Testament Law, all unpaid debts were canceled each seventh year. Deuteronomy warns that a lender is not to hesitate because the seventh year is near, and "show ill will toward your needy brother and give him nothing." Instead the lender is to "give generously to him and do so without a grudging heart" (15:9, 10).

Jesus picks up this thought in Luke. "If you lend to those from whom you expect repayment, what credit is that to you? Even 'sinners' lend to 'sinners,' expecting to be repaid in full" (6:34). The Bible's radical approach is, lend freely "without expecting anything back."

When we put the Bible's teachings together, we find a picture of borrowing and lending that generates surprising guiding principles. In the Bible we discover a way to meet the needs of others without injustice, without massive government programs, and without doing violence to an individual's self-respect. Lending here is not a way in which the wealthy exploit the poor, who must borrow no matter what the money costs in terms of interest. Instead, lending is a way the wealthy can use their possessions in service to their fellow men. The principles that protect this as a truly caring system are:

(1) Borrowing and lending are for meeting real needs. We do not borrow to pre-purchase some luxury or convenience.

(2) Borrowing and lending are family affairs. Needs of brothers and sisters are the special concern of the household of faith.

(3) Borrowed money is to be repaid, if possible. The self-respect of the borrower is protected: he is not seeking charity.

(4) The repayment obligation is limited. If an individual is unable to repay the loan within a reasonable time,

the debt is freely canceled. This is important, for biblical borrowing and lending are intended to relieve pressure on those in need, not to increase pressure by piling on additional burdens of debt.

(5) Borrowing and lending require mutual trust. This is a very personal transaction in the biblical context. The one borrowing must trust the lender not to lord it over him. The one lending must trust the borrower to honestly seek work to meet his own needs and, if possible, to later repay (cf. 2 Thess. 3:6–10). Within this context of mutual trust, borrowing and lending is a way to help bear each other's burdens (Gal. 6:2), while still ensuring that each seeks to carry his own load (Gal. 6:5).

Will the individualized approach to borrowing and lending work in our institutionalized world? I've been a part of one congregation in which it has and have had the privilege of making loans (partly repaid) to meet needs. Along with the privilege of giving, and the help of brothers and sisters in finding others jobs, God's unique approach to borrowing and lending can be applied today. With blessing for all. → **BUYING ON CREDIT**

BRAGGING.   The best single statement on bragging ever made? That's easy. "Who makes you different from anyone else? What do you have that you did not receive? And if you did receive it, why do you boast as though you did not?" (1 Cor. 4:7). Bragging is pretty silly when we realize that everything we have and are comes as a gift from God.

BROTHERS.   The New Testament epistles use the word "brother" some 55 times (NIV). Of these, only two identify those who are brothers by birth. The other 53 identify those who are brothers by the new birth. It's a great discovery for a Christian to realize that, because of Jesus, he or she is a member of a family composed of God's children.

Peter puts the family obligation this new relationship creates in perspective: "Now that you have purified yourselves by obeying the truth [a phrase that here means 'believing'] so that you have a sincere love for your brothers, love one another deeply, from the heart" (1 Peter 1:22). This family relationship makes our differences with other Christians relatively insignificant. We're family, and what links us together is our common Father. That, and love.

BUDGETING.   A budget is a spending plan, designed to help you set goals and allocate your money accordingly. I've gotten along without a budget for 26 family years. For one simple reason. As soon as any money has come in, it's rushed out again. Why worry about a budget when there's nothing extra anyway?

The experts tell me I've been foolish. If I analyze my costs, they say, I'd probably be a lot better off by now. At least I'd have a better handle on my spending patterns, and I would know for sure how I use what money I do have.

I'm not really convinced that a budget would have made all that much difference in my case. But I'm impressed by one thing. As those experts say, keeping a budget lets me *know* what's going on with my money. I'm quite sure that one meaning of that "self-control" the New Testament sets such store by docs involve getting control of the use of my money. "Where your treasure is," Jesus said, "there will your heart be also." Is it possible that at times I've been the victim of a straying heart and never even realized it? It might be good to know.

The chart on pages 84 and 85 gives a sample budget format that lets you compare what you plan to spend each month with what you actually do spend. A person who used the form for six months or so would know more about his or her spending patterns, and maybe would want to rethink those patterns to better reflect his or her values. That's important as inflation constantly erodes our real spending power.

One or two notes on the budget form. It's divided into fixed and variable expenditures. The fixed expenditures are costs that belong in a "can't touch" category, because failure to meet them might lead to serious financial troubles. Many place savings in this category, on the assumption that everyone needs emergency funds to cover three or four months of all expenses. Some Christians might argue that giving, at a 10% rate, also belongs in the fixed expenses category. → GIVING

It is in the variable expenses category that we potentially have flexibility and can shift our spending patterns. After all, even though food is a necessity, eating beef isn't. And if heating costs get too high, I suppose we could shut off some of the rooms in our house and opt for cozy living. Adjusting variable expenses isn't likely to be easy, but at least it is possible.

Have you any flexibility in your present situation? Are you satisfied that your spending reflects your values and your goals? Well, there's a way to find out. Use the form for four to six months and find out. Enter your monthly income here _____, and your monthly expenses there. And see.

FIXED EXPENDITURES	planned	actual	(+) or (−)
mortgage or rent	_____	_____	_____
taxes (other than withholding)	_____	_____	_____
installment debt	_____	_____	_____
insurance premiums			
life	_____	_____	_____
auto	_____	_____	_____
homeowners	_____	_____	_____
health	_____	_____	_____
savings			
emergency	_____	_____	_____
other	_____	_____	_____

VARIABLE EXPENDITURES			
food: groceries	_____	_____	_____
meals out	_____	_____	_____

utilities: gas or oil	_____	_____	_____
electricity	_____	_____	_____
telephone	_____	_____	_____
household expenses	_____	_____	_____
auto (gas, maintenance)	_____	_____	_____
public transportation	_____	_____	_____
clothing: adults	_____	_____	_____
children	_____	_____	_____
pocket money: adults	_____	_____	_____
children	_____	_____	_____
personal care (barber, etc.)	_____	_____	_____
entertainment/ recreation	_____	_____	_____
medical/dental	_____	_____	_____
contributions	_____	_____	_____
miscellaneous	_____	_____	_____

TOTAL FIXED   _____ _____ _____

TOTAL VARIABLE   _____ _____ _____

NOTES:

BUT. All too often we add a "but" after saying something nice about a person. "Sue's friendly all right, but. . . ." "John, I appreciate the good work you've done on this project, but. . . ." Because of the way we use the word, to take away compliments we've just given, it's stunning to see that God uses "but" in just the opposite way. Here are a few of His "but" statements.

● "The wages of sin is death, but the gift of God is eternal life in Christ Jesus our Lord" (Rom. 6:23).

● "'No eye has seen, no ear has heard, no mind has conceived what God has prepared for those who love him'—but God has revealed it to us by his Spirit" (1 Cor. 2:9, 10).

● "No temptation has seized you except what is common to man. And God is faithful; he will not let you be tempted beyond what you can bear. But when you are tempted, he will also provide a way out so that you can stand up under it" (1 Cor. 10:13).

• "Like the rest, we were by nature objects of wrath. But because of his great love for us, God, who is rich in mercy, made us alive with Christ even when we were dead in transgressions" (Eph. 2:3–5).

There are many more "but God" statements in the Bible. Sometime you might want to make a personal study of them. For now though, just think what the "but" statements tell us about God. We use "but" to take away after saying something good. But God uses it to add blessing, after honestly stating our faults or needs.

BUYING ON CREDIT. It's almost un-American not to. Some warn stridently that credit cards are plastic bondage, but most of us know we couldn't own a home or even a car without good old credit buying. Why, credit buying is the foundation of our economy: it's credit that raises our standard of living! So I suppose I shouldn't knock on-the-cuff living. It's our way of life.

Actually, today's Truth in Lending laws have corrected many excesses of the past. At least today we know when we're paying $750 for a $475 TV set. But I suspect there are still some things you and I ought to consider.

Necessities and conveniences. We might consider making a distinction here. We can agree that credit buying is good since it enables us to have a house and car. But that doesn't mean credit is good to use for that new TV set or vacation trip. The house and the car are necessities. The new TV and the vacation are conveniences, or maybe even luxuries. The first two we need. The next two we want. We surely can justify using credit to make sure we have the necessities. But it's not so clear that credit is a good way to go about getting the extras in life.

What's the real cost? This is another question we ought to consider. In the early '80s many people did: they held off buying a new car because they felt interest rates were too high. But many of these same folks hurried out at Christmas to buy several hundred dollars worth of presents at even higher department store rates.

Most of us haven't looked at the cost when credit buying involves relatively small amounts. But look at it this way. Take just $100. If you save it at 10% interest, your $100 becomes $110. If you buy on credit at the typical store rate, that $100 shrinks to $82. The actual difference to you in just one year is $28, or nearly 30% of that $100!

Now multiply that hypothetical $100 by all the hundreds you've used in credit, and multiply that by the number of years you've been in credit debt, and you get a feel for the real cost to you of credit buying. Depending on how much credit you use for your conveniences and luxuries, you can be robbed of a big part of your total income.

Discretionary income. This is another thing to consider. Discretionary income is the amount of money you have left after you pay your basic (food, housing, etc.) bills, to use as you choose. You may use that extra to eat out, for vacations, to put in savings, to give toward missions, or to buy insurance. What's important is that this is "extra" money you can choose to use as you want.

What happens though, when we go on a credit splurge and fill the house with new furniture to replace the old, or take that "once in a lifetime" trip now instead of later, is that you surrender your freedom of choice. Now, for the next three or five years, that "extra" money is already committed to the credit payments that have to be made. When an opportunity comes up to make an unexpected investment, you can't. When a Christian brother or sister has an unexpected need, you can't respond. Credit buying has robbed you not only of freedom of choice, but also of opportunity for ministry.

Tyranny of things. This too needs to be considered and from a Christian perspective may be the most important matter of all. Credit buying today is tightly linked with advertiser's efforts to convince us that if we're to be happy we really "need" the things they offer. We don't. Jesus warned against that fallacy and the foolishness of having treasures on earth that are subject to moth and rust, and where thieves might break in and steal. Our treasure isn't really found in this world. Our heart need not be here either. When we free ourselves of the notion that things can make us happy, we take a giant step toward gaining control of buying on credit.

Are there guidelines a person can follow to help him or her deal with credit buying? These simple principles might.

(1) Use credit for necessities; avoid using it for luxuries.

(2) Set up a savings plan with your discretionary income. You add about 30% to your purchasing power. And you protect your freedom of choice.

(3) Evaluate purchases by your priorities. It's not "wrong" to enjoy conveniences or luxuries. But you don't want the rusty treasures of this world to obscure the really important things in life.

RULES FOR CREDIT BUYING

- Shop for money. Don't sign a store contract when it may be cheaper to borrow the money directly from your bank.
- Make sure every blank in the credit contract is completely filled in before you sign. This should include a description and serial numbers of any appliances or large items you purchase.
- Be sure you understand just how much the interest costs are. New Truth in Lending laws require the rate and the total amount of interest be disclosed before you buy.
- If credit is refused, you have a right to know the reason. If the reason is a poor report from a Credit Bureau, you have a right to see the Credit Bureau's information on you, and to insist they correct their records if they are in error.
- Credit life insurance is relatively expensive. You can usually reduce your cost by increasing your regular policy if a purchase involves a long-term obligation that you believe should be covered.

CALENDAR.

St Augustine laid great store by the calendar. He felt that through festival "and set days we dedicate and sanctify to God the memory of his benefits." Without a structured year, "unthankful forgetfulness should creep upon us in the course of time." Somehow the weeks and months that mark the passage of the year should be cued to turn our thoughts to God.

The notion of patterning the year is common in all cultures. God Himself established the pattern for Old Testament saints. Weeks of seven days recall Creation; the seventh is a Sabbath, on which the people of God share His rest. The Jewish year began in April with Passover, to recall God's redemption of His people from Egypt. Another festival celebrated His goodness at first harvest. For a week God's people camped out under the stars, sheltered in leafy booths, to recall the years of wilderness wandering. Each festival had special times to worship, and times in which they could retell stories of God's acts in history. Thus the pattern of the year constantly directed attention to God's great acts and words of self-revelation.

The earliest church seems not to have had a "Christian year." It probably observed the Jewish festivals. But the week was changed, as the first day replaced the seventh. On the first day of the week our Lord rose from the dead: the eyes of God's people were now focused on Jesus as risen Savior.

In time a special Christian calendar began to develop. It focused on the two major events that set New Testament faith off from that of the Old. Christmas celebrated Jesus' incarnation as a human being. Easter celebrated His death and resurrection. As time passed additional days and times were added to the church calendar. Today liturgical churches link every Sunday with special readings and some historical remembrances.

There's much value in the underlying idea of organizing the year to celebrate our faith and to pattern our remembrance of God. Planning a personal or family Christian year may well help us do what Augustine insisted is so important: "dedicate and sanctify to God the memory of his benefits."

How might we shape a Christian family year? Begin by blocking out two weeks at Christmas and ten days at Easter. Then add other special periods: a week to recall Creation, linked with your vacation. Include two weeks of missions focus, when you read together missionary biographies and/or make a special gift. Another period might be included when you evaluate how you can respond to God's calling to "love and good deeds." And add three days at Thanksgiving to record God's blessings during the past year.

Try to make each celebration special. During Christmas decorate your home, make special foods, sing carols. Work out a series of special Bible readings, perhaps to feature Old Testament prophecy concerning Jesus' birth. Each night as advent approaches, light a new candle, place it around a manger scene. As the night of nights approaches, the scene will be bathed in ever brightening light as new flames are kindled and added to the others.

Build patterns that can be repeated annually with creative variety. Summer vacations can focus on Creation, with psalms that become more special each year as you travel to new locations and see more of God's greatness revealed.

God, by His own acts in history, has given meaning to the past and the future. And He has given meaning to our lives. By planning a family calendar that reminds us of God's great acts, and of our response to Him, we can avoid "unthankful forgetfulness" and bind our lives more closely to Him.

CAMPING.   Lying on the ground with rocks poking at my back and the inside of my sleeping bag caked with sand, I swear I'll never do it again. For years, though, I have. My boys and I raft down some river, or take a boat back up some hundred-mile lake and camp along the shore. The bugs feast on us, the sun peels layers of skin, the food disappoints, and the fish were really hitting—last week.

Publications these days trumpet "carefree camping"

and tout the tents and other equipment that make living outdoors fun for moderns. But I know better. From now on I'll camp out in some motel, where after a day on the water I can take a nice, hot shower, have a restaurant meal, and sleep in a comfortable bed. You'll never get me out camping again. Till next year.

CANCER. Cancer is probably the most feared. of modern diseases. Yet today, early diagnosis and improved treatments save many who would have been lost just a few years ago. The American Cancer Society (1979) reports that its incidence has declined slightly over the past 25 years. This is despite the fact that cancer is associated with aging, and in the past many who develop the disease today would probably have died of other illnesses before developing their cancer.

There are many types of cancer. The most common in men are lung (22% of cancer cases), prostate (17%), colon (14%), urinary (10%), and leukemia (8%). The most common in women are breast (27%), colon (15%), uterus (13%), lung (8%), and leukemia (7%).

Cancers are caused by changes in the genetic material of normal cells. Although the disease is not hereditary, some families are more likely to develop cancer than others. The development of cancer is supposed to be triggered by "carcinogens." These agents may be chemical (such as cigarette smoke), biological (such as viruses), or physical (such as radiation). Many carcinogens are man made. But even if we removed these from the environment, natural carcinogens would remain.

Cancer treatments. Cancer is not a single, or a simple, disease. There are many types of cancers. These types behave differently and are treated differently. Some cancers are responsive to drugs. Others respond to radiation or can be surgically removed. While there is still no "cancer cure," as the 1980s began more than 40% of all victims of cancer were being cured of the disease. Yet several things about treatment typically concern cancer patients. What about costs? How will I react to treatment?

Will there be pain? And how will my sickness end?

Costs in cancer treatment can be very high, both in medical expense and in possible inability to continue work. In 1976, the last year for which figures are currently available, there were more than 1.5 million hospital admissions for cancer, with bills averaging $2,282 per admission. Nonhospital costs averaged 65% of hospital bills. Total direct payments for cancer ran over $6 billion. As several hospital admissions are likely in the treatment of cancer, it's important to have some kind of coverage for major medical expenses.

One disturbing aspect of cancer treatment is that some persons experience side effects. A person may feel sick to his stomach, weak, or lose weight and hair, or become excessively nervous. Sometimes these side effects are discouraging and make it appear the patient is losing ground rather than improving. However, treatments can often be varied, and special nutritional programs can help to offset their impact. One serious problem is that discouragement may lead some to reject medical help and rely instead on supposed wonder treatments or special diets. Such untested alternatives have far less chance of helping than the treatments available through the medical establishment, which today effect an increasing number of cures.

Pain is another concern of cancer patients. Most doctors and hospitals are sensitive to the importance of pain control. At times localized pain may be permitted for diagnostic purposes or other reasons. But no cancer patient need fear a pain-wracked end. Enough drugs will certainly be used to make a person's final months and weeks comfortable.

For some the uncertainty associated with cancer is far worse than any pain. Because of the nature of cancer, no doctor will make confident predictions of the future. But a doctor can provide information, such as 80% of the persons with this kind of cancer are alive and living normally five years after treatment. In addition, a doctor can explain completely the different treatments being used, and what reactions if any may be expected. Both patients and family members should feel free to ask any questions that occur and expect complete answers.

Impact on the family.   Cancer is one of those diseases that has a great impact on the family, as well as on the individual. Because cancer treatment is usually long-term, the patient and family members must live with the impact of the disease for months and years.

There are three major areas in which cancer affects family. First, cancer means that family plans will have to be revised. Vacations will have to be restructured, finances may be seriously affected, and future expectations will be radically changed. Cancer also usually brings a change in relationships and interaction within the home. If Dad functioned as family leader or disciplinarian, his illness will likely require that Mom take on the dominant role. Mom's illness will mean a reorganization of family tasks, with the children taking added responsibility, or maybe cutting activities as her income from outside work is lost. These changes strain relationships, as happens when any pattern is broken, and tend to create additional anxiety and uncertainty. It is very important that family members talk about their feelings and work through together ways in which they can cope. The stress can and often does actually strengthen the family bonds and lead to greater closeness.

The final impact of cancer on the family is the change it also introduces in relationships with groups outside the home.

By working through the changes together, and understanding what is happening to the family members as well as to the patient, the family can be a strong support for a person with cancer. → DEATH AND DYING

Christian perspectives on cancer.   Christian faith is vital whenever an individual is threatened by cancer. But faith is sometimes misused, and can actually create unnecessary problems. For instance, Christian friends may imply that the disease is a punishment from God, or that it demonstrates a lack of "faith" on the part of the patient.

When a person is already under stress, this kind of subtle attack is particularly damaging. → **SUFFERING**

Another dangerous misapplication of faith may come if the disease does not seem to respond readily to treatment. Some Christians may then abandon treatment, intending to rely on the Lord alone for healing. → **HEALING** For many this may be a form of bargaining: an attempt to "prove" the individual has enough faith, and thus ought to be healed. → **BARGAINING WITH GOD**

It is vitally important that the Christian root his or her understanding of illness and current relationship with God in God's own revelation. We need to understand the kind of person God is, and remember His commitment to us as His children. This healthy approach, and a demonstration of how faith helps, is illustrated in an interview with Pat Palau, a cancer sufferer interviewed for *Family Life Today*. Pat expressed three convictions that help her maintain a healthy attitude: (1) God is good. (2) God is with me. (3) God does care about me. Assured of these truths, the Christian above all others can maintain a positive outlook on life, even when suffering from cancer.

Pat also shared a number of Bible verses that comfort her. These range from verses that stress the importance of taking each day as it comes (Matt. 6:34, Ps. 118:24), to verses that give images of God's character (He is a solid rock, Ps. 18:2: a refuge, Nah. 1:7, etc.). Other passages promise strength (Isa. 26:3, 4; 40:31), and recall His commitment to do us good (Jer. 29:11). No believer is immune to natural discouragement and times of being "down." But for each of us, words of comfort and encouragement can be found in Scripture: words that give us continuing hope.

This is perhaps the most important thing for the victim of cancer to remember. God's plan for each of us is good. He weaves "all things" that we experience into a rich tapestry, blending all together that we might come to the fullest possible experience of His presence and working in our lives. Sickness may come. But sickness, even cancer, cannot rob the Christian of his or her confidence and hope.

CANDY. "Buy me the candy, Dad, and I'll do you a lot of good some day." That's what my parents told me I promised my father one day when I was four. I got the candy. I'm not sure I've done him that good I promised. And I'm very sure their indulgence didn't do *me* any good!

Today we realize that sweets, and overeating when young, produce fat cells that guarantee a life-long weight program. I still struggle constantly with gently rolling flab, in part because way back then my folks wanted to be good to me.

We know today that surging sugars in the bloodstream charge up hyperactive boys and girls, and that candy is no favor to them. And if you've lived with a high-strung youngster about to wear you out, you'll probably pay for that candy you make available twice—once in money, once in stress.

Considering all this I've reached the sad conclusion that it just isn't worth it. So Dad, pass the apple. I'll pass up the candy, thanks anyway.

CAN'T. Realistic assessment? Just pessimism? It depends. I know I'm limited. Some of us have tried so many times, and failed, we just accept the fact we can't make it and no longer try. But for Christians, "can't" isn't the last word. We can look away from ourselves, and add a fresh dimension to life: "I can do everything through him who gives me strength" (Phil. 4:13). If I have to depend on my own resources, I say "can't." If I focus on the Lord, I know I can.

CAPITAL PUNISHMENT. In 1976 the Supreme Court announced its decision. "We hold that the death penalty is not a form of punishment which may never be imposed, regardless of the circumstances of the offense, regardless of the character of the offender and regardless of the procedure followed in reaching the decision to impose it." Not every justice agreed. Thurgood Marshall argued that the death penalty is "excessive," and that if the people were fully informed, they would view it as "morally unacceptable."

The arguments. Many polls have shown that the majority, concerned over the increase in violent crime, favor the death penalty. The majority seems convinced that "simple justice" requires punishment, and that the threat of execution is a deterrent to murder.

Opponents of capital punishment raise several arguments. They suggest that execution is just as much killing as the murderer's original crime. How can we take a moral stand against killing, and then kill the killers ourselves? Opponents also note that the death penalty is applied unequally. Nonwhites and poor people are the most likely to be condemned. They also point out that the death penalty is *not* the deterrent most believe it to be. Some states with the death penalty show more murders per capita than other states without it. In addition, some Christians argue that imposing the death penalty is out of harmony with what we know of God's loving and forgiving nature. Surely the idea of retribution does not fit the gospel unveiled in the New Testament.

Proponents of the death penalty disagree. They insist that there is a great difference between an act of murder and the judicial taking of life as a penalty for murder. Proponents also insist that the death penalty *is* a deterrent, at least in some cases. And certainly there is no risk that a person executed for murder will later be paroled to kill again! As for the problem of discrimination, proponents point out that recent Supreme Court decisions contain safeguards against abuse of the death penalty. As for the argument from God's forgiving nature, Christians who believe in capital punishment note that God is just as well as loving. Justice and love must both be affirmed if we are to have a balanced picture of the nature of God.

Biblical evidence. Several lines of teaching in the Bible should be considered when we explore this issue.

• The first mention of capital punishment is found in Genesis 9:5, 6. "From each man, too, I will demand an accounting for the life of his fellow man. Whoever sheds the blood of man, by man shall his blood be shed; for in the image of God has God made man." The force of the passage is to insist that the unique value of individual human life must be affirmed and protected. There is nothing comparable in value to a human life but another life. Thus to establish life's value, the principle of capital punishment is established. Society can affirm the value of life by demanding life for no crime but murder, and by setting a death penalty for murder.

- The Old Testament commandment is, "Thou shalt not murder" (Exod. 20:13). Some have tried to extend this to rule out killing in war or judicial execution. → **PACIFISM** However, the Hebrew word is not a general word for killing, but does specify murder. Thus the Old Testament makes a clear distinction between killing in war and execution by society, and malicious acts of murder.

- The Old Testament also makes a clear distinction between premeditated murder, "with malice aforethought" and accidental (unintentional) homicide (cf. Deut. 19). A number of communities were set aside in Israel as cities of refuge. A person who killed another individual unintentionally could flee to one of these refuge cities and be safe. However, the elders of such cities were instructed to hand over those guilty of premeditated murder "to die. Show him no pity. You must purge from Israel the guilt of shedding innocent blood, so that it may go well with you" (Deut. 19:12, 13). Standards of justice were to be maintained.

- Care was taken to make sure an individual's guilt was fully established. Rules of evidence (Deut. 19:15–21) insisted that witnesses establish the motive as well as the act, and a thorough investigation of witnesses was also called for. The danger of executing an innocent man was thus reduced.

One obvious question is, Why doesn't the New Testament speak out on the question of capital punishment? One possible answer is that the Old Testament principles were well established in law, and did not need to be repeated. However, a more likely explanation is found in the difference between Old Testament and New Testament communities of faith. Israel was not only a faith community, it was also a nation. Thus civil regulations and laws had to be part of its law code. But the church of the New Testament is *not* a nation, for believers live scattered throughout the world, in many nations, governed by many different civil codes. Instructions concerning capital punishment would be moot as far as the church is concerned, for the church neither makes nor administers civil law. Instead, Romans 13 calls on believers to be subject to civil rulers, and to live law-abiding lives.

In American society today, however, the Christian has an opportunity to influence the making of the laws under which he lives. So the Christian citizen must once again deal with the issue of capital punishment, as well as issues like pornography, censorship, teaching Creation in school, etc. What then should a Christian seek to do about capital punishment? For some the answer is: seek to establish laws that parallel those of the Old Testament, and thus affirm the value of individual human life. For others, the answer is: seek to establish laws that isolate the murderer from other potential victims, but permit him to live, in hopes of a later conversion experience.

Whatever your conclusion, the value of each life must be affirmed. And government must accept the responsibility, under God, to administer fair justice.

CAPITALISM. Capitalism is an economic system. The dictionary describes it as a system "in which investment in and ownership of the means of production, distribution and exchange of wealth is made and maintained by private individuals or corporations, as contrasted to cooperatively or state-owned means of wealth." It's popular with some to blame everything from poverty to cancer on capitalism, and insist that in a truly moral society no one would make a profit and everyone would be rich.

The problem with this kind of criticism is that it's naive. The roots of injustice are not found in economics, but in human nature. Sin will warp any system men might devise. Certainly the record of socialism and communism hardly inspires confidence that if capitalism were abandoned, evils would automatically go away.

We can admit that our system has its faults and abuses. But we ought to note two things that make it preferable. First, the system places a premium on initiative and creativity in place of regulation. As a result the society as a whole enjoys a high standard of living, and individuals know they can move upward in society.

The second advantage is even more important. In other systems increasing regulation is required to control individuals, and to determine who receives what benefits from whatever the system produces. Capitalism, however, maximizes individual freedom, as the money persons earn functions as a regulator. Although each of us has more or less money available, each of us has freedom to choose to spend it as we wish. There are things I cannot do because I lack sufficient money. But I can allocate the money I do have to reflect my own values and priorities in life.

CAREERS.
For most of us, life is oriented around our work. Most of our time and effort are invested in our job. Work provides income and a sense of personal achievement, so our career is important in many ways.

For many people these days, life will hold more than one career. Technological changes have forced many changes in lifestyle, opening undreamed-of work opportunities and shutting down old, familiar ones. What do we know about careers and how to choose them that can help a young person starting out, or an older person about to make a mid-course correction?

Geography.
During the '80s certain states will continue population growth, which will create job opportunities. A person willing to locate in one of the growth areas may have a better chance finding a job he or she wants. The best states? Statistics suggest Idaho, Nevada, Utah, Arizona, Colorado, Alaska, Florida, and Hawaii. These are closely followed by Wyoming, New Mexico, Texas, Georgia, North and South Carolina, and Virginia. The first group of states can expect over 30% growth between '75 and '90. The second group of states can expect between 20% and 29%.

Occupations. Studies of trends in occupations also suggest that certain fields offer better opportunities than others. For instance, you're likely to be disappointed if you'd planned to become a teacher, a doctor, an airline pilot, or a file clerk. On the other hand, things are looking up for various medical aides and assistants, scientists, engineers, secretaries, and computer related workers. In blue collar areas things look good for electricians, plumbers, mechanics, and repairmen.

Specific fields with the largest number of job openings expected annually through the '80s are: dental assistants (14,500), medical assistants (27,200), medical lab workers (18,800), registered nurses (71,000), licensed practical nurses (93,000), drafters (17,300), engineering and science technicians (32,000), secretaries and stenographers (449,000), typists (125,000), computer operators (16,400) and programmers (13,000), bank clerks (54,000) and officers (16,000) and tellers (30,000), personnel workers (23,000), air-conditioning and refrigeration mechanics (10,900), industrial machinery repairmen (42,000), maintenance electricians (13,800), barbers (15,200), cooks and chefs (78,600), and police officers (22,000).

You and a career. It's just as important to evaluate your own personality and goals when thinking of a career as to evaluate the job market. What do career counselors suggest a person should evaluate?

• Will you be more comfortable with routine work or work that calls for imagination and ingenuity? The first alternative provides pattern and security. The second brings risk of failure and lots of insecurity.

• Will you be more comfortable in a large or small organization? The first tends to be impersonal, and calls for working through bureaucratic channels. An individual seldom sees the immediate impact of his contribution and has proportionately smaller influence. In the small organization you work through personal contact and see the impact of your decisions quickly.

• Will you be more comfortable working up from

the bottom or starting nearer the top, perhaps as a "management trainee"? Near the bottom you make fewer serious mistakes, but it takes longer to advance. Near the top you're vulnerable to jealousy and have opportunities to make glaring errors.

• Will you be most comfortable as a specialist or generalist? The specialist is trained in a technical or professional field, and is an expert in one clearly defined area. The generalist usually is in management, working with people, with planning, and with coordination of the efforts of others.

Training.   The kind of occupation that interests you and your temperament both help you decide on training. Some occupations call for in-service training or technical schools rather than college. If you plan on college without graduate school, most counselors today suggest focusing quickly on courses that equip you for a career. Many colleges now offer special training courses evenings for older persons who want to prepare to change careers. And of course skills gained in one field may well transfer to a new career field. It's wise to have some notion of your area of interest and your temperament before you enroll in training programs.

The Christian dimension.   While opportunity and personal temperament will play a valid role in the search for a career, the Christian adds another consideration: ministry. In a very real way, every occupation should be viewed as ministry. Work not only pays our way through life and brings personal satisfaction, it also provides an avenue of service to others.

Ministry can take many forms. The job of a builder who creates homes in which families will live, the travel agent who helps plan vacations, and the nurse who gives direct emotional support to patients along with medicine, is as much ministry as the preaching or counseling of a pastor.

Maintaining the awareness of ministry is important for us in our career. For one builder I know, satisfaction comes with providing quality homes at a fair price, in an environment designed to enrich life. Others I know must be in direct touch with people if they are to maintain a sense of ministry.

This then is something you need to consider in finding your career. What is my vision of ministry? What can I do to best serve others through my work? Whatever you choose, you can know that work *is* serving others, so "whatever you do, whether in word or deed, do it all in the name of the Lord Jesus, giving thanks to God and the Father through him" (Col. 3:17).

CARING. A new famous experiment points up something important about caring. A number of students at a theological seminary were sent on an errand, along a route where they would pass a person who appeared to be ill. Some were going to preach a sermon on the Good Samaritan. Others were simply carrying a message for a professor. It didn't seem to make much difference whether a student's thoughts were on the Good Samaritan or the prof. Some stopped to help. Others did not.

But the insight into caring came when the experimenters noted *how* different students helped. Some helped, and then went on their way when the man feigning illness claimed to be better. Others simply would not let him go. They insisted on coming along; on buying coffee or a coke; on hovering beside him even when he insisted he was able now to go on alone. Checking back, the experimenters reached this conclusion. Some helped out of concern for the man. When he was better, they released him. But some helped because they needed to be helpers! They would not let him go because their own psychological needs were met by having others dependent on them.

It's important for Christians to care. But Christian caring focuses on the man or woman in need: Christian caring tries to help others get on their feet, to function with independence and self-respect. Christian caring is *not* using others, keeping them dependent because of our own inner need.

CAT NAPS. I can drop off for 20 minutes, wake up refreshed, and plow back into my work. Waken either of my sons after 20 minutes, and you've got a zombie. How come? Well, maybe my sleep cycle is shorter (the norm is 90 to 110 minutes). Getting waked up in the middle of a cycle is rough. Or maybe my kids drop more quickly into deeper sleep levels, while I drift on the edge. One thing, though. We can't train ourselves to cat nap, or do it by making an effort. So don't feel guilty if you can't cat nap. Envious maybe. But not guilty. It isn't your fault.

CELIBACY. One of the strange notions floating around our society is that sex is a need. "Having sex is just as natural as having a ham sandwich," the argument goes. "Each satisfies a normal human need." Really? Without food, a person would die. Now, *that's* a need. Without sex the survival rate is pretty high.

The whole issue of celibacy is serious, though. Particularly if you remember that possibly one third of the adult women in the United States are currently unmarried, as are a high percentage of adult men. What are their options? Listen to conventional wisdom, and you get the impression they have only two: get married, or find sex outside of marriage.

Despite popular opinion, random sexual experiences are far more likely to create needs than to meet them. And sex is a poor substitute for the fulfilling kind of love that can come through many different human relationships. In fact, *not* having sex is more likely to meet the needs of the single than adopting an increasingly empty playboy lifestyle.

In a 1980 book, *The New Celibacy,* Gabrielle Brown points to evidence that more men and women are abstaining from sex—and enjoying it. Brown argues that relationships without sexual pressures are freer and more meaningful, that more energy is available to invest in work and other interests, and that persons can now be truly loving toward others without mixed motives. When sexual manipulation of or by others isn't at the center of one's consciousness, the rest of life comes into perspective. So

Brown suggests that modern singles consider a decision to go celibate; a decision that may not be easy, but will be rewarding.

Scripture. The Bible simply expects the unmarried to be celibate. When we remember that God wishes only good for us, we realize that celibacy must be a positive, healthy alternative to marriage.

The apostle Paul deals with the issue openly in 1 Corinthians 7. There he points out that sexual drives are not evil, and that one purpose of marriage is to provide mutual physical satisfaction to husband and wife. In marriage, celibacy is not to be practiced, "except by mutual consent and for a time, so that you may devote yourselves to prayer" (7:5).

Paul strongly recommends singleness to those who are unmarried. He believes the celibate life is to be preferred, largely because a married couple must devote time and concern to one another, while a single person like Paul can enjoy the freedom to devote himself or herself fully to ministry (7:29–35).

But Paul realizes that marriage and singleness both are callings from God: alternative lifestyles, each of which is a blessing. He suggests that those who experience strong sexual feelings should consider marriage, accepting this as an evidence of God's calling. But those who are not compelled by their passions will do better, Paul suggests, if they exercise self-control and choose the celibate life (7:8, 9).

The important contribution of 1 Corinthians 7 is that it invites each of us, despite social pressure to marry, to evaluate carefully: What is my particular calling from God? I am not to view marriage as a "good," while seeing the celibate life as an "evil." Both pathways in life are good. Each way is a calling: a gift from God, given to the individuals He chooses to live meaningfully in each state.

So let's ignore the opinions of the world and of men and women driven by passions that will always remain unsatisfied. We can safely ignore their foolish urgings. A human being really is not a ham sandwich, and sex isn't a need. Using others and being used by them in an attempt to satisfy passions is neither healthy nor good.

CENSORSHIP. I just heard about two more cases of censorship. In one a teacher assigned a high-school class readings that some parents felt were indecent. In the other, a hotly fought local election hinged on the promise of some candidates to require a librarian to remove five books a local minister had preached against. As you might imagine, the whole town took up sides and cried out, "Censorship!"

In a free country like ours, the very word "censorship" is suspect. The word carries such negative weight that even those with rational arguments in favor of censorship tend to hang back, a little ashamed of themselves.

Actually, the debate over censorship is an ancient one. It has roots going back to Plato at least. Leaving out for now the question of blatant pornography, → **PORNOGRAPHY** what are the pros and cons of censorship?

Pros. Plato, in his *Republic,* advanced the classic argument in favor of censorship. He believed that society was obligated to promote the moral good and to uphold traditional values. To do this society must stand guard over what children are taught and what they read. Children should be introduced only to that which is right, and protected from corruption by keeping evil thoughts and ideas from them. The goal of Plato's program was a happy, healthy society, with happy, healthy citizens. But whatever Plato called it, there is no doubt that his approach rests on strict censorship.

Cons. Those who object to censorship affirm the liberty of the individual. Any attempt to censor is an attack on personal freedom and the individual's right to make his own responsible choices in life. No one, the argument runs, has the right to control what others may or may not be exposed to. No one has the right to rob others of freedom. What is needed is a marketplace of ideas, where each individual can be exposed to many values and make free personal choices. Thus society must have a tolerance for the beliefs and preferences of others. Otherwise it will never be a truly free society.

Response to the pros. Our Christian perspective raises serious questions about both the pro and con positions on censorship.

For instance, what if the material being censored isn't indecent literature, but presentations of the gospel? We can argue that children shouldn't be exposed to evil. But in the Soviet Union, those in power believe that religion isn't good for the young! If censorship becomes acceptable here, what protection do we have for presentation of religious literature?

We have the same problem in the case of the public school teacher who required objectionable readings. If we challenge her academic freedom, then what about the professor who teaches my youngest son at Michigan State University? He exercises his academic freedom and clearly presents a Creationist view as a reasonable alternative to evolution in his Natural Science courses. But if we tell the literature teacher what she can and can't teach, why shouldn't some other group insist Professor Moore not teach from his Christian viewpoint?

We have a similar concern about the library situation. If we remove the books we don't like, why shouldn't the American Atheist Society demand removal of any religious books they don't like?

Once we permit censorship in a free society, we open the door to the loss of freedom for ourselves as well as for others.

Response to the cons. But our Christian perspective also raises questions about the position of those who reject all forms of censorship.

Governments, in making laws and regulations, always place some limits on the freedoms of citizens. They do this because the concern of government is the well-being of all citizens—not the maximum "freedom" for every individual. In fact a government can only promote the highest good of its citizens if it acts responsibly to establish limits that protect the rights of all.

To insist on a marketplace of ideas philosophy for adults is one thing. But to insist on a marketplace for the young is another. Government must bear some responsibility for determining, for instance, when a child is too young to exercise freedom to drink, even though it permits adults to buy liquor. Isn't government also responsible to set limits on the ideas and values to which the young are exposed? The marketplace of ideas argument might be valid for the public library, but isn't the school classroom something different?

Actually, the teacher who assigns doubtful readings and the librarian who orders books to which some object are not expressing their personal freedom. Each is acting as an agent of government. When their choices are questioned, it is not a matter of censorship as much as it is an examination of whether their actions as agents of government actually express the conscience of those who in our free society *are* (through their representatives) the government!

Dealing with "censorship" issues. It is important when issues like the two described here come up that the debate not become confused and the real issues clouded. Questioning of choices of teachers or librarians must be kept out of the realm of personal attack. The issue must be raised as to whether their actions *as agents of government* actually express the will of the people.

How might a parent, with a teen in the class of a teacher like the one described, handle the situation? A first step might be to let the teacher know that you find the readings objectionable, and that your child will not do them for conscience sake. This can be done graciously, without attacking, and with a request that other readings be substituted. If the teacher should insist or grade your child down, the parent has a basis for taking up the situation with the school administration.

If the Christian parent is concerned about the trends

in the school, he or she can run for the school board. There, as an agent of government himself, he can work to establish guidelines that will set policy to be followed by the classroom teacher.

Censorship is a gray area. Neither pro nor con arguments are conclusive. So to keep the issues in balance, a Christian needs to integrate and act on the following three principles together:

- The Christian must affirm and protect the right of others to be responsible to their own conscience and to God.
- The Christian must exercise his own responsibility to do what is right, for him and/or for his family.
- The Christian must act as a responsible citizen, who is concerned for the health and well-being of his community.

While these principles provide a framework, they do not tell us what we are to do in any given situation. For that, each one of us needs to seek personal guidance and wisdom from God.

CENSUS TAKING. Counting people has a long and honorable history. The Babylonians, in 3800 B.C., had a system for revenue control that called for counting all taxpayers. The Egyptians were busily counting by 2500 B.C., to organize armies of workers as pyramid construction crews. The Old Testament mentions several censuses, the first around 1490 B.C. (cf. Num. 1:2, 3, 19). Biblical census taking included only fighting men over twenty, so we have no Old Testament figures on total population. The largest group reported is some 1,570,000 in the time of David, and this census seems to have been incomplete (cf. 1 Chron. 27:24). The Romans were the best census takers of the ancient world. They kept careful records for more than 400 years. Rather than visiting homes, they simply insisted everyone show up in his or her home town and report to be counted. This is why Mary was forced to make a journey to Bethlehem with Joseph when the birth of Jesus was so near. Then as now, the government wanted a good handle on population, income, and other information that would affect economic planning.

God seems to be the only Person around with no need to make continual census counts. But then, He's already got the very hairs of our head numbered (Luke 12:7). There's nothing about us He doesn't know. And love.

CHARACTER. Social scientists believe that character develops, shaped by continuing choices that conform to principles. There's no such thing as instant character: it must be forged. That's why Romans 5 says, "we also rejoice in our sufferings, because we know that suffering produces perseverance; perseverance, character; and character, hope" (5:3, 4).

CHARITY. The Bible word most closely linked with charity is one that means mercy, or compassion. Some 250 years before the New Testament was written, a noun derived from "mercy" was coined to describe those acts of kindness that came from caring. In time this word developed the specialized meaning of making a contribution for the poor.

Jesus wasn't enthused about the common practice in His day of making a public show of charity (Matt. 6:1–4). But He did commend a caring response that meets others' needs (Luke 11:41; 12:33; Acts 9:36; 10:2). James makes it clear that people who really do care will express their compassion in practical ways (James 2:15, 16). In fact, a personal touch seems to characterize most New Testament charity.

Which makes me wonder. I recently spoke at a conference sponsored by an organization of community churches. In their promotional material they reported on a touching array of shared ministries: foster grandparenting, meals on wheels, and others clearly designed to help those in need. Then I looked at their budget report. All the funds for these ministries came from the federal government. The primary task of one staff member was to write proposals seeking more government funding!

I don't question the motivation of these brothers and

sisters. But what a commentary on our times. We Christians have become so much children of our society that we institutionalize our charity, permitting the government to tax others to pay us to care. → **GIVING**

CHEERFULNESS. "A cheerful heart is good medicine" (Prov. 17:22).

CHILD ABUSE. Child neglect and abuse are nothing new. But they are stunningly widespread. Estimates now suggest that up to 500,000 children suffer cruel or abusive treatment. Some even have called child abuse the largest killer of children in America today. Even when "abuse" is narrowly defined to include only serious physical or mental harm, there are literally thousands of parents and children who need help.

Legally. Federal law, passed in 1974, defines abuse as "any physical or mental injury, sexual abuse, negligent treatment, or maltreatment of a child under the age of eighteen by a person who is responsible for the child's welfare under circumstances which indicate that the child's health or welfare is harmed or threatened" (Public Law 93-247). Individual states have more narrowly defined child abuse and have separated it from neglect. Michigan's Child Protection Law is typical of many states. It defines child abuse as "harm or threatened harm to the child's health or welfare by a person responsible for the child's health or welfare, which occurs through non-accidental physical or mental injury, sexual abuse, or maltreatment" (1975).

Following legislative acts like these, a number of government agencies have become involved. Regulations have been developed, and police or social workers are now able to act to help. Because local laws and enforcement agencies differ, a person who suspects child abuse will need to check to see to what state or local agency it should be reported.

Recognizing the abused child. There are a number of

symptoms that may suggest child abuse. Physically there are the obvious indicators: bruises, burns, or welts. But there are other signs as well: clothing that does not match the weather or provide protection, malnutrition, dirtiness. There are also psychological symptoms, like hostility or destructiveness. Extreme withdrawal, shyness, crying, or fear of adults are other psychological symptoms. Each of these can usually be observed at school, in the neighborhood, or perhaps in Sunday school.

What bothers most people is the question of what to do when child abuse is suspected. Certainly a first step is to check out the resources available in your community to help such children and their parents.

Parents of abused children. It's not possible to provide a profile that fits all abusing parents. But there are common characteristics. ● Child abusers are likely to have been abused when they were children. ● Child abusers are typically immature and see themselves as inadequate or worthless. ● Child abusers tend to view the child as a small adult and have unrealistic expectations of how he or she should behave. ● Child abusers experience great frustration in their relationship with their children and express that frustration impulsively as violence.

A glance at these characteristics tells us at once that abusing parents need help, as do abused children. In fact, in most cases the most practical thing a concerned Christian can do is to help the child by ministering to the parents.

Ministry. What can Christians do to help? Here are some possible steps to consider.

(1) If you sense God's call to minister in this area, pray for several others to work with you as a team. If groups are already formed to work with abusing families, you might volunteer.

(2) Be careful not to develop an adversary relationship with abusing parents. Most are disturbed by their own behavior, but do not know how to change. Be willing to support the parents as well as the children with your concern, for even the children do not want pity.

(3) The most successful approaches to helping parents have involved forming discussion groups, where parents talk with other abusers about their feelings and how they relate to their children. Exploring alternative ways to deal with common situations that lead to abuse does help, as do sessions in which parents learn the characteristics of children of various ages.

(4) The gospel has a particularly vital relevance, as it alone can meet the deepest needs of abusing parents. For those who feel worthless, the gospel comes with the affirmation that they are loved and valued by God. For those who feel frustration and hopelessness, there is the promise in Christ of growing beyond personal limitations. Only Jesus can provide this hope and the promise of self-controlled maturity.

Yes, there will be some situations in which abused children must be separated from their parents. But in most cases, supportive love and growing personal relationships can be used by God to heal the parents, and rescue them as well as the child.

CHILDLESSNESS. Some three-and-a-half million couples in the United States, or one in every six marrieds, are believed to have some problem with conceiving or carrying a child to term. For many, the specter of childlessness seems a threat able to destroy their hopes of a full and meaningful life.

Part of the problem lies in the decision of many today to delay marriage, or put off having children till they are in the late '30s or even '40s. The mid-'20s is the time of maximum fertility for both men and women.

Although having a family has lower priority for the current generation, the discovery later on that a couple *can't* have children may have serious psychological impact.

Medical causes and treatment of infertility. About 80% of those who come to a doctor because of childlessness will learn the cause of their infertility. About half of these can be helped to have a child. About half the time the cause is found in the wife, with the cause in the husband about 30% of the time. In the others there are combined problems.

A woman's fallopian tubes may be blocked, she may have a hormone disorder, or there may be scarring in the reproductive tract caused by venereal disease or an IUD contraceptive device. Abortions may have caused damage, or there may be effects from radiation or chemicals to which she was exposed years before.

The most likely causes of male infertility are inadequate sperm production or the inability of the sperm to reach and fertilize the ovum. The older notion that childlessness could be attributed in many cases to "psychological causes" has not proven to be the case.

Today a number of medical techniques are used to correct medical problems. Couples are taught to keep temperature charts, and to time intercourse for maximum likelihood of conception. Drugs may be used to induce ovulation. Operations may repair blocked tubes or other internal problems. The latest approach, which caused so much press attention, is conception in a test tube (e.g., outside the woman's body), using the wife's egg and the husband's sperm. The fertilized egg is replanted in the wife's womb, and the pregnancy proceeds normally.

Some couples have gone so far as to use artificial insemination with the sperm provided by a donor other than the husband.

As noted, probably 50% of those whose fertility problems are diagnosed can be helped to have their own children. But many other couples will not be helped and must work through their response to the prospect of a childless future.

Psychological impact of infertility. Much stress is created when a couple discovers that they may be unable to have children. Many men and women will have feelings of inferiority, as though they themselves are damaged or defective. One spouse may be furious at his or her partner if the other seems less concerned. Or the infertile partner may feel he or she is "cheating" the spouse. The couple may share a sense of loss of direction: the expected family will never come, and many feel suddenly helpless as though the future were now out of control.

Couples with a fertility problem generally pass through three stages. The first stage focuses on self-feelings and the overpowering sense of worthlessness that often emerges. This will occur while a couple is undergoing the extensive tests and various treatments used today to diagnose and treat infertility.

The second stage occurs when treatment proves unsuccessful. Now the couple comes to a time of mourning what will never be. The mourning may be a shared experience, which brings husband and wife closer. This period also may be a time of examination, in which their goals and values in life are discussed and shaped.

The final stage comes when the couple decides together how they will respond to childlessness. They may choose to adopt. → **ADOPTION** Or they may focus their time and energy on a profession, hobby, or ministry to others.

Biblical insights into childlessness.   Parenthood seems important to most people in our world. Somehow being a woman means being a mother: being a man means being a father. Childlessness attacks these deeply rooted feelings and thus challenges a person's sense of identity.

The Scriptures also show a deep appreciation for family and view children as gifts from God. But the Bible teaches us that our personal worth and value are not linked with our ability to have children. Each person has some share of the image and likeness of God. Because we are His unique creations, and are the object of His love, we each have worth and value.

It's important to note that the Bible commends both the married and single state. Each is considered a gift, or calling, from God. → **CELIBACY** Life is intended to be meaningful for parent and nonparent alike.

The apostle Paul had no physical children, but through his ministry to others he built lasting and intimate personal relationships with many people. These people whom he won to Christ and nurtured along in faith were his children in the most significant sense of all (cf. 1 Thess. 2:7–12). For Paul childlessness was an avenue to even wider ministry and to close relationships with a widening circle of young and old.

How might a Christian couple, with the perspective on life provided by faith in God, deal with possible childlessness?

• Exhaust the possibility of medical aid for contraception if you do want a family of your own.

• Encourage each other by affirming together that God does have a perfect plan for your lives. Express your confidence to God, praising Him for His goodness and love.

• When feelings of worthlessness or inferiority emerge, keep them in perspective by remembering God's great affirmation in Christ of your worth and value to Him.

• Open your lives to God, seeking His direction for your future life together. If you are convinced that your love for children is an indication of His plan, consider adoption. But also consider serving as foster parents, as Big Brother and Big Sister, or working with children in your church and community. Also remain open to the possibility that your childlessness may be part of God's plan for a completely different kind of ministry. Take time in your praying about the future. Remain confident that God does have a purpose for your condition, and expect Him to reveal it in His time.

• Build closer relationships with Christian brothers and sisters in the family of God. Living close to brothers and sisters you will both find and give the love that each of us needs.

CHILDLIKE/CHILDISH. What's the difference? Well, Jesus commended childlikeness when He pointed to a youngster who had come immediately at His call—in contrast to the adults of Israel who held back. Like the child, we're to be responsive when Jesus speaks to us.

Paul is the one who pictures childishness, in 1 Corinthians 13. He describes it as thinking, reasoning, and talking like a child rather than an adult. So when it comes to our relationship with God, we're to set aside judgment and simply respond in faith. But when it comes to living in this world, we're to take a good, mature look around and stop being childish.

CHOICES.   Making choices helps a person feel free, and feel competent. But certain kinds of choices help most. What kinds? Choices that are made between a reasonable number of positive alternatives.

If we limit alternatives, the sense of freedom dwindles. If we make it a choice of negatives, it feels like no choice at all. Too many options, and we feel overwhelmed rather than competent and free.

When we understand these things about choices, we're able to help our children feel both free and competent. We replace that single suggestion "Why don't you play with your blocks?" with a suggestion of half a dozen activities our child enjoys, and let him or her choose.

God follows this strategy with you and me. He invites us to look around and to see a number of ways we can invest our time and energy to serve Him and enrich others' lives. Then God gives us the freedom to evaluate, pray, and make our own choice from His array of alternatives of how to do good.

CHRISTIAN SCHOOLS.   Should you send your children to a public school? Or perhaps they ought to attend that new Christian school? It's sometimes a difficult decision for parents: a decision that must involve consideration of more than the extra money for tuition and the extra miles driving the kids to and from. What do we know about Christian schools, and what should parents consider in making a decision about their children's schooling?

The Christian school movement.   In the '50s, except for parochial schools operated by Catholic, Lutheran, Reformed, or Adventist groups, there were probably only some 350 Christian day schools in the United States.

Moving into the early '80s there were some 4,000, with two to three new Christian schools being established daily! It has been estimated that more than 20% of the population is being educated in private schools, most of them Christian.

In the '50s, few considered sending children to a Christian school. Those who did were moved by strong religious feelings. Most wanted to remove their children from temptations to dance, or the corruption of faith that might come with the teaching of evolution.

By the late '70s there were great changes. Most citizens viewed public-school education as inferior, and saw the public school as a dangerous environment. Parents concerned about quality education sought out private schools, convinced the public school was not doing the job. There seems reason for the view. Test scores of children in Christian schools associated with one accrediting group (ACSI) are generally one to three years ahead academically of scores of children in public education. Religious motivation still existed, but was secondary.

Finances. It's expensive to send children to a Christian school. Tuition fees are likely to run $2,000 a child per year, and more. Even so, teacher salaries are generally only 70–90% of those in public education. Costs are one factor that have kept enrollments down. Should Congress adopt one of several financing proposals—such as a voucher system, permitting parents to use the tax money allocated per child in the school of their choice—enrollment in private and Christian schools will multiply.

Curriculum and staff. Despite the perception of most that education is better in the Christian school, many problems do exist. Most are rooted in the Christian school ideal of integrating Christian faith with the content children are taught. But many Christian schools simply use textbooks published for the public school, which fail to integrate faith and subject matter.

Several organizations publish material for Christian schools, but despite claims the materials are distinctively

Christian, these curriculums—typically using self-study, programed materials—are notably superficial and inadequate.

Another serious problem for Christian schools is the lack of teachers trained to integrate faith and learning. Most teachers are qualified—as teachers. But the task of bringing Christian perspective to subject matter is complex and difficult. Even those Christian colleges currently preparing teachers specifically for the Christian school tend to train in traditional ways, without focus on the distinctives promised in Christian education.

Christian schools can be grouped today into three broad categories, each linked with associations that are trying to improve all aspects of Christian schooling. One group of schools is oriented to Bob Jones University. Schools in this group tend to be militant, legalistic, and separatistic in their approach to faith. Educationally they remain traditional, relying on one classroom teacher with a group of listening students. Another group of schools is related to the Christian Reformed Church (CSI, Christian Schools International). Schools in this group provide high-quality education, with some integration of faith and learning. A third group contains schools linked with the Association of Christian Schools, International (ACSI). These schools seem most likely to promote integration of faith and learning, as well as creative approaches to teaching and learning.

Why Christian schools?   Those in the movement are likely to suggest many reasons why parents ought to send their children to a Christian school. A Christian school will help insulate children from some of the drugs, violence, and sexual activities that so many are convinced characterize the public schools. Secular humanism and evolution will not be taught in the Christian school. The environment of the Christian school will encourage friendships with other Christian children, guided by adults who are caring believers. Christian schools do provide quality education: often better than the education offered in the local public school system. Many Christian educators also promise the ideal: an education in which content is taught integrated with the perspective on life provided by biblical faith. While the movement is weakest in this last vital area, some schools are making an honest effort.

Should my children go?   There is no simple yes or no answer to that one. Certainly the Christian school is no panacea, and will not replace the influence of a strong, healthy family. Complicating our answer is the fact that not every "Christian school" provides a good education. Or even good Christianity! And not every public school has a negative impact on boys and girls. Still, if you are wondering where to send your children to school, you might want to consider the following:

  • What is the reputation of the public schools in your area? Do they provide a safe environment and quality education?

  • What Christian schools are in your area? Do they provide a quality education? What curriculum do they use? What associations or groups are they linked with? It might be good to visit a classroom, and talk with parents who send their children to those schools. What is their assessment, and what is important to them?

  • What is the educational philosophy of the Christian school? What is its approach to faith? Do these fit with what you want for your child and with your own Christian convictions?

  • What are the costs?

  • How does your child feel about his schooling? If going to the Christian school would involve a transfer, would this take him away from close friends? Or perhaps a move would provide relief if control at his present school is lax, and he feels under pressure.

There is no moral obligation to send children to a Christian school simply because it claims to be "Christian." The quality of Christian schools, and public schools, varies greatly. So the process of evaluation is important. How good it is to know that God does have a plan and a place for your child, and that He will lead to what is best.

CHURCH. Finding a local church can be frustrating because there are usually several in a community to choose from. How do we decide?

Now some of us have been brought up in a particular tradition, and just naturally head for the representative of our denomination. Others visit around, to look and listen. Does the doctrinal statement express our persuasion? Do we like the preacher? Is there an active group for our teen? A good choir we might join? We check down our shopping list, look carefully at what each congregation may have to offer, and then make our decision.

I agree that these concerns are important. But I wonder if they are as all-important as we sometimes make them. The Bible's picture of the church may suggest other things we need to evaluate as well.

The church in Scripture. "Church" is a Greek word *(ekklesia)* that was used for centuries before the Christian era to mean an assembly of the people. In the sense of "church" it is used only in the epistles, to identify fellowships that came into being after the resurrection of Jesus. There this "church" is always viewed as a community of believers: as men and women who have responded to God's call to faith in Jesus, and formed ranks together as a witness to the world from which they have come. There's no hint of denominations in the Bible. The church is limited geographically: it is the "church at Corinth" or the "church that meets in your home." God's people are all one company, linked in solidarity with all other believers.

There are two dominating word pictures in the Bible portraying this new assembly. The church is said to be a body. And the church is said to be a family.

• The body presents a living organism, with Jesus Himself as Head. This word picture speaks of an organic relationship between the individual believer and Jesus, and through Jesus with every other Christian. This vision of the church as a body emphasizes the fact that, like parts of a physical body, each member in the spiritual body of Christ has a distinctive function. This stress is found in great body passages: Romans 12; 1 Corinthians 12; Ephesians 4. In them we see that each person is placed by God within the body, and each is given special enablement by the Holy Spirit to fulfill his role there "for the common good" (1 Cor. 12:7). → SPIRITUAL GIFTS Each Christian is to use his or her gift to minister to others, in one of many different ways. Through the active ministry of each person in the body, other individuals and the whole congregation grow toward Christian maturity. And new members are drawn to Jesus and joined to the living church.

This New Testament picture then emphasizes the priesthood of all believers, and insists we Christians understand ourselves as persons called to minister to and serve each other. "Church" is not God's people, seated silently in well-dressed rows, but "church" is God's people ministering and interacting. In the few New Testament portraits we have of the church gathering for a Sunday meeting we see many speaking, many sharing, many offering a teaching, many leading in prayer, many suggesting a song, many encouraging others to committed lives (cf. 1 Cor. 14:26–33; Heb. 10:23–25).

• The family affirms an intimate relationship between believers, with God Himself the Father (cf. Eph. 3:14–19). The New Testament constantly reflects the family character of the church. Believers are called brothers and sisters, and are spoken of in other family terms (cf. 1 Thess. 2:7–13; 1 Tim. 5:1, 2). Over and over each apostle urges Christians to love one another with brotherly love, and to build the intimate personal relationships within which acceptance, encouragement, shared joy and tears, rebuke, reproof, forgiveness, and mutual concern will flourish.

There is no doubt that for the church to fulfill its New Testament promise, local congregations must become loving communities—communities in which believers, called out of the world, link arms in mutual testimony to Jesus' love, and devote themselves to one another and to good works.

These two dominating New Testament images tell us much about the church, and give us clues to follow in our search for a local congregation.

Clues to a vital local church. What are some of the things we should desire in a local congregation, and how can we recognize their existence?

• Loving, intimate relationships. Family and body passages of the New Testament are linked with teaching on love, so this is a good place to begin. Try to get a sense of what characterizes relationships of the people in this congregation. Are the people warm—not just to you, but with each other? When you ask a person about others, like "that couple over there," what kinds of things do they share? Check out the church bulletin too. Are the activities listed there all formal meetings or agency activities? Or do groups that meet for sharing and prayer and Bible study seem to have a place?

• Caring for persons. This is another critical aspect of loving. You can tell a lot just by visiting a Sunday morning service. Does the teaching reflect a personal touch? Are personal illustrations used? Is the Bible related to real-life issues in a positive, encouraging way? Do announcements reflect involvement in the lives and concerns of people in the congregation?

• Ministering by all. This is a vital consideration, reflecting as it does the basic body teaching of the New Testament. Is most of the congregation passive, while the hired staff does the work of ministry? When you talk with people, do they seem to have a sense of ministry; a feeling of excitement about what God is doing in the lives of others? One good indication is the role of the elders/deacons of the congregation. Are they seen as respected spiritual leaders? Or are they viewed more as a board, which meets to vote on the business of the church?

• Testifying to the world. Jesus was quite clear when He taught that a loving fellowship will make it plain to the world that these people are His disciples (John 13:35). Check the perception of people in the community who do not go to that church. How are the members viewed? As distant and "stand offish"? Or as warm and caring?

Making your choice. When it comes to choosing a local church, you and I want to look at the more obvious things, like the doctrinal statement and agencies. But we also want to look beneath the surface, to see the inner dynamics of the people as they live together. Sometimes we'll find that ideal church we dream of. Too often no congregation in our area approaches the ideal. What do we do then?

Earlier I wrote about looking carefully "at what each congregation may have to offer." But should our concern be with what the congregation can offer *us,* or what we can offer in any assembly of God's people? Is "church" just a social service agency, and we go to the one that offers us the most services? Or is "church" really the people of God, and we join them because we are called by God to be with our brothers and sisters, to love and to serve them?

What I'm suggesting is that perhaps the most important thing to do in selecting a local church is to pray and seek God's leading to that group of people whom God wants *me* to serve, rather than looking for a congregation that has everything I believe I want to serve me.

What is really exciting is to realize that the church truly *is* people. That even if people aren't loving now, I can love them. And that if people aren't ministering to others now, I can be God's servant by ministering to them. By being a loving, caring, and serving person, I may find that He has a ministry for me in a congregation that is far from perfect, but which still is made up of people whom He—and I—can love.

CLEANLINESS.   Most of us have heard the saying, "Cleanliness is next to godliness." But don't try to look it up in a concordance. It's not in the Bible. In fact, looking around the house after grandson Matthew goes to take his nap, I'd say cleanliness is next to impossible.

CLERGY PAY.   Bob Girard, pastor of our Phoenix congregation for some sixteen years, always felt uncomfortable about taking a salary. Even the pittance he received. The apostle Paul felt the same way, though he recognized that "the Lord has commanded that those who preach the gospel should receive their living from the gospel'' (1 Cor. 9:14). Paul solved his problem. While he worked to start new churches he lived by making tents and on gifts from distant congregations. He didn't want any of the new Christians to get the impression he sought to win them for his personal profit.

Actually, it's not a question of a pastor being paid to care. It's a question of God's people caring enough to meet the needs of those who devote themselves to their service. Clergy aren't "employees" of the local church. They are individuals who give themselves to serve, and who are given to us by God Himself.

But we're left with that nagging "practical" problem. How much? It almost seems unspiritual to ask. But it's not spiritual to keep our ministers struggling on the edge of poverty, either.

Different congregations have developed a number of systems to help them set clergy pay. Some figure the median income of those the same age with college degrees. Some look to find the average income of a comparable professional, such as a high-school principal. One Presbytery uses this interesting formula.

1. Medial family income of the community $_____
2. Adjustments for complexity (size of
   congregation, inner-city, rural, etc.) $_____
3. Minimum salary $_____
4. Add up to 50% for proficiency or
   experience $_____
5. Fair Salary $_____

In addition, of course, the congregation needs to provide a car allowance, book and conference fund, health and other insurance. And some will pay 15% or so of salary into a pension fund. Put all this together (with housing, of course), and you have what's considered reasonable compensation in this modern age.

Of course, few in congregational ministry get—or expect—anything near this much. Many of us seem to feel intuitively that our pastor's reward in heaven will be in proportion to his financial struggles on earth. So it must be our duty to see he is underpaid. God puts the "must" in a different place. "Anyone who receives instruction in the word must share *all good things* with his instructor" (Gal. 6:6).

CLOCK WATCHING.

"Serve wholeheartedly, as if you were serving the Lord, not men, because you know that the Lord will reward everyone for whatever good he does, whether he is slave or free" (Eph. 6:7, 8).

CLOTHING.

Recent experiments by behavioral scientists have confirmed what we know intuitively: clothes do make the person. Not only does dress mark out high- and low-status persons, but others respond differently to the well- and poorly-dressed. In one fascinating phone-booth experiment, a dime was left on the shelf. A minute or so after a caller entered the booth, either a well-dressed or poorly dressed peson tapped on the door and said, "Excuse me, I think I might've left a dime in this phone booth a few minutes ago. Did you find it?" The dime was returned to 77% of the men and women who were well-dressed. How about those dressed as low-status workers? They got the dime back only 38% of the time!

We might conclude that it pays to dress well. At least then more people will treat you fairly and with respect. But there's another moral here too, one reflected in the New Testament long before there were behavioral scientists. Not surprisingly, people seem to have acted the same way two thousand years ago. But then their actions won a different comment.

"Suppose," the apostle James says, setting up his own experimental condition, "a man comes into your meeting wearing a gold ring and fine clothes, and a poor man in shabby clothes comes in also. If you show special attention to the man wearing fine clothes and say, 'Here's a good seat for you,' but say to the poor man, 'You stand there' or 'Sit on the floor by my feet,' have you not discriminated among yourselves and become judges with evil thoughts?" (James 2:2-4).

The point the modern experimenter makes is, if you want respect, dress well. The point Jesus makes is that it is evil to treat *anyone* without respect, so "Don't show favoritism" (James 2:1).

This all helps us understand a confusing biblical concept: worldliness. Worldliness is neither "doing" nor "not doing" those things that decorate the lists of some of us. Worldliness is adopting the values and ways of the world, so that we live just like those who do not know God. It is certainly not wrong to dress well. But the Christian is taught by God to look beyond clothing, to see each person as an individual of worth and value. Each human being is to be treated with equal respect. No matter where he or she fits into the social niches of the world.

COLLEGE. Young people today are expected to go on to college when they finish high school. We may be uncertain about what college they should attend. And about majors. But for most parents and kids, college is the thing to do. After all, a degree is a passport to getting ahead financially in today's world.

Why not to go to college. Before we herd children off to college, we might consider first whether college might not be a waste of their time and our money. Consider these facts. Professors admit that less than 25% of their students care about classwork. As many as 30% of college students say they are not happy with the whole experience. They're there because they think they have to be to find jobs. Yet most college majors have no relationship to any job a student might find. Only majors devoted to professional training—like accounting or business administration or engineering—prepare for future work. All that traditional liberal arts courses provide is a diploma.

The diploma does make a difference in lifetime earnings. But it's not necessarily that good an investment. Suppose a son is interested in cars. He gets a job after high school at a local garage, takes courses while he works, and becomes a master mechanic. By the time his class graduates from college, he may be making more each year than the graduates will earn. But there's another consideration. Let's suppose the money that would have gone for college was invested. By age 65 that nest egg could have earned enough to more than equal the difference in earnings expected from the degree! It's even possible that he might take that money at age 30 or so, and set up his own business. And really come out ahead.

Of course, what's important is that a person enjoy his work and find it satisfying. That's much more important than cash payoff. So probably the first question we need to ask as college approaches is, Does my child really want to go to college? Or is it just that college is the thing everyone does? Or perhaps even because college is a place to be independent at parent or government expense? Prolonged adolescence may sound nice, but it's not necessarily to anyone's advantage.

College certainly doesn't make a person intelligent or ambitious. It doesn't affect basic personality. And that diploma doesn't open as many vocational doors as it once did. For those who want job training, it's usually better to look at one of the many one- or two-year vocational training schools around. → CAREERS It simply may not be wise to invest time and money in a four-year holding pen, unless a young person really wants to learn.

Choosing a college. These days anyone with barely average high school grades can make it into one of the more than 1,400 four-year schools in the United States. Or start out at a convenient, inexpensive two-year community college, in commuting distance of most of our population.

Those who go to college with a career in mind will want to pick a school with a strong program in their vocational field. But most have little idea of post-college goals. One recent study suggested that career decisions usually are not made until the end of graduate school.

You can get information on colleges from several publications. *The College Handbook* is published by the College Entrance Examination Board, and describes some 2,800 two- and four-year schools. Barron's Educational Services publishes *Profiles of American Colleges*. When looking through them for your school, look for costs, location, facilities, etc. It's a good idea to select perhaps a dozen possibilities and write for catalogs. Then look carefully at courses offered, descriptions of the program and campus, and compare the credentials of the faculty (listed in the back of most catalogs). This process should help you narrow down to a half dozen or less.

You'll find it's worthwhile to visit the most likely schools. This will help parents and teens get a feel for the campus atmosphere, and give an opportunity to talk together about college goals. Talk to students and visit a few classes. Are the students friendly? What is their evaluation of the school? Ask administrators how many students typically go on to graduate school or professional schools. A high percentage may be a tipoff to a competitive academic atmosphere. You'll discover that other schools have the reputation of "party schools," where academics take a back seat to social life. All this information will help you choose a college that fits your own personal values and goals.

It may seem like a lot of bother to go through the kind of process described here. For some it may be unnecessary: Johnny and June just automatically go to Mom and Dad's alma mater, or to the community college so they can cut costs and stay at home. For the rest though, research is a good investment. After all, college will cost the family thousands of dollars. And cost a young person four years of his or her life!

What about a Christian college?   Many parents want their children to attend a Christian college. And many youth want to go to a school where they'll be sure of Christian friends, and have a chance to think more seriously about their faith. Before a quick decision is made, here are facts to consider.

• Bible colleges. This is one type of Christian school. Bible colleges offer liberal arts courses, but tend to stress study of the Bible, theology, and other Christian subject areas. Many offer majors designed for those who intend to go into some full-time ministry, such as missions or youth work or teaching in the Christian day school. Those whose motivation is linked to their religious convictions may find a Bible college the best place to go.

• Christian liberal arts colleges. These schools emphasize traditional liberal arts curriculums, and usually require a minimum number of courses in Bible, theology, and Christian ethics. Those with strong religious commitment may successfully link teaching in areas like philosophy with faith. Few make the linkage in fields like history, the physical sciences, languages, etc. Lifestyle on campus will also vary with the school's religious heritage. So it is important to discover the spiritual atmosphere of the campus if that atmosphere is one of your primary reasons for seeking a Christian school.

• Secular schools. It's a mistake to think of the secular campus as "godless." A number of organizations (like InterVarsity Christian Fellowship) have chapters on college and university campuses. Local churches in college towns may have active college groups. Some denominations maintain campus ministers to provide counseling, fellowship, and Bible studies for students. Many young people have found life on the secular campus forces them to serious evaluation of their own values, and to deeper personal commitment.

Conclusions. Should your young person go to college? This is the first question to explore. The answer should not be an automatic yes. For those who do go, choosing the right school is important. In view of the cost in time and money, working through a careful selection process is a wise investment. Whether or not you include Christian schools (or only Christian schools) in your search is something to judge individually, evaluated together by maturity and values and goals. Don't expect a Christian school to insulate a young person from temptation or from pressures. And don't make the mistake of viewing secular schools as spiritual voids.

Perhaps most important, engage in the search and exploration process together. Then, within the framework you establish together, let the young person decide.

COLOR. London's Blackfriars Bridge was known in the Middle Ages for its suicides . . . until it was repainted a bright green. If you're easily depressed, it can help to repaint those dark brown walls a brighter, cheerful color. Have a hyperactive child? Be sure his walls are painted a restful blue or green. Color preferences have even been used to reveal personality patterns and to diagnose illness (Luscher Color Test). While there is a psychology of color, there seems to be no theology of color. The color black, from ancient times, has represented the sinister and malignant, and so is associated in the Old Testament with judgment (cf. Joel 2:31; Isa. 13:10). White, in ancient Greece, represented the fair, the bright, the clear. In the New Testament it is often associated with the risen Christ (Rev. 1:14) and with purity (Rev. 19:11). While other colors are of course spoken of in the Bible we can draw no general significance from them. Perhaps what is significant is the way God has decorated our world. Here the predominant colors of nature are the cool and the restful; the blues and the greens. Our lives are enriched by the bright and stimulating color trims, but the controlling hues represent peace and rest.

COMFORT AND CONSOLATION. What can you say to a thirty-two-year-old mother of two small children, who is locked in a wheelchair? Or to an angry fifty-eight-year-old divorced father, whose daughter's auto accident the week before was another in a series of personal disasters that flooded him with impotent rage? These were questions that led psychiatrist Paul C. Horton to explore the nature of solace. In his 1981 book, *Solace,* Horton criticizes the current psychiatric world view that denies the existence of any consoling meaning in life, and assumes that every human action must be chalked up to instincts, or to some crooked molecules in the brain.

Horton, writing for professionals, argues that people need, and healthy individuals have, objects or experiences that provide a basis for self-soothing. It may have been a childhood teddy bear, or poems read as an adolescent, or even an experience like a childhood train ride, which helped a growing individual sense a transitional link, re-lating him to the wider world. Somewhere within such experiences, links of meaning were forged, and within the framework of meaning solace—real comfort and consolation—can be found.

Horton's notion is helpful to Christians, because it points us to Scripture's teaching about comfort, where two aspects of consolation are presented. The first is an inter-personal relationship that permits comforting. In 2 Corinthians Paul points out that our own suffering equips us to comfort others. We can know a heartfelt sympathy for others, and we can point them to God, who is "the God of all comfort, who comforts us in all our troubles" (2 Cor. 1:3, 4).

Our ability to comfort effectively begins with making ourselves vulnerable, so others sense that we care, not as "professionals," but as fellow-sufferers who are equally weak.

But we Christians have more to offer than sympathy and shared vulnerability. We have a gift to give: that same confident hope in God that brings us through our own times of distress. Rather than helping a person turn inward in a search for self-soothing, we can affirm the goodness of God, who is life's ultimate link with meaning. While Horton expresses frustration with a secular psychiatry that can offer no consoling meaning to life, we express the confidence of the psalmist, who wrote: "My comfort in my suffering is this: Your promise renews my life" (Ps. 119:50).

We can't give a specific answer to Why to the crip-pled mother, or to the father whose life has gone awry. There are many possible answers to the Why questions, and we might point to some of them in our comforting. →
SUFFERING What we *can* do is to confidently affirm that life still has meaning and purpose, and that even suffering can be reworked for the good of all in the hands of our loving God.

I appreciated reading Horton's book and learning from this secular man the importance to those who are suffering of belief that life still has consoling meaning. I appreciated even more the fact that in Christ we offer a comfort that goes beyond self-soothing. We link hurting people with the true source of all comfort, God. → **COUNSELING**

COMMERCIALS. Many people take a dim view of TV commercials and advertising. For instance: "Hullabaloo, speculation and a mad race for profits have made advertising a means of swindling the people and foisting upon them goods frequently useless or of dubious quality." Before you shout "Amen," check the source. It's the *Great Soviet Encyclopedia,* 1941 edition.

If you're interested, the 1971 *Encyclopedia* takes a more moderate position, and describes advertising as "the popularization of goods with the aim of selling them, the creation of demand for those goods, the acquaintance of consumers with their quality, particular features, and the location of their sale, and explanation of the methods of their use."

This definition doesn't really fit TV commercials. In the 30 seconds or so allotted, few commercials can squeeze in more than 65 words. So how much "acquaintance" with quality can you do? It's hard to do any more than shout "Buy it!" . . . and to do that as subtly as possible.

Their subtlety is probably the most significant criticism of TV commercials. Commercials stimulate a desire for a product by bridging: linking the product with an unrelated desire. They suggest in those 30 seconds that romance comes when you use a dandruff shampoo, and youth is restored by a particular beauty soap. They even present sugar-packed cereals as "part of a nutritional breakfast." I make it a personal practice to note deceptive advertising. And never to buy the product.

Funny, isn't it. Just when the Soviets are ready to adopt a capitalistic approach to advertising, TV commercials make us wonder if their 1941 evaluation might have been right!

COMMUNICATING. Technical books talk about encoding and decoding messages. But most don't help much if we're frustrated because, no matter how hard we try, we can't seem to get others to understand what we're trying to say. What does help? We need to make sure that we provide information on five different levels that make real understanding possible—not information on the one or two levels that people normally talk.

• Information you receive from your senses is first-level information. To clarify how you understand an event you may need to tell what you saw and heard. For instance, the crowd at a basketball game may scream loudly when a player is knocked to the floor and the foul is called on him. But the referee may have seen that player slide his feet and move into the other player's path. The ref called a blocking foul, because he saw something the crowd didn't see.

• Information about how you interpret what you see or hear is second-level information. When Jim comes home and sees Dora waiting for him, her mouth a thin line, he's likely to interpret: "She's mad at me." Or "She's got a headache."

• Third-level information involves how you *feel* about your interpretation of what you have seen or heard. Jim may suddenly feel guilty. Or he may even be fearful at the prospect of another argument. Or if he interprets her tight lips as a headache he may feel compassionate. Or even angry because he expects their plans to go out for the evening to be canceled.

• The fourth-level information calls for us to express our intentions: to say how we want the other person to understand our next actions or words, or express the motives that lie behind them. Dora, understanding how Jim interprets her pained expressions, might quickly say, "Jim, I'm really upset just now, but I want you to know it's not your fault." Or, "Jim, I want to go out tonight, and I've taken a couple aspirin. But I'm not sure my headache will be gone in time."

• Fifth-level information is action information. It communicates expectations about what you or the other person might do, or what you want the other person to do. For instance, Dora might have continued: "Do you suppose you could rub my shoulders for a few minutes?" Or Jim might have volunteered, "Listen, why don't you take a hot bath and relax. I'll feed the kids and then come rub your back awhile."

When one or more of these levels of communication are blocked, persons are forced to operate blindly. Neither can really understand what's happening inside the other person. A person may refuse to express his or her feelings. Or a person may never spell out intentions, or say what actions he or she would like the other to take. When such information is not shared, relationships are uncertain and strained, and the chance of real intimacy is lost.

We can enrich communication and grow closer to our loved ones when we give and receive information on all five levels. So to grow closer, communicate all the information the other person needs. And remember these key questions:

"How do you feel about that?"
"What makes you think that?"
"What is it that you want?"
"What can we do about it?"

COMMUNITY. In the past ten years I've had some close friends who have become enamoured by the idea of community. One couple yearned for the imagined intimacy of a few families, sharing life together on a small plot of land. Two other individuals each saw community in terms of ministry: a small, closely knit group of persons who would live and minister together, earning a common living by common work as they devoted their energy to serving the Lord. The first couple was in search of Utopia, and it has fallen apart around them. The verdict is still out on the vision of the others. But history does provide insights into the way human beings have successfully linked their lives with the lives of others.

Successful but pseudo communities. Simply because people form and maintain a group-living situation does not mean they have approached community. The monastic movement in the Catholic Church historically formed group-living situations. But most did not encourage what moderns think of as community. Strict rules, asceticism, and rigidly patterned hours linked members in lockstep, but not in love. Intimacy was generally limited to whatever sense of closeness to God worship might provide.

Religious communities in the United States that have had even brief success have tended, as the monastic, to regulate sex. Some, like the Shakers of the midwest, called for celibacy. A few others followed the way of many communes of the '60s, insisting sex be shared. Each approach has been taken because, when couples form permanent pairs, loyalty to each other conflicts with the loyalty the community demands be given to the group.

The kibbitz movement in Israel and some communities in the United States have encouraged marriage. But most have insisted that children be raised in common. Research suggests that children raised in this way are generally cooperative and conforming adults, but show less individual initiative and creativity.

Other groups have tried to maintain group loyalty by freezing in time. The Old Mennonites in our country are an example, as are the Hassidic people among the Jews. Each group adopts the dress, lifestyle, transportation, and ways of the century in which it determined to freeze the flow of time. The very difference of the members of this kind of group forces individuals to remain: they are isolated from the rest of the world and must conform.

Each of these more-or-less successful approaches to group living has disturbing elements. Each of them, to maintain existence, calls on members to exchange individual freedoms for controls imposed by the group. Loyalty and conformity become the keys to existence, and these demands rob the group of that free, spontaneous self-giving on which true intimacy must rely. The forming of the community costs the members the experience of community that may have motivated them in the first place.

Biblical insights. Christians yearning for an experience of community are most likely to turn to a passage in Acts that describes life in the early Jerusalem church. Luke writes, "All the believers were together and had everything in common. Selling their possessions and goods, they gave to anyone as he had need. Every day they continued to meet together in the temple courts. They broke bread in their homes and ate together with glad and sincere hearts, praising God and enjoying the favor of all the people. And the Lord added to their number daily those who were being saved" (Acts 2:44–47).

This description is flooded with the warm glow of intimacy and love. No wonder such a picture of true caring awakens desire for a similar experience today. But when we look at the passage carefully, and compare it with other descriptions of the church at this time and place, we see that community is not *structural* in character, but is *relational*. There is no blueprint here for group living. Instead, there is an unveiling of the way to experience interpersonal intimacy.

Note first that community was not achieved by surrendering personal possessions and rights, to live on some commonly owned lands (cf. Acts 4:32–35; 5:1–4). Individuals maintained their own homes. They controlled their own possessions and incomes, rather than surrender them to a common fund (cf. Acts 5:4). It was not structure that made this congregation community. What was the secret?

• They shared concern for each other. People were more important than things. Their attitude affirmed, What is mine is available to you if you are in need.

• They shared worship. The life of these brothers and sisters was focused on God, and they met together to worship and praise Him.

• They shared their lives. Hospitality was a key. They opened their homes to one another, spent time together, and found delight in their fellowship.

What they found through sharing was community in the biblical sense: an experience of true love and caring and mutual support.

Conclusions. The desire for intimacy and love is a healthy one for Christians. All too many of us have an unsatisfied hunger for closeness. But we need to be careful in our search for community so that we are not drawn aside into unfruitful detours.

Structural approaches, which call for special commitments and controls, and legislate loyalty to the group, generally destroy the very closeness and caring they seek to create. It is certainly possible that several families might be drawn together by a common vision of ministry, and link their efforts in a location that involves group living. But this decision must grow out of deepening relationships worked through carefully by all, not some Utopian theory that suggests that ministry will provide a solid basis for relationship.

Perhaps the most important thing to realize is that God has planned to meet our need for community in His church. → CHURCH The church we see in Scripture *is* family: our challenge is simply to experience a relationship which, because of Christ, already exists.

How do we reach out to build community? We might begin with hospitality: with spending time with other believers and coming to know them, and learning to share our lives. We might add worship; taking time to praise God together in our homes as well as in formal church services. And we might personally commit ourselves to the belief that others' needs have priority over our possessions, so that we are freed to give.

Building community may not be easy. And it may not be quick. But, in the brothers and sisters in our own congregation and neighborhood, we already have the basis for the true community of God.

COMPASSION. We all agree it's a warm word, conveying concern. But the New Testament has to use three Greek words to help us really understand it. One word focuses on a pity that moves us to acts of kindness. Another word focuses on a heartfelt sympathy that creates unity because it moves us to identify ourselves with others. The third word pictures a heart contracting convulsively, so deeply do the hurts we see affect us.

When the Bible urges us as God's chosen people to

"clothe yourselves with compassion," it does not call us to charity or to an abstract concern for some distant "them." Instead, Jesus calls us to be like Him: to become sensitive to the hurts of those whose lives touch ours and quickly reach out to help and care.

COMPATIBILITY. The dictionary says that things that are compatible are "capable of existing together in harmony." It's rather fascinating that faith creates one kind of compatibility by destroying another.

What is destroyed is our personal compatibility with impurity and greed and bitterness and anger and malice (Eph. 4:25–31). God does this by reshaping us, providing a whole new attitude of mind, "created to be like God in true righteousness and holiness" (Eph. 4:24).

At one stroke, by making us incompatible with all those corroding inner passions, God has made us compatible with each other! Those things in us that made harmony with others impossible are now out of harmony with our fresh, new personality. Purified within, we are freed to love (1 Peter 1:22).

So if you really want to live in harmony with others, the first place to look is within, to make sure that your responses are really compatible with the new you.

COMPENSATION. In a recent book written to help managers determine fair compensation, the author suggests four factors that should be kept in mind. "The worker (1) must be his own manager, (2) have a say on how he does the job, (3) receive a fair reward for his job in the area of wages and salaries, and (4) receive an equitable share of the profits of the organization." When you think about it, God has designed the ideal. He calls us to serve, but gives us both freedom and responsibility. Once, when the disciples were a little worried about their compensation, Jesus replied, "I tell you the truth, no one who has left home or brothers or sisters or mother or father or children or fields for me and the gospel will fail to receive a hundred times as much in this present age [homes, brothers, sisters, mothers, children, and fields—and with

them, persecutions] and in the age to come, eternal life"
(Mark 10:29–30).

Now that's an offer you just can't refuse!

COMPETITION.

America has a long-standing love affair with competition. We envision a West won by rugged families and individuals who dared to match themselves against vast distances and hostile natives. We see competition as the force that keeps the wheels of industry turning. Competitive sports fascinate us. And winning—whether by getting better grades in school than others, or becoming Miss Arizona—is a primary way by which we measure achievement.

But these days there are growing doubts about competition. How do the Japanese, who stress cooperation, produce cheaper (and some say better) cars? Do competitive sports really build character? Or do they produce immature, irresponsible "jocks," whose egos demand a larger contract than the next player, no matter how ridiculous the salary? And we wonder. Can we really equate winning with achievement? Or is it a greater achievement for a person with limited abilities to pull down a "B" by hard work than for the class valedictorian to make an "A" without effort?

Questions like these make it worthwhile to take a look at competition and the role it plays in shaping our outlook on life.

Economic and political competition. A competitive marketplace for goods and ideas has a positive impact on society. Competition forces innovation and economy: prices are kept within reason, and new products emerge to meet needs and satisfy wants. In the same way political competition encourages citizens to weigh different ideas about how to beat inflation or solve other social problems, and to express their ideas with the vote. Economic and political competition can be misused. But the system of open competition is superior to other systems we might adopt.

Athletic competition. Athletics shifts our focus from competition for allegiance to goods or ideas to competition between persons. Here it's not the best washing machine, or the conservative principles that win. Here it's individual human beings who are the winners and losers.

There is evidence that today girls are adopting the competitive sports orientation long associated with boys. Most of us can and do enjoy friendly competition. But what happens to the personality of those who go on to higher, more intense levels of athletic competition? And what happens to all those who drop out because they were never good enough? The Institute for the Study of Athletic Motivation provides some answers to that first question. Their findings make it clear that competition does *not* build character. Actually there are common traits found in those who are winners. They ● have a great need for achievement; ● are highly organized, dominant, and respectful of authority; ● have a capacity for trust; ● but show low interest in receiving support and concern from others, and a low need to take care of others. Competition seems to block the development of close affiliation with other persons.

Competitiveness in general. Sports are an intense forum for competition, but society encourages the competitive approach to life in general. We compete for jobs and promotions. Usually our success comes at someone else's expense. Competition is stressed in schools, where grading and classroom activities constantly force children to measure themselves against others. One educator describes a situation in which Boris is unable to answer a math problem, even with the teacher's gentle prompting. So the teacher calls on Peggy, who is eagerly waving her hand for attention. He writes, "Thus Boris' failure has made it possible for Peggy to succeed; his depression is the price of her exhilaration; his misery the occasion for her rejoicing. This is the standard condition of the American elementary school."

The situation may be less grim than he pictures. But the principle of measuring ourselves against the successes or failures of others is deeply engrained in society. Persons compete with each other. And for every winner, there will be losers as well.

The biblical perspective. The ancient Greek poet Homer brought the nature of competition into focus when he urged "always to strive for distinction, and surpass the others." This is the core value in the competitive approach: surpassing others. Its roots are not to be found in American society, but in the heart of natural man. Excellence, worth, and value are sought by humanity in surpassing one another.

This whole approach to life is challenged in Scripture, and a different system of values put in its place. We see the Bible's system in several New Testament passages.

● Romans 12:3 says, "Do not think of yourself more highly than you ought," and goes on to show that each believer "belongs to all the others," and is to use his or her different gifts and abilities to serve.

● 1 Corinthians 4:6 warns against taking "pride in one man over against another." Again the point is made that God makes us different on purpose, the better to serve. Differences are not to be twisted into hierarchies of superiority/inferiority.

● 2 Corinthians 10:12–13 ridicules the foolishness of leaders who classify and compare themselves with others in an empty attempt to establish authority.

● Philippians 2:3, 4 calls for an attitude marked by unity of spirit and purpose. "Do nothing out of selfish ambition or vain conceit, but in humility consider others better than yourselves. Each of you should look not only to your own interests, but also to the interests of others."

● Galatians 6:4 calls on us to test our own actions, "then he can take pride in himself, without comparing himself to somebody else."

These passages make it clear. We are to strive to serve others, not surpass them. We are to appreciate the strengths of others, not build ourselves up by measuring our strengths against their weaknesses. We are to excel so that we can take pride in our faithfulness, not to lift ourselves above our brothers and sisters. Affirming the worth and value of each individual, and respecting differences, we are freed to live together in mutual love and compassion, unmarred by any drive to win at another person's expense.

Excelling without competitive drive.   Christianity puts great stress on faithfulness and on excelling in our zeal to follow Christ. But the motivation to excel is stripped of the drive to surpass others, which mars much accomplishment. How do we encourage excellence without the destructiveness of competitive drive?

• Establish impersonal, reachable goals. When my oldest was in grade school we played JARTS (large metal darts, thrown across the back yard to land in plastic circles). Paul's frustration grew as he tried harder and harder to beat me . . . and failed. He competed furiously, and the losing hurt. So I made a simple change in the game. We combined our scores, and then set ourselves the task each round of trying to beat our record high.

This simple shift changed the dynamics of the game. We still competed, but not against each other. We tried to surpass ourselves and our past achievements, not each other.

Helping a child (or adult) focus on personal growth, and to develop a sense of satisfaction at surpassing his own best, is one way we can maintain standards of excellence without the negative impact of interpersonal competitiveness.

• Praise and appreciate differences. Do not compare children or adults with each other. Instead, follow the Philippians' prescription, by looking to the interests and achievements of each, and by focusing on their strengths "consider others better than yourselves." When we help people appreciate their own uniqueness we help them develop awareness of ways they can contribute to others.

In summary.   Let's not rule out all friendly competition in games and sports, as though winning and losing were themselves sin. They're not. What is wrong is that competitive attitude that shapes our view of ourselves and others by demanding that to be worthwhile we must surpass others. That attitude, which has deep roots in human personality, is far from the Christian ideal.

Actually, it is not only those who struggle to surpass and who fail who are the losers when life becomes a competitive struggle. Many studies have shown that those who are the apparent winners in life—the athletic, the attractive, the rich—are losers too. For instance, a study of teenagers has shown that the most popular are often the most insecure! When a person defines himself by his ability to surpass, the threat of one day failing to surpass creates devastating inner stress. Who were the most comfortable and secure teens? Those who had one or two close friends who liked and appreciated them for themselves.

And so we stand again amazed at the wisdom of God. In freeing us from the need to measure ourselves against others, He has freed us to love them and to be loved. And in freeing us to love, God has met our own deepest needs.

COMPROMISE.   It's almost always possible to find a fair settlement if we're willing to make mutual concessions. The only one it's not safe to compromise with is your conscience.

COMPULSION.   This word ranks high on God's list of dirty words. Paul notes in 2 Corinthians 9:7: "Each man should give what he has decided in his heart to give, not reluctantly or under compulsion, for God loves a cheerful giver." We can compel people to do what's right. But God isn't satisfied. He's concerned with the heart and wants us to want to.

CONCEIT.   Any exaggerated sense of our own importance is inappropriate for Christians. No matter how we might compare with others, we fall far short of what we could be. And will be (1 John 3:2).

CONDEMNATION. Condemnation is a fact, a feeling, and a fancy. As a fact, mankind stands condemned for acts of sin. As a feeling, condemnation is marked by restless unease and a nagging awareness of guilt. As a fancy, we pretend we have the right to look on, and to judge others . . . for the very things we do, or would like to do. God deals with condemnation at all three levels. The fact is, "there is now no condemnation for those who are in Christ Jesus" (Rom. 8:1). When we accept the fact by faith, our feelings change and we find peace with God (Rom. 5:1). Accepting the fact that God is the One who both judges and forgives, we surrender our fancied rights to judge others, knowing we "have no excuse, you who pass judgment on someone else" (Rom. 2:1). → JUDGING

I'm sure that it is only by chance each of these truths is found in the very first verse of some chapters in Romans. After all, the verse and chapter divisions were added hundreds of years after the New Testament was written. But even so, it seems appropriate. After all, freedom from the fact, the feeling, and the fancy of condemnation is one of God's number one gifts to us in Christ.

CONFESSION. In a fascinating book on *Writing the Modern Confession Story* for those ten million or so readers of monthly magazines, Dorothy Collett provides the typical "formula." Each confession story will consist of:

1. Narrator's character flaw
2. Motivation for narrator's character flaw
3. Device that creates narrator's immediate problem and necessitates a decision or plan
4. Narrator's wrong decision or plan
5. Result narrator expects or hopes for
6. Action resulting from narrator's decision or plan
7. Unexpected and unfortunate result of above action
8. How this unanticipated result causes narrator to see where and why she was wrong

9. Narrator's remorse and her attempt to make restitution
10. How narrator's remorse and attempt to make restitution unexpectedly bring her happiness after all.

There now. You have all the information you need to write a story for a confession magazine.

Of course, God has a slightly different formula that applies to all believers. It too starts out with flawed characters like you and me. It too features the wrong decisions and actions we take. But here God's plot changes course. Picking up at step 7, God's approach to setting right the sins that mar our lives goes something like this:

7. Narrator experiences inner turmoil, masked by pretense
8. Narrator resists pressures to admit sin to God and others
9. Inner pain finally moves narrator to confess sin to God, and he then finds release from inner turmoil
10. Narrator is restored to fellowship with God, and God resumes the process of cleansing within narrator
11. Narrator is moved to righteous action, to restitution, and in the process finds a fulfilling and godly life.

If you want to see God's formula expressed in Scripture, check Psalm 51 and 1 John 1. Or look at these verses from Psalm 32, and relate them to the steps above: "When I kept silent, my bones wasted away through my groaning all day long. For day and night your hand was heavy upon me; my strength was sapped as in the heat of summer. Then I acknowledged my sin to you and did not cover up my iniquity. I said, 'I will confess my transgressions to the LORD'—and you forgave the guilt of my sin." And then we have the final step. "I will instruct you and teach you in the way you should go" (vv. 3–5, 8).

God's formula for our confession stories is rich and beautiful. We need to return to it often, for we often fall short. In bringing our sins and shortcomings to Him, we open up our lives to the healing power of forgiveness and the dynamic, purifying work of the Spirit of God.

CONFIDENCE.   Confidence grows with experience. I try something, repeat my attempt until I become skillful, and in the process gain confidence. In time my experience of trying and succeeding in many things brings a confident outlook on life: I will be free to try even new and unusual things.

It works much the same way in our relationship with God. We step out hesitantly in trust and repeatedly find Him faithful. In time our experiences with God shape our outlook on life, and we find increasing freedom to risk obedience. Psalm 71 describes the core of the process:

> You have been my hope, O Sovereign LORD,
>> my confidence since my youth.
> From birth I have relied on you; (vv. 5, 6)

The result?

> As for me, I will always have hope;
>> I will praise you more and more (v. 14).

CONFIDENTIALITY.   "A gossip betrays a confidence, but a trustworthy man keeps a secret" (Prov. 11:13).

CONFIRMATION.   A number of Protestant traditions as well as the Catholic Church practice confirmation. In Catholicism confirmation is regarded as a sacrament. It is believed that when the bishop anoints the candidate in the ceremony, the Holy Spirit is given to him or her. In a number of Protestant traditions confirmation involves a course of study for young people. Children, usually of junior high age, attend confirmation classes, after which they are admitted to full church membership. In both systems confirmation serves as a rite of passage: a symbolic moving from childhood to adult status and responsibility. In churches that do not have confirmation, baptism or public profession of faith often have this same impact.

Problems with confirmation. The Protestant traditions that maintain confirmation, officially see it as training to allow a person to take his or her place as a responsible member of the community of faith. Too often however families and young people view confirmation as the end of the educational process, and afterward drop out of church rather than participate in it.

Traditionally, confirmation classes have focused on teaching the basic beliefs of the church. In earlier days, answers to catechisms were memorized. Today no uniform practice is followed even within denominations. Serious questions have been raised about what approach would be most helpful in reaching a church's goals.

Biblical background. Catholic historians agree that no separate confirmation rite was practiced until about the 5th century A.D. The Protestant educational approach was introduced with the Reformation of the 17th century. Thus confirmation does not find its roots in Scripture or in the practices of the early church.

The fact that a practice does not have roots in ancient days does not make it wrong. In fact, there is value in any practice that helps an individual come to a deeper level of personal commitment to God and His people. The question parents need to ask about particular confirmation programs thus should focus on how the experience is perceived by participants. Is this seen as the end of religious training, or a step toward deeper commitment? Do young people continue participation in church after confirmation, or drop out? Are participants helped to understand the nature of Christian commitment and to make personal decisions, or do they simply learn to give answers they do not understand to questions they are not asking?

Perhaps most important, if our children and family have actively participated in the shared life of God's people, confirmation may be a meaningful experience and significant step in consciously linking a child with God's people. If family and child have not actively participated in the church's shared life, no course is likely to have significant impact.

CONFLICT AND RESOLUTION. It's a pretty safe prediction: there will be some conflict in your life today.

One study of executives and managers in business suggested that about 24% of their time was spent dealing with conflict. It may not be that high with you—with your spouse, kids, the neighbors, in-laws, or people at church. But probably the kinds of conflict you experience have the same causes as those listed by business executives. What are the principal causes of conflict? ● Misunderstanding (communication fails). ● Personality clashes. ● Values and goals differ. ● Poor performance. ● Conflicts over who is responsible for what. ● Authority issues. ● Frustration and irritability. ● Competition for limited resources. ● Failure to keep rules and policies.

Conflicts like these are a normal part of everyone's life. There is no way to avoid them. So the issue becomes, How do we deal with our conflicts? Do we approach conflict constructively, so growth takes place in our lives and relationships? Or is our approach to conflict destructive, tearing down relationships and blocking our personal growth? You can tell if the conflicts in your own life are being handled constructively or destructively by checking these lists of characteristics.

CONSTRUCTIVE CONFLICT	DESTRUCTIVE CONFLICT
● brings important issues into the open	● focuses on personalities rather than issues
● results in solutions	● deepens differences
● involves persons cooperatively in efforts to find solutions	● polarizes into "we"/"them" groups
● leads to open communication of feelings and viewpoints	● leads to name calling and fighting
● builds closeness between the people with the conflict	● builds barriers between the people with the conflict

Resolving conflicts. Those who have studied conflict

resolution point to four things that are important to evaluate.

• Evaluate your own reaction to conflict. Here are the most common reactions people have when some conflict emerges. Only two of these reactions are really positive ones. (1) We react by trying to justify ourselves. "Yes, but. . . ." (2) We react by expressing hostility and fighting back. (3) We react by changing the subject and trying to divert attention from the issue in question. "Let's talk about it later. Right now. . . ." (4) We react by trying to avoid the issue entirely. "Well, that's no problem for me." (5) We react by trying to smooth the conflict over. "I think we're both right, and . . . ." (6) We react by surrender. "You're perfectly right. It's all my fault. Can you ever forgive me?" (7) We react by expressing our feelings. "When you say that, I feel. . . ." (8) We react by attempting to negotiate. "Let's work on it and see if we can find a solution."

If we're to deal with conflict constructively we can't avoid or deny conflicts. And we can't defend ourselves, attack, or even surrender. We need to be willing to talk, to share our feelings, and to work together toward some solution that will meet everyone's needs.

• Evaluate your communication. It's particularly important if conflict is to be dealt with constructively and real solutions are to be found, that each person expresses his or her true thoughts and feelings. And that each person listens, to understand the other. For principles of good communication, see → COMMUNICATING.

• Evaluate the relational climate. Most conflicts don't come with isolated incidents. They grow out of repeated series of events. My youngest's failure to do the dishes last night could lead to conflict with his sister-in-law not because he was pushing to finish a college term paper, but because it's happened before!

But the particular pattern that sets up a conflict should not be confused with relational climate. The relational climate is the overall quality of relationships. Do those in conflict see and treat each other with mutual affection and respect? Where warmth and caring exist, there's a good chance of finding solutions. Where suspicion and lack of trust dominate, conflicts are likely to become destructive.

• Evaluate the methods used to resolve conflicts. Experts focus attention on five common methods. (1) Denial. One or both parties try to solve the conflict by pretending it does not exist. This works with unimportant conflicts, and in fact reflects the Bible's observation that when we love we "forebear" (overlook) one another's sins (cf. Col. 3:13). However, when the issue is important to one or both parties, denying that the conflict exists will lead to a buildup of tensions and be destructive to the relationship. (2) Smoothing over. One or both work at maintaining a superficial, surface harmony. But underneath, suppressed resentment will build. Like denial, this is a refusal to deal honestly with the conflict and will ultimately be destructive to the relationship. (3) Power. Here one person or group dominates and simply imposes his or her solution. The power approach may work in the military, where everyone agrees to obey orders. But in life, it means the loser feels powerless and has no way to satisfy his or her needs. The use of this approach is particularly tempting to parents, but it's particularly destructive of relationships, especially with teens. (4) Compromise. Each person surrenders something so each can gain. This attempt to find a middle ground will work when each feels he or she has room to give a little, and where there is mutual trust. (5) Collaboration. All parties work together to seek a creative solution to meet the needs of all. Collaboration calls for time, for honest communication, and for concern for the point of view of all parties. This is the best way to work on solutions to conflict over really important things, where it is worthwhile to spend the time it takes. But it is possible only where each will give that time, and where the persons are truly committed to each other.

We can summarize the appropriate times to use each method on the following chart:

RELATIONSHIP	Very important to me or the others	Not very important to either of us
close, personal, long term	collaboration	overlook; smooth over compromise
acquaintances, temporary	power; compromise	overlook; smooth over

Biblical insights. Secular experts focus attention on our reaction to conflict. Their suggestions for resolving conflict are helpful, but incomplete. Before we apply them, the Bible calls on us to take a close look . . . at ourselves.

The Book of James points to the inner cause of many conflicts. "If you harbor bitter envy and selfish ambition in your hearts," James writes, "do not boast about it or deny the trust. Such 'wisdom' does not come down from heaven but is earthly, unspiritual, of the devil. For where you have envy and selfish ambition, there you find disorder and every evil practice. But the wisdom that comes from heaven is first of all pure; then peace loving, considerate, submissive, full of mercy and good fruit, impartial and sincere" (3:14–17). When the roots of conflict are located in our own sinful desires, the place to deal with it is in our own lives. We can confess uncovered sins and trust God to cleanse, filling us with a wisdom that leads to peace.

Then is conflict itself wrong? No. At times conflict is necessary. Galatians describes a conflict between Paul and Peter. Peter had come to visit an all-gentile church. When some legalistic believers came later, Peter drew back and separated himself from the gentile Christians, as Jews had always separated themselves from pagans. Paul saw this as denial of the gospel, which offers salvation to all by faith alone. Because the issue was so vital, Paul confronted Peter "in front of them all." Later the issue was dealt with by the whole church in a counsel at Jerusalem (Acts 15), and through a collaborative process the principle Paul had been willing to contend for was established. This conflict was a vital and positive element in the struggle of the early church to grasp the meaning of the new Christian faith.

But even the apostle Paul was not immune to destructive conflicts. He fell out with his old missionary companion, Barnabas, when Barnabas wanted to bring along John Mark, a young man who deserted the missionary team on an earlier journey. Paul gave priority to the mission: Barnabas gave priority to strengthening John Mark. "They had such a sharp disagreement that they parted company" the Bible tells us (see Acts 15:36–41). History shows us Paul was wrong. Barnabas did take Mark along, and under the guidance of this older brother Mark became an effective leader . . . and author of the Gospel bearing his name (cf. 2 Tim. 4:11).

What we learn from passages like these is important. We are taught to examine our own attitude first. We are taught not to avoid conflict when issues are important to us. We are taught to guard humility, for even the greatest of us can err. And we are taught that even when we seem to fail, God can bring good through conflict situations and can enrich our lives.

CONFORMITY. Psychologists appropriately define conformity as "a change in behavior or belief toward a group as a result of real or imagined group pressure." The problem psychologists have, like the problem of worried parents and congregations of believers across the ages, is that there are two kinds of conformity. One is *compliance:* outward behaviors that are expected by the group and permit individuals to participate. The other is *private acceptance:* an inner personal commitment to the beliefs and values of the group that also expresses itself in behavior. Just looking at a person's actions may not tell you what kind of conformity exists!

We all know this intuitively. Moms and dads realize it, and worry about how their children will act when they go off to college. Young people realize it, and complain about hypocrites in the church, who act one way when all dressed up for Sunday and another way at home or work.

So we Christians need to ask an important question—and find the right answer! How can we help others conform out of private acceptance rather than out of compliance? How can we nurture that inner transformation that comes from commitment?

Generally we can say that the more a group *demands* conformity, the more likely conforming behavior will be compliance. And the more things a person is pressured to conform to, the more likely responses will reflect compliance. This perhaps is behind the powerful teaching on the Christian community that Paul gives in Romans 14 and 15. There we're told to release others from the necessity of complying: to give each other freedom to differ, even in convictions.

This freedom for diversity within community is basic to our life together as Christ's people. So some eat only vegetables, and others enjoy a steak. All right, neither is to look down on or condemn the other. So some insist that one day is especially sacred, while others hold every day is equally special to the Lord. All right, let each act on his or her own convictions (14:1–10).

Paul sees clearly that setting up rules to which group members must conform will actually put "a stumbling block or obstacle in your brother's way" (14:13). Instead of acting out of conviction (private acceptance) and seeking to please God, people will act out of fear of others' reactions (compliance), and lose sight of the basic reality of our faith: that Christianity is personal relationship to Jesus Christ.

It is in fact our common allegiance to Jesus that brings us together as a group: we are His people. What holds us together, and stimulates our inner growth, is very different from those pressures to be alike that hold mere human groups together. "Stop passing judgment on one another" (14:13), the Bible says, affirming our right to be different from each other. And, "accept one another, then, just as Christ accepted you" (Rom. 15:7). What holds believers together and creates a freeing climate for growth is the fact that we accept and love each other despite our differences . . . for Jesus' sake.

When we give others the freedom to differ, and continue to love, we create a community where conformity comes from within.

CONSCIENCE. Walt Disney has Jimminy Cricket sing, "Always let your conscience be your guide." And contemporary theologian Walter E. Conn argues that conscience "must be understood as the dynamic core of conscious subjectivity that constitutes the very being of the personal self." With endorsements like these, we surely need to pay attention to conscience.

Perhaps the best way to look at conscience is to describe it as our personal sense of what is right or wrong, what is fair, fitting, and good. Researchers in the behavioral sciences have long been fascinated by conscience. How does it develop? What is the relationship between conscience and conduct? What kind of parenting helps conscience develop? There are few solid answers, but there are still important things to say about conscience.

The content of conscience is learned. There is a difference between conscience as the faculty for making moral distinctions and the content of our conscience (what we think is actually right or wrong). The content of conscience is learned, picked up from the beliefs and values of home and society. To Cotton Mather burning witches in Massachusetts was a right and good thing. Most today would disagree. But both moderns and Mather may have strong consciences, even though the content of our consciences differs.

Beliefs and values can be rejected as well as adopted. So psychologists probe for factors that lead a growing person to accept values and make them a part of his or her own conscience. The factors? Parental warmth and affection, clear standards fairly enforced, the example of others who live out the values they teach, and a mild but consistent discipline seem to be important. So we do know something about where the content of conscience comes from, and how that content is internalized.

The conscience itself is part of human nature. The Bible never defines conscience, but it is clear that God created human beings with a moral faculty. All mankind sees certain issues as moral in nature and responds to them by making moral judgments. Paul in Romans 2 teaches that those without the Law (and thus without information from God on what ought to be the content of conscience) are "a law for themselves" (v. 14). That is, they go about setting up as standards their own estimates of right and wrong. With these standards established, "their consciences also bearing witness, their thoughts now accusing, now even defending them" (v. 15).

The Greeks were particularly sensitive to the self-judging aspect of conscience. They spoke much of a bad conscience, relentlessly tormenting its owner with memories of past sins. As Paul points out in Romans, whether the content of our conscience is derived from God's Word or culture, no one has ever lived up to his or her own standards of right and wrong (Rom. 3:9–18). With conscience comes awareness of the great gap that exists between our beliefs about right and wrong and our conduct.

Conscience has an important function in the unsaved, helping them realize their need for a Savior. But conscience is not a reliable witness. Continued indulgence in sin will scar a person's conscience, so it is no longer trustworthy (Titus 1:15).

Conscience does have a role in Christian experience. Despite the fact that conscience will be faulty if its content does not accurately reflect Scripture, the Bible warns us against acting against it (Rom. 14:22–23). And a good conscience (maintained by doing our duty as we understand it) is linked by Paul with a pure heart and sincere faith as the source of spontaneous, free Christian love (1 Tim. 1:5). We can sum up principles that are important to us in Christian living quite simply:

(1) We can help our children and others develop their conscience by providing example, consistent discipline, and instruction, along with a warm, close relationship.

(2) We are not to violate our own conscience by acting against it, even when we are uncertain that our conscience is right (Rom. 14:22–23).

(3) We are not to pressure others to violate their own conscience in order to conform to our convictions. → **CONFORMITY**

(4) We are to constantly test the content of our conscience by Scripture, subjecting our conscience to the Word of God. As we grow in faith and understanding, God will reshape our conscience to conform with His own.

CONSENSUS. The idea behind consensus is simple. We work together at a common problem until we come up with a common solution. Some church boards are committed not to act until consensus is achieved. Some couples work on family decisions the same way.

It usually takes a little longer to reach decisions by consensus, but consensus decisions are usually better ones. And they're carried out.

Still, consensus is often misunderstood. What does it take? (1) A process in which each honestly expresses thoughts, fears, hopes, feelings, and ideas about the problem to be solved and suggested solution. (2) Careful analysis of the problem and suggesting of many options. (3) Agreement by those involved that a particular course of action is the best one to take, everything considered, for now.

Commitment to consensus doesn't mean that you must wait until everyone thinks you've achieved the perfect solution. Instead, it means that, after working together on the problem, if one person in the group honestly says, "I am convinced this is *not* the thing to do," the group will not do it. Usually a group will be able to arrive at a solution to which all will agree, even though not all will feel it's ideal.

We find consensus decision-making in the New Testament. The best illustration is seen in Acts 15, which describes a vital conference of the leaders of the early church. After much prayer and discussion, they reached a conclusion, and wrote, "It seemed good to the Holy Spirit and to us . . ." (Acts 15:28). That's why consensus is especially exciting for Christians. There is always one extra Person in the process. Us and the Holy Spirit.

CONSEQUENCES.

The natural world has been designed with built-in consequences. Step out of a window, and you fall down, not up. The law of gravity makes sure of that. The moral world is designed the same way. "Do not be deceived: God cannot be mocked. A man reaps what he sows" (Gal. 6:7). → JUDGING

CONSERVATION.

When the new Secretary of Interior, a conservative Christian, mentioned the Second Coming of Christ . . . well, it raised a furor! We'd been so used to hearing about planet earth as a tiny spaceship hurtling through the void. We have only limited resources, so the argument went. We can never replace them, and must think of our children's children's children. The remark about Jesus' return, and the notion that we may not need to conserve for eternity, was understandably taken by some as a portent of return to exploitation.

Actually, the debate raises a question for us. In view of prophecy, do we really need to practice conservation? Or just go on as we have been these last hundred years or so?

Nonrenewable resources. Whatever our theology, a 1979 review of earth's resources make it clear they are limited. ● Despite conservation efforts, oil and gas are limited as an energy source. Supplies are measured in decades . . . with no provision for the development of third-world nations. ● Only 3% of the earth's water is available as fresh water for human use. Much of this is locked frozen at the poles; much more is distant from our population centers. Yet water is used in vast amounts (500,000 gallons to make a ton of synthetic rubber), often picking up pollutants in the process. In some parts of the United States the land is sinking as ground water is being used up to meet growing demands. ● Food production, processing, and distribution in the Western world is based in high energy use. This is increased dramatically as we insist on prepacked and frozen foods, and fresh foods shipped from all over the nation.

While we might multiply examples like these, it's clear to all of us that even with forced conservation programs, a continuation of our present standard of living—or significant improvement of living standards in underdeveloped nations—ranges between the highly unlikely and the utterly impossible.

Dominion. The Christian attitude toward environment should not be shaped either by secular doomsayers or by those who promise Christ's return before the 2,000s. Our attitude should be shaped by a responsibility given humanity at creation. In Genesis we read in the Creation story of God's intention for man, "let them rule over the fish of the sea and the birds of the air, over the livestock, over all the earth" (1:26). Psalm 8 picks up this theme and develops it: "You made him ruler over the works of your hands; you put everything under his feet" (v. 6). As God rules over man, so man under God rules the creation.

But the Old Testament concept of rule is not exploitative. God does not *use* the men He maintains dominion over. Psalm 8 expresses the awe of David, who says in wonder, "what is man that you are mindful of him, the son of man that you care for him?" (v. 4). In carrying out humanity's commission to rule over nature we, like God, are not to exploit, but to be mindful of and to care for.

The charter of dominion is a divine commission given us to preserve and to conserve the environment.

Conclusions. We don't know when Jesus will return. But we do know that to be faithful to God's commission, we must deal responsibly with nature's resources.

Responsibility involves us at two levels: a public policy level and a personal level. There are many systems that can be linked with conservation, some even using garbage to produce gas. In Muskegon, Michigan, treated human waste waters are used in irrigation. Dumped, these nitrogen rich waters would pollute streams and rivers with algae growth; used in irrigation they provided a 60% crop bonus. As citizens we can vote and lobby for systems like this one, which work with rather than against the environment.

Individually, we can evaluate our lifestyle. Do we recycle cans and bottles and paper? Do we conserve energy and water? Do we simplify our lifestyle or make it more complex as financial resources increase?

We don't know when Jesus will return. But we do know that when He does, He will be concerned then about our faithfulness. Expectation of His coming will be a poor excuse for rape of the world for which He's made us responsible.

CONSERVATIVE. A conservative is supposed to be committed to old, established values and truths. "We've never done it that way before" isn't the objection of a conservative. It's the objection of a fool, who has confused practices with values. The Bible provides the true conservative with values and truths expressed as principles. It's the challenge of each generation to find new, creative, and meaningful ways to enflesh them.

CONTROL. I have a friend who has a deep need to feel in control. It's reflected in parenting. It's revealed in attention to detail and the insistence that everything be in its place. It's seen in unease in new situations, and anxiety in situations where my friend does not dominate. Comfort comes only when my friend feels in control.

The fact is that none of us are ever really in control. We walk into uncertain futures, subject to an unknown that can radically change our plans. An accident, an illness, the loss of a job; these and a myriad of other possibilities make every life one of risk and uncertainty.

There's really only one source of security for us: relationship with One who is in control. Our future will still be uncertain. But we'll know that whatever happens must pass through the filter of God's love.

CONVERSION. I could read anguish in the two letters I received this year from a Tennessee teen. He'd asked Jesus to save him. But he didn't feel saved. After reading one of my books for young people, he wrote me, expressing his doubts and agonies. How could he ever be sure?

Psychologists have carefully examined conversion experiences, and theologians have explored the theoretical nooks and crannies. But at heart, conversion remains a very personal and very practical issue. What is it? How can I know that I am well and truly converted, and one of Jesus' people now?

The Bible on conversion. Both testaments picture conversion as a fundamental change in life direction. Moved by God (Jer. 18:18; John 6:44), a person turns his back on evil and chooses a new way of life (Jer. 18:18; Mal. 3:7). The convert rejects the old dominion of sin and chooses Jesus as Lord (Rom. 6:11–14). Growing in personal commitment to Christ, the now believing person develops a new outlook and new values, for mind and heart have been renewed so he or she is able to understand and choose God's will (cf. Rom. 12:1, 2).

Both testaments also tell us that conversion's renewal flows from a transforming, inner change. God acts supernaturally to plant new life within the individual, and that new life is the dynamic source of all changes in attitude and action (cf. Jer. 31:33).

In the New Testament the word most closely linked with conversion is faith. This faith is no mere mental assent to abstract information, but a personal response to Jesus Christ as He is presented in the Gospel. → FAITH/ FAITHFULNESS With faith comes that supernatural act in which God gives us His life, and we are in Jesus' terms, born again.

To understand the meaning of conversion biblically each of these elements must be kept in mind. There is faith in Christ. There is God's act of implanting life. There is growth and change as the lordship of Christ is accepted and a life of obedience to Him begun.

Our conversion experience. Christians often seem confused about the conversion "experience." It's no wonder. Some insist we name the date and hour we received Jesus as Savior. Others argue that children should be nurtured in faith from infancy, so they're never aware of a time they were unconverted. Some will tell us of several moments of significant personal decision. And others, like my young Tennessee friend, will wonder why, no matter how many times he makes his "decision for Christ," he still doesn't feel converted. How do we sort it all out?

- We affirm a point of conversion; a moment when God provides us supernaturally with a new life (cf. 1 Peter 1:23).

- We affirm faith as personal response to God, as the human responsibility in conversion (cf. John 3:16).

- We admit not all Christians are aware of the moment of conversion. I can't remember the moment of my physical birth, but I know I'm alive. The real issue for individuals is not "When was I saved?" but "Do I believe in Jesus?" Answer that second question "Yes," and you know you're alive.

- We separate feelings and fact. I am not converted because I feel converted. The Bible says, "To all who received him [Jesus], to those who believed in his name, he gave the right to become children of God" (John 1:12). The fact is, faith in Jesus brings us into God's family, and we have God's word on that. My confidence rests on the promise of a God whose word I trust, not on feelings that I know to be fickle.

- We understand that transformation is generally gradual and involves growth. Conversion will lead to eventual rejection of evil and choice of what is good. "No one who is born of God will continue to sin," the Bible promises, "because God's seed remains in him; he cannot go on sinning, because he has been born of God" (1 John 3:9).

Talk of conversion should not direct our attention into the past, to establish the point of time when our life in Christ began. The good news of conversion is that in Jesus the old is gone. We can look ahead with confidence, all has become new.

COUNSELING. New counseling centers open. Christian bookstores stock counseling books and cassette series. Pastors are overloaded with counseling. Marriage and family counselors advertise in the yellow pages. Churches hold training courses to equip lay counselors. And many of us wonder. What's this movement all about? If you're wondering whether or not you need counseling, take a look at the article on → PSYCHIATRISTS. But if you want to sort through the complex idea of counseling in general, read on.

Types of counseling. Two decades ago the word "psychological" would normally have been linked with counseling. Counseling was for people with personal problems, who wanted help. But today the term "counseling" includes much more.

● Psychological counseling. People still seek counseling for help with personal and personality problems. At times life seems so overwhelming that insights and help from outside are simply necessary.

● Behavioral counseling. "Stop Smoking" and "Diet" centers so popular these days are actually counseling centers. They use techniques developed by behaviorists to help an individual change patterns in his or her life. What a person does, not how he feels, is the focus in behavioral counseling.

● Employment and educational counseling. Batteries of tests are used to help individuals determine the kind of schooling or work they are suited for and will enjoy.

● Marriage and family counseling. Closely knit groups of people are counseled together as a unit. The counseling focuses on the way the persons interact. The counselor helps the group members become more sensitive to each other, and introduces concepts the unit can use to change destructive patterns.

● Group counseling. Groups of persons with similar problems (such as child-abusing parents, or alcoholics) are brought together regularly. The group helps members talk through experiences, to learn ways to change, and to provide each other with encouragement and support.

Theories of counseling.   The counseling process in any of the settings above will depend on the counseling theory applied by the counselor. There are five major theory groups more or less in vogue today:

● Reflective. The counselor sees himself as an outsider. He is there only to act as a mirror, reflecting and clarifying the thoughts, feelings, and values of the counselee. The counselor believes that each individual must ultimately solve his or her own problems, based on personal values, and resists trying to instruct or direct the counselee.

● Relational. The counselor views the relationship that develops between himself and the counselee as therapeutic. Caring and being supportive are vital in his approach to counseling.

● Insight. The counselor believes the counselee needs insights he does not possess. So the counselor will draw from his studies and expertise, and provide information during the counseling process that will better help the counselee understand himself and his situation.

● Directive. The counselor believes the counselee needs answers. And he believes that his role is to provide answers. After listening carefully to define the problem, the directive counselor will then tell the counselee what to do.

● Behavioral. The counselor is not concerned with what goes on inside the counselee. He focuses on specific patterns of behavior that cause the problem. By teaching the counselee how to act to change his own behavior patterns, the counselor believes he can help him solve his problems.

Today there are few "pure" practitioners of any of these theory groups, and a counselor will likely draw techniques from each school. Still most counselors will tend to rely on one approach as his or her dominant method.

Biblical perspectives on counseling. The New Testament does not speak of counseling as we understand it today, nor does it list counseling among the spiritual gifts. But there is much in the Scriptures that is clearly related.

● One anothering. The Bible words translated "counselor" in the New International Version are used most often in the sense of adviser. However, the use of Counselor by Jesus as a name for the Holy Spirit (John 14 and 15) is significant. The name sums up several of the Spirit's ministries, and means "one who comes alongside as a helper."

This may be one reason for the lack of a formalized "counseling ministry" in the New Testament. The Bible describes the life of believers in the Christian community as one of constantly being "alongside" and "helping" one another! Believers shared sorrows and joys. They encouraged, reproved, rebuked, exhorted, taught, listened to, forgave, prayed for, and stimulated one another to growth in Christianity's transforming life. The whole life that God's people lived together involved mutual counseling and support. The need for professional or specialized counselors did not exist, for the community of faith was filled with those who constantly came alongside and helped one another.

● Christ as Lord. Helping is presented in Scripture as a mutual ministry, in which brothers and sisters in Christ offer each other support. One possible danger in counseling as we understand it today is that it often involves a superior/subordinate relationship, in which the counselor is perceived to be "over" the counselee or superior to him. This is particularly true in directive counseling, where the counselor takes it as his responsibility to tell the counselee what he is to do.

The New Testament makes it clear that Jesus alone is Lord, and each of us is to seek direction from Him. We are to relate to each other as brothers only, resisting titles and status that might seem to raise us above others (cf. Matt. 23:8–12). We can make suggestions, share our insights, and provide encouragement. But each individual is to remain personally responsible to Christ for what he or she chooses to do.

• Developing sensitivity. The present movement that encourages Christians to take training in counseling—a training that usually stresses how to listen and encourage —is a healthy thing. In every field, evidence mounts that peer counseling (by nonprofessionals) can be as or more effective than the professional. Building a congregation of people who understand how to care may well help us recover the healing, transforming power of the New Testament community of faith.

Conclusions. Everyone needs help at times. That help often will come from friends or family, or a small group of other Christians with whom we meet for prayer and Bible study. Professional counselors can help too, and it's no shame to seek help. When you do seek pastoral or professional counseling, try to get some idea of the counselor's approach. Generally speaking the reflective and directive approaches will be least helpful. The behavioral can help when you are trying to lick a crippling habit. It is also helpful if people you know can recommend someone who has a good record of success. But don't overlook the possibility that some in your own congregation are sensitive and caring, and that talking things through with a brother or sister may be just the help you need.

CREATIVITY.

Ever wonder if you could be a creative thinker? Or ever wanted your children to be creative? Research gives insights into what creativity is—and how to encourage it. In yourself and in your children.

Most understand creativity as a way of thinking; a way of looking at situations. The logical thinker looks for one right way to do something, and works toward his goal of finding that one way one careful step at a time. He ignores things that do not seem related to his goal or his solution. Picking up a brick, a logical thinker will look around, concerned about the gap in the wall it may have fallen from.

The creative thinker searches for many solutions. He

explores for the joy of discovery, rather than to reach a specific goal. He welcomes even irrelevant seeming data as aids to fresh thinking. Picking up that same brick, a creative person might think of it as a door stop, the foundation for that set of bookshelves he's been planning. Or he might set it down and begin scratching out some complex design for a brick path to build in his back yard.

We need the logical thinker. But we need the creative person too. Creativity has been the source of most invention, and much that enriches us in writing, music, and art.

How do we encourage creativity? With children, the answer is to provide a rich play environment, and to praise unique ideas. Don't buy prepackaged, battery-driven toys. Fill the home with old magazines, tinker toys, blocks, construction paper, string, clay, paper clips, and encourage your children to create. Play pretend games: cut up animal pictures and put them together again all mixed up. Name the resultant tigaphants and giraffaloes, and make up stories about them. Figure out together three ways to do a household task . . . and let your child have the privilege of doing the job as long as he can come up with a different approach to it each day.

The same "play" approach is important if you want to develop your own creativity. Try different recipes in cooking. Find new ways to drive to and from work. Read a magazine you've never picked up, and find three ideas you can try at home or on the job. When you come up with a good solution to a problem, just for fun see if you can invent another that's totally different, but might work. Believe it or not, evidence shows that creativity is learned: we're not "born creative," but we develop creativity.

Why make the effort? Well, creativity helps keep us fresh and interesting. Creative people are generally productive and often sensitive. Creativity helps us solve problems: a creative person can often see a fresh approach that helps him or a group break an impasse when strictly logical thinkers are stumped.

Perhaps most significant to you and me, a look around our world convinces us that God is a truly creative Person. His unmatched imagination is evidenced in macrocosm and microcosm as well. God's own creativity is a clearly engraved invitation to you and me to share His joy.

CREDIT CARDS. Plastic plates padding pocketbooks produce plenty personal problems, plus private poverty. → BUYING ON CREDIT

CRITICISM. There's nothing wrong with a little constructive criticism, designed to correct. After all, being corrected now and then is part of everyone's instruction in righteousness (cf. 2 .Tim. 3:16). Destructive criticism, that tears down, is neither welcome nor right. As for the constructive, Proverbs puts it this way: "Whoever loves discipline loves knowledge, but he who hates correction is stupid" (Prov. 12:1), and "whoever heeds correction is honored" (Prov. 13:18).

That Proverbs advice is helpful when we're on the receiving end of criticism. But how about when we want to give it? How do we help a person listen without becoming angry? The anwer is, love. When another person is so sure we care that criticism can't be mistaken as an attack, our correction is much easier for him to heed.

CURIOSITY. Curiosity is a simple thing. It's a drive to know and find out. Curiosity is most irritating when it's exhibited by a three-year-old, who insists on asking "Why?" It's most dangerous when it's attracted to evils. It's saddest when it's absent.

CURSING. Believe it or not, there's no commandment against swearing. "You shall not misuse the name of the Lord your God" isn't directed against the pagan's occasional "God damn!" It's directed against those who see God's name as an empty, meaningless word and who discount God as irrelevant to life. Even believers can fall into the trap of looking at life as though God were not active, present, and real.

When we come across "cursing" in the Bible, the word is usually used in one of two ways. One sense of "curse" explains the consequences of disobedience to God's law. A person who sins will discover that disaster is a natural consequence. The other sense of "curse" is best understood as a prophetic foreview of disaster to come.

So cursing and misusing God's name aren't really related to profanity. Cursing in our sense of swearing is so stupid God didn't bother to mention it in His law. It should be abundantly clear to anyone that filthy language just isn't fitting on a believer's lips (cf. Col. 3:8).

CUSTOMS. Whenever people get together, they work out unexpressed or written rules to guide them. Some rules, like the "Stop!" on a road sign, take on the force of law. Others, like not pushing into line or how many forks to have at each place setting of a formal dinner, simply are customs.

All such general rules of behavior are helpful. They give individuals and the group a sense of security. After all, with established customs, everyone knows what to expect of others. Even if an individual doesn't keep the rules, we have customs that tell us how to deal with him.

There are two things though that make customs a problem. Times change, and customs need to change with them. Customs that do *not* change can become too important to us.

This is particularly true for Christians and our religious practices. Church services in rural America were timed to fit the schedule of farmers, who needed to get the cows milked, the team hitched up, and then travel to the nearest church. Long after the cows and farmers were no longer a matter of concern, the customary Sunday morning times have been retained. More than one zealous missionary has insisted that "church" in Africa or the Philippines must begin at the correct time, even when customary times in the native culture called for sunrise, midday, or even evening services.

It's interesting but true that the less significant morally a religious custom may be, the more ferociously some religious people will defend it. And will attack any fellow believer who questions the custom, as though he were challenging the Faith.

This is of course the problem Jesus had with the Pharisees. These magnificent hypocrites were quite capable of magnifying customs enshrined as tradition to the point where they were more important than the real issues of faith. "You nullify the word of God for the sake of your tradition," Jesus lashed out (Matt. 15:6). Later He described how they focused on details, carefully squatting by the door to count out a tithe of seasoning herbs, and yet "neglected the more important matters of the law— justice, mercy, and faithfulness" (Matt. 23:23).

The fact that the Pharisees fell so completely into the trap of custom provides us with a warning, and some guidelines.

● Distinguish between moral/biblical principles and customs. Generally customs determine how something is done (meet 9:30 A.M. Sunday, have prayer meeting in church Wednesday night), while principles define what is to be done (meet, pray).

● Remain willing to modify customs, but do not surrender principles.

● As circumstances change, explore with others how customs might be changed to better adapt to them.

Let's spend our energies to maintain unity about what truly counts in life. And leave feuds over customs to the Pharisees.

CYNICISM.

For some 900 years (330 B.C.–A.D. 600) cynics were a disturbing force in Greek society. These social dropouts were simply there, pointing out the meaninglessness of contemporary values and pursuits; arguing for the simple, unencumbered life. The radicals of the '60s, eager to get rid of the establishment, reflected the outlook of the cynic of that earlier age.

Cynicism proved to be only half a philosophy, and never more than half a faith. It echoes the gospel's evaluation that "everything in the world—the cravings of sinful man, the lust of his eyes and the boasting of what he has and does" is meaningless because "the world and its desires pass away'' (1 John 2:16, 17). But it fails to replace the chaff it brushes away with anything that can fill our lives here with meaning. But we have the gospel promise: ''the man who does the will of God lives forever'' (1 John 2:17).

† † †

DANCING. Square, folk, social, disco, modern, ballroom, ballet, aerobic . . . some folks just condemn them all. Others bring them into church for Sunday morning worship. As the Reverend John Cotton observed in 1625, it's not sensible to make a blanket condemnation. ''Dancing (yet, though mixt) I would not simply condemn. For I see two sorts of mixt dancings in use with God's people in the Old Testament, one religious, Exod XV 20, 21, the other civil, tending to the praise of conquorers, as the former of God, I Sam XVIII, 6,7. Only lascivious dancing, and amorous gestures and wanton dalliances, especially after feasts, I would bear witness against.''

DAY CARE. Day care for preschool children has a long history. The movement grew rapidly in the United States after the Civil War as a ''temporary expedient'': an alternative to institutionalizing unsupervised children so poor mothers could gain employment. It flourished again in the '40s. By the end of World War II more than a million and a half children were in 2,800 Day Care Centers, while mothers worked in the war effort. Despite the millions of working mothers and single parents today, capacity today is well behind that peak.

Should parents seek out Day Care experiences for their children? Some of the confusion is caused by differences in the purpose of centers. Some exist to provide a growth environment, to supplement home experiences and provide instruction for involved parents. Others exist as social institutions, to provide care and teaching disadvantaged children would not receive even if they were home. All centers try to provide a danger-free environment and an emotional climate in which a child can grow.

Where a working parent has no choice, a Day Care Center is a great help. Some churches have recognized community needs and have established centers in Sunday school facilities. But how about parents who do have a choice? Are there advantages in providing preschool social and educational experiences?

The weight of the evidence suggests not. Most children over three are ready to participate in some group experiences. But time spent in a Day Care Center will do little to further stimulate the growth of a child who has a varied, nurturant environment at home.

DEATH AND DYING. Today, more than in the past, dying often involves lingering illness. In 1900 some 53% of all deaths in the United States were of children under 15, and the average life span in industrial countries was 47 years. Now life span stretches into the '70s, and the most common causes of death (heart disease, cancer, and stroke) make dying a process. It's particularly important for us to understand how to minister to increasing numbers who suffer life-threatening illnesses.

Responses to life-threatening illness. A life-threatening illness understandably creates many fears. The most common are: ● fear of helplessness; ● fear of being alone, deserted; ● fear of pain and suffering; ● fear of being a burden to loved ones; ● fear of what will happen to projects; ● fear of punishment; ● fear of separation from loved ones; ● fear of the future for those left behind; ● fear of impairment and being unable to care for self; ● fear of the unknown; ● fear others will have to "take care of me"; ● fears associated with money; ● fears of loss of emotional control.

Such fears stimulate reactions that will often appear in sequence. *Denial* is a likely first reaction, as the individual refuses to believe he or she may have a life-threatening illness. *Anger* is common when realization comes. The psalmists too felt anger when facing bitter experiences (cf. Ps. 88). We are free to be angry, and to express our anger to God, knowing He will bring us peace. *Bargaining.* → **BARGAINING WITH GOD** is a common reaction, as is depression. A final state achieved by many as death nears is *acceptance.* For a believer, acceptance is eased by the certainty that God's plan and timing for the ending of life are best.

Caring for the life-threatened. Most of us will live through some months with friends or loved ones with terminal illness. How can we be most helpful?

● Always be truthful. Never belittle or minimize the situation in an attempt to reassure. Integrity and developing a trust relationship are vital to ministry.

● Listen with sensitivity. Be aware of the common reactions (above). Let a person talk out his or her feelings and reactions, accepting each stage as it occurs. This kind of listening can be extremely helpful.

● Respond to expressed needs. There may be ways you and/or others can help with fears related to economic, family, or other needs. Knowing practical issues are being taken care of can bring an ill person great relief.

● Be available. Assure the ill person he will not be abandoned. Cards and phone calls as well as short, frequent visits will help.

● Always offer hope. There may be hope for full recovery. Even when there is not, there is hope that next week the person may be strong enough to go home from the hospital. Or that you will visit tomorrow. There should always be something to which the person can look forward.

● Offer spiritual support. Relationship with God is particularly important now. It is not enough to know God is waiting beyond death. We need to know He is with us in dying. And we have God's promise: "Never will I leave you; never will I forsake you" (Heb. 13:5). Share comforting passages of Scripture, and talk about your own relationship with God.

"Unusual means." One issue that needs to be dealt with in many life-threatening illnesses has to do with the life-support systems available to maintain physical life after hope of recovery is gone, and after a person would normally have died. Many hospitals offer forms an individual or family may sign—a Refusal of Consent for Life-Prolonging Procedures—which permits a person to die naturally and with dignity.

A biblical view of death. Death is inevitable for all of us. But death is welcomed by few. Even believers, sustained by the assurance of immortality and speedy entrance into Jesus' presence, hardly approach death with eagerness.

The psalmist pictures life-threatening situations as dark valleys (Ps. 23:4). Godly king Hezekiah wept at the prospect of death in the "prime of my life." Many psalms appeal for deliverance from death, and the New Testament clearly states that death is an enemy. One day that enemy will be destroyed (1 Cor. 15:26). But until death is "swallowed up in victory" (1 Cor. 15:54), those of us who face it recognize it as an enemy, not a friend.

But death is not to be feared. Christ has freed us from death's ancient terror (Heb. 2:14, 15). He has provided an endless life, which we know will survive physical dissolution. For us death is an interlude, with no power at all to separate us from the love of God which is ours in Christ Jesus (Rom. 8:38, 39).

How well Isaiah expresses the meaning of the death of a believer: "The righteous perish, and no one ponders it in his heart; devout men are taken away, and no one understands that the righteous are taken away to be spared from evil. Those who walk uprightly enter into peace; they find rest as they lie in death" (Isa. 57:1, 2).

DECISION MAKING.
Most decisions you and I make are irrelevant. Wear blue today, or brown? Eggs or cereal for breakfast? For decisions like these, we can just ask, "Do I want to . . . ?" If the answer is "Yes," do it. If "No," don't. But there are other decisions where the instant approach using that "want to" criteria does not fit.

Three kinds of tough decisions. What decisions can't be made by referring to our "want to"?

• Direction-setting decisions. These are important choices because we know they will set the direction of our future. "Shall I marry Beth?" and "Shall I quit my job?" are direction setters. For decisions that affect our future, that "want to" approach just isn't good enough. I have to turn not to my "want to" but to my considered judgment. A better question to ask is, "Will this direction be right and satisfying for me? Shall I do it then?" Hesitancy tells you you're undecided and that you need to gather more information and let your decision ride.

• Moral decisions. Some decisions have a clear moral component. Again the "want to" approach is inadequate. Now the question becomes "Is X right or wrong?" It's not always easy to sort out moral issues. Our thinking can be confused by the (not necessarily correct) opinions of others and by the (not necessarily correct) content of our own conscience. → CONSCIENCE When we are uncertain, it's important to search Scripture for moral guidelines and to ask God to guide us through the gray areas. If we determine that the thing we question is all right morally, then we're back to the "Do I want to . . . ?" or "Shall I . . . ?" questions.

• Patterning decisions. Sometimes "want to" kinds of things, with no moral component and no life-shaping impact, fall into patterns. "Do I want to watch TV?" is an appropriate, morally neutral "want to" kind of thing. But if we answer yes *every* evening, and watching TV becomes a time-consuming habit that affects our lifestyle, a new issue has been raised.

It's helpful every now and then to look at the pattern of our irrelevant decisions. "Do I want that snack?" "Do I want to skip exercise today?" "Do I want to sleep an extra half hour?" In itself each decision is unimportant: as one more in a series of decisions, it ought to be questioned.

Putting it together, three questions provide a simple key in personal decision making.

"Do I want to?" is sufficient for most daily chores.

"Shall I?" is for those serious, direction-setting decisions.

"Should I?" comes into play whenever we think there is a moral issue involved. And every now and then we need to look at the pattern of our "want to" choices, to see if we need to shift some into the "shall I?" or the "should I?" categories.

What about finding God's will?   Christians are rightly concerned in personal decision making with finding God's will. How does God fit into the pattern I've suggested? Beautifully and (super)naturally.

Assuming that you are a believer who is willing to do God's will, you can be confident that God Himself is committed to guiding you through life. Paul puts it this way in Philippians: "It is God who works in you to will and to act according to his good purpose" (2:13). Christ has taken up residence in your life: He is at work in your decision-making process.

Several things strengthen the role of God in your decision making, and help you make that process more effective.

● Your time in Scripture. God has filled His Word with precepts and principles (general guidelines) that help us understand His outlook on the issues of life. The better you understand the Word, and the deeper your insights into God's values, the better your decisions will become.

● Your sharing with others. God intends us to live in fellowship with other brothers and sisters. That's the whole point of His great invention, the church. → CHURCH We're not to ask others to make our decisions for us. But as we share together, we learn much from others' experiences and counsel. The closer your relationship with God's people, the better your decisions will become.

● Your conscious reliance on God. When the people of Israel under Joshua attacked Palestine, they were told to expel the pagans who lived there. One group in the path of the conquering Israelis sent a delegation to make a treaty with Joshua. They carried moldy bread and had worn-out sandals, and pretended they came from a great distance.

Pleased that Israel's reputation as fearsome fighters had spread, the flattered Israelites quickly concluded the treaty. And then discovered they had been deceived! The Bible's comment? They "did not inquire of the LORD" (Josh. 9:14).

God does not direct us in an audible voice, or with a shouted imperative. But as long as you and I maintain an attitude of awareness of God's involvement and of our dependence on Him, we can be sure the Lord will guide us. "Commit your way to the LORD," the psalmist promises, "trust in him and he will do this: he will make your righteousness shine like the dawn, the justice of your cause like the noonday sun" (Ps. 37:5, 6).

When you are growing in your grasp of Scripture and in your fellowship with God's people, and when you commit your way to the Lord, He will guide your answers to the "want to" "shall I" and "should I" questions of your life.

DEFINING BY DIFFERENCE. We do it all the time, and never realize we're falling into one of Satan's snares. I mean we pick out some difference, and then define a person by it. I'm single. You're married. He's rich. We're poor. She has a Ph.D. He never finished high school. And we can go on and on. People are defined by differences in age, in looks, in color, in politics, in denomination or theology, etc. Somehow human beings seem to feel a need for differences to peg and pigeonhole one another.

What's wrong with pigeonholing ourselves or others? Well, when we do we make accidents, essence. We encourage antagonisms. And we create interpersonal distance.

Accidents and essence. The ancient philosophers made a distinction between "accident" and "essence." You could change an accident, and still have essence. For instance, a three-legged horse is still a horse. Maybe not a fast horse. But a horse nevertheless. The missing leg is an accident that doesn't effect "horseness."

It's important to be clear on accidents and essence. The story is told of one school of Greek philosophers who struggled and finally came up with a definition of a human being: a furless, featherless biped. They were quite pleased. Until someone threw a plucked chicken over the fence.

Christians define the essence of "human being" in terms of the image of God. God created us alone with all those attributes of personhood which He Himself possesses: mind, memory, emotions, will, etc. Everything else is accident: age, money, color, sex, singleness . . . these are accidents, which make us neither more nor less human and do not affect our value or worth.

Sometimes we're trapped into making accident so important that we lose sight of essence. Women's Lib does that at times. I can understand why "Black is beautiful." But we all need to realize that being Black is cause neither for pride or for shame. It's our humanness that's our real claim to fame.

Antagonism.   Differences may loom large in our minds. We think we can understand people who are like us, but not those who are different. We fear others because we're sure that if they don't understand, they will never care. So perceived differences lead naturally to defensiveness and antagonism. Union is set against management, and man against woman. Blacks fear exploitation by whites, and whites fear that Chicanos will steal the jobs they need in order to survive. Competition is often cast as a war between "us" and "them."

We see the same thing in the Christian community. "We" are Calvinists: "they" are Arminian. "We" are charismatic. "They" are not. "We" meet only in church buildings. "They" meet in homes. Soon the differences loom so large that we fear rather than appreciate one another, and antagonism replaces love.

Distance.   In the church as well as the world, the natural outcome of focusing on differences is a denial of unity. We fear "them," so we keep our distance. We're suspicious of "them," so we never open our lives or share.

Yet there is an essence in Christianity too. That essence is found in personal relationship with Jesus Christ, through whom we come into intimate family relationship with all who have been born again. → **CHURCH** Surely Christians will always have differences. Accidents are a part of life. But the differences are never to be used by the people of God to define one another.

Conclusions.   It really is important for us to realize that whatever accidents make us differ from others, at the deepest and most significant levels we are the same.

We share common ground with all human beings. "no temptation has seized you," the Bible says, "except what is common to man" (1 Cor. 10:13). All of us hurt, fear, need, rejoice, and desire. Because as persons we are made in the image of God, we must treat one another with concern and respect.

We share an additional common ground with all other believers. "You are all the sons of God through faith in Christ Jesus," the Bible affirms (Gal. 3:26). Because we are family, we must welcome one another gladly and share.

Satan encourages us to look at others and to define them by their differences from us.

God encourages us to look at others and to realize we are one.

DELEGATION.   Delegating responsibility is a good way to help children take pride in work and in themselves. But good delegation isn't easy. We must (1) make sure others understand what is expected, (2) give them some freedom to carry out the responsibility in their own way, (3) provide any help or training needed to enable them to carry out the responsibility successfully, and (4) check, to hold them accountable for doing well, within a specified time limit.

Sometimes parents think of the jobs they give children as delegated responsibility when it's really nothing but slavery. The difference? Slavery is the demand, "Do it my way, now!" Delegation expresses more respect for our children. Delegating effectively means more work for us, of course. But it sure makes life richer for our kids!

DEMON POSSESSION. Demons are real. That's what gives some Christians pause when there's talk about demon possession or oppression. How would you recognize it? Some are afraid. Could I be demon possessed? What should our attitude toward demonization be?

The Bible on demons. The New Testament is our primary source of information on demons. The Old Testament does mention evil spirits, but history's great outburst of demonic activity is associated with the earthly ministry of Jesus, and is reported in the Gospels. This may explain in part the Pharisees' argument that Jesus was in league with Satan. Satanic influence was intense around Him.

Looking into the Gospels it's clear that demons are regarded as personal beings, not "influences." Their activity is linked with human physical and mental illness (cf. in Matt. alone, 4:24; 8:28; 9:14–27, 32; 11:18; 12:22; 15:22). Many believe that the demons of the New Testament are fallen angels, who followed Satan in his ancient rebellion against God. → **ANGELS**

What is exciting to see in the Gospels is that however powerful demons may be, they are powerless before Jesus. Demons were forced to obey Jesus' every command. We also see that Jesus delegated power over demons to His disciples when He sent them on mission (Matt. 10:1). This delegated authority was exercised by Paul in Philippi when he spoke to an evil spirit: "In the name of Jesus Christ I command you to come out of her" (Acts 16:18). However, exorcism is not to be undertaken lightly. It calls for a close, intimate relationship with Jesus (cf. Acts 19:13–17), and confident faith (cf. Matt. 17: 14–21).

For us today. Our day is not marked by the same furious explosion of demonic activity known in Jesus' day. Most of us will have no direct experience with demon possession or influence. And for this we can be thankful. Still, here are some general guidelines for anyone who is concerned.

• Have nothing to do with the occult. Both the Old Testament and the New Testament make it very clear that demonic powers may express themselves through the occult. Believers are never to associate themselves with spiritism. (Cf. Deut. 18:9–14; Acts 19:18–20.) → **ASTROLOGY**

• Don't assume that strong temptation or personal disaster are caused by demons. Our own sin nature is sufficient to cause most of our problems.

• When the absolutely unexplainable happens, don't jump to the demonic conclusion. Fr. John J. Nicola, the Catholic "technical expert" for the film *The Exorcist* and himself an exorcist, insists we look first to (1) fraud or trickery, (2) natural scientific causes (particularly psychological), (3) parapsychological causes, and only then to (4) demonic influences.

• Remember that Jesus has ultimate authority over all spiritual beings. We can respect, but need not fear the demonic.

• Don't try to deal alone with what you believe may be demonic. Look for help from other Christians who take the supernatural seriously. Peter and James both give us God's promise: "Your enemy the devil prowls around like a roaring lion looking for someone to devour. Resist him, standing firm in the faith" (1 Peter 5:8, 9), and "Submit yourselves, then, to God. Resist the devil, and he will flee from you. Come near to God and he will come near to you" (James 4:7, 8).

DENIAL. Denial is a refusal to face the truth or to accept reality. At times denial provides a temporary release from stress. But in the long run, reality presses in, and we have to face it. Extreme denial can be dangerous. There are medical reports of men who, during a heart attack, did pushups or climbed stairs to convince themselves they weren't having one! There's even a report in the Bible that some practice sin, and deny they've slipped out of fellowship with God (1 John 1:5, 6).

DENOMINATIONS. It's good to have roots: to know that our particular expression of Christian faith comes to us as a heritage from men and women committed to God's truth as they understood it, and whose practices reflect their culture and times. We can each be thankful for our heritage. And rejoice in the traditions that are dear to us.

As long as we don't confuse our way with the only way, and our particular expression of faith with Christianity itself.

DEPENDENCY. We don't mind when a toddler cries for mommy. We reach down and lift up a little one who can't quite make it into his chair by himself. But we parents want our little ones to grow up. One of these days they need to take on responsibility for their own actions, and figure out ways to climb into and out of chairs by themselves.

Oh, we'll always be there. And if they need help, we'll give it. But there's satisfaction for child and parent both when a little one is able to do things on his or her own.

Sometimes we forget this in our relationship with God. We think that "depending on the Lord" means doing nothing at all; just waiting for Him to lift us up and put us down. But we're wrong. Yes, God is always there, and we can bring anything at all to Him. → **BABY TALK** But God takes joy in us when we show our trust by stepping out, in faith, to make life's necessary decisions and take life's necessary actions as growing, responsible children. You and I always want to remain dependent on the Lord. But God wants us to be dependent spiritual adults. . . . not dependent spiritual babes (cf. Heb. 5:14).

DEPRESSION. Most of us are down at times; times when ordinary unhappiness makes life seem bleak. Mild episodes of depression are a part of everyone's life. But sometimes depression deepens. We have difficulty sleeping, we lose energy, we seem drugged by fatigue. We feel unhappy about ourselves and avoid being with people. We

181

may find ourselves fearful and irritable. Symptoms like these warn us that our outlook on life is being warped by depression.

Depression is typically associated with some stress or loss. Some depressions have physical as well as psychological roots. The dominant emotions linked with depression are sadness and a sense of hopelessness. Often there are also feelings of guilt or anger.

Medically. Two approaches are generally taken to treating depression. But since a depressed individual already feels hopeless, it is difficult for him or her to seek treatment. One treatment uses mood changing drugs (tricyclic antidepressant drugs), discovered in 1957. A depressed person usually shows some lifting of mood and increased energy within the first week of drug treatment.

Depression is also treated by psychotherapy. The therapist treating a depressed person seeks to establish rapport, and in this relationship of growing confidence and liking, healing may begin. Therapists want to empathize (let the other person know "I understand how you feel"), but do not want to pity. Instead, the therapist seeks to communicate hope. Talking through feelings and problems with another person can help release pent-up emotions. Another person can provide perspective, helping to analyze situations the depressed person must deal with and thus helping him or her to cope.

It is difficult for the family of a depressed individual. Attempts to "cheer up" the person may only irritate. Often the depressive's natural withdrawal is read by the family as rejection or blame. Family members are generally encouraged to follow these principles when living with a loved one in the grip of depression: (1) empathize, but do not pity. Pity tends to deepen a person's feelings of hopelessness and lower his or her self-esteem. (2) Remember that a depressed person really hurts. His or her depression is not a tactic used to manipulate you. (3) Avoid confronting and attacking. Adding pressures tends to deepen depression. It's best to wait until a person is no longer depressed if possible. (4) Offer realistic hope. A depressed person will lack confidence in the future and will not readily accept reassurance. Yet quiet confidence and judicious reassurance from others are vital aids to recovery.

Biblically. We're immediately struck by the fact that our faith is no insulation from depression. Some of the greatest figures of Scripture experienced depression: Elijah (1 Kings 19), Job (Job 6), and even the apostle Paul. Paul openly shares his experience in 2 Corinthians, writing "we were under great pressure, far beyond our ability to endure, so that we despaired even of life itself. Indeed, in our hearts we felt the sentence of death" (1:8, 9). In this open sharing of his experience Paul follows the example of the psalmists, and so brings you and me great release. Depression is not an indication of spiritual inferiority or sin! The greatest men of God have known depression. And while Job's depression was a result of personal tragedy (Job 1 and 2) and Paul's because of hardships, Elijah fell into deep depression at the very peak of his success (cf. 1 Kings 18:16–45).

While we find no explanation of depression in the Scripture, we do gain many helpful insights.

(1) We see how God deals with a depressed person. When Elijah's depression led him to despair, and he ran from his ministry, God was not angry. Instead God actually *provided food to sustain* Elijah while he ran (1 Kings 19:6–9). Then God *spoke* to Elijah *in a "gentle whisper"* (19:12). God *gave* Elijah *a simple task* to do, and also *reassured* Elijah that there were others who were faithful to the Lord (19:15, 16, 18). Finally God *gave Elijah a companion,* Elisha, who would be with him and would one day take on his prophetic ministry.

(2) We see the importance of friends. Much of Job's anguish came when his friends tried to explain his suffering rather than offer supportive love. Elijah's healing was linked with the companionship of Elisha. As Job put it, "a despairing man should have the devotion of his friends" (6:14).

(3) We learn that even depression can bring blessing.

Paul looked back on his dark experience and realized "this happened that we might not rely on ourselves but on God, who raises the dead" (2 Cor. 1:9). Because Paul lived through the depths, he was able to comfort others with similar experiences (2 Cor. 1:3–6). However bleak our future seems when we are depressed, we can know that God will use the darkness to bring others light.

Conclusions.   Christians are not immune to depression. But neither are we conquered by it. We need not be terrified by depression in ourselves or in others.

For our times of depression, meditation on the experiences of Elijah and Paul may be helpful. So can reading psalms of anguish in our Old Testament, focusing on verses that unveil the reality of a hope the psalmist may not have felt, but knew was real. Psalms 43 and 55 are appropriate. Psalm 62 is filled with verses rich in quiet reassurance.

For chronic or intense depression, consider seeing a physician. Your symptoms may have a physical basis. Professional counseling may also help. But consider the possibility that close Christian friends can also provide healing support. You may know someone in your congregation who brothers and sisters go to when they need a person who can listen and care. A person who has come through depression can also help.

If a friend or loved one experiences depression, follow the suggestions given earlier. Keep your own hope and confidence fixed in the Lord. One of the greatest gifts we can give another person in such a time is the gift of believing in God for him or her, until he or she is able again to experience the joy of confidence in God.

DESERTION (NON-SUPPORT).   What happens to children when Dad leaves or parents divorce? Aside from psychological concerns, money is a problem. Courts typically set child support for a parent caring for two children at 33% of the noncustodial (usually the father) parent's income. But the custodial parent needs 80% of the family's former income to maintain the earlier standard of living! Add to this the fact that nationwide probably 50% of divorced fathers make little or no support payment despite court orders, and we get a feel for the problem.

What's being done? Some counties achieve much higher rates of collection than others. These tend to be smaller counties with (1) an automatic system that monitors payments and sends warning notices when a certain amount is in arrears, and (2) when the county or district jails a substantial rate of nonpayers for contempt of court.

As for private collection (a mother hiring lawyers, etc.), if the governmental system does not support enforcement, there will be little the individual parent can do.

Perhaps the best suggestion made to date is to change the child-payment approach, and institute a system of mandatory wage deductions through court orders to employers.

Nationally, making fathers pay for the support of their children after divorce or desertion would provide great savings in the cost of welfare. It should also make a difference in the relationship possible between children and father. Perhaps as significant, it would affirm a basic biblical principle: we remain responsible for the results of our actions and choices. Personal responsibility is something from which no one should be allowed to run.

DETERMINISM. It looks like a comforting philosophy. At least, to those who dislike the weight of personal responsibility. They blandly explain, "It's not my fault. My psychiatrist says it's because Mom wouldn't let me play with the other kids when I was seven." Or they shake their head apologetically, "I just had to do it. I've been hostile ever since I saw Grandpa hit Grandma and they made me eat artichokes."

Of course, the things that happen to us do have an influence. But "make" us hostile? So we "can't help it"?

God's people made the same excuse just before Jerusalem was destroyed by the Babylonians. The prophets Jeremiah and Ezekiel announced God's judgment on their sin, and the people just shrugged. Their fathers had sinned. If judgment was coming, there was nothing they could do. Then they quoted a favorite saying: "The fathers eat sour grapes, and the children's teeth are set on edge" (Ezek. 18:2). By denying personal responsibility they excused themselves for their refusal to repent when God announced judgment. Judgment coming? Turn from our sins? What's the use? It's all been determined anyway.

God's response to determinism is given in Ezekiel 18. There He establishes once and for all that the past provides no valid excuse for today's choices. "You will no longer quote this proverb in Israel" God says, and announces "The soul [person] who sins is the one who will die" (18:3, 4). Each individual is judged for his own actions, not for what others have done.

At first this might look like a pronouncement of doom. Particularly if you feel trapped by your own past. But actually it's a word of hope. Ezekiel goes on to explain that an unrighteous son will not be punished for his father's sins, for he can turn to God and do right. Even a person who has been wicked can turn from his sins to God and will surely live (18:21–23).

Not only does what our parents do not determine our future, what we ourselves have done does not doom us! The past does not fix our future. Each of us has the power to stop, to accept responsibility for our own actions and, by turning to God, to change.

So don't let the determinist fool you. You are responsible and free. You can turn to God and change!

DIET AIDS. These days it takes 8′ by 4′ shelves in pharmacies to hold all the diet aids. Check them out, and you will discover some interesting facts. Most of them work like amphetamines, to speed up the metabolism. Some are drenched in caffeine which stimulates the metabolism and acts as a mild diuretic. Many include an appetite depressant.

Of course, the key is the 1,000 calorie diet that comes with the pills. Follow the plan, and you'll lose weight. Follow the plan without the pills and you will still lose weight. What the plans don't tell you is that the only way anyone loses weight is by taking in fewer calories each day than he or she uses.

They also don't mention (except in very small print) that diet aids are dangerous for anyone with a heart problem or high blood pressure, or under 18. And they never add that hospital emergency rooms are familiar with diet-pill poppers.

What's fascinating, though, is that in a society so concerned with drug abuse, when Mommy wants to lose a few pounds she depends on drugs. It's hard to convince kids that "drug *use* is drug *abuse*," when the society that denies them marijuana and coke depends on diet "uppers."

DIRT. Plato was the Greek philosopher who advanced the notion that there is an "ideal" off somewhere, which all similar things in the material world reflect. He had no problem when it came to arguing for the "ideal" chair, or table, or even human being. But he was bothered by mud. And flies. How could there be an "ideal" for such useless, disgusting things?

The Bible doesn't pay much attention to dirt. Its focus is "not the removal of dirt from the body but the pledge of a good conscience toward God" (1 Peter 3:21).

DISCERNMENT. According to the dictionary, discernment is the ability to see things clearly and with understanding. What does the Bible suggest you and I learn to discern? Not just what is good. "What is best" (Phil. 1:10).

DISCIPLESHIP. So you want to be a disciple, but don't know just how to go about it? Some today suggest you link up with a mature Christian who will "disciple" you. This person will meet with you each week, give you assignments, and review your Bible study and daily decisions. Other people suggest you take a course. Or read a particular book. One leader I know tells you to listen to his cassettes. Pow! Instant disciples.

Not a program, a relationship. Jesus' Great Commission tells us to "make disciples of all nations" (Matt. 28:19). This is a call to a relationship with Jesus, not to establish another church program. We realize that discipleship is for all believers, and from it obeying "everything I have commanded" is to flow (28:20). We sense the relationship again in the fact that Old and New Testaments both link obedience with love: "If anyone loves me, he will obey my teaching" (John 14:23, 24; Deut. 11:18, 22). A disciple then is a believer in a growing personal relationship with the Lord, which results in deepening love and obedience.

Disciple-making. Two New Testament pictures help us understand how to make disciples. Each description is geared to the personal transformation of the individual (cf. Luke 6:40). In the Gospels we see Jesus making disciples. He chooses a group of a dozen, and works closely with them for some three years. They stay close to Him, hear His teaching, discuss, ask and are asked questions, and are sent out together to minister to others. Living together and sharing experiences under Jesus' guidance, they become disciples.

In the epistles we see the church making disciples. Again believers are called together in intimate groups. These groups stay close together and build close, loving relationships. Their members teach and admonish each other (Col. 3:16). As more mature believers are recognized as spiritual leaders, they provide teaching and living examples for our life of faith (cf. 1 Peter 5:3; 1 Tim. 4:12; Phil. 4:9). Living together and sharing experiences, believers become disciples.

Discipleship today. Today as in Bible times, discipleship is for all believers. And disciples are made by the same process. The secret is not a one-on-one relationship or a special course. The secret is simply living together as the church, the people of God, in intimate relationship. Together we share study, life, and prayer. And together we become disciples. → CHURCH

DISCIPLINE.

DISCIPLINE. Facing a stubborn three-year-old or a pouting teen, it's not unusual for a parent to feel angry and frustrated. Or sometimes, like one friend of mine, to feel a little afraid. The confrontations Suzie had with her daughter reminded her of her own willful adolescence, and seemed almost like a challenge. Like many parents, Suzie made up her mind. She would *make* her three-year-old daughter obey!

For some, this sums up their idea of discipline: to break a child's sinful will and force him or her to do what Mom and Dad say is right.

Unfortunately, confrontation may mean parents and children are constantly at odds. Every "You *will* pick up your toys!" or "You *will* finish your peas!" is likely to stimulate an equally forceful, "I *won't.*" Even if a child surrenders before a parent's strength, inner resentment grows. That resentment may lead to rejection of parental values when the child is older.

For Suzie though her daughter would not surrender. She just fought back. Suzie spanked, scolded, screamed, and sent her off to bed, but nothing she did helped the little girl want to obey.

Our goals in discipline. Before we talk about how to discipline, we need to get our goals clearly in mind. Discipline is not a contest of wills, engaged in to force a child to obey. In fact, the real goal is not behavior at all. The goal of discipline is the development of a child's character, to help him or her want to, and be able to, choose what is right.

The Bible's basic passage on discipline is found in Hebrews 12. The teaching is built on the notion that discipline is training: training that is carefully planned. Looking to God the Father as the One who provides us a model, the writer says, "God disciplines us for our good, that we may share in his holiness." Designed God's way, discipline "produces a harvest of righteousness and peace for those who have been trained by it" (Heb. 12:10, 11).

When we understand discipline as training, focused on helping a child build a good character and willingly choose what is right, we're helped to avoid the difficulties that Suzie experienced in her relationship with her daughter.

What are some general principles that help us pattern discipline to work toward God's expressed goals? Here are several, which apply equally to tots like Suzie's daughter and also to teen-agers.

• Listen acceptingly to feelings. Don't take complaints as a personal afront. A three-year-old's "I won't" may come just when she's tired and cranky. Suzie might be better off not shouting "You will!" and saying something like, "I know you don't feel like picking up the toys. I'll bet you're tired. Sometimes I get tired and don't want to do my work either. But you and Mommy do our jobs anyway, don't we?"

What this response does is express acceptance of the child's feelings, try to help her locate the cause of her feelings, and then communicate the positive expectation that like Mom, the daughter will do what is right anyway.

Listening takes more and more time as children grow. But helping a child to express and identify the cause of his or her feelings, and then responding positively pays large dividends.

• Avoid a win/lose atmosphere. This is created when the issue shifts from the thing to be done to personalities. Then "you will!" vs. "I won't!" means that no matter what happens, someone is going to lose and the other person is going to win. Suddenly competition rather than doing what is right has become the issue.

When you or I say "I get tired sometimes and don't want to do my work either" we're telling the child, "I'm with you and not against you." The problem is picking up the blocks, not my determination to force you to act against your will.

Sometimes parents must be willing to give a little. Suzie might help her daughter pick up the blocks, or let her do it after a nap instead of before. Or she might suggest a choice: "Which would you rather do now, pick up the blocks or put your dolls away?"

• Plan ahead for success. This is particularly important. If Suzie has noticed a particular time of day when her daughter is tired, she may need to build a schedule. Picking up may come earlier in the day, followed by the special treat of reading a story book. "As soon as you get your toys picked up we can read" is a different kind of instruction than "Pick up your toys!" And is likely to get a different response.

● Define expectations and limits. As children grow older this becomes more important. Limits can be decided together to avoid any appearance of being arbitrary.

A nine-year-old can be told the hours of sleep children his age need. He can help decide how much time he needs in the morning to get ready for school. He can count backward to the evening hour he should be asleep, and then choose activities he wants to include as bedtime rituals. My kids always wanted to read and sing while being tucked in. By counting up time, it was relatively easy for them to decide when they should start getting ready for bed. The expectations and limits were established together and clearly understood.

● Utilize consequences. Most actions have some kind of natural consequences built in. Parents need to be sure the consequences happen. If you don't eat your peas then no dessert can be a mealtime rule. Just be sure that if the vegetables aren't eaten, the child doesn't get dessert anyway. If that bedtime ritual the children and you plan is missed, the ritual should be forfeited. Helping children understand family expectations and the consequences of failing to meet them is a great aid in discipline. → **CONSEQUENCES**

Is there a place for punishment? If the foregoing sounds somehow "too easy" on kids, remember that the goal in discipline is not retribution, but training. Training doesn't *have* to major on punishments. God's training never relies on power alone.

But the Bible does talk about "spare the rod and spoil the child." Even our Hebrews passage says that "no discipline seems pleasant at the time" (12:11). So where does punishment—like spankings—fit in?

First, recognize that the use of natural consequences in discipline *is* punishment. Second, realize that young children will at times need extra help to be responsive. I found a ping-pong paddle a great help. It made noise, smarted, but didn't cause any real damage. And any fear was associated with the paddle—not with me. Most importantly, the paddle was used to help the child obey, and was not used in anger.

When my kids kept forgetting to close the door one summer (a serious thing because of my wife's allergies), I got out the paddle. "I know you don't want to hurt Mommy, and you don't mean to leave the door open. It's just hard for you to remember. So the paddle is to help. The first time you forget and leave it open, one whack with the paddle. The second time, two. And so on." What a great aid! I never had to whack any of the kids even once. The paddle helped them do what they really wanted to do anyway.

Grounding teens who stay out too late or who keep the car after hours is punishment. And it hurts. But it's a punishment that fits the crime, and rightly administered is designed to help a young person remember the limits and expectations you worked through together as fair.

Punishment does have a place in discipline. But as we discipline wisely, seeking as God does our children's good, we have less and less occasion to use it as our guys and gals grow.

DISCRIMINATION. A massive study on the state of human rights begins with the observation that the human condition "is characterized by an unending series of man-made catastrophies." Working with UN data, and drawing illustrations from around the world, the author catalogs discrimination of all types. He explores discrimination in which rank is given by membership in a social group rather than won by a person's individual qualities. He looks at sex discrimination, racial discrimination, language and religious discrimination, class and caste and legal and political and economic discrimination. In every society, bias for some group and against others seems built into institutions.

The author attempts no explanation for the perversity demonstrated in systematic discrimination. For you or me to explain it as another expression of the sin nature would be correct . . . but it would not be right.

It wouldn't be right because God doesn't shrug off discrimination with an explanation. He knows better than we the root cause. But in Old Testament Law He acts to control it. "The community is to have the same rules for you and for the alien living among you; this is a lasting ordinance for the generations to come. You and the alien shall be the same before the Lord: the same laws and regulations will apply both to you and to the alien living among you" (Num. 15:15, 16).

It's the same in the legal system: discrimination is not to be allowed . . . nor is reverse discrimination. "Do not deny justice to your poor people in their lawsuits." And, "Do not follow the crowd in doing wrong. When you give testimony in a lawsuit, do not pervert justice by siding with the crowd, and do not show favoritism to a poor man in his lawsuit" (Exod. 23:6, 2, 3). In the same context it says, "Do not oppress an alien; you yourselves know how it feels to be aliens, because you were aliens in Egypt" (23:9).

Somehow it's not enough for you and me to cleanse our own hearts of bias. God cares about a just society. And so must we.

DISNEYLAND. It's fun to visit. But wouldn't it be terrible to have to live there?

DIVORCE AND REMARRIAGE. The latest 1981 statistics show that 39% of first marriages end in divorce, as do 60% of second marriages. These facts panic many, who see evidence of the breakdown of the family. They panic Christians, who realize divorce and remarriage have invaded the church. Most important, they tell us there are many hurting people among us who need our support and help.

Why the increase? What do Christians think about divorce and remarriage? What does the Bible say? And, of course, what about *you*?

Society and divorce. There's no question that changes in our society are reflected in the divorce rate. Many who in earlier decades might have felt they had no choice but to stay together realize today there is a choice . . . and make it. Today ● there is less social pressure to remain in an unsatisfying marriage. ● There is no good evidence that postponing divorce helps the children. ● There are jobs for women, so financial dependence is no longer as great a factor. ● There is a high remarriage rate: divorcees have a better chance at marriage than those who have never married! ● High mobility means few roots or supportive relationships that might help a couple work through difficulties. In addition, many women experience unique pressure these days. One researcher points out that relationship-making traits, linked with a happy marriage, are in conflict with the assertiveness and independence women are urged to develop in a quest for personal identity.

Are divorce and remarriage ever right? Hurting Christian couples and church leaders are not so much interested in why the high divorce rate as they are in the moral issue. Is divorce or remarriage ever God's will for us? Are they ever right? There are several differing positions within the Christian community.

  ● Never. This rigid position is taken by those who are convinced the church must take a stand against crumbling cultural values.

  ● Only for unfaithfulness. This traditional position views infidelity as grounds for divorce, and as release for remarriage.

  ● Only if the divorced partner remarries. This position views a divorce as separation, not the end of marriage. Only if one partner remarries is a divorced believer free to remarry, since there is no longer a chance of reconciliation.

  ● Cases must be examined individually. Divorce and remarriage are not viewed as "right," but are understood at times to be best. Biblical principles are understood to provide guidance to the individual but not to express "laws" applicable to all cases (as the three above positions assume).

Anyone considering divorce, and asking for help, is likely to hear one of these four positions advanced. The very fact the differences exist helps us realize that committed believers do honestly differ about how to interpret what the Bible teaches on divorce and remarriage.

What does the Bible say?   There is no question that God's ideal for marriage was and is a permanent, life-long relationship between one man and one woman. Divorce is never seen as part of the ideal, but is recognized as falling short of it. A divorce merely to satisfy one's passion for a new spouse is strongly condemned (Mal. 2:11, 13–16).

With this said, it is also clear that the Old Testament does make provision for divorce, and that remarriage is expected (Deut. 24:1–4). In Jesus' day the rabbis debated valid grounds for divorce. But they never doubted that divorce and remarriage were acceptable to God.

When Jesus was asked about grounds for divorce (Matt. 19:3) He reaffirmed the ideal of a permanent relationship. When asked why then Moses' law permits divorce, Jesus explained. ''Moses permitted you to divorce your wives because your hearts were hard'' (19:8). His point is that sin distorts every human relationship and may harden us in marriage as well. What God designed as an enriching relationship may be distorted by sin and become destructive.

Is divorce and remarriage then right? As falling short of the ideal it clearly involves sin (Matt. 19:8, 9; cf. Rom. 3:23). But it is a ''sin'' for which God Himself has made provision. He understands how hardness can warp a relationship, and that divorce and remarriage may be necessary to heal.

The major passage in the Epistles that deals with divorce and remarriage is 1 Corinthians 7. Here Paul reaffirms the ideal, and tells Christians ● not to divorce (7:10) ● if they do, to remain unmarried in hopes of reconciliation (7:11), but ● if no reconciliation is possible, to consider themselves ''not bound.'' These principles were applied for the Corinthians, many of whom were married to unbelievers. Some argue they apply to situations today in which any spouse refuses to continue the marriage.

Looking at the biblical passages, it's clear that none suggest divorce and remarriage as "the answer" to a marital problem. Instead, the Bible calls on us to seek to heal hurts in any relationship with confession, forgiveness, forbearing, looking to meet others' needs, and love. Divorce is only for those situations where the hurt is great, and one or both persons *will not* follow God's path to healing and reconciliation.

Financial implications of divorce. There are practical as well as moral questions to be considered when contemplating a divorce. One salary may now be stretched to support two households. In dividing assets, unexpected tax bills may come for capital gains. Today child support for two children is set at about ⅓ of the working spouse's income. But 80% of income is needed to maintain the standard of living. As of 1980, some 50% of divorced women work full time . . . but median income, even including alimony, is a mere $10,700! In most cases divorce means financial strain on both parties. Obtaining legal help to work out financial settlements is a necessity.

But what about you? You may have turned to this article out of curiosity. Or because you or a loved one is considering a divorce. Or because you've already remarried. What guidelines might help you?

• If you are considering divorce. Divorce is a last resort, but one that sometimes should be taken. God is compassionate, and is concerned about destructive relationships.

But first, have you tried counseling? Legal separation is also an option. The marriage is not ended, but a court provides for financial support. Separation may convince your spouse you are serious. If both of you face existing problems, counseling can bring reconciliation. Pain in a marriage can be the prelude to healing if both spouses will reach out for help.

• If you are remarried or considering remarriage. Remarriage is likely to be a more difficult decision for believers than is divorce. A book that will help you think through this issue, and help you examine every relevant Old Testament and New Testament passage, is *Remarriage* (L. Richards, Word, 1980).

● Recognize that there are conflicting views on divorce and remarriage in the Christian community. You will receive conflicting advice. Because the issue is so emotionally charged, you may well feel extreme pressure.

The very fact of differences however makes it clear that your decision is too important to hand over to someone else to make. Since honest disagreement exists in interpreting Scripture, you must accept responsibility to study the issue for yourself, and you must personally seek Christ's guidance concerning what He wants you to do. When we trust and acknowledge Him, we know that He will direct our paths (Prov. 3:5, 6). We must then have the courage to be obedient to His leading.

● Refuse to enter into judgment. Each of us should develop personal convictions about divorce and remarriage when the issues touch our lives. But we must also remember that Jesus is Lord. While we are responsible for our own choices, we are not responsible for our brother's or sister's.

Anyone hurting enough to consider divorce needs love and support from others, not condemnation. We are free to share our convictions, but we must do so in such a loving way that others understand we extend to them the right to be responsible to Jesus for any decision they make. We must make it clear that whatever they decide, they are loved.

DOCTRINAL DISPUTES.
We all agree that doctrine is important. And confess that doctrine sometimes seems divisive. But what's a person to do? We're commanded to "keep as the pattern of sound teaching, with faith and love in Christ Jesus," that which we find in the Word (2 Tim. 1:13). Certainly we can't surrender truth in search for harmony.

The tension has been felt throughout history, and many of us struggle with this issue today. Fortunately, the

New Testament shows us how to deal with situations in which brothers disagree about which teaching is correct.

It happened in Corinth. Some of the converted pagans were upset when others purchased meat at temple markets, where it had first been dedicated to an idol. Shocked, they asked these brothers, "Don't you know demons are behind idolatry!" But the meat eaters had an answer. "There's only one true God: idols are just things, shaped of stone and metal." People on each side were sure they were right. And so the unity of the church was threatened by the doctrinal dispute.

Paul did help them work through the doctrine. But first he established an important principle. "We know that we all possess knowledge. Knowledge puffs up, but love builds up. The man who thinks he knows something does not yet know as he ought to know. But the man who loves God is known by God" (1 Cor. 8:1–3).

Paul's thought is this. When we approach a disagreement we can emphasize knowledge, or love. If we say "I *know* better than you," we'll have problems. First, that claim of superior knowledge leads to pride. Second, no matter how much we know, our knowledge is imperfect and incomplete. No one can be absolutely certain "I'm right" and "You're wrong."

What happens though when we emphasize love? Paul says the dispute will then edify, or build up rather than tear down. When we know we're loved (rather than attacked!) we can let our defenses down and honestly explore the issue. We can share our thoughts and listen to others' understandings. In the process, we'll learn and grow.

Paul also implies that loving opens our lives to God so we can be "known by" Him. This reflects the teaching ministry of the Holy Spirit, who is free now to instruct us.

Scripture never suggests that doctrine is unimportant. But the Bible teaches that fighting over doctrine isn't the way to handle disagreement.

Actually, Paul goes on in 1 Corinthians 10 to bring up a point neither side had thought of. In history, as in Corinth, idolatry was associated with immorality (10:6–22). Shouldn't Christians avoid anything so clearly associated with all sorts of sin? Actually, each Corinthian party had been partly right. And partly wrong!

So we need to be sure in our disagreements to give each other love and time. Yes, stand for the truth as you understand it, and present your reasons. But also listen humbly. When believers are willing to keep on loving despite differences, and humble enough to listen when they disagree, God will be at work.

Both sides will learn and grow.

DON'TS.   When young Christians at Colossae became enthusiastic about long lists of "don't do this" and "don't touch that," the apostle Paul wasn't impressed. He wrote them saying, "Such regulations indeed have an appearance of wisdom, with their self-imposed worship, their false humility and their harsh treatment of the body, but they lack any value in restraining sensual indulgence" (Col. 2:23). His observation is important to us when we too go chasing after lists. Such lists are ● self-imposed. And they ● lack any value.

Paul's reasoning needs to be understood. You see, he understands "sensual indulgence" as an inner rather than just physical thing. We set up all sorts of self-imposed criteria for spirituality linked to not doing this or not doing that. But our lists are likely to lead to pride that we're "more spiritual" than others, and to judging them for their indulgence. And *that* (our pride, and looking down on others) is real "sensual indulgence." And thoroughly displeasing to God.

DOUBT.   Doubt is sensible when you consider how little we know, and how easy it is to be wrong. But doubt is unnecessary when we consider God. Still, He doesn't get upset if we continue to be uncertain. He simply invites us, "taste and see that the LORD is good" (Ps. 34:8). →
KNOWING

DREAMS.   Messages from our inner selves? Many are convinced that's just what dreams are. Certainly it's fascinating to note the link of dreams with great discoveries . . . like the role of a dream in diagraming the atom and the role of a dream in the invention of the sewing machine. The Senoi people of Malaysia even use dreams in child rearing. If a child dreams of a monster, he's taught to attack it the next time it appears in his dreams. If he dreams of harming a friend, the next day he must visit the friend and bring a gift. And all positive dreams are to be acted out.

Since Freud, much attention has been given to interpreting dreams, which are regarded as symbolic. You can buy books today that purport to explain what dream objects stand for. But each person's dream symbolism is highly subjective: no one can explain your dreams for sure.

In the ancient world dreams were regarded as omens or messages from the gods. Within this context, it was appropriate for God to speak to Pharaoh and Nebuchadnezzar in dreams . . . and to authenticate Joseph and Daniel as His spokesmen when they alone were able to interpret (Gen. 41; Dan. 2). Even though the New Testament reports incidents in which God guided Peter (Acts 10) and Paul (Acts 16) in visions, these should not be understood as normal dreams. Our dreams? Messages from our inner selves, perhaps. But your dreams and mine are unlikely to be messages from God.

DRIVING. Driving is regarded more as a right these days than a privilege. Kids at 16 insist on getting a driver's license. Moms and Dads cave in, despite knowing what accident statistics and insurance rates tell us about highschoolers' accidents. And despite readily available information on an adverse impact on school grades and acceleration of dating. I suppose in a culture like ours we shouldn't be surprised that drunk drivers don't go to jail. Even though we know that at least 50% of fatal car accidents are linked with drinking. Why should we expect judges to have convictions? Even parents don't.

DRUG ABUSE. Despite a twenty-year furor over drugs, the Drug Abuse Council looked at the '80s and observed, "Drug use and misuse have become among the most compelling realities of contemporary existence." For most, the use of drugs seems merely fashionable recreation. Despite efforts at education and control, each year the age of drug use becomes younger and younger. And the cost, in personal and social terms, becomes higher.

Several terms help us understand the issue. "Addiction" is a pattern of compulsive drug use, in which life is summed up in using and securing the drug, with a high probability of relapse after drug withdrawal. "Abuse" is an intentional use of any chemical substance without full knowledge of likely consequences, as well as wrong use.

Several kinds of substances are included as drugs. Amphetamines are drugs that stimulate the nervous system. Analgesics are pain relievers. Anesthetics produce loss of feeling. Barbiturates act as sedatives or hypnotics. Hallucinogens produce distortions in sensory impressions. Even alcohol is a depressant. Many popular, or street names, are given to these substances and to others.

What may surprise many Christians is the fact that not just cocaine or marijuana are abused drugs. Many of us who would never think of taking an illegal drug—or even a drink of alcohol—have developed a pattern of dependence on Compoz. A quick scan of TV ads for capsules or pills to suppress appetite so we can lose weight illustrates how acceptable the idea of depending on drugs has become in our society.

A 1981 publication on drug use provides these insights into drug use in the '80s. About 65% of high school seniors have used illicit drugs at some time, with marijuana the most common. Some 93% have used alcohol, and 74% cigarettes. Many in the field of drug control believe the drug epidemic began as a consequence of anxiety, and that this is directly related to the breakdown of the family structure in the United States. Today much pro-drug literature and many pro-drug terms are in wide use. These give the impression that the use of drugs for social or recreational purposes is relatively safe. This notion is winning adherents despite increasing scientific evidence that long-term harm is likely, even from the widely-accepted marijuana.

What can be done? Nearly every community has sources of help for drug abusers and addicts. In addition information is readily available: there are books in libraries, hundreds of "how to" pamphlets, and even scholarly journals devoted to the subject. Information about local helping agencies can be obtained at your church or from state/federal agencies.

But the subject of drug abuse may raise another question we should answer. Am I falling into my culture's drug trap? Is my own use of drugs—even if the only drugs I use are sleeping pills—setting an example of dependence that my children or others will extend to illicit drugs?

Two lines of truth in the New Testament invite us to consider a meaningful alternative, and to reflect on our attitudes. One line of teaching stresses the importance of self-control. Two Greek words express the biblical meaning of self-control. One emphasizes self-mastery; a mastery valued as a sign of human freedom. The other emphasizes our capacity to evaluate reasonably and to act sensibly. In the Bible, self-control is never viewed as restrictive. Instead, Scripture affirms that we are most free when we're able to use our faculties to make wise decisions. We are the most in bondage when we have lost control of our lives and of our actions. Writing about those who have become dulled to the meaning and the potential of life, the Bible says, "Let us not be like others, who are asleep, but let us be alert and self-controlled. For those who sleep, sleep at night, and those who get drunk, get drunk at night. But since we belong to the day, let us be self-controlled, putting on faith and love as a breastplate, and the hope of salvation as a helmet" (1 Thess. 5:6–8). To remain alert in today's world, we may well need to evaluate our use of even household drugs.

The other line of Bible teaching deals with the need many feel for drugs, and on the escape from reality drugs offer. This world is certainly not an easy place for anyone. But the Christian faces reality with optimism and hope.

"Do not get drunk on wine, which leads to debauchery," the New Testament warns escapists. "Instead, be filled with the Spirit" (Eph. 5:18). The drugs to which mankind turns offer a momentary escape from a reality that will overtake all. But the Spirit of God, and a life filled with His presence, promises us victory in every reality. If we live in God's presence, we no longer need to flee.

† † †

EACH AND EVERY. Look up "each" or "every" in the NIV concordance, and you'll be disappointed. Neither word seemed important enough to include. But don't worry. "Every" really occurs nearly 500 times in the Bible, and "each" about 25 times. Each and every are still in the Bible. And each and every one of us is still the object of God's love.

EASY. Things that come easy aren't appreciated. Even experimental animals in psychologists' laboratories appear to enjoy working for food pellets by pushing buttons or pulling down bars. They don't have to be rewarded every time, either. In fact, rewards that come in a random pattern, only part of the time, generate more enthusiastic efforts. There's something about things we achieve by our own effort that makes those things sweeter and more meaningful.

I have to struggle to remember this with my youngest. He has lots of talent, but not a lot of discipline yet. I have to watch myself, to make sure he earns his way and I don't make it too easy for him.

God doesn't seem to have my problem. When strapped, I never win a Publisher's Clearinghouse or Mac-Donald's contest, no matter how many hamburgers I dutifully consume. Instead, God just supplies more work for me to do. God is too wise to let us live without the weight of personal responsibility. And too good to let us live a life in which we would not savor earned rewards.

EATING . . . AND
EATING AND
EATING
ECCENTRICS
ECUMENICAL
MOVEMENT

EATING . . . AND EATING AND EATING.

Coach had it plastered with other inspirational signs on the walls of my high-school locker room: "Eat to live, not live to eat."

I found a saying in the Bible that goes coach one better. "Everything is permissible for me—but I will not be mastered by anything" (1 Cor. 6:12).

ECCENTRICS.

You don't have to be like Mad Jack Mytton and ride a bear into your drawing room. Or set fire to your nightshirt to cure the hiccups. To qualify as an eccentric you don't even need to invite a horse to share your fireplace. All you need do is be slightly off-center; slightly out of tune with others in looks or behavior or attitudes. I can't promise any great spiritual advantage in eccentricity. But then, there's no great spiritual advantage in being commonplace, either.

ECUMENICAL MOVEMENT.

We've come a long way from the day reflected in this 1800 church song:

> The Devil, Calvin, and Tom Paine
> May hate the Methodists in vain.
> Their doctrines shall be downward hurled,
> The Methodists shall rule the world.

These days Methodists and Calvinists view each other as being on the same side. Many wouldn't even hesitate to include the Catholics. Today we have a history of decades of cooperation, in Sunday school associations, missions, and service projects. Many denominations and individual congregations have joined the National Council of Churches or its counterpart, the National Association of Evangelicals.

Still, few of us find our lives much affected by either group. Or by Catholic initiatives taken since Pope John XXIII initiated his church's efforts to bridge the ages-long gap with separated Protestant brethren. Even so, we need to think about the issues raised. Our congregation may vote on related issues. Our giving is likely to end up as budget for the NCC or NAE or some other ecumenical group. So we should at least have some idea of the dream expressed . . . and the concern of the critics.

Not uniformity. This is the first reassurance given by proponents. Whatever formula unites the churches will protect theological convictions. One Protestant observer at Vatican II in Rome writes, "The first fact to remember is that in the whole vocabulary of ecumenism there are no such words as 'surrender' or 'compromise.'" There will be no bargaining away beliefs or practices for the sake of unity.

But the critics wonder about *after* unification. After all, some denominations today seem bent on voting away the convictions of minorities who demand rejection of homosexual candidates for ordination, or rejection (or acceptance) of women clergy. If the crushing weight of the vote is used now to enforce uniformity in existing denominations, will an ecumenical church be more tolerant?

But what? Christians generally agree that there is an underlying reality: that the church of Jesus in some vital sense is one. → UNITY But there is little agreement on how that oneness should be expressed. To some it's enough to express unity in interpersonal fellowship. To others, associated with the ecumenical dream, there must be some visible expression or the unity we claim is real will lack authentic expression in the world. Three different approaches to ecumenical unity are suggested. (1) Different denominations and groups work in partnership, without sectarian spirit, on common projects and ministries. (2) There is partnership, plus intercommunion. Each church recognizes the ministry and sacraments of the others, so a common "membership" is understood. (3) There is corporate union, with autonomous denominations superseded by a single organization with some degree of centralized authority.

In a significant sense the National Council of Churches provides a federated structure in which the first understanding of ecumenism is already being worked out.

What does the ecumenical federation do?   National Council of Churches' activities focus on coordination. The NCC: (1) provides a meeting ground for exchange of ideas; (2) produces and publishes materials for all member denominations (such as annual study course in missions education); (3) provides for study and research in areas of common concern; (4) jointly administers projects that call for combined resources and unified direction (such as emergency relief overseas); (5) stimulates experimental and pioneering ministries; (6) serves as a collective voice for member denominations in areas of public concern, issuing "policy statements" on issues ranging from politics to race relations to family life; (7) serves as coordinating agency with Catholic and Jewish bodies; (8) keeps member denominations in touch with secular organizations and movements concerned with human welfare.

Several things about these activities concern the critics. However wise coordination may sound, critics complain that statements made as the "collective voice" of member denominations in areas of public concern often violate the personal convictions of individual Christians. Accusations of socialism and political liberalism have often been heard. At least one accusation has been made that church funds meant for relief were channeled into purchase of weapons for revolutionaries. The loss of control by the individual of the use of funds contributed to God's work, and the pretensions of an organization to speak and lobby for "Christians," seem particularly hard to justify.

Centralized control?   In a way, the issue comes down to one's view of the nature of the church of Jesus Christ, and how its mission in the world is best carried out. Does the body of Christ require institutional expression in the world? Can there be a single voice expressing "the" Christian view of economics, politics, and international relations? Or is it more in harmony with the nature of the church to affirm a real spiritual unity, and seek to work out that unity in the personal relationship each believer builds

with others. Is it better to encourage each believer to contribute generously to whichever of the many Christian organizations seeking to meet human needs and share the
gospel, best expresses his or her own convictions and
concerns?

EGOCENTRISM. When Johnny won't share, or
seems unmoved at another's tears, don't get too upset with
him. It's probably not the sin nature. It's most likely
nothing more than egocentricity.

That's a term that has been coined to express an
interesting fact. A preschool child may be able to see
things from only one point of view: his own. The Golden
Rule—do to others as you would have them do to you—
wasn't stated for preschoolers. Most simply are unable to
separate themselves from their own point of view, and
mentally put themselves in another's place.

On the other hand, the Golden Rule *is* for us adults.
You and I should have matured mentally to where we can
consider the needs and concerns of others. We can put
ourselves in their place and imagine how we'd like others
to treat us. Spiritually, if we've matured enough so that
Jesus' motivations are our motivations too, we'll not only
understand the Golden Rule. We'll live it.

ELDERS. Different traditions give different names to
church leaders. Elder, deacon, bishop, and pastor are all
biblical terms for local church leaders, which we've enthusiastically applied to various ecclesiastical offices.
Actually, the Bible uses the terms interchangeably, so we
probably have the freedom to call our leaders whatever we
want.

But whatever we call our leaders, we need to understand their ministry. The Bible is quite clear on that.
Leaders aren't sharp businessmen elected to manage our
churches like a well-run enterprise. They are spiritual
leaders: persons of maturity and wisdom, called to guide
the spiritual growth of individuals and the congregation.

There are several things to remember when choosing
elders. ● Leaders must meet character criterion. Both

1 Timothy (3:1–13) and Titus (1:5–16) carefully describe leader character. The thought is that those called to lead God's people toward Christlikeness must exhibit a Christlike character themselves. ● Leaders lead by example, not by command. So the New Testament speaks of spiritual leaders as servants, and suggests they live close enough to the people of God so we will know them well, and be able to follow their example (cf. 1 Peter 5:1–3). ● Leaders must understand and be able to communicate the teachings of God's Word to others (2 Tim. 2:24–26). This does not require formal theological education, but it does call for personal commitment to understand and to live by the Scripture's teachings.

The question many ask about women elders isn't answered definitely in the New Testament. → WOMEN IN THE CHURCH

Every congregation will have leaders. A good rule of thumb for you and me in selecting them is to choose persons whom you know well enough to have confidence in, and whose spiritual stature and wisdom you have come to respect.

ELECTION AND PREDESTINATION.

Both words are found in the Bible. But Christians haven't agreed about what they mean . . . or imply. At times strong predestinarians have sneered at missions: after all, if God has predestined the heathen, He'll see to their salvation! More importantly, some today struggle with an apparently unanswerable personal question: Am I among the elect? Has God predestined me for salvation?

A number of different theological positions are taken on the question of election and predestination. It's helpful to summarize them, and then look more closely at the issues they raise.

● Some believe that before Creation God chose (elected) some individuals for salvation, and elected others for damnation.

● Some believe that before Creation God chose some individuals for salvation, but did not choose the rest for damnation.

• Some believe that before Creation God knew who would later believe in Christ. His foreknowledge is the explanation of biblical references to predestination and election.

• Some believe that predestination expresses God's commitment to His adopted children, to bring them to a holy and blameless state, and not to a choice of who will be saved (cf. Eph. 1:4).

• Some believe that God is as helpless in the flow of time as human beings are. He can neither plan ahead, nor act to affect the future of individuals and nations whose choices are free.

The theological issues.   Whenever the question of predestination is raised, we're pushed back to basic issues about our understanding of both God and humanity.

Those who are convinced predestinarians insist that for God to be God He must be sovereign: His control over events in time must be absolute. God may choose to permit sin and rebellion, but He can never be mastered by them. Even evil must ultimately blend into His plan and display the ultimate good.

Those repelled by predestinarian doctrine see such a sovereign God as unfair. If He is in control, why doesn't He choose all for salvation? Selecting some and not others seems to show favoritism. Worse, it appears to make the preaching of the gospel the ultimate hypocrisy if some who hear the invitation are predestined not to respond.

Predestinarians tend to look at humankind as completely lost: so warped and twisted by sin that every impulse drives them away from the true God. Unless God acts with some irresistible grace to break sin's bondage of the will, no one would respond to God's offer of salvation.

Nonpredestinarians look at mankind as flawed but with the capacity to cooperate with God. All are equally able to respond to the offer of salvation; it is by a free act of individual choice that eternal destiny is determined.

There's one difficulty with arguments like these. In making them we slip, unnoticed, into the realm of philosophy. We begin to rely on our ability to reason and develop logical positions to mount attacks on opposing viewpoints. We insist that God must be *either* sovereign or loving. We thunder that man's will must *either* be bound or free. And we never stop to think that God may not be bound by our logic. He may escape into the realm of paradoxes He can resolve, but we cannot.

In making theology an exercise in human logic we forget that Christian theology rests on revelation, not reasoning. God has had to unveil for us hidden realities we could not even guess at. When we turn back to Scripture, we find the concerns of those who are worried that God be understood as sovereign and that God be understood as loving are both dealt with.

What does the Bible say?   This is the question we really need to ask. If we can't quite see how what the Bible teaches fits together, then we must be satisfied to recognize our own limitations. But surely the Bible's testimony is comforting.

● The Bible reveals a sovereign God. The God of the Bible is free to act as He chooses in history and in our lives. There are no limitations on the power of the God we worship (Rom. 9).

● The Bible reveals a loving God. The God of the Bible has acted freely in Jesus, giving His only Son because of His great compassion for rebellious humanity. The suffering of Jesus was for all, for God desires all to be saved (John 3:16; 2 Peter 3:9).

● The Bible reveals that not all will be saved. Some will willfully and willingly reject the gospel invitation: none of these will be coerced against his or her will.

● The Bible reveals that faith is a gift. A faith response to God that bridges the gap between death and life is at the same time an uncoerced, free human response and a gift from God (Eph. 2:8, 9).

Those passages that deal with predestination (cf. Rom. 9 and Eph. 1:3–14) must be understood in the context of Scripture's total testimony that God is both great
and loving.

The personal concern. Some who are troubled about
the idea of election and predestination aren't upset because
of any apparent logical contradictions. They're worried
about themselves and their personal relationship with
God. How, they wonder, can I ever know if I am one of
the elect?

Actually, the question is completely irrelevant.
Scripture presents each individual with only one issue.
The issue is Jesus. And God's promise is that "whoever
believes in him shall not perish but have eternal life"
(John 3:16). God's repeated call to faith and His promise
of salvation helps each of us realize that He is not concerned with how we understand predestination. His concern for you and me is that we place our trust in Jesus, and
thus pass from death to life. If you simply trust Jesus, you
are given life. However you understand election, you are
surely then among the elect.

God wants you to rest easy about your personal relationship with Him. "And this is the testimony. God has
given us eternal life, and this life is in his Son. He who has
the Son has life; he who does not have the Son of God
does not have life" (1 John 5:11, 12). Your salvation is
assured through your faith in Jesus, God's Son.

ELOPING.
It sounds so romantic. And for some, it
can be. But there are several questions worth asking before climbing down that traditional midnight ladder. For
instance: (1) Is the person you plan to elope with an attractive stranger, or is this the culmination of a long-term,
growing relationship? (2) Is the idea a spur-of-the-
moment thing, or have you talked the pros and cons
through? (3) Are you both more or less alone? Or are there
relatives and friends who'd be disappointed not to share
the wedding with you? (4) What are your reasons for pre-
ferring eloping to a traditional wedding?

Eloping can be a special and exciting way to begin a
marriage. So I hope all these questions haven't spoiled the
romantic mood for you. But if it's only a romantic mood,
and you haven't thought through questions like these,
maybe it wasn't such a good idea anyway.

EMBRACING.   One of the few heresies I was taught in seminary by a good brother training us future pastors was, "Never touch a person of the opposite sex." I understand his reasoning (avoid even the appearance of evil), and for a number of years I faithfully followed his advice.

Then one of the college kids who came out for a weekly Bible study in our home dropped into my Wheaton office. Beth was just miserable that morning. As her eyes filled with tears, even I could see there was only one thing to do. I hugged her, and let her tears soak my shoulder.

That's when it came to me. I'd been so busy avoiding the appearance of evil that I'd succeeded in avoiding the appearance of caring. For many people, only a touch or a hug can convey "You're loved," or "I care."

The writers of the New Testament understood this need perfectly well. They knew all believers are drawn together into a loving fellowship, intended to be rich in warmth and intimacy. They knew that such Christian love should be expressed in the warmth of an embrace as well as with smiles and encouraging words. So they not only permitted touching: they commanded it. "Greet one another with a holy kiss," Paul says in Romans 16:16. And he repeats the command (1 Cor. 16:20; 2 Cor. 13:12; 1 Thess. 5:26). Peter puts it slightly differently: "Greet one another with a kiss of love" (1 Peter 5:14).

In the body of Christ, where love is rich and warm and holy, "never touch" is heresy. "Embrace" is God's freeing and good will.

EMOTIONS.   Emotions seem both a plague and a joy. We're troubled by our emotions and enriched by them. Sometimes our emotions seem uncontrollable: they force us into actions we later regret with shame. Other times emotions drop us toward despair, leading us to doubt our relationship with God. But what can a person do? Emotions exist. We can't deny them.

Enriching and troubling, emotions are something we each need to understand and get in healthy perspective.

212   **Why emotions?**   God is the One who made us able to feel. The potential for a full range of emotions, from exhilarating joy and quiet satisfaction to anguished guilt and burning anger, were purposely designed into humanity.

Emotions were necessary if God was to accomplish the goal of making creatures in His image (Gen. 1:26, 27). God too is a person. The Bible speaks often of His love, His compassion, His enjoyment of the good and anger at evil. So our emotions reflect something of the Person who shaped us to be like Him. Our feelings give us some insight into what God is like. Surely none of us can imagine God as some impersonal force or indifferent cosmic mathematician. God is a person who can and who does love.

But while our emotional make-up reflects our Creator, that reflection is distorted by sin. We often link our feelings to wrong objects. We can actually enjoy sin, and feel contempt for what is beautiful and good. God is the source of our ability to feel. But He is not responsible for the specific emotions we experience.

This means that emotions are not a trustworthy guide in life. "I want it" doesn't make something right. And "I like it" doesn't make it good.

Limitations on emotions. The fact that emotions are not a trustworthy guide is only one of their limitations. Even though emotions may feel so strong and real, they are poor indicators of reality.

Imagine a husband who is feeling hurt and upset at being neglected by his wife. "The baby gets all her attention," he mutters to himself. As for his wife, she's depressed and exhausted. And the silent treatment she's been getting from her suddenly uncommunicative husband makes her feel rejected. She's worried too that since the baby has arrived he doesn't find her attractive anymore. All these feelings are so very real.

But suppose they talk. Suppose he shares how he's been feeling, and with relief she tells him of her fears. For the first time he realizes how exhausted she must be. He gives her a warm hug, and insists she go take a nap right now while he takes care of Junior. Suddenly new and warm and loving feelings rush in and replace the old feelings. These new feelings also are "real."

There are several things we see about the limitations of our emotions in this illustration. Emotions are not a trustworthy guide to what is right or to what is good for us. But also:

• Emotions may not be appropriate to the realities of any given situation.

• Emotions can—and will—change. They are not stable or reliable guides.

Noticing these things about emotions, we can see why it's important not to let our emotions rule us or to look to our emotions in evaluating situations. Oh, our emotions are subjectively real all right. And often powerful. But our emotions are likely to be out of harmony with objective reality. To live by the push and pull of momentary, changeable, and unreliable feelings is a very dangerous way to live indeed.

Living with our emotions.   We may not want to live by our emotions. But we do have to live with them. So how can we do that in a healthy and positive way? Several principles help us.

• Accept ownership of your emotions. Don't blame others or the situation. No one "makes" you feel as you do.

For instance, a teen has an auto accident soon after getting his license—right after Dad's lecture on safe driving. When Dad hears, we could understand if he got mad. But it would be wrong to say the accident "made" him mad. He could have reacted differently. For instance, he might have given his son a hug and told how thankful he felt that the boy wasn't hurt.

Boil it down, and we carry responsibility for our own emotions. We own them: no one forces us to respond to life's experiences as we do. So the first step in gaining control of our emotions is to accept ownership for them. What we can't blame on someone else we must learn to deal with ourselves.

• Express emotions to God. The psalms teach us this. God invites us to share our positive and negative feelings with Him. Freely. He already knows how we feel, and still accepts and loves us. We can't shock Him. When we share, He will enrich the emotions that are enjoyable, and gradually transform the emotions that might lead us into sin.

Read through the psalms and you'll see how this works. Jot down feeling words: see how every emotion you've known is shared with the Lord. And note how God gently works within the psalmists to turn thoughts to Him, gradually modifying emotions to bring peace.

•Avoid ventilation of emotions. Recent theory suggests a person gets rid of emotions by expressing them. Even angry verbal attacks on others are justified by taking them as a sign of "honesty."

Actually, research has shown that ventilation doesn't work. Shouting and kicking chairs when you're angry won't make you a less angry person: it will probably just make you able to express anger in destructive ways. Dumping your feelings on a person isn't honesty, it's simply hostility at work.

You can and should "speak the truth in love" as Scripture puts it (Eph. 4:15). But the truth is "This is how I feel now," never "You are a bad person because you make me feel. . . ." Speaking what we feel is "true" now is never to be done when we're dominated by anger rather than by love.

It's good to talk about your feelings. But when you do be sure it is *you* (and those feelings you own) that is being discussed. Not the other person's shortcomings.

• Stand in judgment over your emotions. Emotions are real, and we have to deal with them. But we don't have to be dominated by them. We can evaluate the rightness or wrongness of those acts our feelings prompt.

To do this, begin with the realization that your feelings are not, in themselves, sin. Anger isn't sin, for Scripture tells us when angry to "sin not" (Eph. 4:26). It is the acts that anger prompts that are sin.

As a matter of fact, anger can be an occasion for

significant moral victory. A friend of mine was viciously attacked by a woman in his small Bible-study group. She attacked his motives and behavior, and hurled charges at other group members as well. Then she marched stiffly out of the house.

My friend was hurt and angry. All had seen this woman's critical spirit and judgmental attitude expressed before, but never quite so viciously. At home he cried frustrated tears, and felt anger surge. But the next morning he followed Jesus' instructions and sought a reconciliation. He apologized to her for any hurts, and shared his feelings without blaming. He also tried to help her understand how devastated one young believer in the group had felt about the things said to her.

What happened here? That negative emotion of anger surged. It existed. But my friend stood in judgment over his emotion, and refused to act on it. Instead he was obedient to Jesus and took the first step toward reconciliation, despite his own hurt. The "wrong" emotion, rather than leading to sin, actually stimulated a series of godly choices that strengthened him in his Christian commitment, and which brought glory to God.

So it's not the emotion that is right or wrong. It is how you and I decide to act—surrendering to an emotion's pull, or evaluating possible courses of action in light of God's Word—that has moral content.

Conclusions. Long ago Martin Luther suggested that you can't keep birds from flying around your head but you can surely keep them from building a nest in your hair.

Emotions are like this. We can't choose the emotions that visit us, but we can choose which to welcome, and which we will act on.

Actually, the reality is even more exciting than this. We can express every feeling to God, knowing He understands and cares. We can share feelings with others, without blaming or attacking. And we can make moral choices based on our understanding of the right thing to do, no matter how emotions push and pull. → DECISION MAKING

We need feel no guilt about our emotions. But the

more we learn to live by choice rather than feel, the more God will work within, and the more our emotional life too will come increasingly under His loving control.

ENEMIES.   Maybe you've heard the old saying, "Do unto your enemies what they would do unto you . . . but do it first."

No, that's not in the Bible. But it surely expresses how God's saints have felt at times. Like David, many of us have wanted to cry out, "If only you would slay the wicked, O God!" and, turning back to those who look at us with hostility, add, "Away from me, you bloodthirsty men!" (Ps. 139:19).

David wasn't ashamed of having enemies. He chose them very carefully. "Do I not hate those who hate you, O Lord?" he asked. David's hostility was reserved for those who rebelled against his good God: "I have nothing but hatred for them; I count them my enemies" (Ps. 139:21, 22).

Still, even when our enemies are God's enemies too, something doesn't seem to fit. But it's not until Jesus comes and adds His unique instruction to the hints in the Old Testament (cf. Prov. 25:21) that we really understand what to do about enemies.

Jesus' radical instructions are quite clear. "Love your enemies, do good to those who hate you, bless those who curse you, pray for those who mistreat you" (Luke 6:27, 28). The instructions are radical because the world lives by the norm of reciprocity: the people of the world return good for good and evil for evil, matching their actions to the treatment they receive from others. But Jesus points out that God the Most High "is kind to the ungrateful and wicked" (6:35). Because we are His children now, we take Him as our example and determine to "be merciful, just as your Father is merciful" (6:36).

At first it seems frightening. We're to take the blows and hostility offered us, and return love and mercy? But Jesus goes on and points out the hidden dynamic of His unique approach. We're told not to judge or condemn (6:37, 38) but instead to forgive, and then promised,

"Give, and it will be given to you. A good measure, pressed down, shaken together and running over, will be poured into your lap. For with the measure you use, it will be measured to you" (6:38). When we think about it, we finally understand.

The world runs on reciprocity. So we must break the cycle by which hostility generates more hostility. Instead of returning evil, we return nothing but forgiveness and love. And when love, we establish a new cycle! We keep on loving, until the measure we use with others breaks the old pattern of hatred, and begins to be the measure they use with you and me!

You see, that's just what God did with us. We were His enemies. But He offered us love. We were unresponsive. But Jesus came and died for our sins. And finally when you and I were reached by His gospel of unmeasurable love, antagonism was replaced by hesitant, but growing responsive love for Him.

Oh, not everyone responds. But many will. Just like God, you and I are called on to destroy our enemies . . . by loving them until they are transformed into friends.

ENGAGEMENT. There was nothing quite like our engagement in Old Testament or New Testament times. So there are no specific biblical instructions for us. Engagement is just another step on a societal path that leads to marriage. Because so many marriages end in divorce today, it's important to take each of those steps carefully. What are the steps usually taken in our culture?

• Dating, by which teens and twenties get to know a number of others of the opposite sex.

• Courtship, by which dating comes into focus for a couple, and the two begin to consider if they want each other as life partners.

• Engagement, a more formal period in which the relationship continues to develop with the announced goal of marriage.

• Marriage itself, in which the couple commits themselves to love and honor "till death do us part."

Each of these stages deepens a relationship. The engagement period is particularly important, because it calls for exploring temperament and personal qualities carefully. It's helpful for an engaged couple to share a marriage preparation course, or to have premarital counseling. Engagement isn't for playing at being married. It's for developing an understanding of each other that will help a marriage succeed—or lead a couple to call the wedding off before the final step has been taken.

Probably the most important question a couple has to answer is, how long should we take in each stage. There's no definitive answer. But one word of advice Paul gives in Thessalonians is helpful. He writes about acquiring a wife "in holiness and honor, not in the passion of lust like heathen who do not know God" (4:5 RSV). Paul is not against sex. But he knows that passion is only a part of marriage, and should never force us into hasty action. Couples do need to take time to come to know each other well as a foundation for a lasting marriage. The time required? However long it takes you to come to know each other well, and to be sure.

ENTHUSIASM.

One devastating charge brought against the early Methodists in England was that of "enthusiasm." Of course, the British upper class, trained in the classics, must have understood the roots of that word in a Greek term used for the ecstatic utterances of oracles and epileptics.

Today we relate enthusiasm to normal behavior at sporting events. There crowds feel no embarrassment at all in cheering and screaming for their favorite teams.

If you want a model for Christian enthusiasm, take the crowd at a home game. You can close your eyes, and listening to all the noise, imagine you were there when David brought the ark of God to ancient Jerusalem. Keep them closed and imagine the great king as cheerleader, as he "danced before the Lord with all his might" while the people lining the streets responded "with shouts" (2 Sam. 6:14, 15).

Ever get criticized for too much enthusiasm in your worship? Ignore it. Lift up your hands, and praise the Lord!

ENVY. Xenophon said it a few thousand years ago. "The envious are those who are annoyed only at their friends' successes." Generally, envy involves grudging another person something you want, but don't have. We all know envy is wrong: it's usually found in the New Testament's list of evils generated from man's sinful nature (cf. Gal. 5:19–26; Rom. 1:29).

If you notice a flush of envy, take it as a symptom of mankind's old recurring disease, and hurry back to Scripture for God's cure. There we find just the medicine: God's affirmation that we are so important to Him that He has blessed each of us "with every spiritual blessing in Christ" (Eph. 1:3) and, in the Scriptures, thoroughly equipped us each "for every good work" (2 Tim. 3:17). When we meditate on this, and realize we already possess everything that's truly important, we come at last to Paul's conclusions. "I have learned to be content whatever the circumstances" (Phil. 4:11).

EQUALITY. My, what they're doing with equality these days. Perhaps you've noticed? Suddenly "equality" has been linked with the notion that everyone has a right to an equal share of the nation's financial pie. Some even argue that since equal opportunity hasn't done the job, the government should legislate "equal result," so that people become "more equal in terms of income, education, quality of jobs, and political power." Folks used to call this socialism. But "equality" has the sound of American heritage.

But the issue isn't the political games people play. The issue for us is the way concepts are distorted, and the spiritual impact of the notion of equality.

All people are not really equal. Let's begin here. And realize that even the framers of the Constitution did not imagine for a moment that individuals are equal. They knew as well as we know that persons are not equal in intelligence, in health, in motivation, in occupational responsibility, in income, looks, athletic ability, family background, etc. What the framers of the Constitution affirmed in the assertion that all are "created equal" was that each individual is of worth and value, and that society ought to provide a freedom that gives unequal individuals fair treatment under law, and equal opportunity to advance themselves on their merit. Only in such a society could liberty be guaranteed. The notion that government should legislate "equality of result" and thus level human society was never even imagined much less believed by the founding fathers.

All people are not equal. And all that society can justly do is to ensure inequal human beings of equal access to opportunity to advance themselves to the full extent of their individual ability.

The value of inequality.   What is really fascinating is to realize that it is the fact of inequality that makes a society healthy and whole. After all, what if everyone were to become a doctor? Who would repair cars, or grow wheat? It's because of our differences that we're able to make various contributions to others' welfare.

This is the point Paul makes in 1 Corinthians about the church as the living body of Christ: "If the whole body were an eye, where would the sense of hearing be? . . . God has arranged the parts in the body, every one of them, just as he wanted them to be" (12:17, 18). It is because of our differences that each of us is able to make unique contributions to others: we are important just because we are different.

There is however one additional insight Scripture adds. We are equal in value to God, so differences are not to be ranked in some hierarchy of "best" on through "good" to merely "acceptable." And each of us shares equally in the Spirit, who gives us ability to make our distinct contribution to others (cf. 12:22–26).

The Christian honors others as truly equal, whatever social role or personal attributes they possess. Each person is seen as important and, in the family of God, as a brother or sister to be loved and honored and appreciated.

Equality in an unjust society.   All too often a person's role in life isn't determined by his personal qualities and uniqueness. It may be determined by an accident of birth that places him at a disadvantage.

In New Testament times the institution of slavery forced a large part of the world's population into a strictly enforced and unequal role. In writing to believers the apostles called for no reorganization in society, but instead tried to help slaves and masters understand how to live godly lives. Slaves were encouraged to be the most honest and faithful workers a master could possess (1 Peter 2:18f.; 1 Tim. 6:1, 2), and masters were exhorted to treat their slaves with fairness and respect (Eph. 6:5–9). The point made is important. Whatever one's position in society, his or her responsibility is the same: each is to see his or her role as an opportunity to serve others faithfully as if serving Christ. How a person serves others will differ by his position: the call to serve others faithfully is the great equalizing principle that levels rich and poor, slave and free, as equal servants of Jesus Christ.

There are many people in this world to whom I'll never be equal. I never expect to be equal with my buddy Clyde in wealth. I never expect to be equal with other friends in looks, or athletic ability, or fame. But these are really unimportant. I am absolutely equal in what counts.

I am equal as a member of the one body of Christ, with my own distinct contribution to make. I am equal as a servant, with opportunities to serve others in the role God has given me. And each and every one of the family of God is, in this truest sense, equal with me.

ETERNAL LIFE.   One of the nicest things about eternal life is that we don't have to wait for it. It's ours now. And forevermore.

ETHICS.   Ethics seems to hold a glittering attraction for those addicted to the theoretical. We can trace it back even beyond Aristotle, who wrote carefully on ways to support the practice of virtue against the allures of passion. Today our libraries are full of fascinating tomes, packed with theories about the Good, the Just, and the

Right, as well as treatises on moral obligation (the Ought). Look in a university library, and you're likely to find books on Christian ethics and books on ethics for unbelievers, and with them reformulations of natural law and books promoting moral order for communities and nations. Unfortunately, as one author points out, lofty moral standards based on love for God and man have been recognized in the Western world for centuries. The problem of how to bring them into effect is still to be solved.

This is the most important thing about ethics. It's not that people don't generally agree on what's right. The problem is that we don't *do* what we say we approve

God of course has a solution to the problem. It hasn't been tried by enough people, but it does work. His solution was announced long ago through the prophet Jeremiah, and put into effect with the resurrection of Jesus. God promised through the prophet that "I will put my law in their minds and write it on their hearts" (Jer. 31:33). The ages-old conflict between virtue and passion can be solved only by giving humanity a passion for what is good.

The promised day is here now. Paul recognized it, and writing of the new covenant gloried in the fact that we "are being transformed into his [Jesus'] likeness with ever-increasing glory" (2 Cor. 3:18). When we open our life to Jesus, He begins to shape within us His own passion for good.

ETHNOCENTRISM.

Like many big words, this one disguises a simple idea: we tend to look at and judge others from the perspective of our own culture. To a meat-and-potatoes man from the midwest, the Japanese diet of raw fish and crisp vegetables might not look very good. But it would be much better for him.

We make ethnocentric judgments about faith too. Those who worship in cathedrals may be disconcerted by enthusiastic songs and loud clapping. Those who like informality may be oppressed by dark sanctuaries, with multicolored windows and stately organ music. Some want ministers dressed in robes; others feel a person can communicate only in shirt sleeves.

There's nothing wrong with having such personal preferences. Or in finding a place where we can worship comfortably. It's only wrong if we transform preference into moral issue, and insist that our way is "right" and theirs "wrong."

God, of course, isn't ethnocentric at all. He's been worshiped all over the world, in many languages and many ways. It's not the custom that concerns Him, but the heart. As Jesus once said, "true worshipers will worship the Father in spirit and truth, for they are the kind of worshipers the Father seeks" (John 4:23).

ETIQUETTE.   Once social codes were valued for their snob appeal. One learned to behave like the upper crust to acquire the symbols of status. These days there's a healthier emphasis. Books on etiquette try to help us understand little things to do that will make others feel more comfortable and at home.

Customs and manners are changing rapidly these days. But consideration for others is never out of style.

EUGENICS.   The dream was born in the '30s. With understanding of heredity came the prospect: man might guide his own evolution! "From generation to generation," one enthusiast promised, "there will be a gradual improvement in the biological quality of our people and thus in the whole tone of society."

By the late '70s some still dreamed. And knew how to make the dream reality. A 1976 publication offers chapters on birth control and whole sections on sterilization, artificial insemination, and selective abortion to "eliminate harmful genes" from the human population. If mankind will not give eugenics place as a new religion in perfect harmony with Nature, then surely we can find policies that will permit "population control."

Behind the dream, of course, lies nightmare. Aside from eugenics' evolutionary foundation, and the grim threat of reproduction control by isolated scientists cloaked in white, the movement has another basic moral flaw. It shifts the focus of value from the individual to a mere concept. For eugenics speaks of "mankind" as if that abstraction were real and individuals merely interchangeable units in a real entity.

The facts are just the opposite. "Mankind" has no real existence. But each individual human being does. Each single life overflows with worth and value. When our universe finally flares out of existence at God's command, it will not be "humanity" that stands before God. It will be you and me and every other individual human being who has ever lived. Forever and forever, each human person will continue, self-conscious and aware.

Whatever ways we devise to benefit the race of man, we must never fall into the trap of treating "man" as real, and men or women as insignificant.

EUTHANASIA. The term means "good death." It's been used to refer to a death that apparently benefits the individual → **MERCY KILLING, PREVENTION** and also of killing others for the benefit of society. Hitler's "Law for the Prevention of Hereditarily Diseased Posterity" (1933) and his euthanasia decrees (1939) led to the "good deaths" of at least 275,000 people! God's commentary is simple: "Do not put an innocent or honest person to death" (Exod. 23:7).

EVANGELISM. It means simply, "to bring the good news." But for many Christians it's a rather scary word. We realize the gospel is good news, but we're not at all sure how to bring it to others. Really, what should we do? Pass out tracts? Memorize a sure-fire, four-step presentation? Shouldn't a person know a lot about the Bible before he or she tries to talk about it with others?

We can answer questions like these. But first we need to get a feel for the approach the Bible takes to evangelism.

The Bible on evangelism. The New Testament links three different groups of words to evangelism. Each tells us something important.

• "Good news" words are very common. All through the Old Testament God kept the attention of His people on the future, promising them a deliverer. One day a Savior would appear, to free human beings from the deadly grip of sin. When it happened, angels were the first to announce it as Good News. God's promise had been kept! Before long everyone understood that all of history is focused on the life and ministry of a carpenter in Palestine: that He was the Good News; that the Good News was and is a Person.

● Other words linked with evangelism focus attention on "proclamation." The Good News is a Person, and announcing it means introducing that Person to others who haven't yet met Him. There were certain things about the person of Jesus that the evangelists always included, whether they were introducing Him to crowds in sermons (cf. Acts 2:14-40; 3:11-26; 17:16–34) or whether they introduced Him to neighbors, chatting outside their door (Acts 8:4). They introduced Jesus as a real historical person, who died by crucifixion and was raised again just as the Scriptures had promised. And they explained that He is the One we're to trust for the forgiveness of our sins.

They didn't preach profound sermons. Or explain all the deep secrets of the Bible. They simply told about Jesus; explaining who He is and what He's done, and what faith in Him means for people like you and me.

● The third word group has to do with *witness*. Always associated with "witness" is the idea of first-hand experience. We are to share what we ourselves experience in our relationship with this Person who is Himself God's Good News.

Witness is a particularly encouraging concept, because it includes more than what we say. It includes what we are and do. When Jesus spoke of good works glorifying our Father in heaven, He meant that real goodness, flowing as it does from personal relationship with God, is a vivid testimony to who God is and what He is like (Matt. 5:16). In the same way, close and loving relationships within the Christian community are a compelling witness to those who observe that Jesus lives among His people (cf. John 13:34, 35). The attractive life that is produced when we have a growing relationship with Jesus is a vital part of witness-evangelism.

Very personal evangelism. Few of us have the opportunity of a Billy Graham. We'll preach few sermons in our life. So for us evangelism will be a personal thing, more like chatting with co-workers or neighbors than giving a talk. This is good, because the most effective evangelism really is a very personal kind of thing. We find helpful guidelines in the New Testament's words on evangelism.

• We see that evangelism is relational, not impersonal. It's not wrong to give a stranger a tract. But the most effective evangelism is relational. We sense it in the words linked with "witness." Witness focuses on experience—and on being observed. So we need to build friendships with others in which we can come to know each other. Then, by listening, sharing, reaching out to help, others will begin to sense the hidden reality of Jesus in our wives. When others really know us as people who care, the words we speak have far more impact.

• We see that evangelism is good news, not condemnation. The Bible reminds us that "God was reconciling the world to himself in Christ, not counting men's sins against them" (2 Cor. 5:19). Sometimes Christians feel they must make sure others feel like terrible sinners before they can talk of forgiveness. But "counting men's sins against" others simply hardens them: it raises their defenses against us and what we say. In personal evangelism we're wisest to let the Holy Spirit convict of sin, while we stress the Good News that forgiveness has come in Jesus.

If they know us, they'll never confuse silence with condoning sin. And they'll never be confused about the fact that whatever they have done, we care.

• We see that evangelism is sharing Jesus, not arguing. This is an important principle. It is Jesus who is the Good News. It is Jesus we want others to come to know. Discussing theology and arguing about doctrine isn't part of evangelism.

Because evangelism is witnessing to the Good News we don't have to be able to answer all the questions a person might ask, or even be very advanced in our own understanding of Scripture. We need only to share what we know about Jesus, and what we experience with Jesus daily.

How personal evangelism works. The night Barbara and Charlie joined our little Bible study group, it was clear they weren't believers yet. Oh, they went to church. But it was evident they hadn't met Jesus.

In the next weeks none of us ever hinted that Barb and Charlie were different. We listened to their ideas about the Bible passages we studied, and the rest shared our understandings. We talked about what was happening during the week, and prayed for each other as needs were shared.

Later Barb shared why they had come back week after week. "We'd never seen that kind of love," she said. And she added that they'd begun to feel bad because we apparently hadn't realized what was becoming all too clear to them: that they "weren't real Christians yet."

Then one night when Barb had a couple from our group over for supper, she asked how a person becomes a real Christian. Bill showed her a promise about Jesus in the Bible: "all who received him, to those who believed in his name, he gave the right to become children of God" (John 1:12). Bill told how he had received Christ, and told Barb that all she needed to do was to tell Jesus she believed, and receive Him as Savior, and thank Him for the welcome into God's family.

The next morning, leaning her head against the kitchen door, Barb did just that. And a few weeks later, Charlie followed.

Since then Charlie and Barbara have themselves introduced many people to Jesus. They have built relationships as friends. They have communicated Good News and not condemnation. They have shared Jesus, and not argued religion.

Through the loving witness of simple believers like Charlie and Barbara—and you—people continue to meet Jesus. Through faith in Him they come into the ever-expanding family of God.

EVIL. The problem of evil has always bothered those who want to believe in a good God, but can't quite figure Him out. "If God were both good and all-powerful, they reason, He would never have permitted evil. So either God is not good, or He is not all-powerful." Locked in by this apparent logic, some have simply abandoned the idea of God, while others have struggled to come up with solutions.

It's always dangerous to rely on logic when we already have truth, announced by God Himself, which denies our conclusion. The Bible recognizes evil, yet affirms that the God who shaped our universe is both good and all-powerful. We may not understand how these fit together, but Scripture is surely more trustworthy than our faulty logic.

Various believers have suggested possible solutions. Augustine, who was deeply troubled by evil, concluded that it is a "lack," an absence of good, rather than a thing in itself. When men turn from God they lose contact with real goodness, and the absence of goodness is experienced as evil. This helped Augustine. He was comforted that he no longer had to worry about God "creating" evil. After all, how can anyone create a "lack" or an "absence of good"?

C. S. Lewis was convinced that if we understood the highest Good, we'd realize that an evil world provides opportunities for expressions of goodness and love that would be impossible if evil were not present. With other believers through the ages, Lewis did not pretend to understand, but believed that "in all things God works for the good of those who love him" (Rom. 8:28).

Others have observed an important fact. God is never seen in Scripture as the creator of evil. All evil stems from choices made by free agents. Satan, Adam and Eve, and you and I, are the creators of evil when we refuse to do good. God will use the evil which free agents generate—to punish, to lead to a pain that may turn us from further evil, and in other ways. But evil is the direct result of human freedom, and the evils we experience are the direct or indirect results of our own actions or the actions of others.

The conclusion that has been drawn from this link between evil and the freedom to choose is this: somehow freedom must have such great significance in God's scheme of things that its value more than balances the disasters its exercise has caused.

God could have created us puppets. There would have been no evil then. But we would not really have been persons, either, sharing His image and, like Him, able to choose. Evil may well have been the price it was necessary for God to pay for you and me to even exist.

One last thing. Some might resent that phrase, "the price it was necessary for God to pay." They look around and cry out (as we all should) at suffering, and imagine that God is seated, safe and secure in heaven, an untouched observer of the human scene. They forget that God stepped into our world, suffered with us in Jesus, and in a moment of our time at Calvary took on Himself the infinite weight of all the sin, all the suffering, and all the evil the universe has ever known. You and I can only know one life's worth of suffering. Jesus took on Himself the full weight of all the suffering of all the billions of mankind.

How could a good God permit suffering? Ah, that's the wrong question. The real mystery is, How could there be a God as loving as ours, who gave you and me the freedom we require to exist as human beings, knowing the price of suffering He would have to pay?

EVOLUTION AND ORIGINS. Bills in state legislatures insist a Creationist position be presented in schools along with an Evolutionist position. There are debates on college campuses. "Real" scientists claim that Evolution is science, and Creation just religion. And we wonder what will happen to our kids, and what we should say when they ask us about Evolution and origins. And what should public policy be, anyway?

To sort it all out, we need to understand (1) the nature and limitations of "science," (2) the difference between Evolution and evolution, and (3) how to help others have confidence that it really is intellectually respectable to believe in Creation rather than in Evolution.

The nature and limitations of "science." Science, more than anything else, is an approach to exploring our universe. Data is gathered, theories are proposed to explain the data, and experiments are devised to test the theories and suggest more experiments. The best scientists always realize their data is incomplete, their theories tentative, and there is more to learn.

In using this method scientists rely heavily on observation and repeated experiment. Will water always boil at 212° F at sea level? Boil pots of water over and over. Try sea water. Go up 3000 feet above sea level. Testing over and over again, reliable "laws" (thoroughly established theories) are discovered. Actually, the really trustworthy scientific theories are those dealing with only a few variables (water, heat, atmospheric pressure), and established as these variables are, they are manipulated over and over by the experimenter himself.

This helps us see the limitations of "science" when dealing with subjects like Evolution and origins. There are great masses of complex data. And the theories about Evolution are theories about what might have happened in the distant past, to explain data gathered today. Scientists can gather data. And they can generate hypotheses. But they can't really test them. Come up with the idea that life originated by chance in some warm primal sea, as nonliving chemicals were bombarded by cosmic rays, and you have a totally untestable theory. You can't go back in time to that supposed era and observe. You can't even duplicate those imagined conditions, so you run the experiment over and over again. The most important part of the scientific method—hypothesis testing through repeated experiments with controlled variables—simply isn't available (not really) when it comes to Evolution and to origins.

The difference between Evolution and evolution. The Evolutionary theory of origins was generated when certain mechanisms at work in today's world were noticed by Charles Darwin. He observed changes that took place within species: the shape of birds' beaks, differences in plants and animals from one isolated South Seas island to another. People began to understand how genes and chromosomes control heredity, and how changes take place in mating. It seemed clear to Darwin that those changes that helped a species survive were retained, as individuals with such characteristics lived to breed. And so, out of processes of evolution, which explain changes within species, came the idea of Evolution: the notion that the processes we observe now caused the development of single-celled living organisms into the complex creatures living today. Cells grouped and became fish, fish became amphibians and birds, these became reptiles and mammals and, ultimately, man.

No one now alive observed that process. No fossils of transition creatures have ever been found. But by extending the observed mechanisms of evolution, and adding millions of years, the theory of Evolution—the Origin of the Species—was proposed.

There is no doubt that we can demonstrate, by the scientific method, the theory of evolution. But there is also no doubt that, by the scientific method, no one can demonstrate the theory of Evolution.

Intellectually respectable.   Many Christian scientists —and some scientists who are not Christians—are unconvinced by the arguments for Evolution. Excellent books have been written that show that the theory just doesn't fit the scientific data we possess. On the other side of the argument, other scientists present all sorts of arguments from various data that suggest Evolution does fit the facts we possess.

When it comes to Evolution and origins *neither* position is "scientific." Each believes, taking the unprovable on faith, but is convinced that the position is not unreasonable.

What about the schools?   The obvious problem in our society today is that Evolutionists want their position taught as "scientific," and presented as "fact" rather than theory. In most school systems, teachers who have been raised on Evolution teach from textbooks that assume that

Evolution has been established as the only reasonable concept a modern person can believe.

Unfortunately, some Christians have attempted to counter by presenting what they call "scientific Creationism," and have lobbyed for state laws requiring that Creationism be given equal time. Why unfortunate? Because *neither* Creationism nor Evolution is "scientific." At best Christians should insist that when Evolution is taught, it be clearly labeled as theory. But it is hardly accurate to insist that Creationism be taught as "scientific."

What should we do about children who are taught an Evolutionary view in school, without an explanation of the nature of science or its limitations and without labeling Evolution as a secular faith? Here are some things Christians might consider:

● Parents with young children can explain that no one was there to see the things taught in school: they are just guesses about what happened. But God *was* there, and He's told us in the Bible that He made us.

● Parents with teens might pick up a book or two in a local Christian bookstore. Many good books present the positive evidence for Creationism and discuss the many facts that make Evolution most unlikely.

● Churches might work with the local school system to provide an alternative voice. A presentation in a science class, a short after-school elective, or a released time series on Evolution vs. Creation are possibilities. So is the popular debate format, which might occupy a school assembly.

● Churches might offer elective or regular Sunday school classes on the subject for young teens or high-schoolers, or a special VBS sequence for families with teens.

● Church libraries can develop a section on this issue, and let parents and youth know the books are available.

For very few of us will the issues raised by Evolution be life-shaping, or even faith-shaking. But most youth at some time or other will wonder, and be concerned whether it's intellectually respectable to hold to their faith. Few will want to work through all the evidence. Most will be satisfied to know that evidence exists. Many will be surprised to learn the truth. Faith actually is more reasonable than unbelief.

EXERCISE. I've got good news for joggers. When the Bible talks about "bodily exercise" being of little value (1 Tim. 4:8), it's not referring to your addiction to running at all. In context, the apostle Paul is warning Timothy against ascetics, who looked for moral perfection by exercising strict control over physical drives and needs. I can't guarantee that Paul himself was committed to a regular exercise program. But he may not have needed it. After all, anyone who worked as hard as he did, who spent so much time in prison, was flogged and shipwrecked, in danger from bandits and rivers, in cities and countryside, knowing cold and hunger and thirst as he pursued his mission, must have been in pretty good shape (cf. 2 Cor. 11:23–28)!

Actually, anyone who understands the impact of exercise and believes the body is the Spirit's temple, is likely to be active and involved. Exercise steps up our metabolism 24 hours a day, so what we eat is less likely to go to flab. It helps us sleep, improves rest, and holds back the aging process, so we stay younger physically when we maintain a program of moderate exercise. Exercise makes us look better and feel better about ourselves, giving us a healthier outlook on life. Oh, yes. Exercise of the physical variety *is* valuable. For each of us.

There are many books on exercise in every bookstore. They'll each tell you about the same things. Do a little every day, and avoid strenuous, infrequent exercise. Get your heart rate up and keep it up for some twenty minutes or so. One good form of exercise is brisk walking, and anyone can do that.

There's very little pushy advice in this book. But here's an exception. If you've been spending the last few years in an easy chair, put this book down, now.

Go take a walk.

EXPECTATIONS.

A phrase that is used these days sums up the impact of expectations: "self-fulfilling prophecy." When we expect a person to behave in a certain way, he tends to do it.

Part of the explanation is that we treat people according to our expectations. If you've heard that Georgie is a terror, when he joins your Sunday school class you're likely to jump on him quick, to let him know you're in control. But Georgie isn't dumb. He picks up the fact that you expect him to be disruptive and, obligingly, he is. To some extent at least your expectations have communicated how he's to behave.

The problem comes for most of us when our expectations seem to have a solid basis. After Georgie has misbehaved in class a dozen times, how could we help but expect it? If our kids show again and again they can't remember to make the bed, then we'd be foolish (wouldn't we?) not to check every morning before they get out of the house—and haul them back to do it before they get away.

It's even worse for Christians. After all, we know that everyone has a sin nature. No wonder people misbehave. Perhaps, because we can expect them to do wrong, we need to set up lots of controls, to force them to do right. In fact, many things in our work world and in our churches are structured on just this notion: that we have to be careful to protect ourselves and others against things people would do wrong if only we released our controls.

We have similar problems with ourselves. We expect ourselves to fail, and so we don't try. Or we're so anxious when we make an effort that failure is assured. Our expectations do shape the real experiences we have in the world.

What can Christians expect? Our faith brings with it a brutally honest appraisal of man as sinner. But it brings far more. It shows us a humanity rich in potential, shaped in the image of God. We see a redeemable mind and imagination, and a capacity for sensitive concern. We see in moral awareness the possibility of becoming truly good. Most important, we see that Jesus has already acted to make the possibility a reality for those who come to Him. Because Jesus is real in the life of believers, we are confident. Though Georgie may be disruptive now, and our own kids irresponsible, and we ourselves fearful, we know we'll become very different persons indeed. Under Jesus' touch Georgie will become responsive and loving, our kids thoughtful and disciplined, and we'll even risk obedience. It may take awhile. But because God is involved in our lives we confidently expect the best will come.

This is the great impact of Christianity on our expectations. We know the past does not lock anyone into a predetermined tomorrow. → **DETERMINISM** We know that in Christ we have reason to expect the good, not the bad: the best, not the worst.

So what happens now when Georgie comes into my class, and I expect the best? I greet him with love, and when he misbehaves, I find ways to help him do better. And when I fear failure? Then I remind myself of God's promises and find the faith to try, sure that in time I'll succeed.

Gib Martin, a pastor friend of mine, puts it this way. "People need us to believe for them, until they're able to believe for themselves." You see, Christian faith isn't just about something long ago or far away.

Christian faith is fixed in a living God, who is committed to us in Christ, and who *knows* (not just expects) that we will become the very best we can be, in Him (cf. 2 Cor. 5:21).

EXPERIENCE.   They say experience is a good teacher. But only if we learn → **KNOWING**

† † †

FADS.   Rumors persist that there's a warehouse full of hula hoops, somewhere on New York City's east side. It's definitely no rumor that the popular '60s "Death of God" theology is buried (right next to Situation Ethics?). But not to worry. It's in the nature of fads to flourish, and then die. Pet rocks have come and gone, with CB radios and video games. As also the rush to re-gender God and change half the pronouns in the Bible to Her. It does seem sometimes that the Bible's dry comment on that most famous Greek city fits our age: "All the Athenians and the foreigners who lived there spent their time doing nothing but talking about and listening to the latest ideas" (Acts 17:21).

Taken lightly, salted with humor, fads do little harm. But it is dangerous to mistake fads as solutions to boredom, or some undiscovered answer to life's meaning. The desperate search for something new can indicate that we've failed to recognize answers documented since Moses and which are available today in nearly every language of the world. "The word is near you; it is in your mouth and in your heart, that is, the word of faith" (Rom. 10:8). Looking around for something new will not help. Looking up, and discovering the meaning of that word, "faith," will.

FAILURE. Like death and taxes, we can expect failure. Failure is about as welcome. Still, as some point out, Abe Lincoln was a political failure. He never won an office for which he ran . . . until he won the presidency. Lincoln makes a good object lesson. Failure isn't our problem: it's how we deal with it.

Some children become anxious about failing. They'll work hard to get out of school work—because they're so afraid to fail they simply will not try. Life holds many terrors for anyone who is afraid to fail.

Helping children with failure. It's important to get a head start on developing a healthy view of failure. There are several things moms and dads can do to help. • Don't make a big fuss over your own or your children's failures. Communicate by your attitude that failure can be faced and overcome. For an illustration, look at Psalm 103:8–14. God deals with our sins (those *real* failures of ours) calmly and lovingly. • Help your children set realistic goals, of gradually increasing difficulty. Step-by-step success in little things is the way to build confidence and to learn that failures can be overcome. ● Talk together about failures in a noncondemning way. Talking through an experience helps a child deal with emotions associated with failure. And it can help him or her plan how to succeed the next time (Prov. 15:22).

Helping yourself. Some of us had no one to help us with failure when we were children. It may not be our kids who are troubled and afraid to try, but us! What can we do? We can let God parent us and rebuild our confidence. ● Look at the experiences of Peter reported in the Gospels. He tried hard, and with enthusiasm. Yet he often failed, and Jesus had to correct or restrain him. Yet Jesus never rejected the bumbling disciple. In the end he became one of the most productive Christian leaders. ● Let God guide you to little daily steps of obedience. Don't dream of big victories. Just seek to be faithful in one little thing a day. ● Remember that God doesn't berate you when you fail.

When my oldest was crawling, we lived in a tiny house trailer in Michigan. I remember my wife propping him up as I crouched a few feet away. "Come to Daddy!" Paul, on tiptoes, would stagger a step toward me and fall. I would pick him up, hug him, and say "Good boy! That's right! Try again. Walk to Daddy."

God, the truly good Father, isn't upset when you and I fall as we struggle to toddle to Him. Taking one step at a time, supported by His love, we eventually will leave failure behind and find our way to truly productive lives (Titus 3:14).

FAIRNESS. It seems obvious that a person ought to get what he or she deserves. That's why one story Jesus told, recorded in Matthew 20, troubles some of us. You remember. A landowner went out and hired some men in the morning, and promised them a full day's pay to work in his fields. Later he found others, idle in the town square. When he learned no one had work for them, he sent them into his fields too. At the end of the day the men lined up for their pay, beginning with those who started last. And the landowner gave each of them a full day's pay! But when it came to the people who'd been working all day, he gave them a day's pay as well. Were they upset! They challenged the employer and complained bitterly.

The way Jesus ended the story is fascinating. The employer (who represents God) defended himself. Each person who had worked all day was treated fairly: each got just what he'd agreed to. With the rest, the landowner had simply exercised his right to be generous.

Think about it. Do you really want God to be *fair* with you? Is fairness the best you can do in your relationships with others?

FAITH/FAITHFULNESS.   Anyone can get upset if he feels his faith weakening. Unless he makes an important distinction. The most important thing about faith isn't its subjective strength but it's object. A person can have unshakeable faith in Buddha, but that faith will do him no good at all. Another can have hesitant faith in Jesus and be lifted high.

Jesus once put it this way. "Whoever comes to me I will never drive away," and, "this is the will of him who sent me, that I shall lose none of all that he has given me, but raise them up at the last day. For my Father's will is that everyone who looks to the Son and believes in him shall have eternal life, and I will raise him up at the last day" (John 6:37, 39, 40).

Don't focus your attention on your wavering feelings, and wonder if you have enough faith to hold out. Focus your attention on Jesus, and remember He will never release His grip on you → BELIEVING IN

FAITH HEALING.   It's exciting to realize that our God is "the LORD who heals you" (Exod. 15:26). In Jesus' ministry we see a beautiful expression of that healing power. The blind saw, the paralyzed walked, the leper was made whole, the deaf heard, even the dead were raised. Healing was clear evidence to Israel that their God walked among them (Matt. 11:5, 6). All the ridicule of modern critics, and all the suggestions of psychosomatic cures, have never dimmed the reality. Through Jesus, and after him the apostles, God acted to heal.

Looking into the Gospels and Acts, and realizing that Jesus is among His people now—the same "yesterday and today and forever" (Heb. 13:8)—many are convinced that Jesus continues to heal us. But there are questions. Is healing guaranteed? If so, why aren't all believers healthy and whole? Are there conditions Christians must meet for healing? Is healing channeled through miracle-working individuals, like Jesus and some apostles? Or today does God just work through natural medical processes?

There are many books arguing questions like these. Some insist on yes answers and others insist no. If we or loved ones become seriously ill, we may need help to sort out the issues.

Sickness in Scripture. Sickness is often used in Scripture as an image of man's spiritual condition (cf. Isa. 1). This image is appropriate. Physical suffering finds its origin in man's Fall. In God's Law-Covenant with Israel, material punishments were promised as an outcome of sin, and material blessings were promised should a generation turn from sin to obey God (cf. Deut. 28). Among the punishments is sickness; among the blessings, health.

In the Law then God committed Himself to heal Israel, in the sense of restoring national wholeness, when a generation was obedient. Yet the whole Old Testament looks forward to a time of ultimate healing: a time when the inner sickness of sin, and the suffering associated with sin, would be cured by the coming Savior (Isa. 53:4–6).

Jesus' healing miracles. Against the background of the Old Testament's imagery and its promises linking physical healing with spiritual renewal, Jesus' miracles take on great significance. The healings showed God's compassion for man. But even more, they identified Jesus as the promised Savior. Even His enemies admitted privately,

"No one could perform the miraculous signs you are doing if God were not with him" (John 3:2). Later a man born blind confronted Jesus' enemies openly: "Nobody has ever heard of opening the eyes of a man born blind. If this man were not from God, he could do nothing" (John 9:33).

Some believe the same authenticating purpose is seen in the ministry of the apostles. They point out no later leaders (such as Timothy or Titus) healed, and that while healing is mentioned in the Epistles, it is linked with prayer rather than miracle (cf. 1 Cor. 12:9 with 2 Cor. 12:8; Phil. 2:25–30; James 5:13–16). If the healing miracles of the New Testament had unique purposes, linked with the birth of the church, it may be questionable to assume we should experience such miracles today.

Healing and faith. For many the key to understanding healing is not found in some unique purpose authenticating Jesus as Messiah, but in faith. There's no doubt that many healings by Jesus and the apostles specifically express an important role for faith (cf. Matt. 8:1–3; 9:21, 22; 15:28; Acts 5:16; 14:9). But other miracles of healing clearly take place without reference to the faith or even to the conversion of the individuals healed (cf. Matt. 9:23–26; Mark 6:5; Acts 3:1–10; 8:7; 28:8).

Faith is of course always intimately linked with prayer (cf. James 5:15, 16). But even the prayer of a man with as much faith as the apostle Paul was no guarantee of healing (2 Cor. 12:8–10).

Immunity from suffering. Perhaps this is the crux of the matter. Is salvation intended to bring with it immunity from the suffering caused by illness? Peter's first letter (which uses no less than seven different words for suffering) makes it clear that while believers are shielded by God's power, "now for a little while you may have had to suffer grief in all kinds of trials" (1 Peter 1:5, 6). Peter teaches that suffering is to be expected in this life: Jesus was not immune, and neither are we. We are not to be surprised at painful trials, "as though something strange were happening to you,'' but are to rejoice that we can participate in Jesus' sufferings (1 Peter 4:12–19).

Returning again to Paul, we must be impressed by the fact that when suffering from a tormenting, chronic illness, "Three times I pleaded with the Lord to take it away from me." Instead of healing, God answered: "My grace is sufficient for you, for my power is made perfect in weakness" (2 Cor. 12:7–9). God chose not to heal, that the apostle might experience in weakness a greater measure of the Lord's power than would have been possible for him if he were in perfect health.

Understandings of the Bible's teaching. We can group understandings of the Bible's teaching on healing in several categories. Some beliefs are shared by all Christians. Some beliefs represent different emphases. And some beliefs about healing are contradictory.

● Shared beliefs. God is able to heal. God does act in our lives. Prayer is appropriate when sickness comes as an expression of faith and because God wants us to bring our requests to Him. God does hear and answer prayers.

● Complementary beliefs with different emphases. God works primarily through natural and medical means in healing vs God works primarily through supernatural means. God's attention is focused on inner healing vs God's attention is given to physical healing. The healing made available in the Atonement will be fully expressed in the Resurrection vs the healing made available in the Atonement is for us today. God heals sovereignly, within the context of His plan for the greatest good for each of us vs God heals as a response to a believer's faith.

It's important in evaluating these emphases to realize they are not contradictory. God may use natural medical means in healing, and work through miracles as well. These are "both/and" rather than "either/or" understandings of healing.

● Contradictory beliefs. Some ideas about healing are contradictory, and either one understanding is correct or the other. For instance: God guarantees healing to the trusting believer vs God does not guarantee a believer healing. Or, God must heal if we believe strongly enough vs God is not bound by the strength or even absence of our faith. Or, illness is always an evil vs illness and associated suffering can have a positive, beneficial purpose and thus be good.

When we're sick. When you or your loved ones are threatened by serious illness, it's often difficult to sort out these different understandings of healing. It's only natural to wonder, "Why me?" Under the pressure of normal stress, it's difficult to come to wise conclusions on such a complex subject. Sometimes more stress is added by friends who suggest that it is somehow our fault if we're ill. What then should a person do? Here are some suggestions that may help.

1. Do call on church leaders to pray with and for you. If you are aware of sins in your life, confess them as part of the process (James 5:13–16).

2. Follow the advice of your doctor. If an illness is serious, seek a second or third opinion. Many Bible students understand anointing with oil, mentioned in James 5, to refer to what was then an accepted medical treatment. They believe that James thus implies use of medication in the early church.

3. Express your continuing trust in the Lord. Focus attention on passages of Scripture that reassure you of His love and presence (such as Pss. 23; 145; Rom. 8:18–39, etc.).

4. Be aware that anyone who is ill is vulnerable and may not make wise decisions. Don't act hastily, or on counsel from any single individual. Seek support from several friends, and do not act on suggestions until you have a considered, confident sense that you are being led by God Himself.

You might also gain further insights by referring to related articles in this *Guidebook:* → SUFFERING → FAITH/ FAITHFULNESS → BARGAINING WITH GOD

How good it is when difficulties come to have God's promise: "Never will I leave you; never will I forsake you" (Heb. 13:5).

FALSE TEACHING. How do we recognize it? The Bible focuses on the denial by false teachers of Jesus as God come in the flesh (cf. 1 John 4:2; 5:6–12). Peter and Jude describe a false teacher's personality: there is greed, bridling under authority, arrogance, and, by promising a freedom that does not require a disciplined life of obedience, appeal to the "lustful desires of human nature" (cf. Jer. 23; 2 Peter 2; Jude). What do we do about false teaching? ● Identify it by checking what *anyone* teaches against the Scriptures. ● Present God's truth gently (2 Tim. 2:24–26). ● Rest assured that "their folly will be clear to everyone" (3:9). ● Personally keep on following the teaching laid down in Scripture into a righteous life (3:10–17).

FAME. Ever thought much about the sources of fame? There is fame through looks (Brooke Shields), by name (Rockefeller), by discovery (Salk), by familiarity (Cronkite), by entertaining (Bob Hope), by sports (Reggie Jackson), by notoriety (Manson), by politics (Mayor Daley), by position (Kissinger), etc. Another thing about fame. It's fleeting. A hundred years from now no one will even remember the names I've listed. Doubt it? Try listing 1880s personalities famous for looks, name, discovery, familiarity, entertaining, sports, notoriety, politics, or position.

FAMILY. Perhaps the greatest changes in family life since Bible times have taken place in the past hundred years. We've moved off the farm, away from extended families (closely knit groups including grandparents and aunts and uncles as well as parents and children). Since the end of World War II we've been mobile. Parents and their grown children are typically scattered across the country. Frequent moves keep many nuclear families from putting down roots. Changes in our work force also mean that many moms are now employed instead of at home. Many of the old traditional functions of the family have changed.

Still, recent research documents a vital fact. The

basic function of family has *not* changed. That function? The family is still the primary influence in the development of the personality and character of children. In the context of the long-term, intimate, loving daily relationships the family provides, children shape their beliefs and values and their emotional, intellectual, and interpersonal style.

It's helpful to us to realize that family is for personal growth and development. We moms and dads can be assured that however different is modern lifestyle, we can still be God's agents in the lives of our children. If we invest the time it takes to know and nurture them.

Research on personality growth also helps us understand why the New Testament so often uses family terms in speaking of the church, and why spiritual growth comes through being "rooted and established in love" for other believers (cf. Eph. 3:14–19). In the context of long-term, intimate, daily relationships with other Christians, God helps us reshape our own beliefs and values. His family, the church, helps us develop Christlikeness in thought and emotion and interpersonal relationships.

Family is still important. For our children, and for us.

→ **CHURCH**

FAMILY DEVOTIONS. Many Christian parents are uncomfortable about family devotions. We think they're important. But we've found it almost impossible to carry them off. One recent survey of several hundred Christian parents found 78% couldn't find a regular time, and half couldn't keep the kids interested or do advance preparation. Others worried about finding materials, knowing how, or getting a spouse to cooperate. Though the majority felt family prayer (84%) and times together (74%) were vital, few reported making much progress. Are there any solutions for those who want "family devotions"?

Principles. When my kids were young (they're now past college age) I struggled too. Over years of trying, and making plenty of mistakes, I've reached the following conclusions. ● Nurture can be built into family lifestyle when kids are young, so that "devotions" aren't even noticed. ● "Daily" is not necessary as kids grow older. ● Priesthood of believers must be understood and applied in the family. ● And, setting aside special times during the year is important.

Applying these principles can lead us to a very simple pattern for enriching our nurture.

Between 3 and 8 years of age.   Reserve at least a half hour around bedtime for your children each night. If their ages are staggered, stagger bedtimes too, so each can get his or her own special time with you. Use this time to sing and read. Read Bible story books and missions books (we loved the old Jungle Doctor series). Let your kids go with you to a Christian bookstore to pick out the books. Each week put Sunday school take-home pictures on your child's wall near the bed. Talk about the story and how it applies to you. Use bedtime for listening as well. Let your child talk about school and friends. Build prayers around his or her daily doings. Don't worry if some nights your time together stretches beyond the intended half hour.

It takes a little extra (you may give up a TV show or two) but this is prime time for growing kids.

From 9 years of age on.   Study together a couple times a week. Agree together on a time that fits your kids' schedules and (choke) TV programing. Keep your studies simple. Remember that you and your children are equally believers/priests, so you will share with and teach one another. Actually, it is adults "talking at" kids that turns them off.

What do you do? Work through short passages in Scripture: a chapter of Proverbs, a paragraph in Ephesians, or an event recorded in one of the Gospels. Have each person read the selected passage and look for an answer to one preplanned question. For instance: "What does Dad need to learn from this passage?" "What can you see here that Mom does well?" "What in this passage reminds you of Jim?" "What's the hardest thing here for you to do?" "Tell of one time when you did what this passage says, and what happened." "Explain how you feel when you read this verse, and why?"

This kind of assignment is easy to formulate, and puts parents and children on the same footing. Each can minister to the others, and each is encouraged to share.

Add to these patterns special family events for worship or study related to the changing seasons of the year → **CALENDAR** and you have a simple yet vital structure for your family's devotional life.

FANTASY. In the past twenty years, psychologists have become increasingly interested in fantasy. They've noted that children who can not imagine are likely to act out their passions—often destructively. Daydreaming, that flitting between fantasy and reality which some 94% of our adult population engages in, can have real value. Our fantasies reflect our current concerns, and often so reorganize information we possess that they lead to creative solutions to our problems.

Kept in perspective, the capacity to imagine and to dream can enrich our lives. But fantasy brings problems if we let our imagination run away, and we lose touch with reality. Proverbs notes, "He who works his land will have abundant food, but he who chases fantasies lacks judgment" (Prov. 12:11).

FASTING. The diet aid people seem to be worried about fasts. Recent ads have promised the "quickest weight loss possible except for starvation." Well, fasting isn't starvation. A person can go without food for some time without starvation setting in.

Physiologically. Fasting uses fat stored in the body to fuel it. The stored fat is converted and used rather than those calories a person would normally take in by eating. Because protein is not stored, some healthy muscle tissue is also broken down and the proteins reused.

Fasting does place some strain on the body, so it's good to check with a doctor on your general health before trying to fast. It is also vital to maintain a high level of fluid intake: lots of water is a must.

Many believe that fasts of a week or so are healthy, and allow the body to clear itself of wastes.

In fasting, one's appetite is usually lost after three days or so and does not return until the body's stored resources are near exhaustion. As books on fasting point out, refeeding (beginning to eat again) is critical. Long fasts call for refeeding with nothing but juices for a few days, gradually adding bland foods. I have fasted for up to 21 days, and found fasts of 10 to 14 days have little affect on my own energy level.

Should we fast? Some today fast for health, or to lose weight. Some see fasting as a religious duty, or a way to get God's attention. Looking through the Bible we find interesting insights on fasting.

Most biblical fasts were for a single day, though seven-day fasts are mentioned (1 Sam. 31:13; 2 Sam. 12:16–18). Jesus' forty-day fast at the beginning of His public ministry is the longest recorded (Matt. 4:1, 2). The fact that only after forty days did He begin to hunger indicates the young carpenter could have been on the heavy side: hunger returns to most within 30 days.

The Bible also calls a limited diet of water and some basic foods a fast (cf. Dan. 10:2, 3).

Old Testament fasts are often associated with repentance: the Day of Atonement was a fast day (Lev. 16:29ff.). Fasts might be called when war threatened (cf. Judg. 20:26; 2 Chron. 20:3), or for sickness (Ps. 35:13), or in mourning (1 Sam. 31:13; 1 Chron. 10:12).

The New Testament often links prayer and fasting (Luke 2:37; Matt. 17:21, mg.; Acts 10:30). Paul fasted frequently (2 Cor. 11:27). Yet there are no instructions in the New Testament calling for fasting as a religious or spiritual duty, or as an aid to spiritual growth.

Should you and I fast as an expression of our faith? If an individual is so led, surely. But it's important to keep in mind the answer given in Old Testament times when some inquired about three fasts they had been keeping for years.

The prophet reminded them, "This is what the LORD Almighty says: 'Administer true justice; show mercy and compassion to one another. Do not oppress the widow or the fatherless, the alien or the poor. In your hearts do not think evil of each other'" (Zech 7:9–10). It is not fasting God requires, but holiness and love.

Fasting can be a positive experience, and can enrich our faith. But it is not as close to God's heart as simple goodness.

FAT. Offered on Old Testament altars, fat was considered the choicest part of the sacrifice. Most of us would be happy to sacrifice our fat to the Lord—if He'd only take it quickly and painlessly.

Some fat on the body is healthy, and those older "ideal weight" charts have been shown to be unrealistic. We can all carry ten or fifteen pounds more than the "ideal" they show and be in good shape. But those pounds of flab do raise blood pressure, clog blood vessels, and mean adding miles of networks of tiny blood vessels that increase demands on our heart.

Probably there's significance in the fact that fat is valued on altars. On us, fat can be hazardous to health. →
FASTING → DIET AIDS

FATE. To the ancients as well as to modern determinists,→ DETERMINISM "fate" was grim, irresistible, and impersonal, grinding out the destiny of individuals without consideration of whether their actions were good or bad. The Bible speaks of fate too. But this is fate with a difference. There a person's fate is fixed by personal choice among moral options. "This is the fate of those who trust in themselves, and of their followers, who approve their sayings," the psalmist says. "Like sheep they are destined for the grave, and death will feed on them. . . . But God will redeem my soul from the grave; he will surely take me to himself" (Ps. 49:14, 15).

FATHERING. With apologies to those who lead the rush toward unisex, I have to reveal that growing children need fathering.

It's hard to pin down what makes fathering distinctive. But many studies of the father's role in child development make it clear that Dad is important. The loss of a father hurts an adolescent girl's ability to relate healthily to males. Dad's absence when boys are young tends to lead to immaturity and poor peer adjustment. In general children see father more than mother as setting the direction of the family, as powerful, and as punitive. When Dad participates actively in child care, boys in the family are likely to be more masculine and to achieve more in school. Many studies show that lengthy absence of the father from the home is linked with poor adjustment in children. Absence because of a family break-up has more adverse impact than absence because of death.

Of course, some fathers tear down rather than build up. An aggressive, brutal dad who rejects or neglects a son is likely to produce a delinquent, anxious, or dejected youth. A loving father, who guides but does not arbitrarily impose his will, tends to nurture mature offspring.

Each of the statements in the two paragraphs above has been demonstrated by significant amounts of research. We might not know why fathers are so important. But they are. God's ancient words about Abraham seem just as significant now, some 3,500 years later: "I have chosen him, so that he will direct his children and his household after him to keep the way of the LORD by doing what is right and just" (Gen. 18:19). → PARENTING

Stress on the importance of fathering raises painful questions for many single parents. Some 20% of America's children are now brought up in households headed by women. What can such moms, pressured for time and money and friends, do?

One option is provided by organizations like Parents Without Partners, and Big Brothers. These organizations try to find men with time to give to fatherless children. For Christians there is a nearer remedy. The church, as God knows it, is a fellowship of believers—an extended family of brothers and sisters, of parents and grandparents. Having close Christian friends who are involved and care can't

replace a father, of course. Yet many children without a

father have found that other men in the family of faith can
help fill the void, and guide them in keeping the way of the
Lord.

For a mom bringing up her children alone, reaching
out to build relationships in God's family is important. For
congregations, being sensitive to the special needs of
single parents and their children is part of what it means to
live as the body of Christ.

FAULTFINDING. "Why do you look at the speck
of sawdust in your brother's eye and pay no attention to
the plank in your own eye? How can you say to your
brother, 'Let me take the speck out of your eye,' when all
the time there is a plank in your own eye? You hypocrite,
first take the plank out of your own eye, and then you will
see clearly to remove the speck from your brother's eye"
(Matt. 7:3-5).

Still not convinced? Well . . . how about, "If any
one of you is without sin, let him be the first to throw a
stone at her" (John 8:7).

Did I hear you think, "But. . . . ?" Okay. Try this
one. "Anyone who speaks against his brother or judges
him speaks against the law and judges it. When you judge
the law, you are not keeping it, but sitting in judgment on
it. There is only one Lawgiver and Judge, the one who is
able to save and destroy. But you—who are you to judge
your neighbor?" (James 4:11, 12).

'Nuff said?

FEAR.   Is it all right to be afraid? Or should a Christian
"trust"? And how about children? What can we do to help
when they're afraid? And what about the "fear of the
Lord"? How does that fit in?

It's no wonder if we're uncertain about fear. We need
to do some sorting, to see if there are guidelines to help us
understand and deal with fear. It is particularly helpful to
break the subject down a bit, to look at legitimate fear,
unhealthy fear, and freeing fear.

Legitimate fear.   Legitimate fears are closely linked

with realities. Fire burns, and children must learn not to touch it. One study showed that adults presented with frightening information on smoking tend to cut down. A person going into the hospital with some fear tends to bear up better under the actual experience than a person who has denied or repressed his fears.

Each of these illustrations presents legitimate fears: in fact, helpful fears. Such fears are even spiritually beneficial, for they give the believer fresh opportunities to trust God (Ps. 56:3), and discover that he will in turn be free from panic (Ps. 56:4). After all, "trust" is meaningless if there is nothing to fear.

Several practices can help us deal with fears related to real threats to us or our loved ones. These are:

• Accept the fact of the threat, and do not try to deny it.

• Accept your own feelings of fear as legitimate.

• Gather information that will help you deal with the threat realistically. If for instance you're going to the hospital, find out as much as you can from the doctor about medical procedures, how much they will hurt, medication policy, etc. Knowing what to expect can help avoid panic.

• Express your fears and your trust to God. Let Him deal with panic, as He provided reassurance to the psalmists. God is not angry with us for feeling fear: He knows that fears give us opportunity to learn that we can trust Him.

Unhealthy fear.   Some fears distort reality or are overreactions to possible dangers. When fear keeps us from appropriate responses they are unhealthy. For instance, studies have shown that about 95% of heavy smokers will *avoid* taking lung X-rays after hearing a strong message on the dangers of smoking. A toddler may be terrified by a stuffed animal, or a three-year-old may fear being abandoned by Mom in Sunday school. Unhealthy fears tend to generate unhelpful reactions.

What can help us deal with unhealthy fears and overcome them? In addition to reaffirming trust in God, we can:

• Work toward familiarization. A child has panicked and screams in terror at the sight of a floppy toy. Put the feared toy well out of reach in a familiar room, and bring the child into the room. Stay close to him, playing with him or reading to him. A week or so later move the feared toy to a place it might be reached by the child. Again pay no attention to it, and stay near the child, playing with him. Still later let the child see you touch the toy. Later still, pick it up for a moment or two. After a month or so the child is likely to follow your example and hesitantly touch the toy. Within three months or so of gradual, step-by-step and unforced familiarization, the panic reaction is likely to be gone.

• Rehearsal helps adults. With children, "playing hospital" to practice what will happen there is good preparation for an operation. Adults can rehearse mentally. Think of different "might happen" options, and plan ahead how you will respond. Practice these responses mentally, again and again.

The problem with unhealthy fears is that they tend to create panic, and with it a sense of helplessness. Familiarization and rehearsal help us rethink our impression of reality and build an expectation of self-control.

Freeing fear. Perhaps the strangest thing for us to discover is that God offers us another kind of fear: freeing fear. Both the legitimate and unhealthy fears illustrated above are linked with objects, or experiences that might harm us. Other fears are linked to persons, whose opinion or ridicule we fear. Someone has observed that object fears and person fears have an insidious power. They can make us do what we shouldn't do, or leave undone what we should do.

A person afraid of cancer may put off seeing a doctor and not receive life-saving treatment in time. A person who fears what others think may hesitate to do what he believes is right, or even follow the crowd and do what he knows is wrong. Fear is insidious because it can rob us of the will to make choices we know we should make.

It's in view of fear's insidious power that we recognize freeing fear when we read in the Bible, "The fear of the LORD is the beginning of wisdom" (Prov. 9:10). If we stand in awe of God, the fears that have bound our will and pressured us into evil will be seen in perspective.

Jesus taught the crowds who came to hear Him, "Do not be afraid of those who kill the body and after that can do no more. But I will show you whom you should fear: Fear him who, after the killing of the body, has power to throw you into hell. Yes, I tell you, fear him" (Luke 12:4, 5). Awareness of God and His awesome power is intended to release us from bondage to our terror of others.

But as soon as fear brings its release, God vanquishes any terror of Him. Jesus immediately went on, "Are not five sparrows sold for two pennies? Yet not one of them is forgotten by God. Indeed, the very hairs of your head are all numbered. Don't be afraid; you are worth more than many sparrows" (12:6, 7). With the awe-inspiring realization that God is real comes the discovery that this God of power is a God of love, who cares deeply for us. The fear that awakens us to wisdom is put at rest by experience of a love that casts out fear (1 John 4:18). God teaches us to fear, and then releases us, inviting us to choose what is right not because we are terrified of Him, but because we are unwilling to displease one we've come to love.

Conclusions. Fear comes into every life. Some of our fears will be legitimate, and facing them will teach us deeper trust in God. Some of our fears will be unhealthy and drive us toward panic. These must be mastered. But the most important fear is that which acknowledges the power of God and bows in awe before Him.

When we experience the freeing fear of the Lord, we're immediately led to life's great discovery. The only one whom we need to fear comes to us in love, and tells us not to be afraid.

FELLOWSHIP. In modern church jargon it's likely to mean "social get together." In the ancient world it likely referred to a "common bond" that was supposed to

tie earthly society together in some semblance of brother-
hood. In the New Testament it means "participation": a
sharing of life, rooted in the believer's relationship with
Jesus and, because of Jesus, with other Christians (cf.
1 Cor. 1:9; Phil. 1:5).

Rather pale and weak as it is used today, "fellowship" in the Bible is a bold, vibrant word that makes a
powerful affirmation. It tells us we each have a share in
Jesus' continuing work on earth as well as in the benefits
of His death and resurrection. It focuses on the fact that we
believers have a share in one another's lives. The word
"fellowship" ("share') is even chosen to describe the
Christian's weekly contribution. → GIVING

Understanding the meaning of fellowship, it is most
impressive to read through the New Testament and sense
how intimate is the shared life Christ provides for His
people. As we read we see the giving and receiving of
counsel, encouragement, rebuke, forgiveness, concern,
instruction, correction, and most of all love. We discover
an openness that comes when believers realize they no
longer have to pretend, but can take off the masks and find
true acceptance. We sense the delight that comes from
being together and sharing joys with sorrows. There is in
Christ a fellowship that breaks through the barrier of loneliness that isolates most of humanity. And all this is implied in that New Testament word, "fellowship." The
picture in the New Testament is both attractive and
threatening. → PRIVACY But the warmth and beauty that
glow in the New Testament description draw us, and we
want to experience fellowship for ourselves. We can.
When we become what we truly are, the church of Jesus
Christ. → CHURCH

FEMININE AND MASCULINE.

We all have
some feel for what those words mean . . . and could generate our own list of "feminine" and "masculine"
characteristics. But there's a serious debate in progress
over the "real" differences between men and women. Oh,
there are the obvious ones, like size and muscle structure
and hormones, all of which are linked with sex. But what

255

about all those items on our lists that aren't linked with the physical, but with roles?

Many in the women's movement argue that social roles have been imposed by culture, and are not linked with female or male qualities at all. Parents expect boys to achieve in medicine, engineering, philosophy, and art. So they do. But no one expected or encouraged women to achieve. So history is barren of female Rembrandts, women Einsteins, and distaff Platos. The issue is an important one, especially if we begin with the conviction that women share with men the *imago dei* (the image of God) and are not inferior, but rich in every potential of personhood.

The debate has led to research on femininity and masculinity, in attempts to find out if differences are just social or more deeply rooted. The results? Hard to say. The best that one 1980 book reviewing the research could come up with was to suggest that ● differences in the structure of the brain may be partly responsible for differences in men's and women's cognitive style, ● affiliation patterns seem to have deeper roots than culture. Even 2½-year-old boys show the typical male preference for relating to a number of others (extensive social pattern) while girls prefer to relate to one or two (intensive social preference). ● The activity level of boys and girls differs, with males oriented to the more strenuous.

What does it all tell us? Again, not much. But it does appear that we can't blame all social role differences on society.

There's one more lesson implied, though. If "real" differences are so hard to find, we must take care not to stereotype one another. We must build our appreciation for men and women on the realization that what we share as human beings overwhelmingly outweighs those differences that have seemed so important in the past.

FEMINISM. The growing conviction that women have been and are discriminated against in a male-dominated society is expressed in today's feminist movement. Dozens of books and active organizations express that view. A few men have replied, insisting tongue in cheek that women are really the dominant sex, despite the wisdom of ancient authorities who considered them a necessary evil. They pretend to agree with Confucius that "It is a law of nature that woman should be kept under the control of man and not allowed any will of her own." Women don't think it's funny. And the women have the facts on their side.

Women in the United States. Male domination and discrimination against women has deep roots in our history. In the 1840s married women could not manage their own property, sign legal papers, or control their own income. When the Civil War forced many women into the work force, they were paid low wages or actually not paid at all. Susan B. Anthony's organization, formed in 1868, did not fight for the vote but against economic discrimination. It was not until 1910 that women won that right to vote, after literally hundreds of campaigns on state and federal levels. In 1890 only 17% of the B.A. degrees granted in the United States were awarded to women, and 1% of the Ph.Ds. By 1940 this had risen to 41% of the B.A.s, but still only 13% of the doctorates.

Despite some unfortunate associations (such as the linkage of feminism with a proabortion position), there is no question that the claim of historic and present discrimination against women is valid. And that such discrimination is wrong.

The feminist response. All feminists agree that the problem is economic, social, and political discrimination against women. They agree that this oppression must be corrected. But they do not agree on how oppression came about, or what to do to correct it.

• Socialist feminism sees the origin of discrimination in capitalism, in which the nuclear family is the basic economic unit. Women are oppressed because the system makes the wife economically dependent. Remove private property and class distinctions imposed by capitalism, and women will be freed.

• Moderate feminism (often called Women's Rights Feminism) calls for equality between men and women, and believes men too are victims of society's discrimination against women. Organizations like NOW (National Organization of Women) seek to work within the system toward equal pay, toward the day when traits like independence and tenderness can be valued in both sexes rather than linked with one, and toward a time when child-rearing responsibility will be shared rather than seen as a woman's primary role.

• Radical feminism is ideologically convinced that all forms of oppression (including racism and imperialism) are rooted in male dominance. Oppression of women is the fundamental oppression and calls for revolution. Society must be radically restructured, all sex roles must be abolished, and males must surrender the privileges that have come from their tyranny over half the race.

Biblical insights. Despite the patriarchal cultural background of Scripture, the Bible is supportive of the feminists' call for equality. But Scripture does not support socialist and radical feminists in their evaluation of cause and remedy.

The Genesis creation story stresses the fact that God created male and female alike in His image, and that Adam immediately realized Eve was "flesh of my flesh and bone of my bone." Equality as persons is taught in the creation story: equality was experienced by the unfallen pair.

Only with the Fall does oppression enter. The prophetic observation to Eve that the husband will "rule over you" spells the tragic distortion caused by sin. The divine ideal has been warped: struggle and oppression will turn intended harmony to discord. The fundamental cause of discrimination against women is not found in capitalism, or culture, or a supposed moral order created by God. It is found in sin.

For the Christian two courses of action seem to be suggested. 1. Oppression in society must be fought, though it can never be removed till the curse of sin is taken away. 2. Christian restoration of the divine image through Christ, and God's call back to the ideal, suggest that the body of Christ should become a fellowship in which the ideal can again be seen on earth. There are many challenging questions yet to be answered as to how the ideal can be expressed. → WOMEN IN THE CHURCH → SUBMISSIVENESS →HEAD OF THE HOUSE But surely in our individual and corporate life we must work toward a full expression of the worth and value of women as persons fully equal with men.

FLYING.

It's not fear that keeps one friend of mine from flying, even though 96 separate fears about flying have been reported by hesitant air travelers. With my friend it's the feeling that in a car, at least you have some control. You're not strapped in, completely dependent on some stranger. Other friends point out that if you're in a plane crash, you're almost sure to be killed. In a car accident you might have a chance. Some, if they have to fly, take out lots of insurance. And some insist spouses take a separate flight, so someone will survive to be with the kids.

Actually, that stranger in the cockpit who commands your flight will have as much as or more training than your doctor. Of the 113,000 Americans killed accidentally each year (about 55,000 in cars), only 135 or so will be killed in airliners. What it boils down to is that when you take a commercial flight, you're about 24 times safer flying than driving in your car.

FORGETTING.

It's happened to all of us. That name is right there, on the tip of the tongue. We know it. But somehow we just can't spit it out. We forgot.

Forgetting has done more than cause us momentary frustration. It's led some researchers to devote a lifetime to memory, trying to explain why we forget. The results? "Still no adequate answer can be given." Somehow each of us seems perfectly able to forget what it was we tied that string around our finger for to help us remember. And no one knows why.

There are some things we can do to help us remember. We can repeat a new phone number, over and over. We can write things down. We can say the name of a person we meet several times while we chat. These simple "rehearsal" methods do help us remember until, by using the phone number for several weeks or by meeting the new acquaintance a half-dozen times, we simply "know" them. Then we usually don't have to worry about forgetting.

Really, though, exploring memory leads us to more important issues. What we remember and what we forget tells us much about ourselves. In fact, what we remember and forget can shape our entire outlook on life! And understanding what God chooses to forget can vitally enrich our spiritual life. So let's leave that name on the tip of our tongue, and the string around the finger, and focus on remembered faults, remembered failures, and forgotten sins.

Remembered faults. You've probably heard others do it. Maybe you've done it yourself. An adult tells of his mistreatment as a child. A wife provides lists of her ex-husband's faults. A friend talks about the failings of fellow Christians. Often when this happens you can sense the sincerity of the person talking. It's clear that the person talking is convinced what he or she is saying is true. But don't mistake sincerity for reality.

We are all selective in what we remember about events and people. Some of us are victims of what one French psychologist calls "decoratism"—we have a need to mold reality to fit our pleasure. So we add and subtract from our memory of events until the way we remember it is the way we want to remember it. Maybe we want to remember a parent's failings so we can win sympathy. Maybe we want to remember our spouse's faults to justify our bitterness, or excuse us from any personal responsibility in a failing relationship. Whatever our reason, we decorate the past until what we remember is the way we want things to appear.

Both testaments in our Bible point out that we must

be on guard against the danger of decorated memories. "One witness is not enough to convict a man accused of any crime or offense," the Old Testament states. "A matter must be established by the testimony of two or three witnesses" (Deut. 19:15). The New Testament echoes this principle: "Do not entertain an accusation against an elder unless it is brought by two or three witnesses" (1 Tim. 5:19). An individual who accuses another person may be sincere. But he or she may also be wrong. There must be witnesses to events to provide independent testimony before accusations can even be heard.

The Bible warns us against our own memories when it comes to accusations. "Don't judge," the Bible says again and again. Instead we're to give others the benefit of the doubt, and operate with a memory patterned by Christian love, a love that "keeps no record of wrongs" (1 Cor. 13:5).

Remembered failures. Sometimes it's not bitter memories of others, but dark memories of our own failures that force their way into our consciousness. We can't trust these memories either. Like our memory of others, our memory of ourselves can be distorted and "decorated." For instance, a person with a poor self-image will often focus on remembered failures, and so reinforce his picture of himself. After all, a person who is a failure can hardly be blamed if he no longer tries.

The Bible has two words for us about the dark memories that draw our thoughts. In Philippians Paul writes, "Finally, brothers, whatever is true, whatever is noble, whatever is right, whatever is pure, whatever is lovely, whatever is admirable—if anything is excellent or praiseworthy—think about such things" (4:8). We are to consciously turn our thought to the positive. We are not to focus on our failures. We are to turn our attention to the admirable, and that which merits praise.

Each of us has experienced failures and defeats. But *we* are not failures, and we are not defeated. Our thoughts are more in harmony with reality when we remember the good, and turn away from memories of the bad.

Paul can share this from personal experience. In Philippians 3 he talks of his own early life, and the years in which he concentrated zealously on a religious lifestyle he later came to view as "rubbish." Paul had to turn away from those years, and focus on the future. What Paul saw was that Jesus calls believers to experience Christ's own resurrection power: that we have been raised from bondage to our dead past. "One thing I do" the apostle shared. "Forgetting what is behind and straining toward what is ahead, I press on toward the goal to win the prize for which God has called me heavenward in Christ Jesus" (Phil. 3:13, 14). The significance of our life is found in what's ahead, not in what is past!

Forgotten sins. Despite the way we decorate memory and thus try to remold reality, it's impossible for us to deal this way with our sins. We may try to bury them in some dusty corner of our mind. But they'll crawl out again, disguised as guilt or shame or even as anxiety. We can't hide our sins, or excuse them.

But as we've seen, God doesn't want our thoughts oriented to the past, or focused on faults.

You and I have no way out of the dilemma. Despite the tricks our memory plays with the past, we are unable to change history. But God *can* change history! He can step back into our yesterdays, and when we confess our sins, deal with them. The New Testament Book of Hebrews explores this impact of Jesus' death, and tells us that "by one sacrifice he has made perfect forever those who are being made holy" (10:14). God does this by planting His good Word in our hearts and writing holiness on our minds (10:16). The Bible then adds, "Their sins and lawless acts I will remember no more" (10:17).

How is this possible? The sacrifice Jesus made dealt so effectively with sin that it changed us, and it changed history! When God forgives, it is because the past has been cleansed by Jesus' own blood. That cleansing is so perfect that God Himself forgets our past! The sins are gone. And a forgiven past is totally different than the past we remember.

Summing up. The whole subject of memory and forgetting is interesting—and vitally important. We'll probably never understand *why* people forget. But in Scripture we make freeing discoveries about *what* we can't forget.

• We're freed by Jesus from the pressures that led us to decorate our remembrance of others with the waving pennants of accusation. We no longer need to return again and again to rehearse past hurts.

• We're freed by Jesus from the shame that led us to decorate remembrance of our own actions with row on row of vivid portraits of failure. We no longer need to think of ourselves as we were, but can look ahead now to what we will be.

• We're freed by Jesus from the burden of our past sins, and from the guilt, the shame, and the anxiety that sins produce. In Jesus we have such a perfect forgiveness that God Himself forgets the evils of our past.

Because of Jesus, we can fix our attention at last on the beautiful and praiseworthy, sure that beauty will become the distinguishing mark of our own life.

So if you want to remember something, face it. You'll probably have to rehearse, and write or say it over and over and over again. But if you want to forget. . . . ! Ah, then turn to Jesus, and experience the inner freedom only He can give.

FOSTER PARENTING.   Today more than 200,000 children in the United States live in foster homes, and many more homes are needed for children who can't be reared by their own parents. Various governmental agencies place children and make payments for their care. Yet studies have shown that two leading motives in taking in boys and girls are a concern for children, and a desire to put religious beliefs into action.

Some children fit into foster homes without stress. But since 80% of foster-care children have known rejection from at least one parent, adjustment often is not easy. Typically new foster parents express optimism at three months, some discouragement after six, and after the first year express general satisfaction with a foster child's improvement and their own success in the foster parent role.

What characteristics indicate a couple will make good foster parents? ● The adults are familiar with children (their own, or were raised in large families). ● The adults' own parents provided good models. ● The adults are willing to work closely with social workers and the placing agency. ● The adults have skills in dealing with children, and can relate to "difficult" children. ● The couple tends to make decisions jointly. ● The foster father is sensitive, and seeks to see things from a child's point of view. Couples like this can meet the very real need of many little ones for someone to care, and can help them grow.

There is today a pressing need in most communities for foster parents. Expecially for those who love children, and who realize that "religion that God our Father accepts as pure and faultless is this: to look after orphans and widows in their distress" (James 1:27).

FREEDOM. Most of us make the mistake of connecting the word "freedom" with "from." We say "free speech," and mean freedom from censorship. We say "free press," and mean freedom from government control. Even when an adolescent (of any age) cries out "I want to be free!" what he usually means is free from restrictions imposed by school or parents. He wants to do what *he* wants to do, when he wants to do it.

Freedom is such an attractive word it's often applied in ethics. Libertines prate about freedom from old-fashioned morality, and even homosexuals leap on the "liberation" bandwagon, crying out for freedom to practice their "alternative lifestyle."

All this talk of freedom is deceptive, because we humans are never really free "from." Each of us lives in bondage to all sorts of limitations. Our bodies demand sleep; our work demands our time. We might insist on "freedom" and try to stay awake, or we might quit work and go fishing. But soon we would collapse from exhaustion, or would run out of money. We might act as if we were free from the need to sleep or the demands of work. But we would never be able to do so without consequences.

That's what is so deceptive about the mirage of freedom. Every choice we make carries consequences. We can make our choices and pretend to be free. But we can never be free from the consequences our choices bring.

It's the same with the moral realm. We can laugh at morality and demand liberation from old hang-ups. We can choose to practice sin. But we can never sin safely. We are no more free from the consequences of our moral choices than a person who chooses to step out of a tenth-story window is free from the law of gravity. He is free to step out. But he is not free not to fall.

Actually, when we yearn for freedom, what we really want isn't unrestricted choice. What we really want is the ability to choose what will always be helpful, and never harm. To do what brings us good and not evil. That's why the Bible's teaching on freedom is unique. Once Jesus spoke with the Pharisees about freedom. He promised that if they would live within the restrictive pattern marked out by His words, they would find freedom. The Pharisees were angry. They insisted they had never been slaves. But Jesus replied, "I tell you the truth, everyone who sins is a slave to sin." The choice to sin locks the individual into inescapable consequences that sin must bring. Yet, Jesus went on, "if the Son sets you free, you will be free indeed" (John 8:31–36).

The Christian then has a radical concept of freedom. In Christ we are not promised a "freedom from" restrictions. Instead we are promised a set of divinely designed restrictions, and guaranteed that when we choose them we are freed to find the fulfillment and meaning in life for which we yearn. Slaves to Christ, we become free indeed (cf. also Rom. 6:15–23).

FRIENDSHIP. Slightly cynical about friendship, Dorothy Parker observed,

> Then if my friendships break and bend,
> There's little need to cry
> The while I know that every foe
> Is faithful to the end.

Parker's observation points up the most important quality some 40,000 readers of *Psychology Today* identified: above all, they valued loyalty in friends. With loyalty they wanted the ability to keep confidences, warmth, affection, and supportiveness. Were friendships important? Definitely. Some 51% of those surveyed said they would go first to friends in a crisis rather than to family.

Concepts of friendships. One of the most popular books on friendships is Dale Carnegie's *How to Win Friends and Influence People*. His simple suggestions are linked to popularity and to some levels of friendship. He says:

- be pleasant, and smile
- listen to what the other person has to say
- remember the other person's name, and use it often
- when you can do so sincerely, talk and act in ways that show you regard the other as a person of importance
- avoid being critical
- whenever possible give praise that has been earned
- be genuinely interested in the other person

When we study children's ideas about friendship, we find the very things Carnegie lists are the critical factors. But when children grow older, their ideas about friends will change.

Centuries ago Aristotle outlined three purposes that friendship might serve: (1) utility—we choose friends who will be useful to us; (2) pleasure—we choose friends whose company is pleasurable, or for play activities; (3) virtue—we choose friends whose qualities we admire, and who return our approval and affection. Carnegie's suggestions, like childhood ideas of friendship, fit Aristotle's first and perhaps his second type. But they fall far short of the third.

Building deeper friendships. As we move past childhood, we expect something more than "user" and "pleasure" friendships. Much research suggests that deeper friendships grow when we begin to trust another person, and tentatively disclose something of ourselves (revealing things that are important to us, and make us vulnerable). If the person with whom we share responds with acceptance and with reciprocal self-disclosure, the relationship will deepen. If we share, and the other does not, we'll grow uncomfortable. The friendship will become more superficial or will drift toward mere acquaintance.

Research suggests one other factor. We develop deeper friendships with those we relate to as equals. If one person retains the "right of unilateral imposition" (the right to control what we do and talk about), deeper friendship is unlikely. For instance, few will develop a deep friendship with an employer. And where a pastor is viewed as an authority figure, that pastor will have few significant friendships within the congregation.

For those deeper friendships that adults say are so important, and are a hedge against loneliness, we need to show acceptance, to treat others as equals, and to build trust through mutual self-revelation.

The Bible on friendship. The Bible tells stories of notable friends, such as David and Jonathan. But it actually has little to say about friendship. At first this seems surprising. Why isn't such an important relationship dealt with more fully?

Even the Greek word commonly used for "friend" *(phileo)* is seldom found in the New Testament. What may be even more surprising is to learn that where the NIV indicates an apostle speaking to or of a "dear friend," the Greek word there is not "friend" at all! Instead, the original says, "beloved!"

I said this is surprising, at first. When we understand what the Bible says about the quality of relationships that are to be built with brothers and sisters who make up Jesus' church, it's not surprising at all. The very qualities linked with deeper friendships in the natural world are constantly stressed—in their fullest possible expression—as qualities to be expressed in the life we share with other believers.

Does friendship call for acceptance? "Accept one another, then, just as Christ accepted you" (Rom. 15:7).

There can be no greater acceptance than this. → ACCEPT-ANCE

Does friendship imply equality? Why, we are all children of God, and servants of one another. How can we be more equal? → EQUALITY

Does friendship call for trust and self-revelation? Then to whom are we freer to bare our burdens than to those who care enough to bear them with us (Gal. 6:2)?

Friendship is important to everyone. Even superficial friendships are good. But true satisfaction comes from deeper relationships than these. The deepest friendships possible are made available to you and me in the love we are invited to develop for brothers and sisters in the family of God.

FRUGALITY. I suppose we're most likely to think of a frugal person as the proverbial "stingy man eager to get rich" who is "unaware that poverty awaits him" (Prov. 28:22). Saving money, rather than using it on those good things money is supposed to buy, may seem foolish to us. But what about the shoemaker in my home town, who lived in the back of his shop, sleeping on a cot, so all the money he earned could go to missions? And what about a close friend who lives a very frugal life, because he and his family prefer a part-time salary so he can be free to serve as unpaid pastor and counselor to several house-churches?

Looking at these frugal men—and then around at some of us who work two jobs so we can have money for things—and you wonder. Which lifestyle really provides riches (Matt. 6:20, 21)?

FULFILLMENT. The ad campaign the Army used to tout enlistment captures what a 1981 Yankelovich poll suggests is the goal of nearly 80% of our population: "Be all that you can be!" Some 17% of our population seem wrapped up in an intense search for self-fulfillment. Even those who don't agonize over inner needs and potentials, and give most of their energy to family obligations, work, or worry about the economy, health concerns, the kids' school problems, etc., are no longer convinced that the meaning of life can be summed up in the '50s' values of a nice car and home, a good neighborhood and family, and the hard work it takes to win them.

But where is fulfillment to be found? Some drop out, cut expenses, and take up bird watching. Others cut family ties, and divorce to go out and seek meaning in a less narrow world.

But the Christian's approach to finding fulfillment doesn't involve cut-and-run solutions. It does not focus on material values either. Actually, the Christian's answer goes back to that army commercial. Fulfillment comes when we grow to "be all that we can be" in our new life of faith.

"You have been given fullness in Christ," Colossians 2:10 says, and goes on to point out that God has given us a new life in Him. That new life isn't lived by avoiding the cares of normal existence. It is lived by facing the trivial as well as the crisis in a godly, trusting way. James puts it, "whenever you face trials of many kinds . . . know that the testing of your faith develops perseverance. Perseverance must finish its work so that you may be mature and complete" (James 1:2, 3).

Being complete. That's fulfillment. That is being all that we can be.

FUN.   A good definition of fun? The best I've found links fun to the flow we experience when "we get totally immersed in a sport or creative act" and "lose sense of time and the external world." It's not just play that can be fun. Work, gardening, worship . . . whatever draws you into this highest form of enjoyment will reward you with the fun of having fun.

FUNERALS.   When my mother died after an auto accident, I brought my eleven-year-old home with me for the funeral. He sat quiet and withdrawn in the house where he'd spent so many happy days, now empty of Grandma. Finally, after the funeral, he cried. I hugged him then and I cried too. I told him I'd brought him with me just so he'd have the chance to weep, and to realize, despite his grief that Grandma was gone, that she still lives.

Funerals are important times for all of us, rich in sorrow, remembrance, and hope. They reinforce the reality of our loss, and keep us from retreating into unhealthy denial. They present a dramatic testimony to our loss and our right to grieve. And they reaffirm our confident hope that our loved one survives: that we will be reunited in God's good time.

Much literature in the '70s challenged the funeral and the American way of dealing with death. Funeral directors were cast as sharp businessmen, ready to cheat vulnerable survivors. The cost of expensive funerals was challenged in view of the needs of those left behind. Yet research has shown that most look back after a year has passed and characterize the funeral director as "helpful." And there are many options that are not costly.

The traditional funeral has five elements: visitation, viewing, ceremony, procession, and committal. At times these elements are varied. The ceremony may be held in the form of a memorial service at your local church. Committal may be a private ceremony conducted at another time, especially if the body was cremated. Many feel that the traditional process is best for dealing with grief, visually affirming the passing. Others believe the memorial service is even better, as friends gather to affirm that "John lived, and his life was important to those who knew and loved him." → GRIEF

† † †

GAMBLING. For some people, gambling is nothing more than a pleasant pastime. But for some 8 to 10 million in the United States who find gambling irresistible, it is far more.

Compulsive gambling. The compulsive gambler finds his life dominated by gambling. He wants to win money, and is excited by the pleasure/pain tensions gambling generates. Such gamblers are likely to see their marriages deteriorate, their friends suffer, their careers cut short. Looking ahead to the killing they are sure will come, they ignore the evidence and rush to take even greater risks. They have joined the society of losers.

Why do people gamble compulsively? Talk to the gamblers, and they'll say it's for the fun, or to make money. Talk to psychologists and they will suggest it's more likely a ritualistic response to anxiety (the person feels powerful and admired while gambling), or perhaps that the person wants to lose, because he feels he must punish himself for past sins.

How do we recognize compulsive gamblers? According to Gamblers Anonymous, compulsive gamblers will say yes to at least seven of these questions:

1. Do you lose time from work due to gambling?
2. Is gambling making your home life unhappy?
3. Is gambling affecting your reputation?
4. Have you ever felt remorse after gambling?
5. Do you ever gamble to get money to pay debts or solve financial difficulties?
6. Does gambling decrease your ambition or efficiency?
7. After losing do you feel you must return as soon as possible to win back your losses?
8. After a win do you have a strong urge to return and win more?
9. Do you often gamble until your last dollar is gone?
10. Do you ever borrow to finance your gambling?
11. Have you ever sold any real or personal property to finance gambling?
12. Are you reluctant to use "gambling money" for normal expenses?
13. Do you ever gamble longer than you planned?
14. Do you ever gamble to escape worry or trouble?
15. Have you ever considered committing an illegal act to finance gambling?

16. Does gambling cause you to have difficulty sleeping?
17. Do arguments, disappointments, or frustration create an urge to gamble?
18. Do you have an urge to celebrate any good fortune by a few hours of gambling?

Compulsive gambling is difficult to cure, because the causes seem deep seated. Few even of those who say they want to stop will actually try to get help. But Gamblers Anonymous, established in 1957, uses the same group-support techniques used by Alcoholics Anonymous to help those who do want to change.

Casual gambling. The destructive impact of compulsive gambling, and its tragic impact on others, makes it clear that such gambling is sin as well as foolishness. But what about casual gambling: gambling done just for fun, or engaged in infrequently in the hope of meeting some pressing financial need? After all, playing cards for pennies may be a pastime to some, and actually cost less than the hobbies of those who condemn even light gambling.

Whatever our conclusion on gambling as entertainment, we can have serious reservations on gambling in hopes of winning big money. State lottery records, though, show that gambling take increases dramatically in economic hard times. Apparently many casual gamblers are pressured by need to risk some of the few dollars they have in hopes of a big money win. Some Christians might even argue that such gambling can be an act of faith; a way of trusting God to meet a money need in a direct, unusual way. After all, doesn't Proverbs 16:33 teach that "The lot is cast into the lap, but its every decision is from the LORD"?

If we approach gambling from a simply naturalistic viewpoint, using statistics to figure the laws of chance, the odds almost guarantee we will lose. Gambling in the hope of winning money is not rational behavior: it is a dangerous neurosis.

If we approach gambling from a supernaturalistic

viewpoint, we have grounds for disregarding the odds. If God chooses, He can see that we get the winning ticket. But any person who does approach gambling from this viewpoint must realize that God can provide an intended win through just one lottery ticket. There's no need to spend $25 or $30 a month on tickets. If gambling is an act of trust, it's far better to invest $1 in the lottery, and give the other $29 to missions. The Lord can meet your need with the $1 just as well as with the $30. It should be understood, though, that God doesn't usually use such means to meet the needs of His children.

What it boils down to is that anything beyond social gambling, in which the money is not an issue, involves self-deceit. Gambling is not a realistic way to seek money. As to self-deceit, it might be wise to apply Romans 3:11, 12. "The hour has come for you to wake up from your slumber, because our salvation is nearer now than when we first believed. The night is nearly over; the day is almost here. So let us put aside the deeds of darkness and put on the armor of light."

GARBAGE.   What does the Scripture consider garbage? Ready for a surprise? It's religion without Christ. Talking about the legalistic righteousness he earned in his youth through strict religious observance, Paul sums his religion practices up this way: "I consider them rubbish, that I may gain Christ and be found in him, not having a righteousness of my own that comes from the law, but that which is through faith in Christ—the righteousness that comes from God and is by faith" (Phil. 3:8, 9).

GARDENING.   Francis Bacon said it: "God Almighty first Planted a Garden. And indeed, it is the Greatest Refreshment to the Spirit of Man; without which Buildings and Palaces are but Grosse Handyworks." Not only is Bacon right, but gardening is actually the oldest profession (Gen. 2:15). Humanity's earliest experience of the joy in sharing God's good work of creating beauty was found in gardening.

GENEROSITY. "Good will come to him who is generous and lends freely" (Ps. 112:5). → **FAIRNESS**

GET. "Get wisdom, discipline and understanding" (Prov. 23:23).

GIVING. "Bring the tithes into the storehouse," the pastor used to tell us, quoting the Old Testament. He firmly believed that 10% should go to the local church, and then whatever else you wanted to give to missions. That 10% (off the top, before deductions) we *owed* God. Everything else was "giving."

Many of us have questions about giving. Is the tithe binding on us today? Where should our money go when we give? Are contributions to the United Way Christian "giving"? How do we go about determining what we give and where to give it? Actually, considering how many questions we have, the Bible is surprisingly clear.

The Old Testament pattern. The Old Testament Law established a complex social system for Israel, with many opportunities for giving. There was an annual tithe: 10% of income or produce given to the Lord. This went to the support of priests and Levites, who were to serve the community by serving God. The tithe was to support those who would give full time to ministry.

There were also sacrifices. Part of these animal and grain offerings was burned, part was given to the priests, and part eaten by the offerer. A few were prescribed for special occasions, and others offered as confession of private sins or expressions of praise.

Later in history contributions were collected for building, repair, and upkeep of the Jerusalem temple. By Jesus' day an annual "temple tax" was collected from all.

Another vital element in Old Testament giving is represented in what the Gospels call "almsgiving." Israelites were encouraged to give generously to the poor, as a religious act especially pleasing to God. After all, the Old Testament affirms that "he who is kind to the poor lends to the LORD, and he will reward him for what he has done'' (Prov. 19:17).

Working through the lifestyle laid out in the Law, some scholars are convinced that the Old Testament pattern of giving called for the contribution of some 30% of income rather than 10%!

But it's important to note two things. In that original design no taxes were paid to a central government. This only came later, with the institution of the monarchy. Still, it was never considered to be the role of government to assure the welfare of the poor.

We should also note that no generation, and few individuals proved to be as generous as God invited them to be!

The New Testament pattern.   There are a number of radical differences shown in the New Testament. The early church had no temple to support, and no special class of priests were cared for by a tithe. Giving, and the determination of how much to give, was left up to the individual: the idea of "owe to God" is foreign to the New Testament.

At the same time it is clear there was much and generous giving in the early church. Those who gave themselves to full-time ministry were deserving of support. → CLERGY PAY Wherever famine or need existed, the brothers and sisters in the family of God were urged to share freely. In fact, the guiding principles that replace the tithe system of the Old Testament are clearly expressed in 2 Corinthians 8 and 9.

(1) Giving is a response to need (8:13–15). Individuals (cf. James 2:15, 16) and communities suffering disaster and thus "hard pressed" are to be relieved, "that there might be equality." This is not a principle of income-leveling, but is measured by need (v. 14). God's goal is that the basic needs of human beings might be met, so they can survive and share God's grace with others.

(2) Giving is rooted in relationship with God (8:1–9; 9:12–15). Christ Himself provides the model: He excelled in giving for He gave Himself. In response we give our-

selves to Him. Knowing that we are His, we follow His example and share what we have to supply the needs of His other children, leading to an overflow of praise to the Lord—and prayers offered for the givers.

(3) Giving is an expression of trust in God (9:6–11). When we realize that God will supply all our needs, we are freed to give generously, becoming His channels of blessing to others.

(4) Giving is to be a free and spontaneous act of love (8:8, 9; 9:6–8). God has set no minimum or maximum, and demands no specific proportion of our income. He is concerned about the freedom of our response, and seeks no grudging contributions. Cheerful giving of what we ourselves determine to share because of our love for God and others is basic in the New Testament. At the same time, God faithfully reminds us that He is able to meet our needs so we need not hold back from fear (9:7). We are also taught that any who sow sparingly will reap sparingly (9:6). We are free to do as we choose, but are also reminded that the generous will be treated generously.

(5) Giving is not to be an impulsive act (1 Cor. 16:2). Where we channel our giving is determined by need, but being prepared to give is a matter of discipline. So Paul suggests that weekly "each one . . . set aside a sum of money in keeping with his income" for contributions.

Good stewardship. Today many missions and charities as well as the local congregation compete for our contributions. However much we may set aside for giving, or how little, good stewardship demands we give wisely. The two basic questions to ask are ● Does this gift support communication of the gospel, and/or ● Does this gift effectively and compassionately meet human need— especially needs of those who believe (cf. Gal. 6:10).

Good stewardship also demands we be sure our gifts go to those for whom they are intended. Some religious as well as secular organizations have been found to spend more than 50% of contributions for fund-raising and administration, and one Catholic charity that raised some

$20,000,000 in two years spent less than 6 cents of every dollar on the work for which it was intended. An evangelical tv program was criticized for diverting funds given to missions to pay broadcasting bills. How can we tell if our money is used wisely? Check by writing to the organization, or write for information to the National Information Bureau, Inc., 419 Park Ave. S., New York, NY 10016. Find out: ● Are fund-raising and administrative costs less than 40% of public contributions? ● Are reputable fund-raising methods used? ● Is the organization controlled by an active, unsalaried board, with no paid employees as voting members? ● Is there a complete, clear, independently audited annual financial report available on request?

Blind giving, however good our motivation, is not good stewardship.

Practicing the New Testament pattern today. The theme of New Testament giving is summed up in the Greek word chosen to express it. That word is not "give," as in gift. It is "share," as in fellowship. → **FELLOWSHIP** All we are and all we have belongs to the Lord now. He does not tell us how much to give, or where to give it. He simply makes us responsible stewards, encouraging us to give as an expression of trusting love for God, and compassionate love for others.

It is also clear that New Testament giving is focused on needs—the needs of those who give their full time to ministry and the needs of brothers and sisters who require help to survive.

How do you and I practice the New Testament pattern? These guidelines might help:

● Look honestly at your own needs in comparison with the needs of others, and set aside a generous amount for giving.

● Keep informed on emerging needs, and give responsibly as God guides you.

● Exercise good stewardship, and check out the groups and individuals to whom you channel your giving.

● Where possible, good stewardship indicates giving

should be channeled through your church or another tax-exempt organization. But don't close your heart to a brother or sister in need even though you may be unable to report what you give on your tax forms.

Sharing what God has given us with others, that their needs might be met, is a ministry that is fully repaid by inner joy and a generous Lord, and not just on April 15th.

GIVING UP. "Do not throw away your confidence; it will be richly rewarded. You need to persevere so that when you have done the will of God, you will receive what he has promised" (Heb. 10:35, 36).

GOAL SETTING. Recently I received a letter from an old missionary friend, now pastoring a church in the Philippines. He shared goals they've set for the next year, and among them, 200 conversions. I like his enthusiasm. I know his commitment. But I'm bothered by his goal setting. I couldn't help thinking of James' warning to businessmen who laid plans for their next year and toted up the expected profits. "Why," James writes, "you do not even know what will happen *tomorrow!*" (4:14).

Still, everyone agrees we need to set goals. "Shoot at nothin'" the old farmer is supposed to have said, "an' you'll be sure to hit it." I know I set goals. When I have a deadline I figure out how many pages I have to write to make it, break it down to day-by-day production, and then set out to beat my own daily goals. I suspect if I didn't work this way I'd get a lot less done. But there are some differences between this process and my friend's approach.

● Set goals for level of activity, not results. I can put in disciplined effort, but I can't guarantee results. We can share the gospel with many, but how God uses our witness and how many respond isn't in our hands.

When we set result goals we intrude into the area of God's sovereignty. We can pray. But we're not able to produce results. Actually, setting result goals may create unnecessary guilt. The Bible says of servants that we must be faithful. It does not say that faithfulness guarantees success—or numbers.

278

When I set goals for myself I'm disciplining myself to faithfulness. I need to be faithful, and then trust God for results.

• Set goals as guidelines, not masters. God may surprise us and change our schedule with events we don't expect. Goals we set are to be maintained humbly. Jesus, not our goals, is Lord. (For a classic case, see Acts 8:4–8 and 8:26–29.)

• Set goals for now, not years from now. Goals are helpful in developing discipline for present tasks. They help us live a day-by-day life of obedience.

• Set goals for yourself, not others. I can and should set short-term goals to help me live responsibly. But the goals I set are for my own writing. I can't set goals for my son's painting. He is responsible to God for his life, not to me.

What I can do is to help him work on setting his own goals. Just as I may help a Sunday school teacher think through and set personal goals for visitation or lesson preparation. But I'm not to say to others, "Here are the goals I have set for you." Each believer is a servant of Jesus and is responsible to Him as Lord. Goal-setting is a very special but personal affair.

What about goal-setting then? Well (1) each of us can set goals for himself or herself which (2) bring personal discipline to present activities and (3) lead us step by step into the good future God has planned.

GOD CONCEPT. J. B. Phillips discussed this in *Your God Is Too Small.* The idea we have of God is going to have a whopping impact on our life.

See God as a Policeman, creeping along behind you, eager to catch you in a crime? You're likely to feel guilty—and do the right thing only because you feel you have to. See Him as a Nag, always after you to do things you don't want to do, and obedience will be a chore instead of a joy. And how about the Kindly Old Gentleman? He's doddering now, but so pleased when you find time to visit Him on Sunday. Of course, He's too kind to get upset at your weekday sins.

We can think of other images people have of God. There's the Accountant, always adding up columns of sins and good deeds, to determine what you owe Him. And the Force, that impersonal God of determinists, who rumbles on not even aware of those He crushes.

Actually, Phillips wasn't the first to be concerned about our God concept. The Bible has a lot to say too. For instance, Isaiah ridicules those fools who worshiped idols, never noticing the madness of cutting down a tree, using some for fuel, and then worshiping a carved god made from the rest of the wood (Isa. 44:9–20). What a contrast to the God of the Bible: ever-living Creator, Judge, Redeemer, the One who not only delivers us but who unveils the future even before things come to pass (44:6–8). It is only when we know this God that we appreciate what He can mean to you and me.

What does God want us to learn by unveiling Himself as He does in Scripture? Well, Isaiah's pictures of God as powerful (Isa. 40; 41) lets his people know that God our Helper truly is able to give "strength to the weary, and increase the power of the weak" (40:29). God's unveiling of Himself in Jesus (John 14:10) teaches us, among other things, that He is able to sympathize, so we can approach Him confidently whether it's help we need, or mercy because we've failed (Heb. 4:16). Over and over the Bible shows us a God who shatters all the false images of the Policeman, Nag, Kindly but Ineffective Gentleman, Accountant, and Impersonal Force. God is a person, rich in warmth and love, yet firm in His commitment to the righteous and the good. ·

One important reason to read the Bible is to let Scripture shape our image of God. When we know Him as forgiving, we suddenly realize that we can forgive ourselves and others, and are freed to do good out of love rather than fear. When we see God as powerful, we're released to take the risk that obedience calls for. When we discover that God has only the best in mind for us, we can read the Bible as a warm invitation to an enriching life rather than as nagging demand.

Coming to know God as He really is, stripped of our

misconceptions, is one of the most vital ways to enrich our
Christian life.

How do you build a healthy God concept? One easy
way. Whenever you read the Bible and note a passage that
unveils something about Him, put a "G" in the margin.
Keep on doing this whenever you read. Then every month
or so page through your Bible to find the "G" passages.
Read each one and meditate for a bit on God, letting the
Holy Spirit burn into your heart the magnificent qualities
of our Lord.

GOOD. For centuries now philosophers have put a
"the" in front and capitalized "g." Then they have debated how to define "the Good," and pondered how "the
Good" relates to "the Right."

Fascinating notions have been advanced. Some have
linked Good with human pleasure, and argued that the
Right must be computed. Whatever provides the most
pleasurable life for the greatest number of persons is Good
and Right. Others have insisted that Good is linked to
purpose. A "good knife" is one suited to its function. The
Good for man must be linked with the purpose for which
man exists. Others see Good as adaptation to environment, or contributing to evolution, or satisfaction of desires. But the definitions of the philosophers fall short
whenever they make the Basic Mistake and make Man the
Measure of All Things. The Christian believes that God is
the measure, not man, and that the Good like the Right can
never be known apart from Him.

Looking into the Bible we see three different Greek
words used for "good" in the New Testament, to add
shades of meaning. One term is ethical in emphasis and
evaluates good in terms of uprightness. Only God is truly
Good. But we can model our relationships and values on
Him, and thus display His character (cf. Matt. 5:43–48).
Another New Testament word invites us to see good as
beauty and nobility. When we live a balanced life, glowing with health and beauty because we are in harmony
with God and our fellow men, we are living the good life.
The third New Testament word stresses kindness and con-

cern for others. The good life is marked by caring and compassion.

Such definitions never satisfy philosophers. However, the Christian isn't called to satisfy the philosophers, but to please God. Our challenge is not to define the good life, but to live it. → ETHICS

Where do we find the best simple definition of that elusive "good" life in the Bible? Perhaps a brief passage in Philippians sums up the emphasis of all three New Testament words, and shows us where to concentrate our thoughts and our efforts. "Finally, brothers, whatever is true, whatever is noble, whatever is right, whatever is pure, whatever is lovely, whatever is admirable—if anything is excellent or praiseworthy—think about such things. Whatever you have learned or received or heard from me, or seen in me—put it into practice. And the God of peace will be with you" (Phil. 4:8, 9).

GOOD WORKS.

The concept of good works has always been troublesome. Luther was suspicious of the whole idea. He called James an "epistle of straw," worried that its emphasis on good works would cloud the truth of salvation by faith alone. In the 1920s conservatives charged that the liberals knew only a "social gospel of good works." The idea of having works without faith was infuriating to them.

We're still uneasy about the whole thing today. In fact, a study of adult values by Milton Rokeach showed that people who place high importance on salvation are much less sensitive to social issues than those who do not. But Rokeach wondered. Are the "heavenly minded" really no earthly good?

Still, we have to face it. The New Testament over and over again insists that God's people are to "devote themselves to doing what is good" (Titus 3:8).

Good works and salvation. We might be confused at times, but Scripture isn't. Good works are always linked with salvation, and the nature of that link is made extremely clear.

Good works play no part in winning salvation. Instead, salvation generates good works. "By grace you have been saved, through faith," Paul explains. And adds, "not by works, so that no one can boast." But he immediately goes on to show that, reshaped by God's gift of salvation, we are His "workmanship, created in Christ Jesus to do good works, which God prepared in advance for us to do" (Eph. 2:8–10).

When James wrote his letter, in the early days of the church, he didn't write about salvation but about the life faith would create. He contrasted real faith with a "faith" that exists as mere intellectual assent. → BELIEVING IN How do we distinguish the true faith from the superficial? Why, real faith will express itself in good works. Any other kind of "faith" is dead. When faith plants new life within, that new life struggles to grow and manifests itself in good and righteous behavior (James 2:14–26).

The consistent testimony of Scripture is this: faith brings us new life from God and new life is expressed in good works.

The nature of good works.   Many clear and simple pictures in the New Testament show us good works. We see what this phrase means as we follow Jesus about Palestine, watching as He teaches and heals. We see good works in Dorcas, a simple woman "who was always doing good and helping the poor." Her friends wept when she died, and showed "the robes and other clothing that Dorcas had made while she was still with them" (Acts 9:36, 38). We see good works in the older woman of the Epistles, "well known for her good deeds, such as bringing up children, showing hospitality, washing the feet of the saints, helping those in trouble and devoting herself to all kinds of good deeds" (1 Tim. 5:10). Over and over the emphasis is laid on a simple, caring life: "to be subject to rulers and authorities, to be obedient, to be ready to do whatever is good, to slander no one, to be peaceable and considerate, and to show true humility toward all men" (Titus 3:1, 2).

The gospel's call to Christians to a life of good works

GOOD WORKS is a call to live positive, productive, caring lives: lives that blend personal integrity with active concern for the welfare of other human beings, both within and outside the family of faith (Gal. 6:10).

Good works in doubt.   Even those who agree that good works are integral to the gospel, and who doubt that they are stressed enough in our churches, do disagree. Two particular issues seem to be in doubt.

• Some Christians believe that good works are personal and individual in nature. Others insist the call to do good is a call to social responsibility and involvement. The first group points out there is no social reform taught in the Bible. The other responds that under our government, individuals and groups are encouraged to exercise political rights.

"If you had pulled several sick and wounded individuals out of a river," a Southern Baptist friend of mine asks, "wouldn't you feel it was wise to go upstream, and see if there is some way to keep them from being hurt in the first place?" For him, caring for poor and oppressed individuals isn't enough. The call to good works means to him a call to correct whatever in the political and economic system causes the individual to be hurt.

• Some Christians believe good works must always be closely linked with evangelism. Mere benevolence is not enough. We can meet physical and social needs, but man's deepest needs are spiritual. Good works (such as a medical mission) that open the door to the preaching of the gospel are valid. Because they open the door.

Others doubt that this is Christlike compassion. They argue that we help simply because someone hurts and we care. Doing good is intrinsically valid, and need not be used as material bait to hide a spiritual hook.

How do we evaluate these two differences? On the first we agree to disagree. Some people will insist that good works are personal in nature and not social. Others will focus attention on social causes. Each of us must act on our own conviction here.

The second issue is better understood when we note

the role of witness in evangelism. → **EVANGELISM** Since good works are an expression of our relationship with God, they are also a testimony to God. Jesus said it powerfully: when men "see your good deeds" they will "praise your Father in heaven" (Matt. 5:14–16). Rather than seeing good works and evangelism as separated, or arguing that evangelism justifies good works, we need to see that good works are *both* valid in themselves as an expression of faith, and by their nature a testimony to the loving nature of the God who stimulated them.

In the long run, however, neither of these areas of disagreement touches on the central issue. The issue here is not being "right' in our view of good works. The issue is being about the business for which God has called us to Himself: doing those good works that God has "prepared in advance" for each of us to do.

GOSSIP.

James Fenimore Cooper gets the credit for observing, "Everybody says it, and what everybody says must be true." That's the danger of gossip. Small talk, with or without a known basis in fact and motivated primarily by the ego or status needs of the gossip, can hurt people. Although trivial, gossip is always derogatory. And it's personal: we don't gossip about "the neighborhood," we gossip about a specific neighbor.

The Bible doesn't have a kind word to say about gossip. It is betrayal of confidences (Prov. 11:13), it separates close friends (Prov. 16:28), and stimulates quarrels (26:22). The New Testament finds room for "gossip" in the Scripture's list of dark sins (cf. Rom. 1:29; 2 Cor. 12:20). This pastime of busybodies may focus on trivialities, but gossip isn't trivial at all.

What do we do when we suddenly find ourselves being gossiped to? Well, there are several responses we might make. We might try an honest statement, like, "You know, that sounds like gossip to me." Or a question. "Why are you telling me this, anyway?" Counterstatements often silence gossip. Ignore the nasty little barbs at George, and say "I've always found George thoughtful and friendly. I really respect him." Then there's always confrontation. "Where did you get that information? Did you actually see or hear him, or are you just repeating gossip?"

One thing though. We can't afford to look down on the gossip as though we ourselves were immune. James teaches that the problem we have in controlling our tongue is so great that "We all stumble in many ways." He adds, "If anyone is never at fault in what he says, he is a perfect man, able to keep his whole body in check" (James 3:2). Not being perfect yet, we can't afford to condemn others for a fault we're subject to ourselves.

What can we do about our own weakness? Well, let's begin by being bluntly honest with ourselves whenever we catch ourselves gossiping. It's sin, and calls for confession. Let's also build a healthy attitude toward others, and focus on the good and the positive about them. A good passage to memorize, and then meditate on, is Philippians 2:1–4. The more our attitude is like that of Christ Jesus (2:5), the less gossip will mar our lives.

GRATITUDE. Some people are absolutely sure it is more blessed to give than to receive. For them, receiving hurts.

The one person I know who feels this way most intensely has no problem with gratitude to God. The words of the psalmist ("Praise the LORD, for the LORD is good; sing praise to his name, for this is pleasant") echo warmly in her heart, and praise—always linked in Scripture with gratitude—wells up often. But if she has to receive from another person, warmth is replaced with sudden chill.

I've puzzled over her reaction for years. As nearly as I can tell, she (let's call her Nell) resents receiving because:

• It makes her feel obligated. If someone does something for her, she feels a moral obligation to do something of equal value for that person. And Nell doesn't like being obligated.

• It makes her feel inadequate. Nell has troubles with her self-image. Receiving from others intensifies her feelings of inadequacy, and shouts that she is not capable of doing for herself. Nell hates that.

• It makes her feel diminished. Somehow Nell has the impression that the giver is superior: "up" to the receiver's "down." Nell squirms and resents it intensely when receiving makes her feel inferior.

For Nell, gratitude is almost impossible. Her whole perspective on giving and receiving is distorted by painful emotions that cause resentment rather than thanksgiving.

Gratitude in perspective. Nell's problem isn't that the generosity of others "makes" her feel as she does. → EMOTIONS Actually God intends generosity to "result in thanksgiving to God." and "overflow in many expressions of thanks to God" (2 Cor. 9:11, 12). You and I are most likely to feel gratitude when we understand the foundation on which giving and receiving rest.

We believers, the Bible teaches, have been brought into a unique relationship with each other. We are linked together now as members of a living body. → CHURCH As cells in this spiritual organism we are interdependent in the same way that cells in a physical body must depend on each other. Nutriments of every type, supporting growth and health, must flow freely from cell to cell. In the spiritual body of which we are a member there are many kinds of nutriments. There are teaching, encouragement, rebuke, prayer, money, → GIVING and many other expressions of supportive love.

In the spiritual body as in a physical organism, nutrients flow from cell to cell in a constant, enriching process. Each cell is giver and receiver, and though what we have to give others will differ, within the body each of us is equal. → EQUALITY There are no superior/inferior relationships. Giving does not lift us over others, and receiving does not demean, for we are truly interdependent. Experiencing the joy of a relationship in which sharing is a constant process stimulates our gratitude to God, and our appreciation of one another.

Expressing gratitude. How do we shake off the perspective of the world, and learn to give and receive as Christians? We might begin by following Paul's example and expressing appreciation. Paul wrote to thank the Philippians for a gift they forwarded to him. He was particularly pleased, because their generosity warmed him as an expression of their love. He was glad too that their spontaneous generosity would win them a rich reward from God. It *is* more blessed to give than receive. We have the joy of expressing love, and the promise of divine reward.

You and I can overcome the old feelings by consciously and purposely learning to express gratitude. We can thank God for any gifts He gives us through others. We can write short notes of appreciation whenever someone enriches our life in any way. We can thank God too for good qualities we see in other persons. Practicing the grace of gratitude, understanding the blessings God intends for giver and receiver alike, can help us develop a thankful spirit and grow close to others in the family of God.

GRIEF. Grief is most common at the loss of a loved one. Then we can expect a number of grief-linked reactions. There may be shock, experienced as numbness or blank despair. There may be disbelief, or anger, or guilt feelings. There's likely to be weeping as an expression of sad hopelessness.

During the mourning period a person may lose interest in work and other normal activities, may experience a sense of continued presence of the lost one, or experience illness. This acute grief generally spans some two weeks, although chronic grief may last for months or years.

The Bible views grief at a loved one's death, or at other tragedy, as a normal experience. But Scripture adds that we do not "grieve like the rest of men, who have no hope" (1 Thess. 4:13). Sure that Jesus died and rose again, we know our loss is not permanent. We will meet our loved ones in the Lord when Christ returns.

Ministering to the grieving. Our society seeks to isolate us from death, and too often we feel uncomfortable with another's pain. We withdraw rather than reaching out to help, because we don't quite know how to help. Here are several simple principles for times of mourning.

● Be there. Do not intrude, but let the grieving person know you are there and that you care.

● Remain open to the loss. Don't pretend nothing has happened, or that the loss is not real. Express your own sorrow if you knew the other person well.

● Be sympathetic. Be willing to feel with, and to talk with the grieving person about his or her feelings. Expression of feelings is a vital part of working through a loss.

● Encourage reminiscing. Talking about the past relationship enjoyed with the person who has died helps to acknowledge the death, and yet affirms the vital part the deceased has in the survivor's life.

● Affirm Christian hope. Believers will take comfort in a loved one's presence with the Lord and in future reunion. There will still be grief. But the comforting truths of the gospel help bridge the initial period of intense sorrow.

Grief also brings a need to be alone, as well as need for support from warm and loving brothers and sisters. How good it is that in the family of God we can be sensitive to one another, and minister lovingly. And how good that our grief always includes the affirmation of hope.

GROWTH AND CHANGE. They're closely linked, but subtly different. "Growth" focuses our attention on internal, patterned transition. "Change" focuses our attention on external, sudden, or unexpected challenges. When a teen begins dating, or later as Mom and Dad watch a child leave home for college, great changes are involved. They do involve stress. But these are expected changes; changes made necessary by the maturing of an individual. As research abundantly indicates, it's the deluge of sudden changes—the loss of a job, moving, death of a loved one, a house burning down—that creates those stresses that threaten mental and emotional health.

Groups of people—families and congregations—are much like individuals. Change can be forced on them by external factors. Or change can come gradually, through growth. All too often a parent or a church leader attempts to stimulate growth by forcing change, never realizing that sudden, stressful change is likely to make growth more difficult. Dad shouldn't insist on Little League. And the pastor shouldn't call for everyone to divide up into small groups, to meet in homes next Sunday evening. There are better ways; ways that transform "change" to "growth."

For instance, Dad might get a whiffle ball and bat, and start spending half an hour each evening with Junior. Teach him how to hit, and give him the thrill of succeeding. Later get a mitt and ball. Bounce the ball to each other on the ground and toss it high in the air, to stimulate grounders and fly balls. Play together for a year or so, so that when it comes time for Little League the basic skills are there and the "want to" is there too.

The same approach can be taken with church change. Want small groups developed? All right, give people a taste of what is involved and let them develop skills needed to be successful in Bible study/prayer/sharing in this special setting. Offer six-week electives in "Fellowship Training." Build a retreat around small-group experiences. Try a one-month "break into groups for Bible study and prayer" midweek special. Provide such experiences for a year or so, so when it comes time to launch a small-group ministry the basic skills are there and the "want to" is there too.

What I'm suggesting is simple. That whenever changes can be predicted or are planned, make those changes as much like "growth" as possible. One key to successful change is to accept the fact that what happens inside persons is critical.

What about the sudden, unexpected changes that bring stress into the life of individuals and groups? Well, the key here seems to be quality relationships, which provide support as a buffer against stress. When a person has close, warm relationships with others and feels that he or she belongs, it's easier to handle sudden change—as well as easier to grow. When a person has the opportunity in the context of supportive relationships to talk through his or her feelings and experiences—especially with others who share similar experience—it's easier to transform "change" into "growth."

Two things, then, help us with growth and change. (1) When we deal with planned change, we need to design a gradual process that gives opportunities for inner growth. And (2) we always need those close personal relationships, so essential for support in any time of stress.

GUILT AND GUILT FEELINGS.

Modern psychology focuses on guilt feelings. The Bible focuses on guilt.

There's good reason, of course. Psychology sees the feelings as mankind's problem, while the Bible sees the problem as sin. While the viewpoints are radically different, each recognizes "guilt" as one of the most persistent and destructive of modern problems.

How do psychological and theological understandings differ? And how does each attempt to deal with guilt?

Nature and origin of guilt. • Psychology views guilt as a subjective phenomenon, and is concerned with the experiences of human beings with guilt feelings. The psychological questions are: "Where do these feelings come from?" "What impact do they have on individuals?" and "How do we handle the feelings to enable better personal adjustment?"

The answers suggested are relatively easy to understand. The feelings come from Mom and Dad and others, who praise us when we're little for doing what they say is good, and who punish or condemn us for doing what they say is bad. These early experiences are internalized, so that our conscience keeps on praising and condemning even after we've grown up. Guilt feelings come when we condemn ourselves for violating some socially determined standard of right and wrong. Thus someone has said that "upbringing is a cultivation of the sense of guilt."

The impact of guilt feelings is varied and complex. There may be an intense sense of shame or worthlessness linked with some specific act. There may be a general sense of anxiety, which cannot be tied to any specific failure and yet dominates the individual. There may be self-punishing behavior, an attempt to rid the self of the sense of guilt. None of these reactions—or the throwing off of all restraints to indulge in greater violations of standards—promises "healthy adjustment." Each thus needs treatment.

The psychological approach to treating guilt feelings is focused on the experience and the adjustment of the individual to life in this world. Few psychological theories attempt to deal with culpability. Some even treat the symptoms by suggesting that an individual see his past actions as "determined" by social conditions, by parents' actions, etc. The individual is thus taught to deny responsibility for past actions, and to deny personal guilt. → **DETERMINISM**

● Theology sees guilt as an objective reality, and is concerned with acts of sin that incur real guilt. The theological questions are: "Where does guilt come from?" "What impact does guilt have on the individual?" and "How do we deal with guilt?"

Here too the answers are relatively easy to state. Guilt comes from the fact that we as responsible beings choose to do wrong. We merit punishment which God, in our morally ordered universe, is obligated to impose.

Guilt feelings are a gracious witness provided by God to the fact of our culpability. Social processes may help explain the content of one's conscience. → **CONSCIENCE** But the fact that an inner moral sensitivity exists is a testimony to God's goodness, and to the fact of sin.

Theology is concerned with more than healthy adjustment in this world. Theology affirms that human beings are destined for endless existence, and that guilt alienates us from God in our todays as well as our forever. Thus the destructive impact of guilt on humanity has eternal consequences, and the root problem must be resolved.

Only if guilt is gone, and harmony between God and man restored, can an individual find truly significant answers to either the objective or subjective problems raised by guilt.

Forgiveness. God's solution to guilt and guilt feelings is found in forgiveness, for it is by forgiveness He deals with sin, the source of both. When God forgives sin He removes the objective root of guilt, and lays a basis for the cleansing of our conscience. Hebrews 8 and 10 deal extensively with this great and wonderful revelation.

● Objectively, then, Jesus' self-sacrificial death was payment of the required penalty of sin. With sin paid for, neither sin nor guilt remain. "We have been made holy through the sacrifice of the body of Jesus Christ once for all" (10:10).

This forgiveness is costly, however, in two ways. For God there was the cost of His own Son. For us there is the humbling cost of admitting ourselves to be lost, guilty, and helpless. We surrender every pretense of self-reliance, to rely only on the promised salvation won for us by God.

Once we come to this point and trust ourselves to God, the objective issue is settled. We are declared guiltless by God Himself, for "by one sacrifice he has made perfect forever those who are being made holy" (10:14).

● Subjectively, it may take longer for us to experience the freeing power of forgiveness. Christ's work however does "cleanse our consciences from acts that lead to death, so that we may serve the living God" (9:14). As we are released from the heavy weight of our past, we grow into a renewed experience of life.

The subjective change in attitude from tormented guilt or nervous anxiety is likely to come slowly. Few transformations are immediate. So we need to be careful not to mistake those feelings of guilt that may persist after conversion for real guilt. In fact, there are several steps a person can take to help him or her experience subjective release from guilt's dominion.

● Accept personal responsibility for past wrong acts. Also accept by faith the forgiveness given you by God.

● Study and memorize passages of Scripture that testify to God's forgiveness. Build an inner confidence in

293

what God has promised and done for you. → **FORGETTING**

• Recognize that the new life that salvation brings is to be a holy one, which impels repentance. Consciously turn away from the sins of the past that brought you guilt. Choose new ways that express your willingness to serve God and live His way. → **REPENTANCE**

• Build close relationships with other Christians who give and receive forgiveness and who "spur one another on toward love and good deeds" (10:24). Identifying with the people of God, and experiencing their acceptance, can help you sense God's acceptance and love and make forgiveness more real to you. → **CHURCH**

GUN CONTROL *Life* magazine couldn't resist the pun. A 1982 issue billed gun control as a "controversy that has both sides up in arms." Those for and against federal control of handguns are fiercely, emotionally partisan. Each side feels it has compelling reasons.

The case against control. Opponents of handgun control laws believe that citizens must have the right to own guns for two reasons: protection against criminals and protection against government. The first danger is real and present. "During the frequent periods that I am away from home," one husband writes, "I don't worry about my family, for my wife has a gun that she could use as well, if not better, than I could; and more important than knowing how to use it, she knows when and under what circumstances to use it." Many individuals feel threatened in what they view as an increasingly lawless society. Criminals own guns, so owning a gun and knowing how to use it provides some sense of security.

The second reason is distant and theoretical, but with historical precedent. Nazi Germany and South American rightest regimes have both denied weapons to citizens, and used armed police to brutalize. The possession of weapons by an armed citizenry committed to individual freedom is seen as a guarantee against totalitarianism here.

The case for control. Those who argue for federal

control of handguns view the opposing arguments as slightly foolish. Far more lives are lost by accidental shootings in the home than are saved. Rigorous control of handguns would certainly reduce the nearly 11,000 handgun deaths that occur in the United States each year. If a person is really concerned with security, it's better to have no guns in reach of children or careless adults.

As for the political argument, the proponents of gun-control laws point out that only handguns are at issue: no one is suggesting a law against the hundreds of thousands of rifles and shotguns that sportsmen possess. Handguns, not all guns, must be controlled.

The arguments. Claims and counterclaims abound from both sides. Good presentations that marshal carefully considered evidence can be found in *Restricting Handguns: The Liberal Skeptics Speak Out,* Don B. Kates, Jr. (Croton-on-Hudson, New York: North River Press, Inc., 1979) and *Guns Don't Die—People Do,* Pete Shields (New York: Arbor House, 1981). Some key arguments:

• The constitutional issue. Does the second amendment protect the individual against federal laws that might ban handguns? The strong case made by each side will have to be settled in the courts.

• The violent crime issue. Do handgun laws reduce violent crime? Apparently not. Handgun-banning states have equivalent or higher levels of violent crime than handgun-allowing states.

• The murder issue. Does the availability of handguns increase the murder rate? Or is it really true that where there is motive and intention, the weapon used makes little difference? On the one hand there seems no doubt that the availability of a handgun makes sudden passionate killing more likely. Possibly without guns being there, some shootings would end up as fist fights. Still, comparative cross-cultural statistics suggest that gun control laws are not effective in cutting the homicide rate—not as effective at least as a high clearance rate (quick identification and arrest) and high level of punishment of murderers.

No argument. In some areas there is agreement between the proponents and opponents of gun control. Both tend to argue for immediate, consistent punishment for use of a gun in any crime, with mandatory prison sentences desirable. There is also no argument with the fact that possession of guns all too often leads to accidental killings. Opponents of gun controls feel the individual must accept responsibility for learning how to use a gun safely and keep it out of the hands of children. Proponents feel that such risks are unacceptable, and that it may well be the responsibility of the government to protect individuals against themselves.

Conclusions. Looking at the arguments we're likely to feel confused. Looking at individual tragedies—and especially at the thousands of accidental deaths by shooting that snuff out the lives of innocents, we're likely to urge any steps that offer relief. But today there are some 20,000 different state and local laws, as well as a federal law, which do govern handguns! Can another law really resolve the problem, or deal with the 50 to 60 *million* handguns already in the United States?

For Christians there are other questions not touched on in the pros and cons that dominate the debate. Is it right for a Christian to protect property by means that threaten another's life? Some among us would ask if it is ever right to take a life, even if our own is threatened. → **PACIFISM** → **CAPITAL PUNISHMENT** If someone forced his way into our home, wouldn't it even be safest to simply give him whatever goods and money we have? After all, how can the value of a life be measured against the value of things? So even if we had a legal right to possess and use arms for self-defense, would we have a moral right to?

Some insist Yes. The Christian must resist evil.

Others hesitate.

Most of us will never have that decision to make. Yet, if we live in a high-crime area, and our family is threatened, and neighbors have experienced break-ins, and some have even been murdered . . . then that moral issue must be faced. And a decision made. Prayerfully.

With an honest appraisal of the dangers of owning a gun.
And the dangers of going without.

HABITS.
Have you ever noticed? We almost always add the word "bad" when we talk about habits. Even the New Testament, which only mentions habits twice, speaks of "getting into" habits that are far from commendable. When we look at Daniel's practice of getting down on his knees three times a day to pray (Dan. 6:10), there's no hint this regular action of his was a "habit." Even though he kept the practice up not just for months or years, but decades. What is it that makes "idle talk" (1 Tim. 5:13) a bad habit, but consistent prayer something else?

One difference may lie in the fact that a habit is generally thought of as a more or less automatic response to a situation. It's something you do without thinking. Maybe your habit is taking a second piece of pie with supper. Or an extra spoonful of sugar with your coffee. Maybe it's turning on the TV to watch "Nightline" before going to bed. Or your habit may be gossiping about others when you sit down to lunch with friends. Or honking your horn when other drivers annoy you. The common factor in all these illustrations is that a given situation (having coffee, getting ready for bed, etc.) keys a behavior you do without thinking. Almost always those automatic responses we label habits are bad for us: perhaps not as an isolated act, but harmful when they become a regular pattern.

In contrast, good habits (like prayer, or speaking well of others, or eating nonfattening foods) usually call for self-discipline. We have to consciously work at keeping up the good practices; the bad habits call for no effort at all.

It's because habits are usually thought of as bad that we're much more interested in breaking them than developing them. So how are bad habits broken? There seem to be two basic approaches.

• The modern approach calls for identifying situations that trigger the automatic responses. If pie on the table leads you to reach for a second piece, make sure the pie is cut and put on the plate in the kitchen. Only small, single helpings should be brought to the table. If gossip always starts at lunch, try eating alone. By avoiding situations that stimulate a habitual response, we may break the habit with a minimum of pain.

• The older approach calls for facing the issue head on and exercising will power. We look at the situation and understand the real nature of the habit. That extra piece of pie repeated daily means ten added pounds this year, with increased danger of heart attack. We formulate a clear picture of the ideal: we picture ourselves pushing back from the table, losing weight, and getting into those slacks that hang, useless, in the closet. Desiring to realize the ideal, we change our response by serious and persistent practice. The pie is still sitting on the table. But we refuse to reach for that second piece.

I have a notion some of us will be attracted to the second approach. Brave confrontation, and reliance on will power, seem a little more macho. Actually though, when it comes to bad habits, it seems wise to follow Paul's advice to Timothy. "Flee the evil desires of youth," Paul warned, and "don't have anything to do with foolish and stupid arguments" (2 Tim. 2:22, 23). Avoiding situations in which habit or emotions stimulate an automatic response may be the better part of wisdom. → DECISION MAKING

HANDICAPS. A good estimate suggests some 20 million working-age Americans are "handicapped." Not all handicaps are as serious as blindness or deafness, but more than half the working-age disabled who could work have no jobs.

Prejudice and progress. Things were worse in the past. Yet many stereotypes about disabled persons persist. Minor disabilities are relatively acceptable to the general population and to employers. Partial vision, or partial hearing loss, or even speech impediments and heart con-

ditions are hardly noticed. People feel less comfortable
with amputees, the deaf, or the blind. The least acceptable
to the average person are those with a mental illness and
those with cerebral palsy or paralysis.

Handicapped persons must also cope with paternalism, especially from those in helping professions. In
our culture persons who are ill are treated much like children. They are given little freedom of choice or respect
until they get well. But many handicapped will never "get
well." So those in the helping professions tend to treat
them as "helpless" rather than as responsible individuals.

Despite such inequities, progress is being made.
Laws concerning discrimination against the handicapped
have been passed. And well-publicized studies have
shown that handicapped persons make superior employees. They lose less time due to absence, have equal
productivity, and are less likely to quit or be fired than
nondisabled co-workers.

Mainstreaming (placing handicapped young persons
with other children in school) and other government efforts are designed to reduce discrimination and "nor-
malize" the experience of the disabled. Strong government efforts have focused on reducing architectural and
transportation barriers to mobility of the handicapped. Organizations of handicapped persons have been formed to
lobby for various rights.

Living with handicaps.   Some of us live with our own
handicaps. Others have handicapped loved ones. My 22-
year-old daughter was brain-damaged at birth and will
spend her life in a sheltered community, functioning about
the level of a five- or six-year old. How do we cope with
handicaps?

• Living with the handicapped should begin with rejection of any image we may have of them as "ill" or as
"patients." Each human being lives with limitations. For
the handicapped the limitations may be more obvious or
severe. But each of us, including the handicapped, can
find significance, living to the full within our limitations.
Our daughter, Joy, was encouraged to do everything she

could for herself, and we were excited with her at each new accomplishment. The home/school where she now lives is committed to the principle that each resident be encouraged to use his or her full potential.

It's particularly important to avoid paternalism—that demeaning compulsion to "do for" others. Every individual needs the sense of mastery and achievement that comes only with personal control of his or her own life, as far as that control is possible.

We want to be particularly careful to recognize this in the church, God's larger family. The handicapped among us have spiritual gifts. They need to discover and then use those gifts to enrich others. Other members of the local body must learn to receive as well as to give in their relationship with the disabled.

If you or I are an employer, we need to guard against any tendency to discriminate against the handicapped. It may be that an affirmative action approach to hiring the handicapped can be a vital ministry to individuals as well as of benefit to the employer.

• Being handicapped brings special problems. Some are linked directly to limitations imposed by the specific disability. Others are linked with attitude: attitude toward ourselves, and sensitivity to the attitude of others toward us. What can a handicapped person do? Here are several suggestions:

1. Determine to do as much for yourself as possible.

2. Read stories of how other disabled persons (such as Joni) cope.

3. Evaluate your assets, and determine if you have marketable skills to develop. Training may be available at community or other colleges, and government funds available to assist in your training.

4. Prepare a resume to send to possible employers, asking for a job interview. Stress your positive attitude and skills you have that will make a contribution to an employer. You should be aware that federal agencies and contractors are prohibited by the Rehabilitation Act of 1973 from discriminating against otherwise qualified handicapped persons in hiring.

5. Seek supportive relationships with other Christians with whom you can pray as you seek to cope. Recognize that you have much to offer to others as well, and seek to develop sensitivity to their needs and problems.

6. Write to the Christian League for the Handicapped (PO Box 98, Walworth, Wisconsin 53164) for information on fellowship and the possibility of a local chapter in your area.

7. Keep constantly aware that God loves and is with you. You are important to Him.

Biblical insights. It is perhaps hard to realize, but one of the most significant persons in history suffered a handicap—the apostle Paul. We read of it in 2 Corinthians 12:7–10. Other hints in Scripture have led scholars to believe Paul suffered from a disfiguring eye disease, which affected his ability to read and, in his later years, forced him to sign epistles written by a secretary in large, scrawling letters (Gal. 6:11). Despite this handicap, Paul's love and commitment won him many friends and made him an effective minister of the gospel. Corinthians tells us that he came to appreciate his handicap, realizing that his weakness gave him a unique opportunity to experience the power of Christ in his life (2 Cor. 12:9).

It is strange for us to think of a handicap as a God-given opportunity to experience His power. But the Bible often tells of believers who are treated "unfairly" in this world and know unusual suffering. → SUFFERING No such experience is pleasant. But God reassures us. Living under difficulty in a godly way has great value. It is honoring to Him and merits rich reward (cf. 1 Peter 2:13–25).

HAPPINESS. Happiness is an illusive thing. People can tell you when they're happy. But no one has come up with a good definition of what happiness is. Researchers have tried. What have they found? Happiness is *not* sexual satisfaction, a stressless childhood, education, occupation, a person's religious affiliation, or even whether or not an individual is handicapped. While most people in several studies felt money has a lot to do with happiness, the affluent report about the same levels of satisfaction and frustration with life as the rest of us. Even age seems to have little impact. The young claim to want happiness more than other groups. But young (18–25), middle (40–55) and older (65–79) adults express about the same degree of happiness achieved.

After surveying some 52,000 readers from 15 to 95, *Psychology Today* concluded that "happiness turns out to be more a matter of how you regard your circumstances than of what the circumstances are." Four attitudes were suggested as essential to happiness: ● a sense of emotional security, ● a lack of cynicism, ● the belief that life has meaning, and ● a sense of personal responsibility for and control of events.

The Bible pays less attention to happiness than we do. Perhaps that is because our common notion of "happiness" tends to focus our attention outward, looking for the things or the circumstances that will "make" us happy. In contrast Scripture focuses our attention elsewhere as, for instance, in the Beatitudes. You remember the Beatitudes. They are those brief "blessed are" statements in Matthew 5:1–12, that some versions actually translate "happy are." They proclaim the stunning news that the blessed (the "happy") are really the poor in spirit, the meek, those who mourn, and those who are "persecuted because of righteousness." Hardly things most people seek to make them happy!

Why then are these persons "blessed"? In part because the future is more important to them than their present, for they know that one day they will experience God's richest blessing. But they are fortunate even now— blessed, and even happy—because in a world searching vainly for "happiness," they are anchored in personal commitment to those values that give life meaning.

Secure in their commitment to God, and foolishly believing that goodness carries its own reward, the people described in the Beatitudes have discovered God's way to look at circumstances. Their happiness can come from deep within.

HATRED AND HOSTILITY. Where do they come from, these angry passions? There are different theories. One suggests that hostility is a disease, a carry-over from man's animal origins and an early "fight" reaction once necessary for survival. Others argue that hatred emerges from weakness: we are hostile to those we feel threaten us. Scripture seems to locate the roots of hostility in alienation. When humanity turned its back on God, He came to be feared as someone "other." That same fear spills over into our relationships with persons we see as "other."

Paul in his letter to Titus is sure that believers will be familiar with hostility. "At one time we too were foolish, disobedient, deceived and enslaved by all kinds of passions and pleasures," he reminds them. "We lived in malice and envy, being hated and hating one another" (3:3).

But the tangled web of hatred has been brushed away for these believers: "at one time" they knew fear and malice, but not now! What changed them? Paul goes on to recall that "the kindness and love of God our Savior appeared" (3:4). Through Christ we discovered God is not an "other" whom we have to fear. Jesus took on humanity and died to redeem us. His death made possible our own rebirth and renewal (3:5). Now new life within brings release from the fears that made us react with hostility, and enables us to devote ourselves to good (3:8).

What is the passage saying? That hostility comes from spiritual alienation, and that Jesus has acted to bring us back into harmony with God. We even have a new outlook on other people. Because of Jesus, we no longer see them as threats. Instead we recognize them as merely foolish and disobedient—blind and lost—as we were before we came to know Jesus. Rather than viewing them with fear, we can look on them as Jesus does, with love, and know that they too can be redeemed by "the kindness and love of God our Savior."

When we learn to see others as God sees them, hostility disappears. And we begin to love. → ENEMIES

HEAD OF THE HOUSE. Use that phrase these days, and you'd better duck! To some it's a red flag, and creates instant hostility. For others the phrase is almost sacred; a call for return to moral order in a society gone awry. Those who don't feel strongly are usually just uncomfortable. Does "head of the house" imply male superiority? And female inferiority? We don't like that. How does a man fulfill that head of the house role? We're not sure. And what does it mean for a woman to live in "subjection" to the husband? We just don't know.

Unfortunately, few of us realize that the confusion comes when we misinterpret what the Bible teaches, and impose a secular interpretation on biblical terms.

"Headship" in society. In our society, to be "head" of something implies a position of authority, and a right to control. Speak of headship, and we visualize a hierarchy: a business headed by a president, or an army regiment headed by a general. We sometimes think of churches this way, as congregations "headed" by a pastor or board.

This is certainly the way the Old Testament uses the term. In Hebrew, the top of a mountain is its "head." Military commanders and other leaders are spoken of as heads. And Moses organized the people of Israel into a classic hierarchy with himself—God's chosen leader—at the top (cf. Exod. 18). When both our culture and the Bible portray the head of an enterprise as the decision-making leader, it's not surprising that the phrase "head of the house" conjures up pictures of Dad making the big decisions, while Mom and the kids humbly follow orders.

The whole image is repugnant to many women today, who feel intensely that they have been discriminated against as persons. → FEMINISM Many Christian men draw back from what they too view as a paternalistic relationship with their wives. But doesn't the Bible teach that the husband is the head of the house?

"Headship" in the New Testament. When we move into the New Testament we see a radical departure from the cultural and Old Testament pattern. In the New Testament no human leaders are ever given that "head" title in the church. Instead, a new pattern of relationships and responsibilities are outlined.

The New Testament pattern is based on the fact that the church is the body of Christ—a living organism—with Jesus Christ Himself as the living Head of this body (Eph. 1:19-23). No complex organism has multiple heads: it would be a monster. So it is with the body of Christ. There is only one Head, Jesus Himself.

This calls for a new relationship between members of the body, and rules out hierarchy. Jesus stressed this new relationship several times, as in Matthew 23:8-11.

"You are not to be called 'Rabbi,'" Jesus told His closest followers, "for you have only one Master and you are all brothers. And do not call anyone on earth 'father,' for you have one Father, and he is in heaven. Nor are you to be called 'teacher,' for you have one Teacher, the Christ. The greatest among you will be your servant" (cf. Matt. 20:24-28). The Old Testament's hierarchical pattern is replaced by equality as family. Even leaders are viewed as servants; not "over" but "among" the other people of God. → LEADERSHIP

It seems strange that in the family the old pattern of relationships would be maintained, when in the congregation a new and exciting equality is taught, under the guidance of Jesus Himself.

Ephesians 5:27-33: the husband as head. The one New Testament passage that suggests that one person has a "headship" role in any interpersonal relationship is found in Ephesians. There Paul draws an analogy: "the husband is the head of the wife as Christ is head of the church, his body, of which he is the Savior" (5:23). We need to be sure to recognize this as an analogy.

For instance, to say of a boxer, "He's a tiger in the ring," does not imply he has stripes, four legs, and a tail. It's clear we mean to limit the analogy, and focus on his ferocity. All analogies have limits. To understand an analogy we need to know just what the limits are, and what the analogy is intended to focus our attention on.

Paul clearly limits and focuses this analogy, linking a husband's headship to Jesus' ministry of "saving" the church. Husbands are to love their wives "just as Christ loved the church and gave himself up for her" (v. 25). The purpose of the self-giving is specified: "to present her to himself as a radiant church, without stain or wrinkle or any other blemish, but holy and blameless" (v. 27). It is "in this same way" that husbands are to love and treat their wives (v. 28).

What the passage teaches is that husbands are to model their relationship with their wives not on Jesus' control of the church, but on His self-giving. Being "head of the house" does not mean being boss. Instead it means having Jesus' kind of selfless concern that a wife reach her full potential as a Christian person. Headship is not the granting of a right to command, but a call to concerned and sensitive love.

What about decision making? Misunderstanding of Paul's teaching on headship has done great harm to families. It has supported the fiction that women are somehow inferior, or are unimportant as persons. It has led to the notion that husbands must make all important decisions, while wives meekly "submit." → SUBMISSIVE-NESS It has taken one element of the curse that sin brought on humanity ["he (the husband) will rule over you (the wife)"], and exalted that curse to the place of God's own command (Gen. 3:16). It also ignores the fact that in Christ we are restored now to relationships in which each person is important, with Jesus only the controlling Head.

Rejecting the common idea of "head of the house" for a biblical one raises a basic question. "How then are family decisions to be made?" The answer is found in understanding that Christian decision-making is not to be a question of "who wins." Christian decision-making is not a question of "Do we do what *she* wants or what *I* want?" It is instead a matter of discovering God's will. The question Christians are to ask, for themselves, for families, and for churches, is: "What does *Jesus* want us to do?"

If a husband and wife build their relationship on the

pattern laid down in Ephesians 5, the discovery of God's will becomes excitingly possible. Because the husband loves as Jesus loves, he takes the lead in seeking to understand his wife's needs and thoughts and feelings. Because she responds to his love, she has the same care about his needs and thoughts and feelings. When both truly care, and understand, and pray together to seek God's will, very few decisions they face will not be made together. →
KNOWING GOD'S WILL

HEALTH. Today people are talking about health as "wholeness." For them it's not enough not to be sick. Health is understood as mental and physical well-being; a positive capacity to find enjoyment in the experiences of daily life. What are the major enemies of this kind of health? Not microbes or viruses. Anxiety and boredom are seen as "the twin roots of so many of our health problems" for they "make many people's lives so joyless that they wonder whether anything is worthwhile."

How do we find health? Most answers draw attention to an individual's attitude as he or she deals with reality. You cannot find health and wholeness running away from reality. And you can't find them when your outlook is shadowed by anxiety and fears.

This outlook on health is in close harmony with Scripture. The Bible too sees health in a wholistic way, as positive well-being. But Scripture adds much to our ability to diagnose. There are spiritual as well as physical and mental issues to consider. A person in the grip of guilt has a right to feel anxious—and will never find wholeness until the underlying spiritual problem is dealt with through forgiveness. As the proponents of wholeness point out, we can never find well-being by trying to escape from reality. But when we turn to God, and experience forgiveness, anxiety can be released and wholeness becomes a possibility at last. → **ANXIETY**

The story of the Prodigal Son provides a beautiful illustration. Hurting and hungry, the boy faced the fact of his sins and humbly returned to his father, asking only that he be treated as a servant and provided with food. The father forgave him and welcomed him back rejoicing, restoring him to his place in the family. That total restoration to relationship as well as to physical health is a picture of what God has in store for us when we come to Him and let His Word shape our attitude toward the realities of our lives.

HEAVEN AND HELL. The Bible doesn't begin to satisfy our curiosity about heaven and hell. But it tells us enough to know that both are real. And it tells us enough to understand the necessity of each.

We have to begin with the realization that human life has no ending: that no individual personality can ever be snuffed out. Each of us will exist forever. That "forever" will either be spent in intimate relationship with God, or cut off from Him. In that forever we will live as transformed persons, washed from every taint of sin by Jesus, or as lost persons, still warped by the sin that infects and twists every human being born into our world. To live freed and transformed in fellowship with God is the essence of heaven. To live trapped and twisted in the grip of sin's passion is the essence of hell.

We can read the Bible's description of each and in the bold imagery sense that essence. In describing the eternal state of the saved, the Bible talks in terms of close relationships: "Now the dwelling of God is with men, and he will live with them. They will be his people, and God himself will be with them and be their God. He will wipe every tear from their eyes" (Rev. 21:3, 4). In describing the eternal state of the lost the Bible talks in terms of suffering and alienation. Jesus warns of "weeping and gnashing of teeth," and the most common description of hell is as a place of torment swirling with dark, burning flames (Rev. 19:19–20:15). Heaven and hell. One destiny or the other awaits every individual.

But the Bible's most important teaching about heaven and hell reminds us that our destiny is in our own hands. One vital insight into hell is seen in Jesus' statement that God prepared it "for the devil and his angels"—not for man (Matt. 25:41). In Jesus' death for us on the cross,

God has made it possible for any person to escape. Whoever hears and believes, the Bible says, "has eternal life and will not be condemned: he has crossed over from death to life" (John 5:24).

So we need to be clear on heaven and hell. And we need to be clear on the issues. The question is not "How could God send a person to hell?" but "How could anyone reject the love of God that provides us escape?"

Human beings are too significant to be snuffed out as though they never existed. Human beings are too loved by God for Him to permit them to pass through this life into eternity without hope. God has paid the price to open up the way of escape. We can believe, and live. We can know that, tomorrow and forever, heaven is our home.

HELPING RELATIONSHIPS.
How can you or I really help others? Studies of professional counselors have shown that the key to helping isn't found in techniques or theories, but in establishing a "helping relationship." What characterizes a helping relationship? (1) Am I trustworthy and dependable? (2) Do I express myself in an open, sharing way? (3) Do I really care about others, and communicate warmth and liking? (4) Am I secure enough to let the other person be himself or herself, even when we differ? (5) Can I accept his feelings, and him? → ACCEPTANCE (6) Can I relate to him without judging? → JUDGING

What is so fascinating about these characteristics of the helping person is that each quality describes an aspect of what the New Testament portrays as the normal lifestyle of brothers and sisters in Christ's church. In the body of Christ, each of us is a helper. And each of us is helped.

HELPLESSNESS.
Today helplessness is suggested as a basic explanation of depression. When a person comes to believe that his actions make no difference, he falls into helplessness. Like depression, a sense of helplessness leads to passivity, a loss of appetite and loss of interest in life. What's suggested as the clinical answer? Force a person to steps that reestablish a sense of mastery.

In one way a sense of helplessness is sickness. But in

the spiritual sense, it's only reasonable. Whatever limited successes we may know, we always fall short of taking real control of our lives and future. That's why Jesus reminded His disciples, "apart from me you can do nothing" (John 15:5). Like a branch cut off from the vine, without vital relationship with Jesus our life will produce nothing of lasting value.

John 15 is no call to conversion. It's written for believers, to call us to a life rich in meaning and fulfillment. The prescription Jesus gives us against an empty, meaningless life is a simple one. We are to remain close to Him. "If you obey my commands, you will remain in my love, just as I have obeyed my Father's commands and remain in his love" (15:10). The antidote to helplessness is not a struggle to regain control, but a willing surrender of control to Jesus. We are to focus on simple, daily steps of obedience.

The result? Well, these actions *do* make a difference. When we concentrate on obedience we know joy (15:11). And we "bear fruit—fruit that will last" (15:16). We discover then that we're not helpless at all!

HEREDITY. Once people blamed everything on heredity. They believed that, like red hair, madness and personality came directly from Mom or Dad. Later people blamed everything on environment, and believed that every personality trait and every choice an individual makes in life can be traced back to how a child was treated by Mom and Dad. It was convenient to blame the folks. But a person's choices are his own.

Mom and Dad may be responsible for red hair, and heredity may even be linked with a high-strung or phlegmatic personality. But Mom and Dad aren't to blame for what you and I choose to do with what we inherit. Those choices are ours. Our folks don't get the blame. Or the credit.

HIERARCHIES. Like jungle gyms in a school playground, hierarchies are fun to swing around on. You can go up them, and get the thrill of being on top. But you can tumble too, and suffer on the bottom. Because most hierarchies are like pyramids, there are always more people on the bottom than on the top. Even so, we still like to play around with them. We pretend our families are hierarchies, → **HEAD OF THE HOUSE** and we enthusiastically organize our churches into hierarchies. But we do so at our peril. Why? Well, listen to what Jesus said about the religious hierarchy in His day, about those people who loved to be "up" even when it meant others must be "down."

"But you are not to be called 'Rabbi,' for you have only one Master and you are all brothers. And do not call anyone on earth 'father,' for you have one Father, and he is in heaven. Nor are you to be called 'teacher,' for you have one Teacher, the Christ. The greatest among you will be your servant. For whoever exalts himself will be humbled, and whoever humbles himself will be exalted" (Matt. 23:8–12).

In one saying Jesus flattened this playground of the human ego, and taught us that in the family of God servanthood is greatness. The way up, is down.

HINTING.   It doesn't appear on any Bible list of deadly sins. But if you've ever been close to someone who will never come out and say what he or she wants or means—but will get very upset when you don't guess— you probably feel about hinting the way I do. I couldn't find any proof texts condemning hinting. But I did find a good example for us to follow. "We have spoken freely to you, Corinthians," Paul writes in his second letter to that congregation, "and opened wide our hearts to you" (6:11). How good it is to know people who are completely open and honest with us. And what a gift to give to others. Let's stop hiding behind hints, and treat others with an openness that builds love and respect.

HITCHHIKING.   There is all sorts of evidence that it's dangerous to pick up hitchhikers, and almost as dangerous to be a hitchhiker. So it's hard to understand why otherwise cautious adults stop to give strangers rides. The only person I knew with a good reason was a gal with

YFC, who said she picked people up because the Lord wanted her to witness to them. OK. But knowing that of 28 hitchhikers picked up along the New Jersey turnpike by an unmarked patrol one afternoon, over 80% had active criminal records, suggests we'd better be sure it is God's leading when we put on those brakes. After all. We can witness to our neighbors just as well. They'll even be around later, so we can follow through and build a winning relationship.

HOLINESS. If you want an insight into holiness, just imagine Jesus at a party. There He is now, surrounded by the outcasts of His society. Look, there's a group of tax collectors off to His right—those sharp businessmen whose wealth everyone knows comes through fraud. And say, aren't those . . . yes! Why, those are call girls, permitted in Israel (although of course publically condemned). Look at them, gathered around Jesus, drinks in hand. Listen! They're actually laughing. And look at them bend forward, listening to the gentle rabbi who attracts them so strongly.

Now look outside, at that knot of men in fringed robes standing there in the street. See, they're peering inside, and muttering angrily to each other. We can almost hear them, complaining about this upstart prophet who dares associate with the dregs of society. Look. They're hitching up their robes. Not even the dust on the street outside the home Jesus is visiting will contaminate *them*. We know who they are. They're those religious people who have such strong convictions about how to please God. Pharisees, they're called.

Looking at that scene, sketched for us in Matthew 9:9–13, we make an important discovery. There is only one holy person in that picture: Jesus. Not the tax collectors. Not the prostitutes and sinners. And not the scrupulous, religious Pharisees. The holiness we see in Jesus is far different than their contemptuous withdrawal from contact with the lost of the world. It is far different than the angry, condemning spirit with which the Pharisees widened the gap of hostility between the "good" and the "bad." What we see in Jesus is a dynamic, attractive holiness, which glows with a love and compassion that have a strange attraction for those who know their lifestyle has led them far from God.

We learn more about this peculiar holiness when we read the Book of Colossians. There in the first chapter we're confronted with the stunning image of the Creator of the universe stepping personally into a world tainted with sin. Colossians goes on in chapter 2 to warn against hollow philosophies that deceptively link holiness with ritual or with submission to ascetic rules. And we are led on, into chapters 3 and 4, to discover that true holiness means living our lives in this world clothed with "compassion, kindness, humility, gentleness and patience" (3:12).

How do we recognize a really holy person? We do not discover holiness in the religious who stand aside from life and criticize. We do not find holiness in the lists of dos and don'ts they follow, so they will never brush up against the tainted of our world. We find holiness in the person who relates lovingly to everyone in the human family, who glows with a compelling warmth that attracts even those most tangled in sin.

The secret of holiness is discovered in the wonder of Jesus' continuing incarnation. True holiness is God in our flesh, living out the beauty of His goodness, and drawing all men to Him (cf. Col. 1:24–27).

HOMOSEXUALITY.

In 1969 homosexuals began to slip out of the shadows. It was the beginning of the gay liberation movement: the demand by homosexuals that their particular sexual preference be accepted by society as an "alternative lifestyle," and that every kind of discrimination cease. Since then vocal homosexual groups have influenced legislation, become a political force in some cities and organized churches, and avowed homosexuals have demanded ordination as ministers of the gospel. Multiplied books and articles have been written, and many parents have experienced the shock of hearing a son or daughter tell them, "I'm gay." Laying out all we need to know to understand this growing societal and personal issue isn't possible in this brief article. But some of the basic facts we need to understand can be sketched.

Causes of homosexuality. In the Middle Ages homosexuality was explained by demon possession. A century ago it was viewed as a vice, calling for public condemnation and humble repentance. About seventy years ago the explanation was physical: it was thought to be caused by neurological decay, a fate fixed by heredity. A quarter of a century ago homosexuality was a glandular imbalance, and treatment involved the injection of hormones. In the sixties and early seventies it was an emotional problem, usually blamed on a dominant and overprotective mother. Today, on the basis of widespread research across cultures as well as in the United States, homosexuality is simply viewed as learned behavior. Youthful experimentation with sex is followed in our permissive, experience-oriented society by additional experiences. The pressures exerted by society lead the individual to identify himself or herself as "homosexual," and to adopt the homosexual "lifestyle."

Characteristics of homosexuals. Before 1973, when the American Psychiatric Association officially declassified homosexuality as a "disease," it was assumed that homosexuals were emotionally disturbed if not mentally ill. This resulted in part from the fact that psychiatrists who saw homosexuals saw only those who were mentally disturbed, and generalized this picture to all homosexuals. Others have suggested that, since the concept of sin is no longer fashionable, people knew no other way than sickness to label behavior of which they disapproved.

Much recent research suggests that homosexuality isn't necessarily linked with emotional maladjustment. While the argument of some gay-libbers that homosexuals are actually better adjusted than the general population can't be justified, neither can the idea that homosexuals are less "well adjusted" than the general population. Nor is it true that homosexuals eagerly proselytize others.

Homosexuals are as capable of holding a responsible job as heterosexuals, and in fact share with the heterosexuals the general values found in society.

Gay "liberation." What is it the vocal advocates of the homosexual lifestyle are agitating for? In broad, general terms it can be summed up as removal of all forms of "discrimination." Some states have laws against solicitation or homosexual acts between consenting adults. Some employers do not want to hire homosexuals. Some individuals have been discharged from the military because of their sexual preference. Many parents' groups are concerned about permitting homosexuals to teach school, or to serve in other roles (such as librarians) where they might use their position to influence others to their way of life. Of course, some homosexuals have insisted that ordination to the ministry must also be open to them, and that "marriages" between parties of the same sex be given religious and legal recognition. In essence the demand is that "straight" society surrender its prejudices, and admit that homosexuality is a socially valid and approved alternative lifestyle.

The Bible on homosexuality. The Bible speaks clearly about the meaning of sex. It is placed in the context of a life-long commitment between a man and a woman. Outside of this marital relationship, sexual activity is unhesitatingly identified as sin. Sex is sin between unmarried members of the opposite sex (adultery), and sex is sin between members of the same sex (homosexuality, or sodomy). Homosexuality is identified as a detestable perversion that defiles the individuals involved (Lev. 18:22, 23). This Old Testament condemnation is bluntly repeated in the New, where the behavior is said to come from "the sinful desires of their hearts," which lead to "sexual impurity for the degrading of their bodies with one another" (Rom. 1:24). The passage continues, describing homosexuality as "shameful lusts" and saying: "even their women exchanged natural relations for unnatural ones. In the same way the men also abandoned natural relations with women and were inflamed with lust for one another. Men committed indecent acts with other men, and received in themselves the due penalty for their perversion'' (Rom. 1:26, 27).

However we may relate to persons who are homosexuals, it is clear that homosexual acts are sin. God has identified this "alternative lifestyle" in His Word as "shameful," "unnatural," "lust," "indecent," and a "perversion." We can care for the homosexual, as for every sinner. But we can never retreat from God's evaluation of this practice or pretend that it is not sin.

Evaluating issues related to homosexuality. Accepting God's judgment of this sin as we accept His judgment of other acts as sin, how do we respond to issues currently raised in society by the vocal minority of gays who call for "liberation"? How do we deal with individuals who have been caught up in this particular pattern of sin?

First, for parents or loved ones of homosexuals who are gripped by a sense of guilt, afraid that they might have "caused" a child or spouse to turn gay: ● Recognize that homosexuality is not a sickness or mental illness. It is learned behavior, developed as individual choice is exercised in a series of sexual adventures. A 1977 survey of the San Francisco gay community showed that one half the white homosexual males interviewed had had more than 500 different sexual partners! Mom or Dad didn't "make" a child grow up gay; that pattern of life was imposed as the individual chose to surrender to lust in growing promiscuity. ● Recognize that the individual would be just as great a sinner if he or she was promiscuous with the opposite sex. In each case, the individual has surrendered to lust and is in the grip of sin—and is personally responsible for his or her actions.

Second, for society and community, let's recognize that "sin" and "illegality" are separate, though linked, issues. Not everything the Bible identifies as sin is enacted in our legal codes, or even expressed in the conscience of a community. Yet the community certainly has the right to express its moral convictions in codes of law. The same law that makes solicitation for prostitution illegal can make homosexual solicitation illegal. A community that would not hire as teachers those openly practicing promiscuous heterosexual behavior surely has a right to proscribe hiring those who admit homosexual promiscuity.

Third, Christians need to take a stand with God in naming this behavior as sin—and in reaching out in love to the individual. We want to invite every individual to come to Christ and so find cleansing from sin. As for those who insist on practicing homosexuality, we must make them feel accepted as fellow Christians in a local congregation. God's instructions for church discipline clearly apply. Any individual who confesses to what God calls sin and who struggles to find release, must be accepted and supported lovingly by brothers and sisters. Even when that individual stumbles and falls many times. But any individual who refuses to admit that homosexual behavior is sin must be lovingly disciplined by brothers and sisters who care, as we are instructed in 1 Corinthians 5 and 6.

Fourth, as for those outside the body, we are not called to judge homosexuals but to love them (1 Cor. 6:17). Instead of drawing back in horror, we need to reach out caringly, as we would to any other human being, communicating by our love the love of Jesus, who wants every sinner to come to Him to find salvation, and release.

HONESTY. Honesty isn't the best policy. It's the only policy. → **LIES**

HOPE. The object may be totally unlikely—like winning that state lottery—but hope keeps people going. In fact, many psychologists feel that having something to look forward to is what keeps individuals from drifting into despair. Even looking forward to a phone call from a friend, or fresh strawberries for breakfast, seems to give life a tinge of meaning.

The subjective value of hope is something we ought to always keep in mind. Our children find it easier to take that nap when promised, "You can take Teddy with you." One of the most powerful medicines a doctor can offer is "You'll be well enough to go home for Thanksgiving." Picking out something to look forward to tomorrow, or next week, or this summer, helps us keep a positive outlook on our life.

But "hope" means even more in the Christian's vocabulary. Our hope isn't related in any way to desperate wishful thinking. Instead "hope" spells out our confidence that God is in charge of the future. Tomorrow and eternity are filled with His good gifts, so we face life with confident expectation (cf. 2 Thess. 2:16; 1 Thess. 4:18).

Hope helps you and me maintain that positive outlook that makes our experience of life so rich and full. No, we don't "hope against hope" for some unlikely lottery win. We look forward to the sure grace and goodness of our loving God.

HOSPITALITY.   Always a valued quality in the ancient world, hospitality was especially honored in the church. Each New Testament passage giving instructions on selecting leaders insists those so recognized must be hospitable (1 Tim. 3:2; Titus 1:8). Believers are commanded to practice hospitality (Rom. 12:13; 1 Peter 4:9; 3 John 8). But when we do have people over, there's one thing we should remember. "Hospitality" doesn't just mean inviting others into our house. It means inviting them into our lives.

HOW TO.   Our "how to" orientation is the blessing and the curse of American society. Because we're so practical, we have a unique ability to get things done. We've done well enough for our nation to have the highest standard of living the world has ever known. But our "how to" outlook has another side. If we can't see the "how," we tend to reject an idea as impractical. "It won't work" is the phrase pronounced over the grave of many a good idea, and indicates our contemptuous dismissal.

This makes it particularly hard for us Christians. So many biblical concepts are strange to us. In a world of dynamic leaders it's hard to grasp what the Bible means when it speaks of servanthood. "It'll never work here," one board member says. The others nod and quickly hurry on to apply the newest practical ideas for management-by-objectives to the body of Christ. Or we discover in Scripture that nurture isn't related to schooling. "Huh," someone says, "we could never make anything like that work the way our Sunday school rooms and curriculum are laid out." Nodding agreement, the CE board hurries on to order the new equipment they hope teachers will use to impress Bible truths on young lives.

The Bible takes a different approach. God does not ask us to evaluate His truth by applying "how to" criteria. He challenges us to understand the truth He reveals; to ask "what," not "how." "What is God's approach to leadership in the body?" "What does the Bible teach about the nature of teaching and learning His Word?" And then the Scriptures become truly radical. They ask us to commit ourselves unhesitatingly to what God says is to be done—even when we don't yet understand how to do it!

God isn't worried about the how to. He's given us the Spirit to guide us, and has planted creativity in our hearts. But God undoubtedly weeps when you and I look into His Word, see what it teaches, and then turn our backs when the "how" seems difficult or obscure.

HUMANISM.

Some Christians in Texas are organizing to fight humanism in the schools, and putting up big money to do it. A number of influential believers there are convinced that creeping humanism is the chief enemy of the church.

What's humanism? Well, an author of the 1950s simply says that "Humanism is concerned with man in society." He sees humanism as a movement devoted to exploration of the values that man establishes, and the reasons for the values. "Humanism looks at the religions, the philosophies, the sciences, and the physical world and its inhabitants and tries to make use of all the aids it can find to advance the living-together of people."

The 1980s variety is a little more confrontational. As in other historical periods, humanism today focuses attention on man as the measure of all things, and "God" is

319

dismissed as outmoded superstition. "Today, one who describes himself as a humanist implies first of all that he has no faith in revealed religion." But humanists are very moral people, in active search of ethical systems without theological anchors. Ethics, they believe, can be established by a careful, scientific study of the nature of man and by generalizations about social relationships. With "God" set on the shelf to gather dust, modern humanists look enthusiastically ahead to a new world, won by the harnessed emotional vigor of those willing to build a positive moral order.

Most humanists are what we would call good people. They're unlikely to agree with every biblical perspective on right and wrong. But they do want to see caring relationships established in a just, moral society. So what's wrong with humanism?

When the rich young man came to Jesus and asked about goodness, Jesus quoted the commandments that govern relationships between human beings (Matt. 19:16–22, esp. vv. 18 and 19). "All these I have kept," the youth answered. "What do I still lack?" There was a moment's pause. Then Jesus told him. "Sell your possessions and give to the poor. Come, follow me." The Bible says the young man went away when he heard this. He was sad because he was unable to tear himself away from his great wealth to follow the word of his God.

The young man illustrates the problem of the humanist. Knowing what is good, and choosing to do it *when it costs the individual something important to him,* are two different things. The young man was good to others, for it cost him nothing. But his goodness could not change the self-centered focus of his character.

We don't need revealed religion to show us how to be good to other human beings, and to treat them fairly. Every culture and society has realized that moral behavior is important, and has made good guesses as to the content of morality. → **CONSCIENCE** But neither humanism nor "religion" can change the selfish focus of a human being's life, and free us to follow Jesus down the path to true goodness. It takes the dynamic power of Jesus Christ in our life to reshape us from within, to make that dream of an ideal world or ideal relationships even approach reality.

Is humanism a danger? Only for those who foolishly imagine that they can be good on their own.

HUMILITY. Now we know. Some 1979 researchers have shown that nearly everyone sees friends, neighbors, and co-workers as pretty inferior compared with him or her. And that nearly everyone expects greater than average rewards in pay and praise. Successes? Directly related to ability and effort. Failures? Just bad luck.

This assumption of superiority is the antithesis of humility, which is something like self-forgetfulness. The truly humble person doesn't display false modesty. Instead he or she accepts strengths with joy, and praise with appreciation, and then finds satisfaction in following Paul's advice to the Philippians: "Do nothing out of selfish ambition or vain conceit, but in humility consider others better than yourselves. Each of you should look not only to your own interests, but also to the interests of others. Your attitude should be the same as that of Christ Jesus" (Phil. 2:3–5).

HYPNOSIS. No. It's not a parlor game. Nor is it "the scientific key to mental control, the open sesame through which we reach the innermost recesses of thought." Actually, while hypnosis is used by responsible therapists, no one knows for sure just what hypnosis is or how it works. There's no way to measure objectively the nature of a hypnotic trance, and persons under hypnosis need not be "asleep" nor surrender their will. Some of us are particularly suggestible and easy to hypnotize and others simply are not.

Although hypnosis is sometimes used to enhance the memory of witnesses to crimes, testimony under hypnosis is not acceptable in a court of law. Hypnosis can be used to block pain reactions and affect a variety of symptoms of illnesses. But there's no evidence it is linked with the cure of problems that are physically based.

Hypnosis is most often used in psychotherapy. Two

professional groups have been formed: the American Society of Clinical Hypnosis and the Society of Clinical and Experimental Hypnosis. Hypnosis has been recognized by the American Medical Association since 1956 as "valuable as a therapeutic adjunct."

While there seems no reason to reject hypnosis when used as part of a course of treatment by a trained clinician, it surely is nothing to toy with. Neither stunt nor satanic, nor miracle solution, hypnosis is another healing resource people today are still struggling to understand.

HYPOCRISY. Picture the sculptor, furtively looking around as he rubs wax into the marble, trying to hide the gouges his chisel made in the unforgiving marble. The wax filled in the grooves. Deftly smoothed, the stone figure now seemed to glow in white perfection. Later, in the heat of summer, the wax would melt. Then everyone would know. But then the sculptor would be far away.

Today's hypocrite follows the age-old pattern established by long-dead Greek sculptors. He tries furtively to cover the flaws in his character, hopeful that pretense will make him appear to be what he is not. But every human contact generates some warmth, and the wax runs, leaving streaks that are visible to everyone but him.

So pity the poor hypocrite. He lives constantly with the stress of pretending. And all the time his flaws are glaringly visible to all he knows.

† † †

IDEALISM. Like perfectionists, idealists often fall into a trap set by their strength. Idealism is a strength because we need visionaries: people able to see clearly how things ought to be. The trap is that some idealists become so caught up in the dream of "should be" that they can't handle reality. And are hard for the rest of us to live with.

322

What are guidelines for idealists? • Don't surrender

your ideals. Your vision is vital, in society and the church.
• Learn to value process. No ideal is realized overnight.
At best we can make progress. God recognizes this, and is
committed to bring us through a gradual process in which
we become more like Jesus (cf. 2 Cor. 3:18). • Be gentle
with people. James reminds us that "We all stumble in
many ways" (James 3:2). All of us are imperfect. All of
us must live with something less than the ideal.

In fact, there is only one ideal to which an idealist
should make a total commitment. That ideal? Love. For
"Love is patient, love is kind. It does not envy, it does not
boast, it is not proud. It is not rude, it is not self-seeking, it
is not easily angered, it keeps no record of wrongs. Love
does not delight in evil but rejoices with the truth. It always protects, always trusts, always hopes, always perseveres" (1 Cor. 13:4–6).

IDENTITY.   "You are all sons of God through faith in
Christ Jesus, for all of you who were baptized into Christ
have been clothed with Christ. There is neither Jew nor
Greek, slave nor free, male nor female, for you are all one
in Christ Jesus" (Gal. 3:26–28). This is our identity. From
it everything in our relationship with God and others grows.

IDLENESS.   McGuffy captures the attitude of our
founding fathers when he included in his famous Readers,
"The Devil finds Work for Idle Hands." Long before
that, the apostle Paul laid the foundation for that insight.
He wrote to the Thessalonians, "We hear that some
among you are idle. They are not busy; they are
busybodies. Such people we command and urge in the
Lord Jesus Christ to settle down and earn the bread they
eat" (2 Thess. 3:11, 12). Idleness just isn't God's will for
us. Or His best.

IMITATION OF CHRIST.   For centuries believers
have been fascinated by that idea, and more than one book
on the theme has captured the imagination of a generation.
But is it realistic to think we might live in our world as
Jesus would?

The idea seems to have biblical roots. "Whoever claims to live in him," John says, "must walk as Jesus did" (1 John 2:6). And Paul calls on the Ephesians to "be imitators of God, therefore, as dearly loved children, and live a life of love, just as Christ loved us and gave himself up for us as a fragrant offering and sacrifice to God" (Eph. 5:1, 2). Even so, most of us are a little uncomfortable with the notion of patterning our life on Jesus. We can try. But it seems impossible that we would act as Jesus would if He were here.

If He were here? That, of course, is the Bible's jolting surprise. Jesus *is* here! We Christians are not called to mimic Jesus, but to let Jesus live through us. The New Testament speaks of this reality as a mystery, kept hidden for ages and generations but now revealed to us: "God has chosen to make known . . . this mystery, which is Christ in you" (Col. 1:27). In personal terms, Paul writes "I have been crucified with Christ and I no longer live, but Christ lives in me. The life I live in the body, I live by faith in the Son of God, who loved me and gave himself for me" (Gal. 2:20).

The secret of living as Jesus would in our world is not imitation, but incarnation. Jesus really is present within us. As we live by faith in Him, responding to the promptings of the Spirit, it is Jesus who shines through our words and actions.

IMPULSIVENESS. The dictionary identifies impulsiveness as acting, or being likely to act, suddenly and spontaneously. The New Testament words most closely related suggest we need to view impulses with suspicion. The inner passions that drive us toward another person, or an object or experience, are all too likely to be rooted in our sinful nature.

But impulsiveness isn't always bad. Watch, for instance, as a leper hesitantly approaches Jesus (Mark 1:40–42). Fearfully he creeps near. In Israel as in the whole Middle East, healthy persons draw back in horror from anyone with this dread disease. On his knees in the dirt, the leper begs Jesus to make him well again.

At other times Jesus will heal with a word or from a distance. But now, filled with compassion, Christ reaches out impulsively and touches the leper. That spontaneous loving act, that touch, communicated to this man, whose years alone were empty of human contact, the healing love of God. Jesus' words, "Be clean," restored. But Jesus' touch communicated love. Yes, we want to guard against selfish impulses. But it's hard to go wrong when we follow an impulse to reach out, spontaneously, to care.

INDIFFERENCE. Hate isn't the opposite of love. Indifference is. Only indifference has the power to demean, communicating powerfully "I simply do not care."

It's no wonder some children misbehave purposely, just so parents will punish them. Being noticed—even to be punished—is better than being ignored.

Being ignored is such a terrible thing that the New Testament emphasizes it over and over again. We are to love one another, fervently and actively. God wants each of us to realize that we are important. To others, and to Him.

So if you can think of someone in your family or church fellowship you're cool to, or who others ignore, recognize that indifference for what it is. Confess the sin of indifference, and hurry to him or her with love (1 Peter 1:22).

INDIVIDUALITY. Looking over research on individual differences generates a fascinating number of terms used to describe various traits. Care for a partial list? Well, try: submissive, acquiescent, ambitious, competitive, aspiring, friendly, good-natured, argumentative, independent, stubborn, resolute, determined, adventurous, deferent, respectful, assertive, decisive, dramatic, timid, cautious, sensitive, shy, nervous, sympathetic, gentle, protective, organized, neat, precise, playful, easygoing, exclusive, aloof, sensuous, sensitive, dependent, helpless, intellectual, curious, logical, creative. . . . And there are more. But this partial list is enough to remind us how greatly individuals can differ.

It's good to appreciate the fact of individual differences. We don't want to fall into the trap of viewing Christians as members of some cookie-cutter brigade, all lined up, just alike, surrendering individuality to fit in. You and I can be ourselves, each with our own differences, and still experience "unity among yourselves as you follow Christ Jesus, so that with one heart and mouth you may glorify the God and Father of our Lord Jesus Christ" (Rom. 15:5, 6). → ACCEPTANCE

INFERENCES.   An inference is a conclusion drawn from the words or actions of others. History has recorded a number of rules for drawing inferences. For instance, one rule says choose the simple explanation over the more complex. The Bible suggests a stunning rule of inference for Christians. It's rooted in the principle of love and seen in 1 Corinthians 13's reminder that love "always trusts." What's the rule? When we make inferences about others, we are to draw the conclusion that gives the other person the benefit of the doubt, and puts the best possible construction on his or her actions. → JUDGING

INJUSTICE.   It's popular these days to blame injustice on social and financial conditions. Simply change conditions (for instance, redistribute wealth) and all injustice problems will be solved! The notion is theoretical and naive. Even though the Bible shows great concern with establishing a just social order, → JUSTICE Scripture takes a distinctive approach to the question of injustice.

The nature of injustice.   In Scripture, "injustice" is a relational concept. It is not to be found in some theoretical leveling of wealth or power, for such a leveling can never happen in our world. Instead, justice and injustice are located in the responsibility of each person to treat others rightly, according to his or her station.

For instance, the Old Testament employer is told in the Law to pay his workers daily, so they will be able to meet daily needs for food and shelter. It's not injustice for some to be wealthy, and others not. But it is injustice if the wealthy hoard their riches, and fail to pay the workmen who mow their fields (James 5:1-6).

There are social differences in every society. Some are widows; some are judges. This is not an injustice, even though it involves inequity. But if a judge fails to act to protect a widow from those who would defraud her, that is injustice (cf. Luke 18:1-8).

Slavery involves great inequity. Yet in Bible times slavery was a way of life, and a large percentage of the world's population were slaves. The basis for emancipation was laid in the gospel's great affirmation of the worth and value of every individual. But the New Testament does not agitate for social reform. Instead, it calls for justice within the system, insisting that masters "provide your slaves with what is right and fair, because you know that you also have a Master in heaven" (Col. 4:1), and in the same spirit, that slaves give their masters their wholehearted best (Eph. 6:5-8).

In each of these illustrations injustice is not rooted in the different place society provides for different persons. Injustice is when persons fail to relate fairly to others from within their role. Whatever our place or position, the Bible's call to justice requires that we treat others with honesty, respect, and consideration.

When others aren't fair to me.   God holds no brief for societies where injustice is institutionalized. Yet we all must realize that injustice is epidemic in every culture. Injustice will be found in institutions and found in individuals. Parents will treat children unjustly. Grown up, children will respond in kind. Business will treat labor unjustly. And unions will unjustly conspire to keep minorities out. Sin's web entangles all our institutions and grapples with each individual.

In this world of ours injustices will exist, and this fact has a dual impact on believers. On the one hand, we are to do all we can to establish justice. → JUSTICE On the other hand, we will have to respond in a godly way when we are treated injustly. How are we to respond? The Bible's prescription calls for commitment to a most difficult course.

It's summed up in Peter's first letter: "It is commendable if a man bears up under the pain of unjust suffering because he is conscious of God" (2:19).

● "Bearing up" under the pain of injustice teaches us to neither give up nor strike back at those who hurt us. We are to continue doing good, whatever others may do to us.

● Being "conscious of God" reminds us of two great truths. First, God never permits purposeless suffering. He intends each experience for our own and others' good (cf. 1 Peter 3:13–17). Second, God takes personal responsibility for the judgment of those who treat others unjustly. No one "gets away with" injustice. "God is just: He will pay back trouble to those who trouble you and give relief to you who are troubled" (2 Thess. 1:6).

The apostle James' words to those who suffered under the oppression of the rich of his day sums up the guidance Scripture gives us: "Be patient, then, brothers, until the Lord's coming. See how the farmer waits for the land to yield its valuable crop and how patient he is for the autumn and spring rains. You too, be patient and stand firm, because the Lord's coming is near" (James 5:7–8).

IN-LAWS. The key word for both sides is "responsibility." A newly knit couple has left dependence on Mom and Dad to establish a new, mutually responsible relationship under God (cf. Gen. 2:24). Getting along in the in-law relationships this drastic change introduces is likely to hinge on one thing. Can the parents resist the temptation to feel and act as if they were still responsible for their child? And, can the young husband and wife resist the temptation to avoid responsibility, and run to Mom and Dad?

In-laws can be close, warm, and supportive friends. But they cannot be responsible.

INSTITUTIONALISM. In an individual we'd call it habit. For a person or an organization it's all too easy to keep on doing things just because we've always done them that way.

Every organization is formed with some purpose in

mind. Its members figure out ways to reach those goals, and go to work. As time passes, the way things are done becomes entrenched. Finally the way we do things becomes sacred, whether or not it really helps us reach our goals. No organization is immune to institutionalism. Some, like a church, are particularly susceptible.

How do we know when we're stricken with institutionalism? When someone makes a suggestion, and the majority object because "we don't do it that way here," institutionalism has struck. When someone says, "Hey, this meeting we have every week isn't deepening our prayer life," and everyone is as shocked as if he'd launched an attack on the deity of Christ, institutionalism has struck.

What do we do about institutionalism? We hurry back to basics. We define again (in writing is best) the goals and values for which our organization exists. We honestly look for the best ways to reach those goals, and enflesh those values today. Then we act, even if it means doing something different and new. Only by constant evaluation, and by a constant focus on goals, can we overcome the paralyzing impact of institutionalism.

INTELLIGENCE TESTS.   What does it mean if your kids score in the 99.8 percentile on IQ tests? Probably not much.

Once such tests were looked on as "the most important single contribution of psychology to the practical guidance of human affairs." Now the value of IQ and mental tests is heatedly debated. What is the nature of intelligence? How does cultural background influence scoring? What aspects of the mind (such as creativity) do our tests ignore? Do these tests have any predictive value? Oh, we can measure things like verbal comprehension and rote memory and reasoning. But we can tell very little from such measures about how a person will react in real-life situations, or about his judgment and personality.

Recent suggestions focus attention on intelligence as competency: they say that *knowing how* is more important

INTERDEPENDENCE than *knowing that.* But competency is hard to test with a paper and pencil.

Still, the suggestion to focus on competency brings us closer to Scripture, for the Bible emphasizes wisdom, not intelligence. And wisdom is the ability to evaluate situations and to make right choices. Of wisdom, daily life is the only real test.

Some people might be interested in labeling themselves or others "intelligent." Christians, like God, should be more concerned with labeling them "good."

INTERDEPENDENCE. "Dependence" suggests surrender of personal significance. "Independence" suggests rejection of close personal relationships; a decision to go it alone. "Interdependence" guards both individuality and relationship.

This is the thrust of the Bible's teaching about spiritual gifts and about the church. Each believer has his or her own unique contribution to make to others. Each believer needs what others can contribute, to enrich his or her personal growth.

It's fascinating that in 1 Corinthians 11, a passage often thought to put down women, Paul guards against such an interpretation by an appeal to interdependence. He argues from culture and from the order of creation that men and women are different. So women who demand "equality" on the basis of a supposed sameness as men are in error. Then Paul immediately guards against distorting what he says by adding, "In the Lord, however, woman is not independent of man, nor is man independent of woman" (11:11). In the body of Christ, a woman can accept the cultural symbols that mark her as female (such as long hair) without any shame. In Christ, "different" does not mean inferior! The relationship between all believers is one of interdependence, each individual sharing from the strengths in individual differences what others need for growth.

What does interdependence mean as a practical matter? Attitude. It means respect for others. Consideration for others. Listening to others. Appreciation for what others contribute. Sharing with others. It means living out the conviction that your life and mine take on meaning when we build close personal relationships in which we give. And receive.

INTUITION. Intuition, one credulous contemporary author gushes, can't be described in words "simply because intuition must be understood *by* intuition." Yet the author goes on for some 70 tightly packed pages, concluding finally that whatever intuition is, it brings a person to "the rarified atmosphere of truth" and a "quiet vision" that "stops all speculation and striving, all doubt and uncertainty."

This writer trudges along faithfully in the footsteps of many philosophers who, unable to prove their theories, have argued that they rest on intuition. Classical Intuitionism fondly held that intuition could penetrate to reality directly, avoiding reason and logic. Contemporary Intuitionism retreated a bit and suggested that some truths (though not Truth) are just "seen" by human beings. Most recently, Inferential Intuitionism rejected both earlier theories, to view intuition as the faculty by which we select from various possible inferences and arrive at a sense of subjective certainty (which often proves objectively correct).

We've all seen intuition at work. "I just don't like him," someone may say when meeting a stranger. Later, if the stranger proves to be a swindler, intuition is credited for giving insight into the "real" person. Or "I just know I'm right," an individual is likely to say. He or she can't explain, or give reasons for the feeling, but intuition has brought that awesome sense of certainty, which nothing can shake.

One of my friends divides humanity into "rational" and "intuitive" persons. She doesn't trust the rational people (she's intuitive, of course). Because her intuition brings a sense of certainty that isn't related to reasons, when she "just knows" she is right no amount of evidence will sway her.

Does the Bible have anything to say about intuition?

Can we really trust it? Well, if you'll pardon a rational approach to the subject, several things make me very uncomfortable about intuition. ● The Fall corrupts all. Admitted that human reason was affected by the Fall, and sin has warped that ability. But we should also admit that the faculty of intuition must have been affected too. In that case we should subject intuition as well as reason to the objective revelation of Scripture. ● Be sure humbly. Because we are fallible creatures, we're forced to live by faith. We do our best, but we must admit that we may be wrong. The very certainty intuition claims should warn us against it.● Quickness and prejudging, particularly of other persons, is neither wise nor right. We need always to give others the benefit of the doubt, and seek to learn their strengths. We need to gather as much information about things and issues as we can, and make decisions only after careful exploration.

Putting these together, I can't say "My intuition tells me not to rely on intuition." My judgment does.

IRRESPONSIBILITY. It has been called "decidophobia," and means a dread of making significant, life-shaping choices. People with decidophobia squirm, and then adopt strategies to help them avoid the stress of taking responsibility for their lives.

How? ● Monasticism. This involves making one grand decision that frees us from the need to make others. Whether in the religious monastery or the military, some may choose a life regulated by rule. ● Status Quoism. We make all choices according to conventional wisdom, and by what others expect. If others have a new car every three years, we do too. ● Drifting. We simply do what we feel like doing. We refuse to make any big decisions that require taking conscious control of our life. ● Joining a movement. We let the leader or the party doctrine decide. ● Pedantry. We focus on the insignificant details of life. We become so absorbed with detail we never have to consider anything else. ● Becoming religious. This is an escape for some. Life is now regulated by dos and don'ts, or our elders make significant decisions for us. ● Getting married. This is a solution for some women. They abandon responsibility for their big decisions to their husbands, arguing that they are supposed to be submissive.

There's one thing that won't help you if you have decidophobia. That's acknowledging Jesus as Lord of your life. He won't give you simple rules to apply. He won't let you run away from personal responsibility. In fact, He'll thrust you into complex situations that affect not only you but others as well. Though you have the Word to guide you and Spirit to lead, you'll be called on to apply principles when you can't be *sure* that you're right. You'll learn to walk by faith, very conscious that faith is not sight, and that responsibility always involves the risk of mistake.

It would be simpler if God just told us right out what to do. But He doesn't give us that kind of escape from faith. Why? Maybe it's the same reason why, though I find great delight these days in my 1½ year-old grandson, I don't want him to stay in diapers. I know from bringing up my own sons that they're a great delight at every age, and that each year older is a year better.

Is it really surprising that God wants us out of spiritual diapers? I don't think so. And the fact is, it takes responsibility for us to grow.

† † †

JEALOUSY. We envy people their things. But jealousy, that flash of anger mixed with hurt, is strictly personal.

The anatomy of jealousy. See your spouse laughing with friends, or reaching out to touch another person, and you may experience a jealous flash. Or you may feel the warm glow of pride, glad that he or she is a caring, friendly person. Like other emotions, jealousy isn't in an act but in our reaction.

Some jealousy is a momentary thing and may represent nothing more than a feeling of being left out. But when jealousy is persistent fear, it is a symptom of more serious problems.

A number of things affect jealousy. If we feel good about ourselves we're less likely to be jealous. Feel depressed or dissatisfied, and jealousy is more likely. If we are unhappy in a relationship or unsure about it, jealous feelings are probable. Jealousy is complex, but never pleasant.

The Bible links jealousy with quarreling (1 Cor. 3:3), anger (2 Cor. 12:20), and with hatred (Gal. 5:20). Clearly feelings of jealousy can stimulate sinful actions that are more destructive of relationships than the jealousy itself.

Dealing with jealousy.   Each of us is sure to feel jealous at some time. What we want to be sure of is that we handle jealous feelings wisely, and don't let them spill over into sin. What can we do?

• Admit the feeling to ourselves. Neither denial or angrily striking out at another person is helpful or right.

• Recognize jealousy as a sign that we feel threatened, and try to discern why. If the flash of jealousy is unusual, and comes when we're feeling particularly down, it's probably just an extension of our mood. If the feeling comes often, something much more serious is involved.

• Talk over your jealousy with your partner. Don't attack or accuse. Later, when out of the situation, candidly express how you felt, but without blaming.

Talking through the kinds of actions and the people that are likely to trigger jealousy, and getting the same information from your partner, can help you each understand the other's expectations and feelings. Good communication is important in every close relationship.

• Be willing to visit a counselor. If the jealousy is persistent, and linked either with strong negative feelings about yourself or deepening fears about the relationship, view that jealousy as a warning to seek help.

Godly jealousy.   Paul uses the phrase in 2 Corinthians

11:2. "I am jealous for you with a godly jealousy," Paul writes to this straying congregation. In so writing, Paul returns to an Old Testament expression rooted in God's covenant relationship with His people Israel. Warning Israel against worshiping idols or other gods, the Lord says through Moses, "I, the Lord your God, am a jealous God" (Deut. 5:9; cf. 6:13–15). God has called His people to Him and established a unique relationship with them: in that relationship He is committed to them, and they are to be committed to Him.

God's jealousy is distinctive in that He is not merely jealous *of* us but is jealous *for* us. Only through an exclusive relationship with Him can we human beings find fulfillment and the good God yearns to provide. Wandering from our relationship with God is sure to harm us. And God cares far too much for you and me to be unmoved at that prospect.

The jealousy of God helps us to realize that some human relationships are intended to be exclusive. Jealousy is no evidence of a partner's fault, but it does warn, telling us to pay attention to ourselves. And to the relationship.

JOGGING. It's all right for some. But a brisk walk is better for most, and safer. → EXERCISE

JOY. God doesn't intend us to live huddled under a blanket of boredom. He wants us to know joy.

But we need to realize that joy is different from mere emotion. Joy has a dynamic, sustaining quality: it is a characteristic of the Christian life. Three New Testament word groups are associated with joy. One group deals with outward expressions of joy, as in public worship. A second group resembles happiness, expressing a subjective merriment associated with good times. But the most significant word group calls us to look beyond external situations. In fact, this astonishing joy is often linked in Scripture with tribulation and with suffering. Joy can be drawn only from the deep wells of God's love, and enjoyed through fellowship with Him (cf. John 15:11f.).

Sometime use your concordance. See how often joy

is linked with distress, and with closeness to Jesus. The lesson we learn is important. We don't find joy in externals. We find joy in the Lord.

JUDGING.

It's confusing. In some places the Bible asks "who are you to judge?" (Rom. 14:4). In another Paul actually writes, "I have already passed judgment on the one who did this" (1 Cor. 5:3). And he calls on the local congregation to join in condemnation! What's it all about, anyway? Are we to judge, or aren't we?

When not to judge. The Greek word for "judge" is much like our own. On the one hand "to judge" means to discriminate: to look at an issue or a situation and to distinguish good from bad, right from wrong, best from better. On the other hand "judge" has a judicial meaning, and implies bringing a person to trial and condemning him.

This distinction helps us immediately. It's a very different thing to judge (evaluate) situations, and to judge (condemn) people. When we look at major passages dealing with judging, we see how directly this distinction applies.

● Jesus instructed us not to judge others (Matt. 7:1, 2), for we are limited to fallible human standards (John 8:15, 16).

● The Book of Romans forbids us to judge others' personal convictions. Each individual is responsible to the Lord in those broad areas of life in which there are no clear, authoritative commands (14:1–10).

● In 1 Corinthians Paul remarks that he is not even competent to judge his own motivations, much less those of others (4:3).

● Both Galatians 2:6 and Colossians 2:16 warn that appearances give no valid basis for judging others. And James calls judging others an intrusion in an area clearly reserved to God alone (James 4:11, 12).

In each context the word "judge" is used in the sense of calling a person into court and then condemning him or her. In each context we are told not to treat one another in this way.

When to judge: church discipline. First Corinthians 5 and 6 outlines two situations in which believers are told *to* judge. The one case involves lawsuits between believers. Paul instructs the congregation to appoint panels of judges to examine the issues, evaluate, and settle the disputes.

The second case involves open sexual immorality. God has announced in Scripture His own judgment on certain actions, identifying them clearly as sin. Paul calls on the Corinthian congregation to take a stand with God, to identify the brother's actions as sin, and to discipline him appropriately.

It is important to realize that this "judging" does not involve condemnation. Instead it involves love. Sin always drives a wedge between God and man. Only confession of sin can restore shattered fellowship. When the local congregation takes a stand with God on sin and cuts the unrepentant individual off from fellowship, that congregation acts out on earth the reality of the spiritual relationship. The goal of church discipline is always restoration, not punishment. In the Corinthians' case discipline had just this result. The individual repented and confessed the sin he had earlier denied. Paul immediately guides the congregation to "forgive and comfort him, so that he will not be overwhelmed by excessive sorrow. I urge you, therefore, to reaffirm your love for him (2 Cor. 2:7, 8).

Church discipline, then, is not condemning a brother or sister but is (1) evaluating actions that God has identified as sin and (2) acting to cut off the individual from fellowship if he or she will not repent (cf. Matt. 18:15–17), (3) with a view to bringing the individual to repentance and restoration of fellowship with God. Church discipline is (4) to be followed on confession by immediate restoration to the loving fellowship of the congregation.

Judging, as a critical or condemning attitude toward other persons, is forbidden. Judging, as correct evaluation of situations, is commanded, and is especially needed when disputes between brothers and sisters arise and when fellow Christians turn aside to live in sin.

JUNK FOOD. Some folks say "we are what we eat." If that's true, who wants to be a soft, mushy, sticky-sweet Twinkie? Wouldn't you really rather be a firm, crisp, luscious apple?

JUSTICE. It's a complex and puzzling topic, justice. Yet anyone who has read the prophets is sure that justice is close to God's heart. Amos, like many others, thundered against those who "turn justice into bitterness" by oppressing the righteous and depriving the poor. Time after time the prophets express God's yearning for a time when justice will "roll on like a river, righteousness like a never-failing stream" (cf. Amos 5). Because justice is important to God, it's important for us to have some idea of what "doing justice" involves.

Personal dimensions of justice. In one aspect, justice is a very personal and individual kind of thing, rooted in a basic relational concept. Every interpersonal relationship carries with it responsibilities to others. An employer has a duty to give a fair day's wage. An employee has a duty to give a fair day's work. Husbands and wives have duties to each other defined by their relationship. Parents have duties to children and children to parents. Neighbors, friends, and strangers are knit together by common bonds of due respect. In this personal sense, justice is "to each his due," with every individual having those benefits and burdens that are appropriate to his personal circumstances and his relationships.

Social justice. The prophets of the Old Testament did more than speak to individuals. Their primary message was to the community, calling the nation back to God and to the vision of social justice so boldly outlined in the Law. Exodus, Leviticus, and Deuteronomy laid the foundation, in well-defined social order, for a just, moral community. Although no generation of Israelites ever put that system into practice, Law provided the background of all the prophets' calls to justice.

We cannot bring Old Testament social order forward

and impose it on modern society. But we can see principles in the Old Testament that can apply to our modern social/legal justice systems.

● Personal responsibility. The social/legal structures of the Old Testament stressed the personal responsibility of each individual. Persons were responsible to work and earn their own necessities. Even those without land, granted the privilege of gleaning [picking up the scattered grain left] in the fields of others, were expected to go out to gather for themselves. At the same time, well-to-do individuals had a personal responsibility to help the less fortunate, through generous loans and in other ways. In the area of legal justice too the principle of personal responsibility was stressed: one who witnessed a wrong was to report it, and everyone was called to give unbiased testimony in any dispute.

Modern social systems can also stress personal responsibility, and never rob individuals of the sense of worth that only personal accomplishment can bring.

● Needs to be met. The social/legal structures of the Old Testament system were particularly sensitive to the needs of individuals. Many "safety net" features were built into Law. One unique net was the provision that an Israelite unable to make his own way could sell himself for seven years into what amounted to apprenticeship to a successful fellow-countryman. After the seven years the individual was released, given seven years pay (his new capital) and, now trained, was again permitted to be personally responsible.

Modern social systems should also provide structures to meet the needs of all, but should do so creatively, with a view to equipping the individual for productive personal responsibility.

● Deserts. The social/legal structures of the Old Testament system stressed the application of appropriate consequences. This is seen particularly in the criminal justice system. While violent crime against the person was dealt with punitively, nonviolent crimes were handled through restitution. For instance, a person who stole was to repay the debt and to pay double or triple damages.

Certainly this principle alone would revolutionize our legal justice system, empty our overcrowded prisons of nonviolent criminals, and put them to productive work making restitution to their victims.

The Christian and social justice. No one doubts that God's Old Testament call to "do justice" lays on the contemporary Christian the obligation to treat other individuals in a just and loving way. But there is debate over the Christian's responsibility to society. We live in a secular world, not the theocratic world of the Old Testament. Are we called to affect the structures of a non-Christian society, and to impose biblical values in a world that does not recognize the authority of the Word?

Christians who say no emphasize the importance of individual justice, and expect social justice to exist only when Jesus comes. Christians who say yes stress the fact that in our free society they have the right and obligation to influence the political process, and communicate as effectively as possible God's vision of good to all mankind.

† † †

KNOWING. It's deeply planted in the spirit of our age, this feeling about "knowing." Somehow it's obvious to moderns that we can't really "know" unless we try something for ourselves. Knowledge that comes through rational deduction, or the testimony of others, isn't quite as good as knowledge that comes by sensation.

The tendency to rely on experience isn't as dominant in the '80s as it was in the '60s. But deep down it's still there.

This view of "knowing" is linked intimately with the use of drugs and alcohol and with modern attitudes toward sex. We can present evidence that drink and drugs are dangerous, and that extramarital sex will hurt. But in this age of sensation, individuals are likely to insist, "I've got to find out for myself. I can't know until I try it."

Knowing by trying. The notion is absurd on its face.
Just a moment's thought shows several reasons why:

• We don't apply the principle to all experiences. If the "I can't know unless I try it" argument is correct, why isn't it applied to things like fire and speeding cars. No one sticks his hand in a flame because he wants to "know" if he'll be burned, or steps in front of a speeding car to find out if he'll be hurt. Yet there is evidence that drink and drugs and illicit sex are dangerous, just as there is evidence that fire burns and speeding objects hurt.

• We don't apply the principle to distasteful experiences. No one says "I can't know until I try it" when refusing to take a job as window washer on the world's tallest building. It's only when we think an experience will provide pleasant sensations that we insist on trying it "to find out."

• We only apply the principle to experiences with delayed bad results. A person may decide to try promiscuous sex so he can "know" if it's good for him. But the guilt (or the pregnancy, or the disease, or the warping of a later marriage) shows up later. The only immediate evidence a person gets is from the sensations accompanying the experience. He might say "I like it" or "I don't like it," but trying it will provide no evidence to help him know whether action he's taken will ultimately do him harm.

That kind of knowledge simply isn't available through experiences—until it's too late.

Trying what we know. The Bible reverses the whole process. Instead of trying to gain knowledge through experience, God shows us in Revelation how to have a good and meaningful life.

This is an exciting difference.

• If knowing comes through experience we can never be sure of what might hurt until it's too late.

• If knowledge precedes experience, we can live confidently, sure that the choices we make are the best for us.

But Scripture's promise of safe passage is rooted in

the fact that "knowledge" and "knowing" are not the same. We may have information, and even believe it, without "knowing" in a biblical sense. There is something unique about the truths unveiled in the Bible. God has given us His Word in order that we might obey it. In living a life patterned by the Word, we come to know by personal experience how trustworthy that Word is.

It's only when you and I put the Word of God into practice that we truly "know" the full meaning of that Truth that sets us free. → TRUTH

KNOWING GOD'S WILL.   What college shall I go to? Should we move and take that new job? Should we have another child? Is this the time to buy that new car? These, and many other genuine concerns, move Christians to wonder about God's will.

The concern need not come from any unwillingness to take personal responsibility for our choices. We're concerned about God's will because we believe He wants to guide us in our life-shaping choices. We believe God has a "best" for us to experience (cf. Ps. 32:8). But at the same time, we're confused. How do we come to know God's will? Is there a process through which He guides us to make our necessary choices?

God's will, and God's will.   Let's begin by understanding that "God's will" is used in at least three senses in the Bible. It's used in the sense of a principled will, a prophetic will, and a personal will.

   • Principled will. Colossians 1 reports a prayer of the apostle Paul. In verse 9 he asks that believers might be "filled with a knowledge of his [God's] will." What is he saying here? His reference is to the fact that God has shared with us in the Scriptures specific precepts and principles by which believers are to live. The Scriptures give insight into what is right and what is wrong, as well as into the values that are to infuse our lives. This is the principled will of God: a great body of revealed truths that we are to study and to apply.

Often an answer to our question, "Is this God's will

for me?'' is found in God's revelation of His principled will. You've fallen in love with a nonbeliever. All your emotions insist that this is the one. But a look at 2 Corinthians 6:14–16 and 1 Corinthians 7:39 show you God's principled will, and you know that, however much you pray and ask God for a sign, the marriage simply is not His will for you.

Living by God's principled will calls for our full commitment. God will not force us to be obedient, and we can resist. This aspect of God's will focuses responsibility squarely on you and me. God will not force us against our will to do what Scripture teaches is right. But when we do commit ourselves to obedience we both glorify God and choose paths that lead us to His very best.

• Prophetic will. Some Scriptures tell what God has determined *will* happen, whatever individual human choices are made. The best illustration of this is found in prophecy. Over and over in the Old Testament we find God announcing beforehand what will happen. The Babylonians will carry Judah into captivity. The Messiah will be born in Bethlehem and die on a cross. History's march will end with a great tribulation. Jesus will return. These grand announcements of what God has determined rest on the foundation of His sovereign purpose, and will come to pass. God's prophetic will does not invite us to respond with obedience, for there is nothing we can do to cooperate or to resist. Revelation of God's prophetic will calls on us to recognize His awesome power, and worship Him.

• Personal will. God's personal will is distinctively different from both the principled and prophetic will. We see illustrations of God's personal will in many stories of the Bible.

Abraham's servant was guided to Rebekah as a bride for Isaac (Gen. 24). Isaiah and Jeremiah were called to special ministries, and Amos was led away from his herds to serve as a prophet to Israel. Paul was led to go to Macedonia, and finally led—against the advice of many friends—to that return to Jerusalem which led to his imprisonment. In each case, at a turning point in life, God acted to lead these believers into special personal paths.

While you and I are not Isaiahs or Amoses or Pauls, we are important to God. And His Spirit is present to guide us in the significant decisions of our lives. God does have a personal will for you and me. He will help us find it.

Discerning God's personal will. This is the discussion we began with. When you or I have a significant decision to make how do we go about it? How does God make that personal will known? There are—if you'll forgive the continued use of "p" words—several issues to identify. There are perversions of, prerequisites to, and patterns for discovering God's personal will.

● Perversions. Some treat finding God's will as something magical. But we should not say "If the phone rings in the next 20 minutes, God wants me to. . . ." And we should not open the Bible with eyes closed, punch our finger at a verse, and call it guidance.

We also want to be careful not to extend the search for God's will to trivialities. God may be interested in what tie you wear tomorrow, but He is quite willing to leave the choice up to you. Most of the daily choices we make are ethically and theologically irrelevant: they make no real difference in the ultimate scheme of things. We should be willing to take responsibility for all such decisions, and exercise good sense and good taste.

● Prerequisites. It's important to understand that there are certain prerequisites to discerning God's will.

God has a basic will for non-Christians: to come to know Him. Becoming one of His children is the first step, for personal guidance calls for personal relationship.

Beyond this you and I need to approach the search for God's personal will with an attitude of commitment. Willingness to do God's will is basic. Sometimes what we call a desire to know God's will is nothing less than a desperate search for permission to do something we already know is wrong. To discover God's will, obedience is essential.

● Patterns. Personal guidance does not come magically, but is discerned in the overlapping patterns of our life.

The first pattern is found in Scripture, where God's direct commands and principles help us understand His values. We know, for instance, that sexual immorality is never the will of God, so whatever our emotions or temptations we never have to look beyond the pattern laid down in Scripture if this is the choice we're considering (cf. 1 Thess. 4:3; 5:15–18). Our choice may lie between two jobs, one of which gives us a special opportunity to serve the needy. This value of God's may be impressed on us as we pray, and provide leading.

Circumstances provide another overlapping pattern. What are our skills, or our likes and dislikes? What doors are open to us, and which are closed? It seems unlikely God is calling us to be a doctor if study is hard for us, we dislike chemistry, and no med school will accept us because of low grades.

The counsel of those who know us provides another pattern we need to consider (cf. Prov. 27:17, 19). As Christians we are members of a body, surrounded by those who know us, our strengths and weaknesses, and our gifts. We need to share the process of making life-shaping choices with such others, and listen to their counsel.

How do we really know?   There will be no voices from heaven. And when we make our choices, we may not be sure then that what we choose is best. How then can we know if what we choose is God's will for us?

We can be confident that God is at work in us as we look at the patterns that help us sense His direction (cf. Phil. 2:12, 13). Knowing that Jesus lives, we can remain confident that, if we are committed to pleasing Him, He will guide. We may not "know" as we make our choice, for our life must be lived by faith. But we do trust.

Probably the Bible's most quoted guidance verse applies after a decision is made. Colossians 3:15 speaks of peace ruling within, acting as an umpire to assure us deep down that we have chosen rightly. At times we'll know constant turmoil and distress after making a decision.

That's the time to go back and reevaluate, for God may be telling us we've taken a wrong turn.

Putting it all together, discerning God's personal will is a supernatural but not a mystical process. We study the Scriptures and circumstances. We consult our own strengths and mature Christian friends. We then accept responsibility to act in faith, and make the necessary choice in the firm conviction that God is with us in the process of deciding, and that Jesus will act to change our direction if we are wrong. → DECISION MAKING → CONSENSUS

† † †

LABELING.   Have you ever noticed that labeling may provide a false sense of security?

"My, she's behaving strangely," someone remarks. "Oh," another says, "It's just a touch of paranoia." Everyone relaxes. We've named the problem, now we can safely ignore it. But labeling is diagnosis, not cure.

A similar thing happens some Sunday mornings. We hear the Bible taught powerfully, and are struck with God's call to personal holiness. "My, that was a disturbing sermon," someone remarks. "Oh," another says, "that was the Wesleyan doctrine of sanctification." Somehow we all relax. We've pinned a label on God's truth, and now it seems safe to ignore it.

It's not wrong to use descriptive terms to label diseases or doctrines. But we do need to be alert to the deceptive impact of labeling. Pinning words on problems or on truth is no answer. We need to go on, to solve the problems. And to live the truth.

LAITY.   When the Greek word *laos* was corrupted and laity set in contrast with clergy, a great distortion entered the church. Even today the body of Christ is warped by the notion that believers are divided into an active "ministering" class and a passive "ministered to" class.

No such division is found in the Bible. That word *laos* simply means "people," and Scripture provides us with a powerful portrait of the people of God. Among us, every member is viewed as gifted, → SPIRITUAL GIFTS able to touch others significantly. Among us, there is no such thing as "just a layman." Among us, each person is enabled by God to minister and to serve.

LATE. In some parts of the world, you're expected to be late. Everyone knows a dinner invitation for 8:00 means no one should arrive before 9:30. In other places lateness is associated with status. Only low-status individuals come on time. The more important you are, the later you are supposed to be, and the longer you keep others waiting.

Here, though, while some may use lateness for their own ego/status games, lateness means something else. Thoughtlessness. For believers, late is a four-letter word.

LEADERSHIP. Leadership is often defined as the art or skill of getting things done through other people. The leader is viewed as one who plans and organizes, assigns and delegates and supervises, and so accomplishes tasks. This concept of leadership is appropriate in government, in business, in the military, and in clubs or work groups. But it's not appropriate in the church or the family. It's important for us as Christians to have a biblical understanding of the leadership God expects us to provide in these relationships.

People building. This is the first consideration. Secular leaders focus on getting tasks done. Spiritual leaders focus on helping people grow. Secular leaders are concerned with controlling behavior. Spiritual leaders are concerned with motivating for discipleship, so believers willingly respond to Christ's leading and His commandments. We must understand spiritual leadership not as organizing people to get jobs done, but as "preparing God's people" for works of service, "so that the body of Christ may be built up . . . and become mature" (Eph. 4:12, 13).

In just the same way, a parent is concerned not with using children to do jobs around the house, but with the healthy growth of those children to a maturity in which they will be responsible for their own lives and work.

Bluntly put, leadership designed to get people to do tasks and leadership designed to build people to maturity are different kinds of leadership indeed.

Leading. There are some parallels between good task-leadership and good spiritual, people-building leadership. But there are also distinctive emphases. What's involved in the ministry of the spiritual leader, in the church or the home?

• Close, intimate relationships. Spiritual leaders are called to live among (not over) others, and to build close, caring relationships. Coming to know others well and being known well are both basic to effective spiritual leadership (cf. 1 Thess. 2:7–12; 2 Cor. 1:3–9; Matt. 20:25, 26).

• Clear, consistent example. Spiritual leaders are called to live the Word of God, thus providing examples of the way of life toward which they guide others. As 1 Peter 5:3 puts it, the church is to have no little tin gods, for elders serve "not [by] lording it over those entrusted to you, but being examples to the flock." The importance of example is constantly stressed in the New Testament. We are even taught to recognize as leaders only those whose lives show clearly that they have taken God's truth to heart (cf. 1 Tim. 3; Titus 1). → MODELING

• Gentle guidance. Spiritual leaders are called to share the Word of God, explaining it to show others how to live godly lives. → TEACHING

There are other keys to effective spiritual leadership. → EXPECTATIONS →ACCEPTANCE →FAILURE But the basic tools are relationship, example, and guidance.

The work. This view of spiritual leadership troubles many. They see so much to be done in our world. There are human needs to be met. There are the lost who need to hear the gospel. There are wrongs to be righted. Overwhelmed by this vision of the task, they are likely to adopt secular approaches to leadership. They organize to manage rather than to build people, and lead in ways that control behavior rather than motivate growth toward discipleship. But how else is the work to be done?

The answer is found in two lines of teaching in the Bible. (1) Jesus is head of the church. As living head, He directs and guides believers into various ministries and into those ''good works'' that God has prepared beforehand for us (Eph. 2:10). Human leaders are not called to be heads of Jesus' various enterprises. (2) It is the mature believer who is alert to Jesus' leading, and able to minister effectively. Human leaders are called to work with God's people to nurture them to responsible maturity (see *A Theology of Church Leadership*, Richards/Holdetke, Zondervan). With nurture as the focus of both parents and spiritual leaders, we seek not to control but to influence—in God's way. Linked with others in love, providing teaching and example, spiritual leaders in the home and in the church build the people through whom Christ will reach the world.

LEARNING. There's a lot of difference between learning the alphabet and learning to drive. It's good to remember the difference when we approach the Bible. It's one thing to learn to repeat what the Bible says. And another thing entirely to learn to live it.

LEGAL ADVICE. Our American legal system is an adversary system. In it each party to any controversy presents its case, and a judge or jury makes a determination. Our system classifies cases as criminal or civil. Criminal cases are those in which the government, acting through a prosecutor, charges an individual or corporation with a crime. Civil cases involve a complaint by one private individual or company against another, often seeking money damages or settlement of some issue in dispute. Because of the complexity of criminal and civil law, most of us will need to consult a lawyer at some time.

But most of us have questions about legal advice.

When should we consult a lawyer? How much will legal advice cost? How do we find a good lawyer? And some Christians, troubled by 1 Corinthians 6, wonder if it's right to be involved with the courts.

When we need legal advice. If we're charged with a crime, or are being sued, we clearly need to hire a lawyer. But the greatest value of legal advice is preventive: consulting a lawyer can help us avoid later disputes.

Despite a rash of do-it-yourself legal books, because of differences in state laws you should have a lawyer help you draw up a will, incorporate a company, and read any contracts or legal documents you are to sign. Real estate closings should also be handled by a lawyer. If you believe you have reason to initiate a suit, a good lawyer will advise you if you have a case and whether a suit would be too costly.

What will a lawyer cost? Fees vary widely. Generally they are lower in small- or medium-sized cities. Lawyers may charge by the hour, or at a flat rate for a particular job or, in the case of civil suits, may contract for a percentage of any settlement won. Lawyers will be specialists (as in tax law, or corporate law) or generalists. If you draw up a simple will, for instance, a legal clinic or small practitioner can draw it for you for a very reasonable fee. If your estate is large or complicated, you'll want a specialist who is familiar with estate planning. The specialist will cost more, but can save many thousands of dollars in taxes that might otherwise be charged to your estate. It's appropriate when you contact a lawyer to check on his fees, and compare them with other lawyers offering similar services.

In the early '80s, after a 1977 Supreme Court ruling allowing lawyers to advertise, a number of legal clinics developed. They offered fixed prices for standard legal work. Several chains of franchised law clinics now exist, and studies have shown that their clients are very satisfied with their services in simple or standard legal matters.

Choosing a lawyer. Check with your local bar association if you need a specialist. Most associations have a
referral system that will provide names. This referral is not
a recommendation or endorsement of the quality of a
lawyer's work. You may ask for recommendations from
any lawyers you know personally or who are members of
your church. When you have several recommendations,
visit them to find out the kinds of case each handles and
the cost. The more complicated your problem, the more
important it is to locate a specialist who spends much time
with similar matters. You will also want to be comfortable
with the lawyer as a person, particularly if you'll need to
work with him or her over a period of time.

Christians and the law. Looking back into 1 Corinthians 6, some Christians have been doubtful about using
our legal system. There Paul writes about two believers
involved in a dispute. Each felt he had been wronged or
cheated. Rather than working through the problem as
brothers, the disagreement became so heated that it was
taken to the courts in lawsuits. Paul was shocked. Such
bitterness should not have been permitted to grow within
the body of Christ. Even then, it should never have been
taken into pagan courts, shaming the believing community. Paul wrote that a committee of fellow believers
should have been set up to settle the dispute.

Two things are important to note. (1) This does not
suggest withdrawal from society, or rejection of the legal
system. Paul himself was quick to assert his legal rights as
a citizen (cf. Acts 16:35–40; 22:23–29). (2) This does
establish a principle. When believers have disputes they
cannot settle, other members of the body should be called
in to help them make a binding decision. The legal approach implied here is inquisitorial, in contrast to adver-
sarial. The inquisitorial approach uses a panel of three or
more judges, who have access to all information and
question all witnesses. On the basis of what they discover
they make a judgment.

While this approach to resolving disputes between
Christians is seldom used today, it should be seriously

considered if you experience a dispute with another believer.

LEISURE.   For the first time in history, our "time for living" exceeds "time working for a living." We may never have thought of it that way, but our "time for living" is our leisure time.

Some people are uncomfortable with free time. They bustle out to fill it up. They take on church or club duties, or bury themselves in a mass of daily doings. Even vacations are taken in a hectic rush. Others seem stupefied by free time. How can they ever use it up! So they settle down dully to stare at tv, spending that leisure time in half-hour blocks, vacantly chuckling when the laugh-tracks cue them that something funny has been said.

According to classical writers, leisure time is the basis of culture. When human beings do not *have* to be occupied, they have time to think and grow and create. Ancient Christian writers saw leisure as celebration: a time for self-enrichment, when the person at peace with God could find relaxation in contemplation. In those days, leisure was viewed as a mental and spiritual attitude, not as "spare time" demanding to be filled.

Biblical guidelines.   The best place to look for insights into leisure is to God. After all, as children we're to imitate our Father (Eph. 5:1). How then does God approach leisure?

We see best in the Genesis creation story. There we discover these guidelines:

• Enrichment. God expended creative effort in His work. All His imagination and all His creative energies went into the design of our complex, wonderful world. Sometimes the time we must give to working for a living binds us to repetitious, empty tasks. If so, we can give priority in our free time to those things that use creative capacities and enrich life. We may study. Or make things in a workshop. Or serve others in some person-to-person ministry. Whatever our particular abilities may be, giving some of our leisure time to them to enrich ourselves and others is our first guideline.

• Enjoyment. God paused after each day's work. He examined all He had done, and pronounced it good. For us too, time to reflect on what we've done, and time to enjoy our accomplishments, is a vital contribution of leisure. This enjoyment may take on the tone of celebration and worship, for you and I acknowledge God as the source of all we have done.

• Rest. A full night passed between each day of creation. The seventh day was set aside by God to rest. We human beings, shaped by God, need rest, and we have Christ's word that the Sabbath was made for man (Mark 2:27). Rest, with its capacity to recharge us with fresh energy, has high priority for every believer's use of leisure time.

• Sharing. Leisure time is for relationship as well as for enrichment, enjoyment, and rest. God's creation culminated with human beings, and He sought out the first pair for fellowship (Gen. 3:8). We see the same theme of fellowship in God's creation of Eve and provision for an expanding human family. It is not good for a person to be alone (Gen. 2:18). We also need to spend some of our leisure time with friends, enjoying their company. And to spend leisure time with God, enjoying Him.

Ultimately, our use of leisure time will determine the quality of our life. Our work is important. But whether or not we become the persons we can be will depend to a great extent on how well we learn to enrich, enjoy, and to share our leisure hours.

LIFESTYLE. We hear the word almost every day. Actually it's a sociological term that has crept into popular speech. What does it mean? It focuses on a group phenomenon. A person's lifestyle is not his unique, individual pattern of behavior, but the pattern he shares with others. So we speak of adolescent lifestyle, black lifestyle, the lifestyle of the drug culture, or even of a swinging lifestyle.

Lifestyle (which may vary with age, with region of

the country, sex, etc.) is typically marked by common values and a common way of looking at life, as well as common patterns of behavior.

Which raises an interesting question. Is there a Christian lifestyle? Is there a pattern to the lives of those who belong to the community of faith? There is. We can find that lifestyle clearly described in Romans 12–15, in Ephesians 4:17–6:20, and in Colossians 3:1–4:6. We can even sum it up in a single phrase, reflected over and over in the New Testament passages. That phrase? Just this: "live a life of love" (Eph. 5:2).

You can't live love alone.

So none of us can build a truly Christian lifestyle apart from close, growing relationships with the people of God.

LIES. We usually divide them into "little white" and the other kind. As nearly as I can tell, popular wisdom has it that lies told to achieve selfish ends are wrong. But unselfish lies are "white," and probably all right.

For instance, we may lie intending to avoid hurting someone's feelings, or to keep a friend out of trouble. "No sir, I didn't see Jim here tonight. Not tonight." We may even bend the truth to build morale. "Get out there and fight, team. They can be beat!" We may lie because we want to achieve fairness: the other guys shade the truth, so we need to also, to balance things off. All these reasons for our little white lies rest on a common assumption. If our goal is praiseworthy, and our intention good, the lie itself is relatively unimportant.

There are just two things wrong with this approach. First, God shows an uncommon interest in means as well as in ends. He wants us to do good all right. But He wants us to do good His way. Lying just isn't ethically neutral. So we have to follow God's instructions, and "do not lie to each other" (Col. 3:9).

Second, any approach that appeals to intentions to justify actions is downright foolish. Why? Because we can never guarantee any outcome by our actions. Just because we *intended* that lie to save old Jim some trouble doesn't mean things will work out that way. Even if we could guarantee things would work out the way we intend, we couldn't justify a lie. But to try to justify lying by how we *hope* things will work out is just foolish.

Of course, we Christians have an edge on other people when it comes to the future. No, we can't look into it any more than they can. But we rely on a God who holds the future in His own loving and good hands. Because we know that God is in charge of the consequences of all actions, we abandon ourselves to do good, rejecting wrong means as stepping stones to hoped-for ends. We have confidence that God will see to it. What is right will lead to what is good.

LIFE INSURANCE. Most Christians buy life and other insurance as a matter of course. But some do not. They view buying insurance as a lack of trust; a misuse of the funds God has provided. Certainly our age is unique. In most eras believers were forced to live "by faith." No such thing as insurance was available to them.

What then about insurance? Should we take it out, or not? If we decide insurance is for us, what factors should we consider in taking out policies?

The pros and cons. What arguments do believers advance to support buying or not buying insurance?

• The pros. Those who opt for insurance point to biblical injunctions that call on us to provide for our own families (cf. 1 Tim. 5:8). Insurance is seen as a way to fulfill this responsibility. They suggest that planning ahead is commended (cf. Luke 14:28–30), not condemned as a "lack of faith." In fact, lack of foresight and a refusal to accept responsibility for our own, is more like presumption than faith.

• The cons. Some who question insurance point to several arguments. The Lord's coming is drawing near: shouldn't our funds be used in ministry rather than funneled into insurance? It is certainly true that we can trust ourselves and our loved ones to God. Isn't He committed to meeting their needs (cf. Matt. 6:28–34)? Somehow the purchase of insurance does not sound like seeking "first his kingdom and righteousness," sure that "all these things will be given to you as well." Isn't buying insurance worrying about tomorrow: something we are not to do (Matt. 6:33, 34)?

• The New Testament church. Each of us must come to a personal conclusion about these two points of view. But it may be helpful to realize that a unique form of "insurance" existed in the early church. We see it in Acts, as the first believers share their possessions to meet the needs of brothers and sisters, and provide food for widows (Acts 4:32–35; 6:1–4). Some thirty years later in an all-gentile church, we see the same pattern (1 Tim. 5:3–10). With the Christian community gathered around to meet the needs of the destitute, the church itself was a form of insurance. → GIVING

Buying insurance. Suppose you determine that purchasing insurance is God's way of wisdom for you. What are some things you should consider?

There are many kinds of insurance. Life. Mortgage. Householders. Medical. Major Medical. Income Replacement. Auto. And so on. Most suggest three simple principles for selecting insurance.

• Identify the most significant risks you and your family face, and insure them according to potential loss. If you're young and unmarried, you probably need no life insurance. If you have a large young family, you'll need to consider how much it would take, beyond any social security benefits, to meet their needs during the growing years.

• Insure big losses, not small ones. Taking out $500 deductible on your car means big premium savings over $50 deductible. Shaping a health policy with significant deductibles for normal illness, but full coverage for major illnesses like cancer or heart disease, means great yearly savings and you are still protected against major loss.

• Compare costs and coverage offered by several companies before you buy any insurance. There are significant price differences between companies offering essentially the same kind of policy.

Life insurance. There are many types of life insurance, but they fall into one of two categories. "Cash value" types call for a fixed premium, based on your age at purchase. That premium is greater than the company's cost of insuring you during the early years, so the extra, plus interest the extra earns, goes into a reserve. You may borrow against cash value at a good rate of interest or, if you cancel the policy, take out the surplus. "Term" insurance gives you the lowest initial cost, but every few years the cost is increased. Many companies do not offer term insurance for those in their 60s or 70s. If your goal is to provide the largest possible coverage for your family during their vulnerable, growing years, you can buy more coverage for your dollars with term.

How much life insurance should you carry? Most suggest that to decide you need to: ● Estimate the income your beneficiaries would need if you were to die now. ● Subtract the income they could expect from social security, salaries, or other sources. ● Fill the gap with insurance.

This simple procedure however is filled with uncertainties. What will inflation run? If you invest the insurance money, what interest can you expect it to earn? Will the surviving spouse work? Will he or she need training, and what level of earnings can be expected? There is no way to know these factors for sure. And whatever coverage one buys must be evaluated by how much income is available to spend on insurance.

No one can decide for you if you should have insurance, or if so, how much. In this dimension of life as in every other, you and I must seek God's leading, remembering that we are responsible ultimately only to Him.

LISTENING. Whenever I write, I turn the TV on for background noise. I don't listen to it. I just like the drone, which drowns out household sounds. Of course, when one of my kids comes in, I have to stop typing, lean back, and listen. My TV is never hurt if I ignore it. My kids may be.

Books have been written on different kinds of listening. It's important, they say, because while 32% of our verbal communication involves talking, some 42% is listening (reading and writing accounts for the other 26%). Maybe my TV noise would fit in there somewhere. I'm not sure. But I am sure that there is one kind of listening the experts write about that really is important. Some call it "social-serious" listening: listening in an "informal nonstructured communication setting." Boiled down, you and I would want to call it conversation, or just talking.

What makes just talking so important? Simply the fact that to the Christian, people are important. Good listening when we talk with others communicates respect, and is a key to close, loving relationships. But "good listening" isn't easy. It calls for concentrated effort and the development of several skills. We can describe good listening as active, reflective, and responsive.

Good listening. What should we concentrate on if we want to become good listeners?

• Active. Sometimes when we're with others we focus on what we're going to say next, not on what they're saying. Active listening focuses on the other person. It listens not only for what is said, but for feelings. Tone of voice, a nervous laugh, a tightening of the lips, all can convey information about how the person feels about what he says. When we want to understand and care, we need to listen not only to what is said but to how it is said.

• Reflective. Reflective listening means we respond to the feelings expressed as well as to concepts. We reflect the feelings we think we hear. We don't reflect all the time, of course. But when a friend says, with her features reflecting stress, "Jim was late again last night," it's appropriate for us to say, "You sound concerned."

A reflective statement may miss the mark. Our friend may not be concerned, but hurt at Jim's thoughtlessness. But on target or off, our attempt to reflect her feelings is an invitation. It lets her know that we're willing to talk about that deeper, more significant "feeling" level of life that is so often ignored. We let her know that our concern isn't superficial relationship; that we really care about what is going on inside.

In a real sense reflective statements, which pick up and restate feelings we think we've heard, communicate love. They tell the other person that he or she is important to us.

• Responsive. Loving relationships are never one-way. If we only listen actively and reflect feelings, always on the hearing end and never on the sharing, others become uncomfortable with us. Once we move beyond the superficial, we need to be willing to communicate our feelings and experiences as well as to hear these from others! → COMMUNICATING

The whole process of sensitive listening is deeply imbedded in the Bible's description of how we are to live with one another. Caring, sharing, sensitivity, non-judgmental acceptance, bearing of others' burdens, all these are woven through the New Testament's portrait of the Christian community.

You and I can ignore our TVs. But we can never ignore the human beings God has called us to love.

LISTENING TO GOD.   Listening to others means giving them our full attention, and being responsive to what they share. → LISTENING Look through a concordance, and you quickly discover that listening to God also implies response. A specific response. Biblically speaking, if you or I fail to *do* what God says, we've neither listened nor heard.

LONELINESS.   According to one national study, it seems that within any four- or five-week period more than a quarter of all Americans feel painfully lonely. Surprisingly, people from their late 60s on are less lonely than adolescents and young adults.

Loneliness and being alone are different things. Some persons look for prolonged isolation. And all of us find we need some time to be alone. But when loneliness does come, with its rush of sadness and longing, we know how much it hurts.

Causes of loneliness.   Psychological researchers define loneliness broadly. Some speak of "loneliness of the inner self," and of "spiritual loneliness," which comes when life seems to have no meaning. → ALIENATION Most of us experience loneliness as a social thing: a sad emotion that comes when we feel separated from others, and from the warmth and caring so vital to healthy human experience.

Researchers believe that two kinds of social links provide a hedge against loneliness. One is social *attachment*. We feel attached when we are living in family. For most adults, the sense of attachment is provided by a spouse, or by being in love. The other link is *community*. The sense of community is provided by a network of friends who share our interests and values.

Loneliness is common today, researchers suggest, because our society has little neighborhood stability, and because of family breakdown. Children and youth are thrown by divorce and frequent moves into situations where they experience loneliness often and intensely. Adults too live less and less connected lives. So loneliness becomes a symptom, warning us that the foundations of our society may be breaking down.

Cure of loneliness.   All of us are likely to experience loneliness at times. But loneliness need not be a permanent or even common experience.

• Attachment. Attachment relationships are those we view as permanent, which provide stability and closeness. While marriage is the primary attachment relationship for most adults, it is not the only one. Nor is sexual component essential. For some, attachment needs are met by roommates, with whom singles have shared households for many years. Some believers tell of a growing sense of closeness to God, through which He meets their need for a sense of permanent relationship. David expresses this in Psalm 27, sharing his confidence that "though my father and mother forsake me, the Lord will receive me" (27:10). Others have found the need for attachment met in a ministering relationship: years invested in caring for children as a foster parent or nurse, or working with unwed mothers in a half-way house. The giving and caring focused through such relationships form bonds to places and persons, which offer a deep sense of attachment.

• Community. We all need networks of friends with whom relationships are more than superficial. Here God's provision for us is found in the church, not as an institution or building, but as fellow believers. Becoming a Christian means entering a relationship with other persons as well as with God: a relationship that offers us the possibility of a rich community experience. → **CHURCH**

The blessing of loneliness. Loneliness is never pleasant. But feeling lonely may be a blessing. It may be God's way of letting us know that we haven't yet experienced all the benefits of our relationship with Him. Loneliness may be God's way of stimulating us to reach out, to build relationships, and to find in that process the richer, fuller life God wants us to know. → **FRIENDSHIP**

LOVE. My daughter-in-law's teenage niece, who's living with us this year, is in love again. She bubbles happily to Beth about her delight in the new boy (Mark, I think it is this time). But probably even she knows that, by this time next week, it will be someone new. Even so, being in love is so exciting.

No one can quite define the nature of this love that makes us bubble. "Romantic love" is the usual designation. But whatever term we use, this love is the feeling (some call it the highest, most intense feeling) that a particular person or experience is wonderfully good.

Romantic love can be wonderful. But it can be dangerous too. Particularly if we fail to realize that different people have different ways of loving. And if we fail to measure our experience of romantic love against "real" love.

Ways of loving. Because being in love is such an exciting experience, most of us never stop to wonder if being in love means the same for others as for us. Actually, several different ways of experiencing and playing at love have been suggested.

• Beauty love. For some, love is linked to the lover's ideal of physical perfection. When attracted to someone who approaches that ideal, passion erupts into intense desire. This kind of lover seeks an immediate sexual relationship. But the search is for an ideal rather than a real person. Disappointment soon sets in. A person who falls short will quickly be dropped.

• Love as a game. Some enjoy playing at love as others enjoy playing a game. Courtship is a pleasant pastime: brief affairs are simply scores. The person who plays at love doesn't want to become seriously involved, and does not want to share. The player shys away from talk about the future, and feels most secure when dating several persons rather than just one.

• Love as affection. Some love slowly, with feelings birthed as acquaintance ripens to friendship. The exhausting, flitting forms of love hold no attraction for this kind of person. His goals are a stable, comfortable marriage marked by deepening appreciation and shared enjoyment of the basic things in life.

• Love as obsession. For some, love strikes unexpectedly and against all reason. The obsessive lover is likely to not even like the one he loves. But however foolish he recognizes this to be, he feels caught, helpless in "love's" grip.

• Love as shopping. For people like this, love is simply the recognition that marriage and family are an important part of life. This person looks carefully at the values desired in a mate, and goes about looking for likely prospects. Love feelings can grow later. But marriage and mate selection are too important to leave to the emotions.

It's clear that romantic love, as hard on us as it generally is, really becomes a problem if a person with one way of loving becomes linked to another to whom "love" means a very different kind of thing.

Measuring love. Most of us can make quick and solid value judgments between these ways of loving. Some are clearly selfish: the lover loves for what he or she gains. Others seem to open the door to something more.

In one sense, romantic love is intended to be selfish. That is, God gave us the capacity and the desire for love. He shaped us so we might experience its mystery, its wonder, and its delight. Each of us can be enriched by loving and by being loved, and we are meant to be. So, in the sense that romantic love is intended to be enjoyed, what we gain in loving is important and right.

But what we gain can never be the only measure, for a simple but important reason. We can see it if we imagine ourselves sitting in the living room, glancing at a favorite rhododendron, and suddenly realizing we're in love! We slide close to the plant and reach out shyly to touch its palm-like leaves. Then, thrilled, we sit close, and together watch our favorite TV show.

Ridiculous, isn't it. You can't fall in love with a plant. Or even a favorite pet. Love demands relationship with a person who is like us.

This is the key. Because loving relationships involve another person, I can't be concerned just about me. My feelings are important. But that other person has feelings too; I must respect them and her.

What is "wrong" about some kinds of love is not the pleasure felt in it, but the fact that some loves *use* other people.

The Bible's standard of love is unveiled in Christ, and is more like romantic love than most of us have been taught. Surely *agape* is no cool, impersonal, passionless decision to act for another's good, as it is sometimes made out to be. No, God finds much joy in His relationship with us, and calls us His precious ones (cf. 1 Peter 2:4). His joy wells up as we respond to Him. Like any lover, God is enriched as He cares. But what sets God's love apart is its sensitivity to the needs of the beloved, and His willingness to give as well as to receive. God's love never uses us, but finds deepened joy by enriching our lives, even as our love enriches His.

Someday my daughter-in-law's niece may bubble happily about *the* boy. Someday she may discover a love that is for real. That love will still be wonderful, filled with mystery and delight. But it will only be real if she and he, thrilled by their own enjoyment, learn to show just as much and even more concern for the well-being of the other. The love that recognizes the beloved as a person to respect, and reaches out to give, is the only love that will last or can fulfill.

LUCK.   Why isn't the word found in the Bible? Because none of the writers ever imagined for a moment that *anything* happens by accident.

LUXURY.   A luxury is something we miss only after we've had it, but can get along very well without, because when we don't have it, we discover it doesn't make any real difference in our life.

† † †

MANIPULATION.   I've just read a fascinating book on the art of manipulation. The author comes right out and says that manipulation is managing to get what you want from others. He insists on judging what he writes by only one criterion: does it work? He then provides a steady stream of illustrations on how to get the opposite sex into bed, how to sell inferior products at inflated prices, and how to steal promotions. Then, on the last page, he warns against selfishness and suggests "applying the golden rule as you manipulate people."

I wonder. Who's he trying to manipulate with that ending? God?

MARRIAGE.   In these days of "living together" and quick divorce, many young adults question the meaning of marriage itself. With others it's still popular to question the value of a marriage ceremony. After all, marriage is just a license for sex, and sex is a private thing. Why involve everyone in an expensive show when the marriage may not even last?

We can add to this attitude marital stress caused by

new problems. Today the old sex-role stereotypes of Mom in the kitchen doing dishes while Dad is in the living room smoking his pipe and reading the evening paper, are challenged. And many women find the homemaker role unfulfilling. Today, sacrifice—the belief that "we" should be put ahead of "me"—is also resisted. So it's no wonder that many have lost sight of the meaning of marriage, and of how to build a successful husband-wife relationship.

Biblical roots. To understand marriage we have to go back to the ideal established in Scripture. The story told in Genesis 2 is the foundation for our understanding. God created Adam and set him to exploring Eden. Adam delighted in his garden, and in observing the birds and animals, which he named. But he increasingly became aware of an emptiness: in it all "no suitable helper was found." When Adam was fully aware of his lack, God took a rib from him and from it shaped Eve. The message was not lost on Adam. He immediately realized Eve was not someone different from him, but was his equal in every way, sharing his identity as shaped in the image of God. This message echoes in Adam's words: "This is now bone of my bones and flesh of my flesh" (Gen. 2:23). Genesis goes on, "for this reason a man will leave his father and mother and be united to his wife, and they will become one flesh" (v. 24).

This passage instituting marriage establishes the ideal. ● Marriage is a relationship between two individuals who share a common identity, rooted in an equal share of the image of God. ● Marriage is a helping relationship, designed for the growth and enrichment of each person. ● Marriage is a "we" relationship, in which the couple learns to live its life in this world as a unit (as "one flesh"). ● Marriage is a relationship between equals, for only equals can become "one." → **HEAD OF THE HOUSE** It is only later, with the entrance of sin, that marriage is distorted into hierarchy, with the husband "ruling over" the wife (Gen. 3:16). ● Marriage is a commitment relationship. The old bonds of each partner to parents are broken, and a fresh, lifelong commitment is made to each other.

Essence and accident. The philosophers of old made an important distinction between that which is vital to the very nature of a thing (essence) and that which is not vital (accident). You can change accidents and have nothing important lost, but you dare not modify essence, or the very thing itself becomes different in nature.

This is our problem today with marriage. We retain the terminology, but we confuse essence and accident, and in too many cases the essence itself has been lost. This happens when we confuse marriage as nothing more than licensed sex, or as a bondage designed to keep women as slaves to men. Marriage is far more than a license that society provides so people can enjoy sex without guilt, and it is something very different from a way to enslave.

● The essence. Looking at the biblical roots we can state it clearly. *Marriage is a lifelong commitment to a "we" relationship, in which each person, as an equal, commits himself or herself to be a helper to the other*. If we change or deny this essence, marriage can neither be understood—nor experienced.

● The accidents. Should a wife work? Should the husband help with housecleaning? Should we move whenever a better job offer comes for Dad—or for Mom? How will a couple make its decisions? Every society has its own current notions on the "right" answers to questions like these. Most Christian communities also have stereotyped ideas about appropriate roles for husbands and wives. But it's important for a couple—and for the Christian community—to recognize such issues as accidents, and not essential to marriage. Each couple must have freedom to work out its own solution to such questions. But they must do so in ways that maintain the essence of marriage: a commitment to consider the needs and feelings of each, and arrive at a "we" decision of what is best.

The marriage ceremony. Against this background we can see more clearly the rationale of the marriage ceremony. Marriage is not an announcement that two people are going to have sex. → SEX Marriage is a public commitment: an announcement to the community that from now on the issues of life will be met by "us," not just by "me." Marriage is a public commitment promising that whatever the future may hold—sickness or health, better or worse—the future will be met together, with each individual there to help and support and to love and respect the other.

The public announcement of this commitment in the marriage ceremony is important to the couple and to the community. "I do" spoken in solemn vows before God, in public, in the light of day, means far more than "I love you" whispered at night in the back seat of a car. The ceremony is an affirmation of trust: a mark of commitment each to the other.

For the community the ceremony is important too. It means that another couple has stood to testify that life holds more important things than personal gratification: that "we" truly *is* more important than "me," and that God's plan for meeting our deepest needs is the best plan after all.

MARRIAGE ENRICHMENT.

This is a specialized ministry, but is sometimes confused with other types of marriage counseling.

Marriage enrichment seminars were developed to help couples with good marriages enrich them by learning better ways to communicate with each other. The seminars—usually in the form of weekend retreats—help participants develop skills in sharing and in becoming more sensitive to each other. M.E. seminars, first stressed in the Catholic community, are now widely offered through Protestant churches as well. Marriage enrichment seminars are not intended to correct serious marriage problems, and do not replace counseling or therapy.

When one or both partners are concerned about their marriage, it's wise to see a counselor. A skilled third party can often help a couple work through potentially serious problems together. Today there are thousands of marriage counselors and marriage and family clinics. However, there are many different approaches to their counseling, and few states require licensing for those who advertise as counselors. The best way to locate someone to help? Call three or four pastors for recommendations. Most ministers will be aware of counselors in the area with a significant success rate in helping with marriage problems, and can refer. → COUNSELING

MASTURBATION.

Legend has it that masturbation is harmful. For several hundred years, stimulating one's self to orgasm was considered sinful as well. A brief history of society's view helps us put this sensitive issue in some perspective.

The last three centuries. Little public attention was paid to masturbation before the last three centuries. Then in the 1700s an anonymous English clergyman penned a terrifying tract that associated masturbation with frightening judgments by God. His tract failed to mention that he also marketed a patent medicine promising to counter the most terrible of the supposed harmful mental and physical effects.

The theme was picked up in the mid-1700s by the French physician, Tissot. He was not a medicine salesman, but he was an ascetic. He claimed that *all* sexual activity was dangerous to the body, but focused his attention on masturbation. He considered this deadly, because it could be engaged in by youth and because it was likely to be done "to excess." Since Tissot considered masturbation a major moral crime, he taught that the guilt generated would lead to mental illness, to fits, idiocy, paralysis, and to impotency. His views were picked up by the medical community and permeated our society until around 1900.

Several facts have led to a gradual change in attitude toward masturbation. For one thing, sex has ceased to be regarded as evil in itself, and the importance of sexual feelings became recognized. It also became clear that the specter of terrible illnesses to follow masturbation was without substance. In fact, sex research showed that masturbation was normal rather than abnormal: that 92% of the men in Kinsey's 1953 research and 63% of the women reported masturbating at some time in their lives. The supposed link with madness and impotency could no longer be maintained. The sexual revolution of the '60s actually carried the issue to the opposite extreme: some in society began to actively promote every kind of sexual experience as necessary for good mental and physical health!

No one today claims that masturbation is the most meaningful expression of our sexuality, and few Christians hold that sex is sinful in itself. But it still took a great deal of boldness for Charlie Shedd, a well-known Christian writer on sex and marriage, to write that we should look on masturbation as a gift of God. Shedd argues that in situations in which sexual expression in marriage is not possible, masturbation is a valuable way to find relief from sexual stress and from physical or mental tension. Masturbation then represents God's provision to help human beings resist temptation to immorality.

A biblical perspective. It is particularly difficult to agree on "the biblical perspective" on masturbation, for neither the Old Testament nor the New Testament deal with the issue. The passage often turned to as prooftext against the practice is found in Genesis 38:8–10. There the story is told of Onan, who "spilled his seed on the ground" rather than father a child by his dead brother's wife (an obligation in that age and society). God was displeased, and Onan died.

It's likely the story reports an incident of coitus interruptus rather than masturbation. But it is clear that God's anger was roused by Onan's refusal to carry out his moral duty, rather than by the method he chose to avoid the obligation.

With no explicit teaching, we're forced to turn from precept to principle for guidance. What do those who argue the pros and cons suggest?

• Pro. Picking up Shedd's theme, the pros argue that masturbation is one "way of escape" that God provides to guard us from sexual temptation. Sexuality is not sinful: sex is in fact one of God's gifts to us. Since masturbation is not mentioned in the extensive lists of sex sins in the Old Testament and the New Testament, we should assume that it is not wrong. Certainly masturbation can never replace the sexual fulfillment to be found in marriage. And it certainly should not become an obsession. But it is wrong to condemn it, and so create a burden of guilt over an act that God Himself has not clearly identified as sin.

● Con. Sex is always placed in the context of marriage in Scripture, with the purpose of deepening that relationship. Masturbation, however it is identified, is sex outside of the marriage relationship, and thus wrong. Also, masturbation is normally associated with sexual fantasizing. Christians are to focus their thoughts on what is good and pure, noble and right (cf. Phil. 4:8), and not even imagine other persons as objects to be used. As far as the tension and stress arguments are concerned, male physical pressures are released by nocturnal emissions ("wet dreams"), and need not be released by masturbation. A much better way to handle sexual pressures is found in sublimating—releasing those energies by concentrated physical or mental efforts in sports or some creative hobby. God may not have identified masturbation as sin, but there are many biblical principles that indicate the practice is neither wise nor edifying, and should be abandoned.

Conclusions. As in every situation where Scripture does not speak with a clear, authoritative voice, we find ourselves in the land of convictions. As Romans 14 teaches, in such areas we have no right to demand that others conform to our views. → **CONFORMITY** At the same time, we are each bound individually to come to a personal conclusion in the matter, responsible to Jesus as living Lord.

God is comfortable leaving many personal but disputable matters up to the individual. And each of us must free others, and accept personal responsibility for ourselves.

MATERIALISM. As a philosophy, materialism teaches that the physical universe is all there is. As a way of life, the materialist acts as though possessions give life meaning.

Jesus dismissed materialism as foolishness when He told the story of a rich farmer who stuffed his barns full of goods and settled back to enjoy life. That night he died, and all he'd gathered went to someone else (Luke 12:16–21).

But there are other reasons why materialism is foolish. The materialist is forced to focus his energies on getting food and clothing and luxuries. He must worry, for he has only himself to depend on, and life is uncertain. In a world of inflation and unemployment, with war a breath away and tomorrow uncertain, the materialist lives with gnawing fear.

So, after telling of the rich but foolish farmer, Jesus instructed His disciples (Luke 12:22–34). Disciples are to look beyond this world, and see a God who loves them far more than He loves birds and flowers. This God will meet the daily needs of Jesus' followers. Released from worry and fear by the watchcare of God, disciples can focus their energies on living as citizens of His hidden kingdom, investing not in riches but in righteousness.

You and I, who are not materialists, need to hear this message over and over. Why? Because although we believe in the unseen kingdom, we may not be enjoying the full benefits of our citizenship. Hearing Jesus' good news about release from materialism's bonds, we are freed to live now ● without worry, for God will meet our needs; ● without fear, for we know that God loves us; ● without setting aside the significant issues of love and caring in favor of things. Living this way we find life's real treasures, which are locked in the kingdom of our God.

So let's hear His good Word.

And let us set out to live as citizens of the kingdom of God.

MATURITY. Prayers for maturity produce unexpected answers. Why? Because maturity comes only through a long, painful process. James, who describes the process for us, lets us in on a comforting thought. It's worth it. We can "consider it pure joy, my brothers, whenever you face trials of many kinds, because you know that the testing of your faith develops perseverance. Perseverance must finish its work so that you may be mature and complete, not lacking anything" (1:2–4). So go ahead. Pray for maturity. Welcome your trials. It's worth it all to be complete.

MEDITATION. It has a suspicious ring, that word. To many of us it has an eastern sound, and conjures up visions of brainwashed youth clothed in yellow robes muttering endless repetitions of nonsense syllables. Only if you're Catholic are you likely to know that meditation has a long Christian tradition as well.

Christian meditation has a different focus than the practices of eastern religions. While both may suggest a mild asceticism, the heritage of Christian meditation is found in its emphasis on contemplative prayer. The goal is not to tear the individual away from the real world or from life's struggles. The goal is instead to focus attention on the reality of Christ, seeking to develop a constant sense of His presence. The Celtic St. Columba expressed in a seventh-century poem the goal of linking God to all of life and all of life to God:

> That I might bless the Lord
> Who conserves all—
> Heaven with its countless bright orders,
> Land, strand and flood,
> That I might search the books all
> That would be good for any soul;
> At times kneeling to beloved Heaven
> At times psalm-singing;
> At times contemplating the King of Heaven
> Holy the Chief;
> At times at work without compulsion,
> This would be delightful;
> At times picking kelp from the rocks
> At times fishing
> At times giving food to the poor
> At times in a solitary cell.

In its best expression meditation is no withdrawal from the world, nor is it a method or system. Instead, meditation is an attitude. One who seeks to draw near Jesus seeks in the contemplative attitude a growth of trust, reverence, and joy.

What does this long Christian tradition suggest as aids to meditation? Those aids testified to across the centuries are:

- Use psalms and other Scriptures to focus thoughts on God.
- Focus thoughts on the passion, death, and resurrection of Jesus
- Set aside time to be alone, in silence. Direct thoughts and prayers to God at such times, expectantly awaiting the sense of His presence.

MEEKNESS. We might not be so suspicious of "meekness" if we realized that it really means kind, gentle, and considerate.

MENTAL ILLNESS. What is "mental illness" and how do we deal with it? Here is some basic information.

Types and causes of mental illness. Mental illness can be divided into neuroses and psychoses. Neuroses are mild and, while they may bring anxiety or depression, do not necessarily keep a person from functioning in daily life. A neurotic person is not enjoying mental health. But he or she would not be considered insane. Psychoses, on the other hand, are severe mental illnesses. Psychotics lose contact with reality, and suffer from delusions or hallucinations that are expressed in "crazy" behavior.

Mental illnesses are often classified by cause, as organic or functional. Organic mental illnesses are linked with changes in the structure of a brain. A chemical imbalance, a tumor, or even a vitamin deficiency (as in pellagra) may cause mental illnesses. Functional mental illnesses are those that cannot currently be traced to physical changes in the brain. For some reason the person is not functioning in a normal, sane way.

Treatment of mental illnesses. Organic mental illnesses can sometimes be corrected by drugs or hormones. Functional disorders can also often be helped by drugs. Counseling and psychiatric therapy is another approach that helps many.

Those suffering from mental illnesses are often placed in mental hospitals. Today nearly a million persons in the United States have been so hospitalized. Despite the fact that mental hospitals provide a valuable service, several criticisms have focused on the way we treat mental patients.

• Commitment to mental hospitals has been criticized as a form of involuntary imprisonment. Many functional cases are not so much "sickness" as deviations that make family or friends uncomfortable. Commitment may be sought not because it is the best for the individual, but because it removes a strain on the family. The fact that the Soviet government commonly commits dissenters as mentally ill warns us that we need to protect from placement in a mental hospital persons who should not be committed.

• Mental hospitals are crowded, and patients are not able to receive sufficient therapy from overworked doctors and staff. In many cases extensive counseling is not required, and healing comes with time. Even so, critics point out that more must be done to make mental hospitals a place of healing rather than simply a place for custodial care of society's outcasts.

• Potentially violent or suicidal persons are often released when their condition has been "stabilized" rather than when cured. This is the reverse of the easy commitment problem. More than one released patient has committed acts of violence that later investigations have shown were predictable.

Attitudes toward mental illness. Our difficulty with mental illness is magnified by the discomfort and fear felt by most around anyone labeled "mentally ill." We don't know what to do or say, or how to react when their behavior is "strange." Today too the very words "mentally

374

ill'' call up images from a dozen horror movies. It's no wonder that most of us are frightened by mental illness, and that great strain is placed on the family of anyone who suffers a mental illness.

Because mental illness does place such strain on the family, it is important that family members insist on specific help from an institution when a loved one is released, or from a doctor if a loved one is in treatment. Information needed includes ● What kinds of behavior can we expect? ● How should we respond to our loved one? ● Is there anyone who family members can talk with for more guidance, or for help in working through our own feelings?

At one time mental illness carried a greater stigma than today, and it was believed that Christians could not suffer from such problems except as punishment for sin. Mental illnesses were also commonly blamed on heredity, and were thought to be passed on through the generations.

Today most of us realize that, like twisted ankles and broken bones, mental illness can strike anyone. And, like sprains and breaks, mental illnesses can be healed. Although mental illness continues to be feared, we are better able to deal with it today than at any time in the past.

The Bible on mental illness. Scripture has little to say. Some stories in the Gospels make it clear that mental and physical illness may be linked to demonic activity, but are not necessarily so. → DEMON POSSESSION Only two other incidents in the Bible are linked with insanity. David pretended to be insane when visiting the land of the Philistines (1 Sam. 21:13, 14). And the Roman governor, Festus, hearing Paul tell of the resurrection of Jesus, accused him of being insane (Acts 26:24, 25). The oft-quoted verse from 2 Timothy, pointed out as evidence of the Christian's protection from mental illness (''God has not given us a spirit of fear, but of power and of love and a sound mind'' KJV) is correctly translated in the NIV, ''God did not give us a spirit of timidity, but a spirit of power, of love and of self-discipline'' (1:7).

We must then view mental illness as a possibility for

375

those within the family of faith. We also must realize that this, like all other tragedies, provides God's people with fresh opportunities to trust. As we rely on God we will discover the ever-widening limits of His faithfulness to us.

MERCY KILLING. Can a Christian ever consider mercy killing? On the one hand believers affirm the significance of each individual life, and see purpose even in suffering. We know that God can turn every experience to good for those who love Him. And we realize that eternal issues may be involved in lingering death that we cannot yet understand. But on the other hand, we also affirm God's mercy and compassion, and want to express His loving concern in our relationships with others.

The conflict in our beliefs and values becomes very real when someone we know and love—a parent, or spouse, or child—is involved. We can certainly identify a number of situations in which an end to life appears to be mercy; even situations in which continuing life would appear cruel. But are we qualified to judge? Are our intentions of merciful love enough to justify a killing, or assisting to suicide a person who asks help?

Theologians and doctors make a helpful distinction here. They point out that there is a difference between permitting a person to die, and causing his death. Medical science has developed ways to prolong physical life far past the point an unaided individual would have died. Prolongation, after hope of cure is gone, has rightly been called useless torture. Refusing to prolong life by special medical means and taking action to end life are clearly two different things.

Pro and con arguments culled from the literature on mercy killing can at least help us focus on some of the issues involved.

• Pro. A person has a right to end his or her own life when it becomes meaningless or burdensome, and the right to ask a loved one to help if he or she is unable to do so alone. A person who suffers intensely should be released when death approaches. It is cruel to keep such a person in torment. A person's own wishes should be given first consideration in making a decision like this.

• Con. God is the giver of life, and the only One who should take it. We cannot call any life meaningless, even if it is burdensome, for God can use suffering to teach and nurture us. To aid another person to end his or her life or to act alone to take it usurps the role of God. Since death is not the end for an individual, and life is preparation for eternity, ending life before its time may deprive the individual of some significant work God intends to do in his or her life.

As for pain, doctors and hospitals today use drugs freely in terminal cases to relieve physical suffering. Mental stress associated with life-threatening illnesses can be used redemptively by God. Ultimately the believer affirms that God is vitally concerned with each individual, and must be trusted in tragedy as in blessing.

MESSIAH COMPLEX.

Pastors may be the primary group susceptible. Symptoms are easily recognizable. The infected person must be at every meeting (to make sure someone doesn't mess up), must respond immediately to every call from a stranger or parishioner (because they really need him), and must work furiously fifteen hours every day (saying "hi" to his family as he rushes off to save the world).

Cure is often difficult. He or she must stop rushing around long enough (1) to remember that Jesus also works through others in the local body of Christ, (2) to establish personal and family priorities as well as work priorities, and (3) to come to a realistic appraisal of his calling as one of many ministering as a servant (not savior) in the kingdom of which Jesus is living head.

Cure brings the sufferer great release, although it also means a painful deflation of his ego. It's worth the cost. But since people with a Messiah complex are really on an ego trip, and are working furiously to maintain an exaggerated sense of their own importance, many just refuse to come back to reality.

It's too bad.

There's already one Savior. We don't need another.

MIRACLES. Most Christians are almost comfortable with miracles. Almost, because while we believe that miracles *can* happen, we're not so sure that we can depend on them. Some Christians seem to though. And it's not unusual to hear miracles discussed on Christian TV networks as if they were commonplace and, sometimes, as though only second-class believers with second-class faith fail to experience miracles regularly. So it's helpful to be clear on how this term "miracle" should be used. And whether God performs them these days on our behalf.

Miracle. The naturalist insists that the material universe is all there is. Whatever happens *must* then be the result of natural laws, and miracles simply cannot happen. Reports of God's mighty acts in Old Testament times and of Jesus' miracles are either rejected out of hand, or some energy is expended trying to figure out reasonable natural causes to explain them away.

The supernaturalist believes that there is a reality beyond our material universe. The Christian, basing his or her faith on God's self-revelation in Scripture, has confidence in a God who is Creator and Sustainer of the physical universe. We also realize that there is no uncrossable gulf fixed between the natural and supernatural. God has bridged the gap often, and has shown that He is completely capable of acting in the material world.

Looking through history and Scripture we find two ways in which God has demonstrated this capability. ● God has performed *obvious miracles,* which seem to involve suspension of natural laws. ● God has performed *hidden miracles,* which involve shaping events using only processes that are apparently natural.

Obvious miracles. These are events to which everyone agrees the word "miracle" should be applied. "Nobody has ever heard of opening the eyes of a man born blind," argued one beneficiary of Jesus' healing (John 9:32). There was no question in the minds of the witnesses. Something supernatural had happened here. Even Jesus' enemies, burning with frustrated fury, couldn't deny that something had happened that could not be explained by appeal to any natural process.

It is important for us to realize that obvious miracles are concentrated in specific periods of Bible history. There are obvious miracles associated with the Exodus period (1450–1400 B.C.). There are obvious miracles associated with the ministry of the prophets Elijah and Elisha (875–825 B.C.). There are many miracles associated with the ministry of Christ on earth, and the early ministry of the apostles (A.D. 30–45). But apart from these three periods, miracles are *not* the commonplace experience of God's people. Overriding natural law, or acting against the flow of natural process, just is not the typical way that God works out His will.

Hidden miracles. What we do find in Scripture, and especially in prophecy, is that God is secretly at work in our world. The Old Testament tells how He used even enemy invasions to discipline Israel when she sinned. At other times God used disease or rumors to save His people. The Old Testament is full also of specific prophecies concerning Jesus' birth, life, and of the events surrounding His death and resurrection. All these came to pass just as foretold. While we must believe that God had a hand in guiding events to their foreordained conclusion, there is usually no hint of obvious miracle. Cause and effect followed in natural sequence; the persons involved acted freely, moved by their own passions. No one looking on would have reason to point and say, "Look! There's evidence of God's intervention."

Hidden miracles then are recognized by the eye of faith, and easily dismissed by unbelief. There is nothing obviously supernatural about them. Instead, God's hand is disguised by the seemingly natural flow of natural event following on natural event.

Miracles today? "And then," the TV talk show guest says breathlessly, "when the doctor took X-rays again, my cancer was *gone!*" And the host declares in awed tones, "It was another miracle." "Yes," she says, "a miracle."

What do they mean? Talk with doctors, and they'll all admit to sudden remissions and amazing recoveries they can't explain. You can call it a miracle. The doctors will tell you things like this happen all the time. You claim it for faith. The doctors will tell you of pagans to whom it's happened as well. But neither you nor the doctors will compare that personal miracle with the obvious miracles of the Bible.

It can't be compared with the darkness that struck the whole land of Egypt, or the death of all their first-born. It can't be compared with the sea rolled back as all Israel watched in amazement. It can't be compared with fire falling from heaven to consume sacrifice and altar on Mt. Carmel, as all Israel watched and then cried out, "The Lord, he is God." It can't be compared with the healing of the man born blind, or Jesus' feeding of the five thousand. It can't be compared with the supreme miracle of the Resurrection. Bluntly put, what we like to call "miracles" today simply are *not* miracles in the fullest sense.

But are they "miracles" in the sense of the hidden miracles? Are they miracles in the sense that God has quietly worked shaping circumstances to bring you His best? Certainly. But in that sense, everything is miracle. God is always at work in your life, gently guiding natural processes to keep you in the center of His will. God works out His plan for you through the family into which you were born, through the schools you attended, the spouse you met and married, the work you do, the neighborhood you live in, the church to which you belong. The eyes of faith see God at work in everything. Even in the cancer that *isn't* cured.

Even tragedy, in the sense that God is at work through it, is miracle to the one who believes. → **FAITH HEALING**

God *can* perform the obvious miracle today. But He probably will not. Still we can rest assured. We are surrounded by the loving care of a God who is quietly at work in every detail of our lives.

MODELING. The Bible word is "example." Both mean a pattern or blueprint, something that gives direction and shape as a person builds his or her life. The behavioral sciences have rediscovered how important modeling is. Beliefs, values, attitudes, and behavior are all picked up from other human beings. In fact, when it comes to living, we learn more from our relationships with others than from any books or classes. No wonder then Paul told young Timothy to "watch your life and doctrine closely" (1 Tim. 4:16). Providing an example of truth taught is essential to the role of Christian leader, or teacher, or parent. → **LEADERSHIP**

The idea that God has called us to be models frightens many of us. For two good reasons. We aren't sure how to go about modeling. And we're honest enough to know that we're not always *good* models. How do we deal with these two problems?

• your influence is greater if you have frequent, long-term contact with another

• your influence is greater if you build a warm, loving relationship with another

• your influence is greater if the other person sees you in many different life settings and situations

• your influence is greater if you share your inner feelings and thoughts with another

• your influence is greater if you live out what you say you believe

• your influence is greater if you talk about the beliefs that guide your life

A person who builds this kind of relationship with others, whether family members or members of a class or sharing group, will be a model whom God uses to powerfully influence others for good.

Our inadequacies. No single individual can be a perfect model, or serve as a model of every Christian grace. That's one reason for the church: in our brothers and sisters we see a number of godly traits modeled, and find that different persons help us with different areas of growth (for instance, one of my friends is a good model in prayer, another in giving, etc.).

But there is another dynamic at work in modeling.

This dynamic takes into account the fact that each of us, as a sinner, is imperfect. So we never are asked to *pretend* in our effort to model. Instead we are told to be real, and let even our blemishes be known. The Bible explains why in 2 Corinthians 3:12–18. There we are told to be "very bold," and to remove our masks so that others can know us as we are. Why? Because we know that we "are being transformed into his [Jesus'] likeness with ever-increasing glory" (v. 18). The strength of our influence isn't found in others mistaking us as perfect, but because—knowing us as we are—they see Jesus at work transforming us over-time.

When you and I have the confident assurance that Jesus *is* at work in us, we find the courage to be real. Then, sharing ourselves honestly within the family of faith, God will use us as a model to help others grow.

MODERN.   Browsing in a university library last month, I made a fascinating discovery. Dozens of books written in the '40s have the word "modern" in their title. It's strange to pick up a dusty volume no one has looked at for four decades and read that word "modern." Without even looking, you know many of the views expressed on its pages are so out of date that now they seem slightly ridiculous.

But that's the problem with words. "Modern" sounds so fresh and new and exciting. It means the very latest thing. It's hard for us to realize that modern does not mean lasting. And that it certainly doesn't mean right.

MODERN MUSIC.   If you want something that will split the generations, just turn to modern music. To the young contemporary music is everything that modern means—new, up-to-date, ours. To the older generation it often means noise, or more likely, fear.

We've seen it in every generation. Every five years or so a new sound appears, youth respond, and the older generation is paralyzed with fear. We've been frightened over "jungle rhythms" that are designed to rouse passions and lead to immorality. We've been frightened over songs that glorify the drug culture. We've been frightened over songs that glorify rebellion against authority. And as I write, some are frightened that songs carry satanic sound. In fact, one bill has been introduced in California's legislature to ban certain '82 music because, played backward, it supposedly carries a satanic message that will twist the behavior of our youth!

How do we respond to the frightening charges regularly made against contemporary music? And what should Christian parents do? I remember how important the question seemed when the Beatles first appeared and my kids were teens. Then a member of our church became quite popular, going around to youth groups and holding seminars that explained why even listening to such music was the doorway to great sins.

Music, and music. To sort it out, we need to begin by noting that music in itself is neutral. The "sound" is neither good nor bad.

History provides fascinating illustrations. Many of the songs we now sing in church are the very tunes of England's dance halls. You can't pick up a Methodist or Salvation Army hymnal without singing songs that correspond culturally to the sound of the Beatles or Simon and Garfunkle or of other popular groups. The sound, associated with sin but so very popular in Britain in those days, was stolen and sanctified and used to carry the gospel message.

Contemporary Christian artists typically pick up the popular sound, and use it in their own compositions or arrangements. It is the sound that attracts the listener; the message is shaped by the artist.

While this is generally true, and we should not automatically label a particular style of music wrong, it is also true that some music (for instance, acid rock in contrast with general rock) is closely linked with a particular lifestyle. We should be able to distinguish between music styles that are simply new and popular with youth, and those that are tightly tied to a particular philosophy of life.

A parent's guide. If we accept the notion that music styles are essentially neutral, so the "sound" isn't wrong in itself, what guidelines can help a mom or dad who hear frightening talk about contemporary music, and realize their kids are actually listening to it? Here are some things to do . . .

● Have your son or daughter pick up a "good" (in his or her view) tape or record. Play it together, and talk about what it's saying. (I once spent three days driving across the country with my youngest, listening to his tapes. For a lover of classical music, it was kind of hard at first.)

● Ask about the music with "bad" associations. What are the themes? Which groups are distinctly "unchristian." You may be surprised at how clearly your teens can distinguish between groups. You may also be surprised how much their particular music is associated with the "good guy" kids at school.

● Encourage your children to exercise good judgment in the music they listen to, and to evaluate the themes.

● Talk now and then about the themes most popular in the current top ten. This will keep you in touch with how youth think and feel, and will also let your teens have the fun of instructing you in something in which *they,* not you, are expert.

You and I don't have to like contemporary music. But we shouldn't get carried away with hysteria. And we shouldn't forbid our children something we haven't first tried to understand.

MODESTY. Without modesty, we attract attention —to the wrong thing. Take the gal who wants to be popular, and so dresses to draw the male eye. She'll get attention all right. But it won't really be *her* the fellows who gather around are interested in. To top it off, the men she attracts won't be the ones she'll want if she's wise.

MONEY. Maybe you've puzzled over one story Jesus

told. It's called the Parable of the Shrewd Manager, and you can read it in Luke 16. It's about a manager who'd been dipping into company funds. When the owner heard rumors, he warned him that an auditor would soon appear. In panic, the manager called in all the company creditors and rewrote the books. A person who had a bill for $20,000 got it cut to $10,000, and another who owed $18,000 got it readjusted to $12,000. Later the owner commended the dishonest manager for being so shrewd. Jesus commented, "For the people of this world are more shrewd in dealing with their own kind than are the people of the light. I tell you, use worldly wealth to gain friends for yourselves, so that when it is gone, you will be welcomed into eternal dwellings" (vv. 8, 9).

What's He saying? Simply this. Let's never be foolish and mistake money as riches. Money is just something to use, to help us prepare for the future. The wise person recognizes this fact, and spends his money with eternity in view.

"No servant can serve two masters," Jesus concluded. "Either he will hate the one and love the other, or he will be devoted to the one and despise the other. You cannot serve both God and Money" (v. 13).

MYSTICISM. Mysticism is the belief that the finite human spirit can directly experience God. History records the report of many, believers and unbelievers alike, who have had mystical experiences in which they sensed the touch of Ultimate Reality. Believers have spoken of touching God: nonbelievers have used other terms.

How do we react to the claims of the mystic? We have no particular problem accepting a mystic's affirmation that he has had an experience. The subjective reality can go unchallenged. Our problem comes when the mystic tries to describe his experience in objective terms. It is the claim of some mystics to have learned truth that creates our problem.

It's one thing to affirm that God has stepped across the void and communicated to us in words spoken by the prophets and recorded in the Scriptures. It's one thing to affirm that God came in Christ to show us more fully who He is. It's another thing entirely to say that we crossed the void and have come back again with new information from God's hidden realm.

What's best? To realize we have no need to challenge a mystic's claim to have experienced God. But to realize too that the one trustworthy source of knowledge we have about reality is God's revealed Word. → TRUTH

NAGGING.   Everyone hates it. And no one listens. But some people just continue to nag. The fact is that it takes ten positive statements to a person to counter the impact of one negative statement. If you really want to influence another person, the *only* way to do it is *not* to nag. → CONFIDENCE →MODELING

NATURAL.   That's the magic word in advertising these days. Why, people even claim you can keep your sweets and still lose weight if you stick to "natural" sweeteners. And many of us buy those extra-expensive hothouse tomatoes that are "natural grown."

The thing is, "natural" has become a code word these days, guaranteed to create a knee-jerk reaction. Take those "natural" sweeteners (fructose) that are supposed to be so much better than table sugar (sucrose). In the first place, both are "natural," for each comes from plant material. In the second place, advertising to the contrary, fructose isn't "nature's own" sweetener that unlike refined sugar is free of "empty calories." Calories are calories and sweets are sweets. The only real difference is that when table sugar was selling for $1.50 for five pounds, fructose was selling for $5.00 for one pound. The people who really benefit from natural sweeteners are the ones clever enough to find millions of gullible consumers who are willing to pay for the false security provided by an empty word.

NEATNESS. It's all right if you like it. But give me the cluttered comfortable disarray that says Children Live Here, or Someone's at Work.

NO. Watch out for that word if you're a parent. You'll find that it's the easiest thing to say when one of your kids rushes in and says, "Mom, can I . . . ?" It's easy because saying no means we don't have to stop and listen, or talk a possible problem through. Saying no means we take no risks; later we won't have to worry if letting Suzie stay overnight or Jimmy ride his bike may have been a mistake. And saying no gives us a feeling that we're still in firm control.

Because saying no is so much easier and has so many apparent payoffs, some parents say it automatically, to every request. But saying no means something for our kids, too.

Saying no means to Suzie she's not important enough for us to stop what we're doing, and listen with love. Saying no means to Jimmy that our comfort is more important to us than his excitement about his ride. Saying no means that we don't trust our children, or release them for the freedom they need to grow strong and tall.

Saying no may mean one thing to us. But it means something entirely different to our boys and girls.

Oh, we don't have to say yes all the time. Kids don't want or expect that. But we do need to listen and consider carefully before we say yes *or* no. When we listen, whatever we say, our kids will know we really care.

NUDITY. That statement in early Genesis is intriguing: "the man and his wife were both naked, and they felt no shame" (Gen. 2:25). It gives us a sense of wonder, and an insight into the age of mankind's pristine innocence. To look on beauty, to enjoy, and have no sense of shame. . . .

Genesis is very careful here. It says nothing about a sense of desire. Sex surely had its intended role in the life of the first pair: Adam and Eve were called to be fruitful and to multiply (Gen. 1:28). Sight and touch must have had their intended impact: desire glowed. But innocence is seen in the free spontaneity of their passion, and the fact that in no caress or touch was there the seed of shame.

It's different now.

The Playboy philosophy leads the rush back to the undraped form. But the object in view isn't to restore lost innocence. It is to pose in such a way that all the passions we know to be shameful are focused, and our imagination is drawn into a twilight world we'd never dare to share with anyone whose life we viewed as pure.

The sophisticated response to objections to the nude human form is a delicate sneer, and the observation, "It's all in the eye of the beholder." The remark is meant to silence every complaint, and to suggest that if only you were as pure in your thoughts as I, you'd see no problem. Of course, the point is absolutely right. It *is* in the eye of the beholder. There's nothing wrong or sinful about the naked form: God has shaped the human body and it's infused with warmth and beauty. But sin has shaped the eye of the beholder. And no one is pure.

So out of concern for others we want to dress modestly, and affirm the need of our society to maintain the standards that today are so lightly tossed aside. Not because the body is sinful. But because sin has infected the human race, and the eye can no longer look on beauty and desire without shame.

"Woe to the world because of the things that cause people to sin," Jesus said. "Such things must come, but woe to the man through whom they come" (Matt. 18:7).
→ **PORNOGRAPHY**

† † †

OATHS. "Do not swear at all: either by heaven, for it is God's throne; or by the earth, for it is his footstool; or by Jerusalem, for it is the city of the Great King. And do not swear by your head, for you cannot make even one hair white or black. Simply let your 'Yes' be 'Yes,' and your 'No,' 'No'" (Matt. 5:34–37). Jesus' point? If we're trustworthy, no one will have to ask us to promise.

OBEDIENCE. I've been surprised at recent questionnaires I've given to parents. Earlier generations were sure: obedience in children is very important. But in the late '70s and early '80s parents placed much less stress on obedience. Why the change? Are kids more responsive, so Mom and Dad have no trouble with obedience? Do parents give kids more freedom, or expect less from them? Do parents see children as individuals with rights, and so don't ask? Does the spirit of our age go counter to the exercise of tight controls? I'm not at all sure. But I do know two things. Obedience is important. And parents are called to help but not to "make" children obey.

The importance of obedience. An infant lives by impulse. He feels, he wants, he moves, he reaches out. He doesn't make choices, but reacts to what he sees and feels. Then Mom and Dad begin a long process. They say "No" when he stretches out toward a delicate vase. They say "Let's go to bed" when he's tired. Because he lives by impulse, they have to choose for him. They give structure to his life and guide him toward what will help and not hurt.

In time he learns. But all through childhood Mom and Dad provide guidance. They say "No" at times, and "It's time for bed," and "Let's do the homework first," and "You have to be home before dark." Even when a child knows what he or she ought to do, Mom and Dad are needed. Their reminders help him go against his "want to" to what he knows is right.

Later, when a child grows through adolescence into adulthood, Mom and Dad won't be there. Then the child will either have developed internal character and motivation, and choose the right over the "want tos" of life, or he will turn back toward infancy and live by impulse. He feels, he wants, he does. He won't make choices, but simply react to what he sees and what he feels. Such a person will drift into a life full of sensation, but empty of everything that gives life meaning and purpose.

But if a child has developed internal character and motivation, he will be able to choose against the "want tos" that bombard us all. He may realize that God Himself has taken over the place of Mom and Dad—that God's words in Scripture now give him needed guidance. Then comes the grand choice to be obedient to God. And God leads him into a life rich in meaning and purpose.

That's why obedience is so important. We must learn to control our "want tos," and freely choose to do what is best, as first Mom and Dad, and then God Himself, provide the guidance that gives structure to life.

Making children obey. Not too long ago parents took obedience seriously. Many of the Christian college kids I taught in the early '70s grew up with parents who were ready to make their children obey. These parents tended to rely on rules. When kids seemed slow to respond, they tended to say very loudly, "I'm your *father*. . . ." That position carried the right to control. Often the kids were told they should do this or not do that "because I say so. And no back talk, young man!"

Some of my early counseling with parents of preschoolers focused on the frustrations of that power struggle, as parents yelled and slapped and sent to bed two- and three-year-olds, whose sin nature seemed to them the cause of their toddlers' unwillingness to jump on command.

Unfortunately, parents who fail to learn that we are not called to *make* children obey keep on trying, and all too often produce rebellious teens and turned-off adults. That's what's wrong with the force approach. We can use force to control behavior. But force will never shape the person within so that a person freely, joyfully chooses to obey. Jesus put the issue this way: "If anyone loves me, he will obey my teaching. . . . He who does not love me will not obey my teaching" (John 14:23, 24).

Helping children obey. Children and adults need guidance. Neither boys and girls, nor you and I are wise enough to live our lives without it. At first we need Mom and Dad to point out the best way. Then, for all our lives, we need God to take that role and give direction.

Children who have been helped to obey find warmth and security in doing what they know is right. They find little difficulty later, shifting to obedience to God. So it's important to know how we help our children obey.

• We build a relationship rich in love. We listen, care, and give firm guidance, which children know comes not from our impulses, but from our commitment to their best.

• We try to make it as easy as possible for children to choose what is best. → DISCIPLINE

• We demonstrate in our own lives that we do not live by impulse, but seek to do the will of God.

OCCULT. Yes, Virginia, there are spirits. If there weren't, dabbling in the occult wouldn't be so dangerous. It would still be wrong, of course. It would be wrong because turning to the occult has always been a slap in God's face; a denial that God cares for us and provides the leading we need. When we fear, or doubt, or are troubled about the future, we're to bring our cares to God, sure that He cares for us.

How about the occult, then? The Old Testament carries God's blunt, clear message to His people of every age. There is to be no one among us who "practices divination or sorcery, interprets omens, engages in witchcraft, or casts spells, or who is a medium or spiritist or who consults the dead. Anyone who does these things is detestable to the LORD, and because of these detestable practices [Moses told Israel at the conquest of Palestine] the LORD your God will drive out those nations before you. You must be blameless before the LORD your God" (Deut. 18:10–13).

OPINIONS. Someone has said that facts are what we know to be true, beliefs are what we consider to be true, and opinions are what we wish to be true. That may explain why people tend to get mad when their opinions are challenged, are mildly upset at a challenge to their beliefs, and calmly explain when someone is mixed up on the facts.

Wouldn't it be interesting to carry a scorecard around for a few days, to see if the theory proves out for us? What's most likely to get you upset with your kids or spouse? What generates the most heat at church business or board meetings? It is really the less important but more personal things that people fight over. → CONFLICT AND RESOLUTION

ORTHODOXY. It's an important word for Christians, but one that can't stand alone. What does it need with it? Orthopraxy. The one affirms we believe right. The other that we live right. We can no more have right beliefs without godly lives than we can have God's kind of faith without His kind of good works. → GOOD WORKS

OUGHTS. Oughts are like pets that lie around every house, and now and then show their temper by taking a nip at exposed ankles. Some folks I know are never bothered by Oughts. They accept them as friends and are glad to have them around. I've known others who Oughts always attack. They bark in fury, eager to dig their sharp fangs deep into the conscience.

What makes the difference? It's probably the way we view our Oughts. If we see Oughts as good things to have around, they seldom bother us. But if we glance at our Oughts and imagine they're watching, waiting for a chance to attack and condemn, why, they almost surely will. Malicious Oughts can make a human being feel like a total failure, never able to do anything right, and undeserving of any affection at all.

The problem comes from the particular breed of Oughts we keep around us. Kantian Oughts were specially bred by Immanuel Kant, a philosopher of an earlier age. He developed a breed of pure Oughts that insist on immediate obedience and gnaw on the conscience for any failure. The breed expresses Kant's own conviction that only an action undertaken from a sense of stern obligation is a moral act. There's no joy or spontaneity in his breed.

There are two families in the biblical breed of Oughts, each of which is very different from the Kantian. One is the Appropriate family. Often when we read "ought" in the New Testament, the original language is actually saying, "It is appropriate." For instance, we "ought to love each other"—because it's appropriate that we who are now linked together as brothers and sisters in God's family should warmly care.

Another family of biblical Oughts is that of Necessity. For instance, if we say "a fish ought to be in the water," we're not arguing moral obligation. We're making a statement of fact. The nature of a fish calls for it to find its home in the water. Many Oughts in the Bible are just like this. We might say "a Christian ought not to sin." In his first letter, John writes that anyone born of God actually cannot continue in sin. Jesus' life within us is so dynamic it will surely break sin's stranglehold. There is a grand necessity in Christianity that we be loosed from sin's power.

What should we do, then? Well, we need to examine the breed of Oughts we let into our lives. The Kantian Oughts will look at you piercingly, bark in furious demand, and quickly attack you if you fall short. The biblical Oughts are very different indeed. Instead of focusing their gaze on you, biblical Oughts act like pointers. They direct your attention to choices that are appropriate because you're a Christian now. Or to choices that define the realm of goodness where our new life makes it necessary for us to live.

You'll find one other wonderful difference too. Biblical Oughts don't bite. If we fail, these wonderful little friends snuggle up to us, and remind us that forgiveness is available, along with the strength to try again.

Why are biblical Oughts such special friends? Because God is their breeder. And His Oughts are filled with His love.

OURS. You can tell when a marriage or a church is healthy. Just listen awhile to how the people talk. When they don't mention "my" but keep talking about "our," you know everything will be all right.

PACIFISM. Pacifism has a long and honorable history. Many early Christians were martyred rather than serve in the Roman army, testifying with their blood to the conviction expressed by Lactantius of Bithynia around A.D. 310:

> When God prohibits killing, He not only forbids brigandage, which is not allowed even by the public laws, but He warns us not to do even those things which are legal among men. And so it will not be lawful for a just man to serve as a soldier . . . nor to accuse anyone of a capital offense, because it makes no difference whether thou kill with a sword or with a word, since killing itself is forbidden.

The logic used in support of pacifism is not always compelling. For instance, the commandment often quoted, "Thou shalt not kill," would, if translated strictly, read "Thou shalt not murder." → **CAPITAL PUNISHMENT** But the issue raised by pacifism isn't so much a matter of marshaling arguments as it is one of individual struggle, to come to a personal commitment to what God wants each individual to do. For even if some wars are justified, it does not follow that every Christian ought to go to war. Nevertheless, it is helpful for us to consider the common arguments, and then to consider the options.

"It can be right for a believer to go to war." All realists recognize the inevitability of war. We live in a world moved by sinful passions; history's pages are blotted with the ugly evidence that war visits every nation. The question the Christian pacifist raises is not "Can we stop wars?" (we can't) or "Are wars wrong?" (they are) but rather "Is my going to war ever justified?"

Many believe that there are times when going to war is right, and even an obligation. They insist that the believer is called to resist evil. Surely going to war to defeat Hitler's Germany, with its brutal treatment of all races, was a moral necessity. One committed to good cannot stand by and contribute to evil by refusing to resist.

Many point to the Bible itself for support. They point out the clear distinction made in the Old Testament between murder and killing in war. Different Hebrew words are used, and while murder brings guilt, killing an enemy in war does not.

Many also look at the function of war in Old Testament times. Godly men were warriors—men like David and Jonathan and Joshua. God is specifically said to have used wars for His own purposes, including executing His judgment on the sin of peoples whose wickedness was institutionalized as national policy (cf. Gen. 15:16; Deut. 18:12; 20:1–20).

It may well be then that an individual will conclude going to war is not God's will for him. But is it possible to conclude that going to war is always wrong?

"It can be right for a believer to refuse to go to war."
When we move away from the absolutist's "wrong/right" approach, the question rightly focuses on the issue, "Is it right for me to refuse to go to war?"

Government, which recognizes the rights of conscientious objectors, refuses to let them base their plea on whether or not a particular war is a just war. The conscientious objector must be against all war—the war against Nazi Germany as well as the war in Vietnam. On what do believers who are pacifists base their personal convictions?

Many believe that while "thou shalt not kill" focuses on murder, it also affirms the importance of human life. That implicit affirmation is far more compelling than the competing notion, "Thou shalt fight for freedom" or "for your country." In a competition between values, the pacifist comes down squarely for the primacy of human life.

Some argue that the Old Testament's "angry God" has been supplanted by the New Testament's "loving God," and thus the Old Testament is not binding. But others are unwilling to so twist the Bible. Instead they point out that in Old Testament times Israel was a theocratic nation. Whatever we may say to justify war today, we can hardly identify any modern country as the "people of God."

There is another concern pacifists often express. Trust in weaponry is non-Christian in its moral assumptions. To live in the kingdom of God calls for decisive rejection of the kingdom of man, and the values that shape it. Only by personal commitment to live out the moral vision of such Scripture passages as the Sermon on the Mount can a Christian give testimony to God.

The options.   If we refuse to argue the absolute rightness or wrongness of war, we're freed to focus on the personal issue expressed by the pacifist. Christians in the military honestly believe that good men must be willing to stand against evil, and that godly men can be warriors. They see defensive war justified today as in Old Testament times. Other Christians refuse to serve in the military, and honestly believe that the value of human life must be placed above other values. They do not believe modern war is parallel to Old Testament wars involving Israel. They do believe that their radical commitment to a kingdom lifestyle testifies to God's new and better way.

If you as an individual reach the first conclusion, and are called to military service or choose to enlist, you have that freedom under the lordship of Christ. If you reach the second conclusion, and believe that going to war is wrong for you, you have options. If drafted you can file as a conscientious objector. You will not be compelled to serve. But you may be required to perform some other service, or offered the opportunity to become a military medic. You would not carry weapons. You would carry comfort—and perhaps life itself—to the wounded on both sides.

396   **PAIN.**   The simplest way to look at pain is to see it as

God's early warning system. The flame burns us, and we jerk our hand back before we can be seriously injured. The tragedy of leprosy is that the sufferers lose the capacity to feel pain, and as they go about daily activities literally wear their fingers and toes away.

That's the simplest way to look at pain: as a gift from God, to keep us from serious injury.

But we can't fit all pain into that gift-wrapped package. Take chronic pain—the nagging backache that sells so many Doans pills, or the migrane that persists for weeks. This kind of pain drains life of all joy. Is this pain too a gift?

In some way all things, even pain, work together for good in our lives, for God uses them to shape us toward Christlikeness (Rom. 8:28, 29). But relief from pain can also be a great gift. So let's focus on healing. Is there relief these days from chronic pain?

Doctors and researchers are increasingly finding ways to release us from pain. Pain clinics are becoming relatively common in our country. A number of techniques are used to help. There are bio-feedback, acupuncture, electrical stimulation, hypnosis, drugs, exercise, and other means to deal with the physical roots of our pain. But the evidence mounts that this kind of treatment isn't enough. Personal reaction to pain is proving one of the most significant factors for recovery.

All too often pain brings little, hidden benefits. A wife may show extra affection when her husband is in pain, and unconsciously he's willing to suffer a little for that reward. A nagging backache is likely to persist—if it means a person can stay home from a difficult, boring job. The pain is real. But we're less willing to fight to overcome pain if it has some subjective payoff. Studies have shown that people who live exciting, active lives are seldom incapacitated by pain. It's not that the person with chronic pain pretends, or even that he wants the pain. It's just that the overall quality of his or her life has a significant impact on recovery.

Looked at this way, it may be that even chronic pain is a gift from God. Persistent pain may be God's invitation to reevaluate. Is return to our normal life important to us? Or is it possible that our "normal life" isn't as full of meaning as God intends it to be?

If we suffer chronic pain, it's vital to get medical help, of course. But it may be spiritually vital to let pain stimulate us to look at our life, and see if God is inviting us to stretch out toward something more.

Oh, one more thing. The particular pain most often mentioned in the Bible is the pain of childbirth. Out of agony, a fresh new life is born. Just so, pain may be a prelude to a fresh new life for you.

PARENTING.   A psychiatrist provides a healthy reminder: "We are beginning to see that parents have, in the past, too often blamed themselves for the way their children behave. . . . Parents do have a tremendous effect on their kids, but kids are also born with personalities that affect their behavior." However our children turn out, we can't take all the credit. Or accept all the blame.

In fact, what parenting requires is that our children are brought up in a climate in which they are most likely to grow: a context Ephesians 6:4 calls bringing them up "in the training and instruction of the Lord." This Ephesians emphasis isn't on content. "Christian nurture" is not simply providing information about God. Christian nurture is distinctive because it seeks to bring children up with *the same kind of training and instruction* the Lord uses with us!

What guiding principles seen in God the Father's parenting of us can we apply to life with our children? Here are four principles stressed in Scripture that are also stressed in modern research on child development.

• Parents can help build a sense of personal worth. God never hesitates to let us know that He loves us, and that we are important to Him. To follow His lead we must help our children feel loved and important. One important aid: praise. Anyone who is nagged or constantly criticized grows up feeling unsure of himself and doubting his worth. Studies have shown that children are particularly sensitive to criticism. One Christian researcher suggests it takes ten incidents of praise to counter one angry criticism. Following God's pattern will lead us to stress encouragement and affirmation. → EXPECTATIONS

• Parents can help by providing consistent discipline. Looking to God, we immediately see that "discipline" isn't "punishment." Instead, its focus is loving guidance, which sets limits within which children can be secure. Discipline calls for real commitment by Mom and Dad: we need to care enough and be wise enough to help our children live successfully within meaningful limits. → DISCIPLINE

• Parents can help children develop lasting values. God boldly communicates His values to us. In Jesus He comes and lives out those values, so we can see and follow Him. The Bible and the behavioral sciences agree that communicating values is more a matter of relationships than of providing information. When Mom and Dad build warm, loving relationships and share thoughts and feelings with their children, values are communicated, and lives are shaped. → MODELING

• Parents can help by providing a spiritual framework for life. God in Scripture helps us see beyond man's horizons, to understand the basic issues of life. God helps us find meaning and purpose, by linking every experience with Himself. God first becomes real to children as they sense His reality to Mom and Dad. In many ways parents can help children develop an awareness of God's presence and His importance. → FAMILY DEVOTIONS

There is nothing you and I can do to "guarantee" how our children will turn out. Each human being has, and exercises, the freedom of responsible choice. But when we pattern our parenting on God's way of dealing with us, we have confidence, and a promise. We can "train up a child in the way he should go, and when he is old he will not turn from it" (Prov. 22:6).

PASSION. You can tell a lot about anything by the words with which it keeps company. For instance, you never see "passion" with companions like "mild" or "calm." Instead "passion" always hangs around with

399

"overwhelming" and "towering" and "ungovernable."

Some people connect "passion" with sex. It certainly can be used to describe ardent love and sexual desire, but actually, passion describes emotions of every sort, as distinct from reason. That phrase "distinct from reason" is important. We never expect anyone "in the grip of passion" to stop to think or to be reasonable. Passion demands instant action, on impulse.

A quick glance in the Bible suggests that passion isn't a very respectable word. It's not that emotions and feelings are wrong. → EMOTIONS It's just that the New Testament epistles view the roots of passion as sunk deep in the old nature. So Galatians 5:24 speaks of "the sinful nature with its passions" and Titus 2:12 and 3:3 mention "ungodliness and worldly passion," as well as being "enslaved by all kinds of passion."

The last phrase gives us the clue. Enslaved. Whenever any emotion grips us so strongly that we're overpowered, forced by our heated emotions to act, we've lost our way. No wonder God says the passions that grip us are in conflict with the Spirit, who wants us to walk a different way.

So next time you feel your passions aroused, stop and do this simple check. That same Galatians passage says that the fruit produced when the Spirit is in control is "love, joy, peace, patience, kindness, goodness, faithfulness, gentleness and self-control" (Gal. 5:22). Any passion that crowds out the crop of goodness had better be abandoned.

PATIENCE. "Patience" is a word that sounds pale, almost sickly. It suggests a wilted person: an empty person, crushed by life, marking time because it's no use struggling any more. Patience is such a passive grace.

In English, perhaps. But in the Bible? Never! In Scripture, "patience" has a bold, courageous ring. To communicate it requires several Greek words, but the underlying meaning of "patience" is confident endurance. The patient man is undefeated. He stands firm, buffeted by life, but quietly persistent in doing good.

We need to understand what patience means. When our toddlers annoy, patience reminds us that we can endure and remain calm. When our efforts fail, patience reminds us that we need not surrender, but can overcome. When others misunderstand or accuse us, patience reminds us that grace is longsuffering, and so we can keep on caring.

Perhaps 1 Corinthians 15:58 sums up the grace of patience and our calling as well: "My dear brothers, stand firm. Let nothing move you. Always give yourselves fully to the work of the Lord, because you know that your labor in the Lord is not in vain."

PEACE. One day there will be peace everywhere—when God personally intervenes. This is the message of the prophets for a world torn by wars. And there's a similar message for individuals who churn with inner turmoil: peace cannot be found apart from God.

It's important to realize that both testaments view peace as inner well-being rather than quiet circumstances. Peace, as inner well-being expressed in social harmony, went astray when mankind turned from God to try life on it's own (cf. Rom. 1:28–32). Isaiah describes the personal impact of that choice when he writes, "the wicked are like the tossing sea, which cannot rest, whose waves cast up mire and mud. 'There is no peace,' says my God, 'for the wicked'" (57:20, 21).

Because peace is an inner issue for the individual, God can deal with it now rather than waiting on Jesus' return.

Numbers 6:24–26 records the blessing God commanded to pronounce over Israel:

> The LORD bless you
>   and keep you;
> the LORD make his face shine upon you
>   and be gracious to you;
> the LORD turn his face toward you
>   and give you peace.

Jesus expands on the blessing and makes us this promise: "Peace I leave with you; my peace I give you. I do not give to you as the world gives. Do not let your hearts be troubled and do not be afraid" (John 14:27).

God never promises us Disneyland. But He does promise that when we turn to Him, no matter how harried or tense our circumstances, we can know peace within. How do we find peace? We stop looking at and fretting about our circumstances. We trust ourselves to God, who knows our every need.

PERFECTIONISTS. I once employed a perfectionist as a writer/editor. It was a strain on both of us. She agonized over every project, gathered much more information than she could ever use, wrote and rewrote every page, and puzzled over words, tormented by the thought it might be better to use a synonym.

She put off starting on new projects: she needed to be sure she'd done enough research. She put off starting the day's work: she had to go over what she'd done the day before, and find some file to straighten. It was hard for her to turn in a final draft: she felt compelled to re-edit it one more time. As a result, she never met her deadlines, and I ended up doing my work and much of hers too. As I said, it was a strain on both of us. She felt worse and worse about not getting her work done. And I wasn't too happy about late nights, working to do her share after finishing mine.

Looking back, I think it was probably harder on her. It must be terrible to feel you have to do better than you can. How freeing it would be if perfectionists could realize that God knows our weaknesses and can work in spite of them. All any of us can offer others is the best we have, even though that best falls short of what it might be if we were perfect. The good news of the gospel is that God takes our efforts, sanctifies them by His Spirit, and uses them to touch the lives of others. The effectiveness of our effort does not depend on the perfection of our product, but on the working of the Spirit of the living God.

There's a freeing prescription for perfectionists—particularly perfectionists in any kind of ministry. "Do the best you can in the time you have." And stop taking yourself so seriously. The One you need to take seriously is God.

PERSECUTION. Christians have always been a target for persecution. At times persecution has been society-wide, as in contemporary Russia. At other times it's a private affair: a mild concoction of glances, gossip, and discrimination. At times Christians invite persecution by being self-righteous and condemning others. But it hurts when we're only trying to live quiet and godly lives, and goodness itself seems to goad those around us.

If you've felt the hurt of private persecution, two passsages of Scripture are worth memorizing. Here they are:

"If the world hates you, keep in mind that it hated me first. If you belonged to the world, it would love you as its own. As it is, you do not belong to the world, but I have chosen you out of the world. That is why the world hates you. Remember the words I spoke to you: 'No servant is greater than his master.' If they persecuted me, they will persecute you also" (John 15:18–20).

The other passage is from Peter's first letter. "It is commendable if a man bears up under the pain of unjust suffering because he is conscious of God. But how is it to your credit if you receive a beating for doing wrong and endure it? But if you suffer for doing good and you endure it, this is commendable before God" (1 Peter 2:19, 20).

PERSUASION. I like the dictionary definition: "to win over to a belief or course of action." I like it because it focuses responsibility where it belongs. The individual we seek to persuade must be respected as the one ultimately responsible to make his or her own decision. It's all right for us to try to win others over. It's wrong to insist.

One passage in Paul's second letter to Timothy (2:24–26) explores the art of persuasion. Here's what the apostle says: "The Lord's servant must not quarrel; instead, he must be kind to everyone, able to teach, not resentful. Those who oppose him he must gently instruct,

403

PLASTIC SURGERY in the hope that God will grant them repentance leading them to a knowledge of the truth, and that they will come to their senses and escape from the trap of the devil, who has taken them captive to do his will.'' We won't always be trying to persuade others about revealed truth. But whenever we seek to persuade, this passage suggests guidelines to remember.

● We must not quarrel. Persuasion isn't competition, in which we win if the other adopts our beliefs or chooses our course of action, and lose if he does not. This is particularly important when dealing with loved ones. We are to care—but not to take things so personally that we become resentful or angry. Instead, we must guard the other person's sense of personal freedom: we appeal, but never demand.

● We must care. In persuasion, the needs of the other person and his or her best interests are paramount. Opposition must not move us from gently suggesting thoughts the other can use in evaluating his own best course. If we remain gentle and unthreatening, the other person is more likely to hear what we say, and to realize we're concerned about his or her needs rather than our own.

● We must release. In persuasion, our hope is that God will lead others to the best decision. Even persons trapped in Satan's web must be given the freedom to be personally responsible for their own actions. We can never *make* a person believe or choose what is best. We must communicate our own conviction that he is free to choose, and then we must trust God to work in his life.

Each of these three principles is important in our relationships with others. By caring, by speaking gently, and by releasing others to God, we follow God's prescription for a winsome persuasion to what is best.

PLASTIC SURGERY. Someone has suggested that plastic surgery is ''undoing nature's mistakes.'' It certainly can ease the ravages of time. But interestingly, vanity isn't the primary reason most seek cosmetic surgery. For many, an operation is undertaken because it's felt to be important to a career or social life. There's no question that plastic surgery may have a positive psychological effect as well. It does help some people feel better about themselves.

Today plastic surgery is inexpensive enough to be in range for most people. Nearly 90% of all cosmetic surgery is done on the head and neck, and involves relatively minor procedures. Much is actually done in the doctor's office rather than in the hospital. What are the most common procedures? Improving the shape of the nose, correcting receding chins, removing facial scars, and tightening sagging facial skin (face-lifting).

If you do decide to check out plastic surgery, be sure anyone you consult is certified by the American Board of Plastic Surgery. Visit his or her office, tell clearly what you hope for from the surgery, and get information on all crucial details—any risks, chances of success, length of recovery time, fees and other costs. It's not out of line to ask to talk with a doctor's former patients. Plastic surgery is something like art, and talent as well as training counts!

How about spiritual issues? Some are sure to argue it's not "nature's mistake" that plastic surgery undoes, but rather it seeks to change something God has purposefully given. For those with this point of view, cosmetic surgery involves going against God's will.

Others have an interesting response. No one hesitates to correct a physical defect like a club foot or cleft palate. Why are cosmetic defects so different? God has given us the means to control many things in our environment. Should we reject air conditioning because God has given the South a hot climate? Why, when cosmetic surgery can correct a feature that makes us emotionally uncomfortable, shouldn't we use it, and be thankful to God who has made it possible?

This issue, as so many things in life, boils down to a simple thing. In no "disputable thing" (Rom. 14:1) can we make rules for other people. So we are each free to consider the options before us, and ask God what He wants us to do.

PORNOGRAPHY. As Judge Wagner of New York

observed in 1924 about "obscene" and "indecent," it seems unnecessary to define pornography. "These words are in common use and their meaning is readily comprehended by men of ordinary intelligence." Perhaps. But the courts since have had great trouble with all these words that "defy misunderstanding." It may be because such material is aimed at the glands as much as the mind. At any rate, the courts have carefully shied away from attempts to define, and instead have appealed to that questionable construct, the "conscience of the community." Pornography, like the obscene, is not judged by the supposed impact on the young or susceptible, but its relationship to the attitudes of that modern myth, the "Average Man." Even then if a film or book has "redeeming social value" it will not be challenged, although no one quite knows how to legally define social value either.

What's a reasonable Christian view of pornography, and a citizen's reasonable response? We can hardly venture to impose our conscience on an admittedly pagan culture. But there must be some grounds on which to take a stand.

The problem with pornography. A number of fears have surfaced as our society has had increasing experience with sex and violence in the media. Specific cases have been documented in which individuals have acted out rape and other violent acts they have read about or seen on TV. The field of socialization suggests that we can expect individuals to imitate actions they see modeled again and again in films or in print. Statistics show a parallel between crime statistics, and violence and sex in the media.

An excellent book by H. J. Eysenck and D. K. B. Nias, published jointly in the United States and Great Britain in 1978, examines *Sex and Violence and the Media*. The authors carefully study the multitudes of experiments done to evaluate the impact of exposure to violence and pornographic representations, and reach several conclusions. While pornography may have different effects on different individuals, they argue that "effects on viewers and readers can no longer be disputed." There is clear evidence that some are provoked to antisocial sexual behavior, and even to aggression and violence. This is particularly the case when perversions are represented: such things as incest, sadism, and rape. Brutalized portrayal of human beings, and portrayal of pornography, "has effects on many people which cause them to interfere with the lives, health and happiness of other people."

The authors conclude with an appeal to society and the courts to weigh the "amusement, enjoyment and delight viewers may derive from such presentations against the injuries, degradation and even deaths which may be caused to innocent victims who become subject to the perverted sexual and violent urges in part produced or increased by these portrayals."

The individual and pornography. There's little need to suggest that Christians pass up any "amusement, enjoyment and delight" pornography may appear to offer. Colossians 3:5 calls on us to "put to death whatever belongs to your earthly nature: sexual immorality, impurity, lust, evil desires. . . ." The more difficult question is how to deal with pornography when it surfaces in a community. Some groups picket X-rated theaters and "Adult" bookstores. Usually this succeeds only in giving these enterprises free publicity. Another approach seems called for.

• Research. What state or local laws govern obscene or pornographic materials in your community? What prosecutors are charged with enforcement? How common is possession of such materials in the high schools? (In some communities, school lockers are filled.) Have there been any incidents of which police are aware linking crimes with pornography?

• Educate. Do not make pornography a religious issue. Seek to inform of documented links between pornography and harm to innocent victims. Much information is available in the Eysenck book mentioned above, published in the United States by St. Martin's Press, New York.

Seek ways to present your concerns and the evidence to city councils, through the newspapers, and in other ways. Make it clear that this issue is not motivated by a puritan conscience but by deep concern for those who are innocent victims.

● Agitate. The courts have been hesitant to appeal to possible harm to others in evaluating pornographic materials. They have simply tried to apply the test of whether or not material would be judged obscene or pornographic by the typical member of the community. Expressing concern to local judges, and presenting evidence of harm to others, becomes particularly important.

Our world today is one in which the community conscience is rapidly deteriorating. People consider acceptable today things that would have shocked and horrified their parents. It may well be essential for Christians to take a stand for the hidden victims of our society's rush toward indecency. You may even find, to your surprise, that the one called to make that stand in your community is you.

POSSESSIONS. John Wesley, founder of the Methodist Church and fulcrum of the 50-year revival that reshaped England, was concerned about one impact of his ministry. The converted turned away from sin and settled down to live productive lives. As a result, they began to make and to save money. Gradually these hard-working Methodists were becoming wealthy.

So Wesley wrote a warning, explaining the only way the converts could maintain their zeal and purity and full commitment to God. Wesley's advice is simple. Believers should work as hard as they can, to gain as much as they can—so they can give as much as they can. Then and only then would these believers be safe.

When Wesley himself died after five decades of ceaseless evangelism, his only possession was the silver spoon with which he ate.

He left it here. And went to claim the mounds of treasure his own commitment to God had won for him in heaven.

POTENTIAL. "I could be a writer . . ." an acquaintance was fond of telling me. I agreed. I never question anyone's claim to have potential. I know that God made us wonderfully and well: tremendous potential is part of what it means to be a human being and redeemed.

But my acquaintance who is sure she could hasn't, and probably never will. Jesus' familiar story of the talents illustrates why. Each received a different treasure entrusted to him and was told to invest it. Each who did so was praised: he had been faithful in using what he had. The individual who wrapped his talent and buried it took no risks. But won no praise.

It's not our potential that counts. It's what we do with it that concerns God.

POVERTY AND THE POOR. We have mixed feelings about the poor. On the one hand, we care. Everyone should have basic needs met. On the other hand, many of us feel a little put out. Aren't most of the poor to blame for their own situation? If they'd just go to work, they could find some way to support themselves rather than sponge off society. At least, that's how many Americans feel.

The Bible has much to say about the poor and the oppressed. We need to read carefully, because we want our own attitude to reflect God's as closely as that is possible. So here's a simple quiz.

Poor quiz. Mark a plus beside each of the following statements with which you agree. If you agree strongly, put a couple of plus marks. If you disagree, use a minus sign.

1. Poverty is a state of mind more than anything else.
2. Most poor people lack ambition.
3. Society should accept responsibility for maintaining a moderate standard of living for the poor.
4. Those who work should not be forced to support those who are able-bodied but will not work.
5. Rather than giving welfare, society should insist the poor do community service work in return for their money.

409

It's surprising to see how much there is in the Bible about poverty. Here are just a few verses from one book— Proverbs. Read them carefully, and then go back over your responses to the poor quiz. Is there anything in these verses that seems to confirm your responses? Is there anything in these verses that might lead you to change an answer?

- A poor man's field may produce abundant food, but injustice sweeps it away. (13:23)
- The poor are shunned even by their neighbors, but the rich have many friends. (14:20)
- He who oppresses the poor shows contempt for their Maker, but whoever is kind to the needy hon- - ors God. (14:31)
- Better to be lowly in spirit and among the oppressed than to share plunder with the proud. (16:19)
- He who mocks the poor shows contempt for their Maker; whoever gloats over disaster will not go unpunished. (17:5)
- Better a poor man whose walk is blameless than a fool whose lips are perverse. (19:1)
- A sluggard does not plow in season; so at harvest time he looks but finds nothing. (20:4)

There are more verses in Proverbs, but this is a fair example.

Always with you. Jesus once observed that "you will always have the poor among you" (John 12:8). It's not that Jesus didn't care. In fact, if the blueprint the Old Testament outlines for Israel's society had been followed, it would have solved the problem of poverty (Deut. 15:4). But while the Bible recognizes that some are poor because of their own sloth, most Old Testament references to poverty suggest that its root cause is oppression. Whenever people love material things rather than care for others, misery will stalk a land.

The causes of poverty are so complex in our society that no simple solutions can be found. We can't blame poverty on the poor, and absolve the institutions that oppress them. We can't blame poverty on the system, and absolve the individual of responsibility. And we dare not let our attitude toward the needy harden.

This is perhaps the most important message for you and me. Look back over that quiz once more. Do your responses to the statements suggest that your own heart is tender, or hard? Do you keep on caring, or do you begin to blame and condemn, and so deny responsibility to relieve the misery of other human beings?

Every now and then God will throw you or me into contact with those in need. When that happens, there may be few guidelines to tell us how—or whether—we are to be involved. But one principle is clear. We do need a tender heart and an open mind, for "whosoever is kind to the needy honors God."

POWER.   Power is a fearsome word, all too often associated with exploitation, force, and repression. We get an insight into the nature of power when we try to visualize a warm, close relationship with a truly powerful individual. Somehow "warm" and "close" don't quite fit with "power."

Attempts by behavioral scientists to develop theories about power tend to emphasize conflict. Power is applied when people differ, and someone wants to win.

Just look over these traditional concepts of power, and sense the relationships each suggests.

• Person A has power over person B to the extent that A can get B to do something he would not do otherwise.

• Person A has power to the extent he can change person B's probable behavior. This power resides in person A by virtue of greater physical, financial, informational, charismatic, or other resources.

• Person A has power when he controls the resources that person B must have to satisfy his wants or needs.

• Person A has power to the extent he can force person B to act in ways that accomplish person A's goals.

• Person A has power to the extent that he is able to affect person B's ability to reach his own goals.

Each of these power theories makes me uncomfortable. Each shows person A treating person B as an object, not as another human being. No one, not even a child, enjoys being treated as an object and thus robbed of respect.

Sometimes the kinds of power just described are held by institutions rather than individuals. Governments, industries, unions—even churches—are likely to bring power to bear on citizens, workers, or members. All too often the group that controls the institution seems an arrogant gerontocracy, misusing its position to maintain personal privileges rather than carry out the mission of the institution.

No wonder "power" is hardly the favorite word in most people's vocabulary.

The Bible on power. One New Testament word representing power picks up the coercive theme: it reflects the use of violence to impose one's will. But other biblical terms carry a different message. Many words of power call our attention to strength, or health, or ability. These words contrast power with impotence, and point to Jesus as the One who gives us strength. While God will use His strength to scatter the proud, He also stoops to make that same unimaginable power exercised to raise Jesus, available to us (cf. Eph. 1:19). Other New Testament words for power focus on inherent ability, and convey the exciting news that God's power enriches our lives.

When we read what the Bible has to say about power, we're struck with the contrast between divine and human power theories. Mankind is excited at the prospect of power to gain control over others. God is excited by the potential of power, to release human beings from the control of sin, of Satan, and of one another.

Power is used by man to enslave.

Power is used by God to free.

When we have power. One of the most important things you and I can learn by examining power from these two perspectives is how to use any power we may have.

We're to reject the temptation that power brings to use or control others. We are to accept the responsibility that comes with power to follow God's example, and to serve others.

We shouldn't use parent power to make our children obey. We need to use parent power to help our children grow. → DISCIPLINE

We shouldn't use employer power to make subordinates do things our way. We should use employer power to help employees become effective and productive, with a maximum amount of self-determination.

We shouldn't use power as church leaders to make decisions that commit others to tasks we assign. We should use leadership power to help others grow, and find their own leading from the Lord.

Power for Christians is a means for enabling, and for providing release. It is only in the world that "power" is distorted, becoming chains that hold others in bondage to our will.

PRAISE.

Shout with joy to God, all the earth!
Sing to the glory of his name;
offer him glory and praise!
Say to God, "How awesome are your deeds!
So great is your power
that your enemies cringe before you.
All the earth bows down to you;
they sing praise to you,
they sing praise to your name."
Come and see what God has done,
how awesome his works in man's behalf!
He turned the sea into dry land,
they passed through the river on foot—
come, let us rejoice in him.
He rules forever by his power,
his eyes watch the nations—
let not the rebellious rise up against him.
Praise our God, O peoples,
let the sound of his praise be heard.

413

These verses from Psalm 66 (2–8) capture the nature of praise. Praise focuses our attention on God and all He has done, kindles a sense of wonder and joy, and finds expression in telling God how awed and thrilled we are at who He is.

Praise is perhaps the purist and most appropriate response of man to God.

It's possible to point out many benefits of praise. One of the most important is that when we focus on God's qualities, recalling the ways that quality is expressed in Creation and Redemption, we build a vital image of who God is. A person whose eyes are filled with the greatness of God is unlikely to be terrified by mere men. A person who has praised God for miracles is unlikely to be discouraged by difficulties. A person who has expressed joy in the saving love God has poured out is unlikely to feel depressed or alone. There are great and wonderful benefits to us when we learn to praise. But they are hardly the reason why praise is so important. That reason is utterly simple.

He is worthy.

PRAYER. I've read many books on prayer. Too many of them approach prayer as if it were an obstacle course. God's answer is a prize to be won, but only if we overcome hurdles He's placed in our way. Spoken of usually as "conditions" for answered prayer, authors insist we must ● believe when we ask, ● not regard sin in our hearts, ● ask in God's will, ● have no selfish motives, and so on.

Reading these stern interpretations of phrases found in God's Word, prayer seems to become a tense, threatening chore. Our technique must be just right. God, the all-seeing Judge, gives points, and when we fail to clear the hurdles He is quick to withhold the prize.

What bothers me about such interpretations is that they're hardly honest to God. They distort the vision given in the Bible of a loving, welcoming God; a vision we see reinforced again and again when we read the Bible's words about prayer. Listen, for instance, to the tone of just three New Testament passages:

• "We do not have a high priest who is unable to sympathize with our weaknesses, but we have one who has been tempted in every way, just as we are—yet was without sin. Let us then approach the throne of grace with confidence, so that we may receive mercy and find grace to help us in our time of need" (Heb. 4:15, 16).

• "And when you pray, do not keep on babbling like pagans, for they think they will be heard because of their many words. Do not be like them, for your Father knows what you need before you ask him. This is how you should pray: Our Father . . ." (Matt. 6:7–9).

• "Ask and it will be given to you; seek and you will find; knock and the door will be opened to you. For everyone who asks receives; he who seeks finds; and to him who knocks, the door will be opened. Which of you, if his son asks for bread, will give him a stone? Or if he asks for a fish, will give him a snake? If you, then, though you are evil, know how to give good gifts to your children, how much more will your Father in heaven give good gifts to those who ask him?" (Matt. 7:7–11).

The God who invites us to come to Him in prayer is the warm, loving Father we know so well in Jesus—not some distant Judge who is more concerned with our technique than with our need.

What about those so-called "conditions"? Why, instead of hurdles, they are promises and reminders. When we ask, and are inexplicably filled with a sense of peace and assurance, God's Spirit is telling us we have been heard. When we're invited to pray in Jesus' name or in God's will, we are being assured that God the Spirit is our prayer-companion: He will guide our thoughts and desires so our prayers can be answered. When we're warned about clutching sin close or about selfish motives, we are being told honestly that our choices prevent us from experiencing God's best. No, God isn't threatening us. He doesn't treat prayer as a carrot-stick affair, to force us on toward greater efforts. God isn't that kind of person at all.

To understand prayer, we simply need to look up at the character of our God. We need to see the loving Father. We need to hear Him invite us to share every need and confess every sin. Catching the vision of God as He is unveiled in the Bible's great passages on prayer, we realize that prayer is not "spiritual exercise." It's not an obstacle course. It's not a religious duty.

Prayer is nothing less than responding to the warm assurance of God's love, and accepting His invitation to come to our Father and to share.

PRIDE. Pride is born as a tiny thought: "I'm better than. . . ." It may be nothing important. "I'm better than Joey at imitating owls." Or, later, "I'm better than anyone at math." Whatever, that infant pride grows by comparison. We look at others, and pride swells when we observe, "I'm better than. . . ."

Paul looks at the men who compete for "better thans" in life and notes dryly, "When they measure themselves by themselves and compare themselves with themselves, they are not wise." We can always find others we surpass. But Paul concludes, "Let him who boasts boast in the Lord. For it is not the one who commends himself who is approved, but the one whom the Lord commends" (2 Cor. 10:12, 17, 18).

God never commends us for being "better than" someone else. He simply commends us for being faithful with what we have.

PRIORITIES. We all know they're important. And actually, it's quite easy to set them. Just follow these simple steps:

1. Make a list of the things you commonly do each day, or each week.
2. Jot down beside each item the amount of time you typically spend daily or weekly.
3. Put a check mark beside "must" activities (√).
   Put a plus mark beside three "most important" activities.
   Put a minus mark beside three "least important" activities.
4. Write down your three most important personal relationships.

416

Now, look over the list with its times, checks, pluses, and minuses, and underline activities that specifically enrich the three important personal relationships you identified.

In setting priorities, time is the key. That check list should give you guidance, helping you see where you can rearrange your use of time to focus more on the relationships or things that are important to you.

Putting this kind of evaluation down on paper is important. But it won't make any difference, unless you go on to engrave those priorities deeply in your heart and life.

PRIVACY. The group broke up when Dan and Ellen wouldn't share. At least, that's what the others claimed.

The five couples had been meeting together weekly to share and study the Bible. They had started because each yearned for intimacy and Christian caring—something none felt they found at church. They began with a covenant: each promised to be there, to pray, and to share.

That was the problem. As the weeks passed the others began to feel uncomfortable with Dan and Ellen. They came each week. But they seemed to hold back when the others shared. Finally there was a confrontation, and the two were accused. Ellen responded angrily. "What you really mean is that we've got to be like you to be accepted."

Dan and Ellen were private people, and sharing wasn't easy. But privacy wasn't permitted in that little group.

The right of privacy. "Privacy" has been defined as "each person's exclusive access to a realm of his or her own." Usually we assume others have the right to set their own limits: they can invite others into their private space, or not. No one can demand indiscriminate disclosure; demands debase rather than enrich intimacy.

The little group Dan and Ellen met with made the same mistake often made by secular Encounter Groups, and by other Christian small-group fellowships. Members demanded disclosure, denying the right of privacy. They were unwilling to take the slower route to intimacy, which respects each person's freedom and counts on a gradual development of trust to bring a refreshing transparency.

Parents sometimes make the same mistake with teens. Mom or Dad will slip into a teen's room—just to look around. And then pick up a diary, or glance through a letter. Such invasion of privacy whether or not discovered distorts relationships, and stunts the growth of trust.

The one essential: trust. There is much in the Bible that promises us freedom to share even our private and personal experiences. Often we hurt inside and need the prayers and the support of people who know and care. Teens need it. Adults need it. And God intends us to find freedom to share in the warm, supportive fellowship of God's family.

But God's invitation in Christ to discover deep and freeing personal relationships is no license for forcing our way into another's private space. It is only by respecting others fully, loving them freely, and sharing ourselves that the confidence grows: here are very special people indeed, whom we can trust with our inner selves. → ACCEPTANCE

PROCESS. The day after the seeds were drilled into the ground, the field seemed only barren dirt. Later yellow-green sprouts appeared: Later still you could see that the sprouts marched in rows. When the corn plants were inches high, I rode a horse-drawn cultivator, guiding the blades to root out the weeds that grew between the rows.

Later I walked through the field with a hoe, cutting weeds between the plants. By July 4th the plants were knee high.

At summer's end the stalks eared out, as plump kernels budded within nestled green husks. Finally the silken tassels began to brown and stiffen. Then, on brisk October days, I walked with my uncle and grandfather, husking the ears from the stalks and tossing the bright yellow cylinders on the flat-bedded wagon that moved alongside.

Only then, when the process was complete, could we measure the harvest.

Sometimes it's hard for parents and preachers to remember. People are God's tender, growing things. We can't force premature harvest, or measure the richness of their lives before its time. All we can do—all we are to do—is tend the process, loving freely to enrich the soil in which they grow. Life is a process. We farmers, whether we grow corn or nurture human lives, are called on to have patience and hope. → EXPECTATIONS

PROFANITY. Just a cursory glance at the history of swearing suggests it is as old as language. For some, profanity seems to be a social necessity: swear words are used to decorate relaxed conversation. For others it's a verbal convenience: swear words release tension, or serve as verbal aggression. It is rather fascinating that while some sins seem to produce at least momentary pleasures, swearing offers no particular reward, although one political scientist suggests that diplomats be encouraged to use swearing in international affairs as a substitute for war. I suppose it would be good to find some use for what George Washington, in a General Order to the American Army in 1776, called "impiety and folly . . . a vice so mean and low, without any temptation, that every man of sense and character detests and despises it."

PROPHECY. Jeanne Dixon. Edgar Cayse. And all others quoted so often in the national tabloids. Are they really modern-day prophets? Some think so. And wait breathlessly for their next pronouncement.

But believers are given clear guidelines in Scripture on how to identify true and false prophets. Deuteronomy 18 tells us that a true prophet will: ● come from among the company of believers (v. 18); ● speak only what God has commanded, and speak in the Lord's name (vv. 18, 20); and ● *everything* he announces as a prophecy will take place (v. 22). If what he foretells does not happen, "that is a message the Lord has not spoken. . . . Do not be afraid of him" (v. 22).

It's certainly possible for false prophets (those not speaking God's message) to be right about future events some of the time, especially if the "prophecy" is stated in general enough terms. But the pages of the *National Enquirer* and the *Star* hardly merit the serious attention given Scripture.

How then about Christian groups that believe in modern-day prophetic utterances? These are believers. And they do claim to speak in God's name.

Some believe that Paul's expression in 1 Corinthians 13:8 ("where there are prophecies, they will cease") indicates that when the New Testament was completed, God no longer needed to speak to us through prophets. They argue that this ministry no longer operates, although it did operate in the early church (cf. 13:2). Others insist that prophecy is a spiritual gift, and does occur today as well as in New Testament days. But all should agree on two things. ● No contemporary prophet would have a message that changes or contradicts the Scripture. And ● the ancient test must still apply. The words a prophet speaks as God's message to His own must actually come to pass, or the speaker is to be disregarded: the Lord is not prophesying through him or her.

PSYCHIATRISTS.   Most of us have heard psychotherapy referred to as "the secular religion of our age." We've heard talk show personalities refer to "my analyst" as another person might speak of "my pastor." It's not a great surprise then that Christians are often suspicious of psychiatrists. Some of us, if asked whether a believer should go to one, would respond with a quick no! That answer may be too quick. And not the right answer at all.

What is a psychiatrist?   A psychiatrist has an MD degree and has specialized in the treatment of mental illness. A number of treatments may be used by a psychiatrist, including prescription of medication. But most tend to rely on psychoanalysis or psychiatric therapy; long-term processes in which the doctor and patient meet frequently to talk about the patient's experiences, thoughts, feelings, wishes, and problems. In that exchange a number of things may happen that help to heal the patient and enable him to function in society.

Many studies have been completed that "demonstrate repeatedly that psychotherapy does bring about positive changes." Although psychiatrists operate from different theoretical frameworks and use different techniques, there is no doubt that it does provide one avenue of ministry to broken lives, both of Christians and non-Christians.

In the past two decades many of the therapy functions that were once reserved for psychiatrists have been taken on by counselors, psychologists, social workers, and others. While the medical training of the psychiatrist sets him or her apart, there is still some claim that psychiatric treatment is unique. → COUNSELING

Theoretical framework of psychiatry. In its early years psychiatry was dependent on the ideas of Sigmund Freud. Many Christians found Freud's ideas about human nature in conflict with Christian beliefs, and so felt believers should not seek help from psychiatrists. Today the theoretical base has been broadened and modified by leaders like Carl Rogers and Albert Ellis. The thinking of each of these about the nature of man differs significantly from the Bible's picture. But each does stress some aspect of the biblical view. Many Christians who go into psychiatry as a ministry/profession retain helpful secular insights, but seek better integration of their faith with their professional practice.

While the discipline of psychiatry itself cannot be called "Christian," it is hasty to reject it as entirely unbiblical. Two Christian psychiatrists I know personally have developed solid reputations for helping, and wisely use the skills gained in their training.

Where and when to go for help. It's common these days when pastors recognize the existence of a serious problem to refer individuals to a good psychiatrist. If anyone suspects mental illness, it is better to seek help from a psychiatrist than from another kind of counselor.

How do you find a reliable psychiatrist? Probably the best way is to check with several local pastors or family doctors. They are likely to know which psychiatrists have a good record of success.

As Christians, we of course rely on God's healing power. But reliance on God does not require cutting ourselves off from those He might intend to use as channels of His work in our lives. → FAITH HEALING

PURPOSE. "I press on to take hold of that for which Christ Jesus took hold of me. Brothers, I do not consider myself yet to have taken hold of it. But one thing I do: Forgetting what is behind and straining toward what is ahead, I press on toward the goal to win the prize for which God has called me heavenward in Christ Jesus. All of us who are mature should take such a view of things" (Phil. 3:12–15).

† † †

QUALITY. My youngest, Tim, who has worked with me on this book as my researcher, has some thoughts on quality. He reacted to an essay on quality read in one of his Michigan State University classes. The writer claimed that "quality cannot be defined" even though "you know what quality is." Tim calls his argument pathetic, and responds, "Quality is measurement; discriminating between similar items. It may be difficult to agree on criteria by which to judge aesthetic value, workmanship, construction, functionality, or other characteristics. But it is nonsense to suggest that quality can be known and not defined."

Tim's right, of course. And wisely focused on the real issue: not the definition of quality, but the criteria by which we measure. God does the same thing in suggesting that there is such a thing as a quality of life. In the end, the Bible says, "the fire will test the quality of each man's work" (1 Cor. 3:13). God's point is clear. We are the builders, He is the judge. He encourages us to build wisely and well, for we know that He cares about quality. And knows very well what it is.

QUESTIONS. Questions have a special character all their own. Many are neutral, simply designed to solicit information. "What's our assignment this week, Miss Saunders?" "When does your plane get in?" Neutral questions like these—gathering information about the when, what, where, why, and who of things—are the foundation of the news industry, and are greatly valued by reporters.

Other questions aren't neutral. They are veiled barbs, designed to hurt or accuse. "Johnny, did you do that *again?*" "Will you never learn?" "Why can't you be like Harry's wife?" "Did you cook this, or find it in the back yard?"

Then there are nurturing questions. Questions that communicate caring and concern. "Where does it hurt?" "How can I help?" "Do you want to tell me about it?" "Is there anything I can do for you?"

I suppose we could go on and add to the list. But instead, let's conclude with the most important question in the world, asked by Jesus long ago.

"Who do you say I am?" (Matt. 16:15).

QUIET TIMES. I don't know how long the phrase has been around. When I was converted nearly thirty years ago it was well established, and every Christian was encouraged to have a personal quiet time every day. It's a good idea: taking time out to start the day, or finish it, with prayer and God's Word. → **UNDERSTANDING YOUR BIBLE** In today's noisy world we need our quiet times.

RACE AND RACISM. Just look around a busy city street, and it's obvious. Human beings don't look alike.

They come in different shapes and sizes, with different colored hair and skin. For as long as we have grouped each other by such characteristics, we've insisted there are "races."

People have tended to classify the other races as inferior, and then struggled hard to find a basis for their claim of superiority. Darwin was used to justify British colonialism: evolution justified machine-gun diplomacy by which the "superior" European societies overwhelmed "inferior" Black and Indian cultures. In the Bible belt, Genesis was twisted to make it appear God intended the colored to serve the superior whites. Even today we hear echoes of the once common notion that the brain size in Negroes is not quite up to the size of the Caucasian brain. And this despite the fact that the frontal lobe, regarded as the seat of the intellect, has been shown to be the same average size in all races, and that black IQs are not really inferior to whites. Struggle as we will, it just is not possible to find valid basis for a claim to racial superiority. The Bible's quiet word is consistently demonstrated to be true: "From one man he [God] made every nation of men" (Acts 17:26).

Racism. Despite the evidence, people persist in characterizing members of other racial groups. Institutions like school systems and labor unions—and churches—discriminate against individuals on the basis of racial group membership. Even where racism is not openly practiced, stereotypes exist that are subtly reflected in our attitudes.

We know there is no basis in fact for the notion of racial difference. But we also know that racism is a fact of life in every society, and will be as long as human beings bear the taint of sin.

The critical question is, what can we do about racism? There were minority groups in ancient Israel even as there are minority groups in society today. Old Testament Law made it very clear to God's people: "The community is to have the same rules for you and for the alien living among you; this is a lasting ordinance for generations to come" (Num. 15:15). Each individual is to receive equal treatment, regardless of his or her position in society. → DISCRIMINATION

How do we counter racism and prejudice? Individually, we learn to recognize and reject stereotypical racial thinking. But the most important single way to overcome personal prejudices is to come to know persons in stereotyped groups as individuals.

What do we do as a society? Some argue that the impact of racial discrimination is so great society must take affirmative action to bring things to a fair balance. For instance, minorities should be given promotions before majority group members. The argument is that when you're starting a mile run it's hardly fair to ask some contestants to start 100 yards behind the others. The argument is that society is obligated to take action to bring minority groups up to where others begin in the competition for jobs, education, and power.

The problem is that to take such action the majority of individuals will suffer from a sort of reverse discrimination. Can two wrongs make a right? Or will every human society have inequities which, whether racial or otherwise, will never be completely removed?

It's easier to deal with individual prejudice than with institutionalized inequities. There we find no easy answers. But Scripture's call to the believer is a clear one.

We reject racism, for all humankind is one.

And we are committed to living in such a way that every person—whatever his or her race or creed or sex—is treated with a fairness God commanded long ago.

RAPE. Legally, rape is usually defined as sexual penetration of a woman without her consent, often with the added proviso, outside of marriage. For the victim, rape is a traumatic experience, often followed by intense lingering feelings of anger, guilt, rejection, anxiety, and helplessness. No mere "social problem," rape is a deeply personal problem for victims, who often need special help. To understand the problem, it's important for us to know something of the rapist's motivations, what to do to prevent attack, and what to do after an attack has taken place.

The rapist. Since rape involves sexual assault, it's not surprising that many people believe rape is caused by passion or sexual stimulation. On that assumption, many victims of rape have been questioned insensitively, looking for something the woman did or said to "cause" the rapist to attack her. But research has demonstrated that most rapes are not impulsive acts, or responses to a supposed irresistibility of the victim. Most rape is assault: it is motivated by anger and aggression, not "love." The rapist is more likely to respond to a victim's apparent helplessness than to sexual suggestiveness.

As this motivation is better understood, women receive more supportive treatment from police officers than in the past, although complaints of rape by women of minority groups, women with bad reputations, and prostitutes are likely to be ignored by legal authorities. In most states, women raped by their husbands have no recourse in law.

Attempts to treat rapists for the hostility expressed in their acts have had some success. But at present, few attempts are made to rehabilitate perpetrators and thus keep them from raping again.

Preventing attack. A surprising number of rapes involve victims who are acquainted with the attacker. Rape may occur at work or in the home as well as on the streets. What can be done to prevent attacks? Today suggestions range from the traditional "dress respectable and avoid the wrong places," to taking a self-defense course, to learning how to talk to a rapist. Understanding a rapist's motivation helps us see why it is important not to look or act helpless. Many women carry personal tear-gas containers or police whistles, but it may be the sense of confidence such resources provide, reflected in a woman's carriage and attitude, that is her best defense.

What should a woman do if threatened with rape? Some say comply and avoid being beaten. However, studies of attempted rape show that a good number of women escape. The three most effective reactions are (1) run away, (2) fight back, and (3) scream and cry out.

If none of these responses is possible, some have talked rapists out of attacking them. When a number of rapists were studied and asked what reaction by the women would be most likely to deter them from completing a rape, they identified the following:

1. Appeal to a bodily weakness. Tell of illness, cancer, pregnancy, or some disease.

2. Statement of acquiescence. Say you refuse to fight, but question: "I just don't understand this. Can't you tell me why? I don't love you, and you don't love me. What's sex without love?"

3. Moral appeal. Talk about the rapist's intentions, but do not refer to standards. "You don't want to hurt me, right? You know this isn't the right thing to do. You know it. Please, you know this isn't the right thing to do, so don't do it. You don't want to hurt me, and . . . ."

Understanding rape as a hostile act—often as a way of striking back at some dominating female figure in the past who has made the rapist feel helpless—the probable reason for the effectiveness of these responses can be understood. In each case the woman refuses to play a dominant role, thus destroying the goal of the act, mastering someone who represents a hated master.

It's hardly surprising that those responses the rapist judged least likely to deter were those that involved verbal attack. By threatening or calling a rapist names, a woman takes a dominant role and stimulates him to complete his attack.

After rape. A number of communities have established Rape Crisis Centers, to which women who have been raped can call or go for help. Crisis-center experiences suggest the following needs must be met:

• The need for a supportive relationship. Often a victim needs to experience empathy and warmth, and to talk about her feelings before she can evaluate decisions that need to be made.

427

• The need for medical examination. A medical examination should be encouraged as soon after the experience as possible. The exam is important in case legal action is taken later, in case venereal disease has been contracted, and because "Morning After Treatment" medications that prevent pregnancy must be started within 72 hours.

• The need to report the rape to legal authorities. Even in situations in which the victim does not want to prosecute, rape should be reported. The rapist needs help, and other possible victims need to be protected from him.

A sense of shame, or fear of either reprisal or a husband's/society's misunderstanding may keep a victim from reporting rape, and leave her to struggle with emotional and other problems alone. This is one reason why establishing a community Rape Crisis Center, or developing a Rape Crisis Center through a local church, can be a significant ministry. An excellent 1977 text is available to help planning for such a center. It is the *Rape Intervention Resource Manual,* compiled by Patrick Mills, with contributions by Lee Sachs, published by Charles C. Thomas, Springfield, Illinois.

READING.   Never mind school grades. If the children read, they'll do well in college, and have a head start on life. But how does a person pick up a desire for reading? Here are a few things parents can do.

• Be readers yourselves. Your love for reading is catching.

• Read aloud to your children. Start as soon as possible, and keep it up at bedtimes through childhood. I often read aloud to my family up through my youngest's junior-high years.

• Buy your children pre-reader and early reader books when they're young. Get them a bookshelf for their own room.

• As soon as your children are old enough, get each his or her own library card. Schedule regular trips to the library, or be ready to go "on demand."

- Let your kids read widely, and be available to talk about whatever interests them now.

- Subscribe to magazines that match your children's interests. Getting their own magazines, to explore personal interests, is a good way to stimulate reading. And don't overlook comic books as reading stimulators.

I suppose we've spent thousands of dollars on magazines and paperbacks during the boys' growing up years. History, science fiction, adventure, art, science, a very few westerns, and every other genre clutter up the boys' rooms, and flood over on family room shelves and, now and then, to piles on a spare chair or even the corner of some room. Each of the kids has done an honest job in college.

They read.

REASON. We've done a lot with reason. We've reached the moon. We've harnessed the power of the atom. We've produced millions of books and scientific papers, analyzed our problems, and struggled toward solutions. We should never downgrade the importance of reason, or the potential that God has built into humanity to understand and to master the universe in which we live.

It goes without saying what reason can't do. Reason has not enabled us to master ourselves. And reason has not enabled us to know God. The Supreme Court to which we must appeal on these central issues in life is not reason, but God's Word.

REBELLION. It's not right, but there are reasons for it. That's what the Colonies insisted back in the 1770s. That's what sullen, angry kids insist in the 1980s. Actually, it's relatively easy to stir up a rebellion of your own. Here are a few simple rules, guaranteed to work:

- Keep careful count of another person's failures and sins.

- Hold every failure against him, and let him know you know it's the 10th, 11th, 12th, 13th, etc. time this week!

- Always demand and insist rather than ask.

• If he does apologize, stay angry as long as possible afterward.

• Never let a person who says "I'm sorry" doubt that, though you grudgingly accept his apology, you'll not forget.

• Always act as though the other person is the only one who ever sins or makes mistakes, and that you are perfect.

As I say, rebellions are easy to stir up. And almost as easy to avoid. If you want to know how to avoid them, just read on. About reconciliation.

RECONCILIATION. The word means to bring into harmony. Thinking of friends who've had a falling out, a definition in one of my dictionaries is "to make friendly again."

As a theological word "reconciliation" speaks of what God has done in Christ to restore our broken relationship with Him. Because of Jesus' cross, we are turned away from sin, back to the Lord.

But the Bible is also filled with truth about person-to-person reconciliation. We find principles that tell us how to "make friendly again," and how to stay friendly. The principles work in any close relationship—husband and wife, parent and child, brother and sister, neighbors, fellow Christians, etc. The key principles are found in two New Testament passages.

2 Corinthians 5:11–21: becoming reconciled. This passage explains God's own reconciliation process in Jesus. The death of Christ provides the basis, and communicates a unique message of love to humanity. In our personal relationships we can apply each of the three principles expressed here:

• Not counting their trespasses. God in Christ announces that He will not keep a record of the wrongs we do. He will deal with us on the basis of love and forgiveness.

• Not counting against them. God in Christ announces that though sins are known, they are not held against humanity. In Christ God offers the prospect of a new life, which will be lived "for him who died for them and was raised again" (5:15).

• We implore you. God, who could demand we turn to Christ, instead presents the fact of His love and invites. He cares. But He will not force us to respond against our will.

In our personal relationships these same attitudes are necessary if we are to experience reconciliation with those we care for.

Matthew 18: staying reconciled. How does a person stay in harmony with other human beings, in view of the fact that we each sin against and hurt those we love? Jesus deals with this question in three stories told in Matthew 18.

• Restoring when one goes astray. Jesus says we are like sheep, sure to wander off at times. But a lost sheep is looked for, and brought back "rejoicing." Rather than anger, joy at restoration is to mark our relationships with others.

• Offering unconditional forgiveness. Jesus says we are like family, in which brothers may often sin against each other. But sibling hurts are to be dealt with by unstinting forgiveness. We are to remain willing to give our brother or sister a fresh start.

• Remembering our own fallibility. Jesus reminds us that we are servants who have been forgiven a great debt by the Great King. We who have been forgiven so much can only be humble, and as ready as He to forgive when others hurt us.

Staying reconciled and in harmony with others calls for us to remember how imperfect every person is, and to be quick to forgive, so that we can again find joy in mutual love.

By the way. In case you didn't read the item on rebellion just above, it's good to note that rebellion and reconciliation are mirror images. By living God's reconciliation way we maintain interpersonal harmony. Acting against this way stimulates rebellion and destroys harmony. Which pattern best expresses the tone of your own relationships? Perhaps the chart below will help you tell.

RELATIONSHIPS THAT TEND . . .

Toward Rebellion ← →	Toward Reconciliation → ←
• Keep a mental record of other's sins/failures	• Forget past sins/failures
• Feel angry and hostile if failures are repeated	• Don't hold on to the past; keep on forgiving.
• Demand and insist the other conform	• Encourage and invite the other
• Stay angry after the other apologizes	• Accept apologies with joy and thankfulness
• Forgive, but never forget	• Forgive unconditionally, as often as necessary
• Act as if you never make mistakes: let the other know anything wrong is always his or her fault	• Ask forgiveness when you fail, and remember your own imperfections when you relate to the other person

RELAX! Now we know. Learning to relax may be better than pills for people with high blood pressure.

Of course, teaching a person to relax is harder than prescribing pills, and most doctors lack the time as well as the skills. But relaxing is interesting. You lean back, visualize yourself floating in a canoe on the surface of a calm northern lake. You can almost feel the sun warming you; almost hear the clear waters lap comfortably against the aluminum skin. You can almost hear the distant cry of the loon.

And they call it medicine!

The problem is, we can't spend our whole life laid back. We have to open our eyes and return to our pressure-packed daily life. Then our blood pressure may rise again.

What it boils down to is this: it's not so much the time-outs that make a difference; it's how we handle the daily pressures that make so many people tense and worried.

Here Christians have the advantage. We don't all use it, but that extra edge is ours if we want it. You see, we can live with pressures, but without anxiety. How? The Book of Hebrews promises us that we can enter God's rest (4:1–11). In that passage the writer explains that God's own work "has been finished since the creation of the world." He is not saying God is inactive. Instead he points out that nothing can happen in the whole course of history for which God is not prepared. The Creation takes every possibility into account. Thus there is no problem you or I can face for which God has not already worked out the solution.

Why then do we worry? God knows the way through our wilderness; all we need to do is follow.

When we grasp this great truth and trust our problems to the Lord, we find rest. We turn from reliance on our own efforts (Heb. 4:10) and find the wonderful freedom to relax despite the hectic pace of our anxious world.

REPENTANCE.

Repentance is more than a cheap "I'm sorry," or a moment of sorrow. As language scholars observe, repentance is always associated with the choice of a new direction for life.

When repentance is real, there is a change of lords: Jesus replaces even the most inviting sins. There is a new outlook and life has a new objective: we learn to live to please God.

This understanding of the Bible's radical view of repentance isn't something to use as a weapon against others. We don't say, "If you were *really* sorry, you'd . . . ." → RECONCILIATION Instead, words about repentance are God's personal message to us. Do we know God in that deep, true way that truths like "conversion" and "repentance" invite us to understand? Paul says it this way: "Examine yourselves to see whether you are in the faith" (2 Cor. 13:5).

RESOLUTIONS.

Are those New Year's resolutions we make, or the promises to ourselves to watch our diet, helpful or harmful? Should we make resolutions, or are they like promises made to God that only make us more guilty when we break them?

Part of our confusion arises when we look back and see our past littered with shattered resolutions. It makes us feel helpless, and even guilty. Often there's shame: what must God think of us?

There may be no easy answer to that resolution question. But there is a sure answer to the question of what God thinks of us. He knows us and remembers we are dust (Ps. 103:14). He knows our temptations and is able to sympathize with our weaknesses (Heb. 4:15). He understands and reaches down to help us up whenever we fall.

Personally, I think resolutions can be good for us. We need to set personal goals, to try. As long as we are as willing to forgive ourselves when we stumble as God is and are willing to get up and stumble on again, progress is assured.

RESPONSIBILITY.

It boils down to just one thing: Do I face the fact that *I choose* to do, and to be, what I am? Blaming others or fate may seem to offer an easy way out. But the fact is that each of us bears personal responsibility for our every act. Galatians 6 sums up the Bible's teaching succinctly. "A man reaps what he sows. The one who sows to please his sinful nature, from that nature will reap destruction; the one who sows to please the Spirit, from the Spirit will reap eternal life."

It's good to know that God gives us freedom to choose. And that when we choose life in the Spirit, He adds this promise: "At the proper time we will reap a harvest if we do not give up."

RESURRECTION.

Resurrection is something we can all look forward to. But it's more than God's promise of an endless eternity. God's promise of resurrection offers us new life, now. Paul explains it in Romans 8:11. "If the Spirit of him who raised Jesus from the dead is living in you, he who raised Christ from the dead will also give life to your mortal bodies through his Spirit, who lives in you.''

Resurrection is ahead, and now.

God's resurrection power is available to enable us to live His kind of life, even though we're locked in bodies that are all too mortal now. Coming to know Christ involves coming to know the power of His resurrection today (cf. Phil. 3:10).

RETIREMENT. Books and articles on this subject talk incessantly about money. The retiree, they say, can get along on less but will still need 60–65% of preretirement income to maintain an established standard of living. ''In large measure,'' the experts suggest, ''retirement planning is arranging affairs so you have enough money when those regular paychecks stop.''

Planning retirement finances is too complicated to discuss here. It's much better if you just pick out one of the paperbacks on the subject at bookstores. If you're 45 or so, do it when you have the chance and look ahead twenty years. (If you're much over 50, don't finish this article. Rush out and buy a retirement book now!)

Of course, after studying up on annuities and social security and tax law changes and IRAs, you might start thinking about the most important issue of all. This: Whenever you retire, you have many years of life ahead! Not just to exist. To live.

The chart on page 436 shows government life-expectancy figures. For instance, if your retire at 50 you can expect 23.3 years if you're a man, and 28.9 if you're a woman. Even if you retire at 70 you can expect another decade. And these will be years when you no longer have to use your time making a living. All that time will now be yours to *live!*

The real meaning of retirement is found in the prospect of decades of free time. Some people are completely happy using that time for leisure. → LEISURE Others need to be occupied. And many find great fulfillment using free time to reach out to others, to help in volunteer work or through churches. → AGING

So what does retirement hold for you? Now may be the time for you to begin to look ahead, not just to plan finances, but to seek God's leading toward a new life and a new ministry/career that retirement can bring.

Age	Life Expectancy		Age	Life Expectancy	
	Male	Female		Male	Female
50	23.3	28.9	63	14.3	18.4
51	22.5	28.0	64	13.7	17.6
52	21.8	27.2	65	13.2	16.9
53	21.0	26.3	66	12.6	16.2
54	20.3	25.5	67	12.1	15.4
55	19.5	24.7	68	11.6	14.7
56	18.8	23.8	69	11.0	14.1
57	18.1	23.0	70	10.6	13.4
58	17.5	22.2	71	10.1	12.7
59	16.8	21.4	72	9.6	12.1
60	16.1	20.6	73	9.2	11.5
61	15.5	19.9	74	8.8	10.9
62	14.9	19.1	75	8.4	10.4

REWARDS. The kind of rewards you tend to rely on will depend to a great extent on your view of human nature and God's redemption plan. It's common these days for some to use a technical jargon, liberally inserting such terms as "reinforcement" and "conditioning." Man is an animal, and by organizing outside stimuli an individual can be pulled or prodded or manipulated into ways determined by others to be good. What happens outside—the techniques we use and how persons behave—are the realities we must consider. What happens within is not only mystery, but irrelevant as well. Man is an animal, and words like freedom and dignity have no meaning at all.

The other way to look at human beings is to view what happens within as the basic reality. With this view we suppose that a person's inner states—satisfaction, altruism, values—are the real stuff of life, and the key to motivation and character. Rather than stand outside and pull strings, the person with this view of humanity is convinced that those rewards that really count are the rewards that come from the inner conviction that we have done right and well, and have pleased the persons who are important to us.

It sounds very abstract, I know. Until you're sitting in an airport and hear a mother say, "If you sit still I'll give you a piece of candy," while another one says, "If you don't shut up this minute, I'll slap you 'till you can't see!"

And you recall trips with your own kids. You remember giving one a hug: "You've been so good on this trip!" And saying to another, "I know it's hard and you're tired. You're being very brave to hold back the tears."

RIGHTS. We all have them. And we all want to keep them. It's no wonder some people bristle when they feel someone is infringing on their rights. Our fiercely protective attitude toward personal rights is certainly one of the basic causes of conflict.

Scripture never suggests that individuals have no rights. The Bible never even hints that it's all right for you or me to trample on the rights of others. What the Bible does do, in the New Testament, is ask us to stop and think a moment before insisting on our own rights.

Three passages are particularly instructive. In 1 Corinthians 9:12 Paul speaks of his own right to be supported by those to whom he ministers. Yet he says, "we did not use this right." He wanted to model in his own life the fact that the gospel is free.

In 1 Corinthians 10 Paul writes to people who believed they had a right to eat meat sacrificed by pagans in their temples. All right. But Paul points out while everything may be permissible "not everything is beneficial. 'Everything is permissible'—but not everything is constructive. Nobody should seek his own good, but the good of others" (10:23, 24).

In Romans a similar conflict developed when those who felt it wrong to eat temple market meat became upset. The meat eaters had their rights. But Paul says, "If your brother is distressed because of what you eat, you are no longer acting in love'' (14:15).

The point is simple but profound. We have rights—but our rights are never as important as the persons God has placed us among. People of the world may fight for their rights. But the Christian has the privilege of choosing to give up personal rights, in the interest of love.

† † †

SACRED AND SECULAR. Ever notice our tendency to divide up occasions and places and things, labeling some ''sacred'' and others ''secular''? It's true that the Old Testament does this. The temple, the altars, the ark, the days of worship, the very dishes and equipment used in worship, were sacred. Because they belonged uniquely to God, they were different in nature from the secular things, which belonged to humankind.

But a great shift is reflected in the New Testament. ''Sacred'' is stripped away from things and places and rites of worship: the mantle of sacredness is instead settled firmly on the shoulders of the people who have received new life from Christ, and are now home to God's Spirit. ''God's temple is sacred,'' Paul teaches in 1 Corinthians 3:17, and then affirms, ''and you are that temple.''

What does it mean that ''sacred'' no longer applies to days or places or buildings or religious activities, but to us? It simply means that everything we touch and do is holy, and ''secular'' has lost its meaning. Our work is sacred, because God's Spirit within us expresses Christ in the way we do our job and relate to our co-workers. Our family life is sacred, our leisure time is sacred, our worship is sacred, for the Spirit is within us to sanctify every moment of our lives.

SAFETY BELTS. We've had them for years, but in this country we don't know too much about them. Only .9% of our citizens use them, so it's hard to get statistics.

It's different in Canada, where wearing seat belts is mandatory, and at least 65% of the population complies with
the seat belt law. This means that Canada has some pretty
accurate figures on what happens in a collision when you
wear seat belts—and when you don't. What do the Canadian figures show? Without seat belts, deaths per thousand
people in accidents runs 2.38%. With lap and shoulder
belts, deaths per thousand people in accidents runs .85%.
Seat belts reduce death in accidents by considerably more
than half! And have an equally dramatic impact on reducing head injuries.

Seat belts are particularly helpful in head-on collisions and roll-overs. They are less helpful but still important in side collisions. But they are no help at all if we
don't wear them.

SAINTS. For anyone in the Catholic tradition,
"saint" may conjure up the image of an ancient ascetic,
whose exceptional holiness has gained so many extra
points with God that he or she can win concessions for
normal people like you and me. Protestants do not expect
favors from saints. But like Catholics, Protestants often
reserve the term for men or women with exceptional qualities and kindness. We'd all like to be saintly. But that's a
destiny we feel is reserved for blue-ribbon Christians.
Most of us would be more than happy to settle for honorable mention.

This common notion doesn't fit the Bible's use of
"saint" at all. The New Testament, and particularly Paul,
extends that word to include every Christian (cf. Eph. 1:1;
Col. 1:4, 12, 26, etc.).

You see, what makes a believer a "saint" isn't what
he or she does. That word reflects the fact that God has
acted in Jesus to set us all apart for Himself. We have been
"made holy through the sacrifice of the body of Jesus
Christ once for all" (Heb. 10:10). This is the exciting
news about sainthood. Because Jesus has died and made
us saints, we all have the potential to live blue-ribbon
lives. We don't become saints by being saintly. Because
we *are* saints, a life that expresses Jesus' own qualities

439

and loving kindness becomes possible for each one.

The next time you want to see a saint, don't visit a shrine. Look in a mirror. Then let your actions express who you are: one of God's own set-apart and special people, enabled by Him to live out exceptional love.

SALVATION. I wonder. How many signs and billboards in the United States announce "Jesus Saves," or quote "Believe on the Lord Jesus Christ and thou shalt be saved"? I've seen them painted on barns, lettered crudely on home-made signs in Arkansas, and shining in bright neon outline over rescue mission doors. I'm certainly not against them. Still, I wonder. What does that word "saved" mean to those who pass by? For that matter, what does it mean to us?

God's Old Testament people had a pretty clear idea of salvation. Old Testament references reflect the quiet conviction that God acts in history to help His people. Israel looked back, and had so much to remember. She recalled the soldiers of the oppressors, dead on the Red Sea shore, and knew: "That day the LORD saved Israel from the hands of the Egyptians" (Exod. 14:30). So "saved" was full of meaning. It expressed the conviction of the believing Israelite that God Himself acted to deliver . . . from sickness, the wicked, from troubles, and from the threat of death. Every foe, whether physical or spiritual, must surrender to the power of God.

Salvation was an exciting word then. Human beings might be weak. But God is great, and willing to help. "Salvation" brought a sense of warm closeness to this great, caring God, who belonged to Israel because Israel belonged to Him.

In the New Testament the underlying Old Testament theme is given an expanded emphasis. The meaning of "salvation" is applied in depth to spiritual deliverance. It is not only the external enemy from whom human beings need rescue; it's from the enemy within. Within lies the guilt of past sins and the overmastering urge to commit new sin. So the New Testament trumpets the good news: God who acted in history also acts within man. Because of

Jesus individuals have been saved, are being saved, and will be saved.

Those tenses sometimes bother us when we read the New Testament. But they're important. They tell us that when God acts to meet our spiritual needs, He is completely thorough.

● We have been saved, speaks of the fact that through Christ's death our sins are forgiven. There is no more guilt, because our sins themselves are gone. The past is no longer held against us, for Jesus has worked a startling miracle and wiped out our past (Heb. 10:17, 18) →
GUILT AND GUILT FEELINGS → FORGETTING

● We are being saved, speaks of the fact that the living Jesus is with us, to lend His own resurrection power and break the grip sin has on our motivation and will. Because God acts within us, we can now begin to do good. It is present-tense salvation that Paul writes of to the Philippians: "continue to work out your salvation with fear and trembling." We may find life a struggle. But we know that "it is God who works in you to will and to act according to his good purpose" (Phil. 2:12, 13).

● We will be saved, speaks of the fact that in the future, at the Resurrection, the last stain of sin will be cleansed from our personalities. Then we will be like God in unblemished purity (Eph. 5:27).

When we put the message of the two testaments together, we have a full and stunning picture of what that word "saved" means. It means that God has chosen to become fully involved, willing and able to meet our every need. God acts to deliver us from dangers without, and He acts to deliver us from the blows aimed by sin within. We are weak. But God is great, and will help. And this great salvation is ours when we step into personal relationship with our great, caring God, who belongs to us when we choose to belong to Him.

SCIENCE AND SCIENTISM.

"Science" is a way of going about the study of the universe we live in. "Scientism" is a religion: the belief that there is nothing beyond the material universe, and that thus human existence and life's meaning must be explained without reference to "God." Science particularly ought to be treated with respect. Science, a method of gathering information, conducting experiments, and applying what is learned to control our environment, has given us space travel, television, heart transplants, wonder drugs, abundant energy, computers, and everything that makes our modern world what it is. Focused on the present, this method has tremendous power to give us control over nature. But the method of science becomes less helpful when we leave the present and try to use it to explore the distant past or predict the distant future. You can't go back and observe Creation. And you can't design an experiment to replicate over and over again some supposed spontaneous generation of life.

It's here that science drifts unacknowledged into scientism. Persons holding scientisms' "no God" belief have to explain origins and meaning by constructing theories that leave God out. So they develop theories, reasoning from what we now know of nature as we observe it. All too often the practitioners of this nature religion claim their beliefs are "scientific."

Here is where we have to lose some respect for the practitioners of scientism. By pretending that their theories are established fact, they practice deceit. A person who says "Here are my reasons for my beliefs, and the fact that my arguments are based on evidence gathered from within the physical universe makes my beliefs scientific," is either a fool or dishonest. Christians who believe in Creation by God also give reasons for their beliefs, and can marshal many arguments based on evidence gathered from within the physical universe. But this doesn't make biblical faith either "scientific" or "unscientific." *Science* is a way of dealing with the physical universe. But theories about origins constructed on information gathered from the physical universe alone are not therefore *scientific*. → **EVOLUTION AND ORIGINS**

The Bible has an observation about scientism, and its insistance that God be ruled out of humanity's calculations. "Ever since our fathers died, everything goes on as it has since the beginning of creation" such scoffers are quoted as saying (2 Peter 3:4). The divine commentary is this: "But they deliberately forget that long ago by God's word the heavens existed . . . and by water also the world of that time was deluged and destroyed. By the same word the present heavens and earth are reserved for fire, being kept for the day of judgment and destruction of ungodly men" (3:5–7).

SECOND CHANCES. Tarshish was about as far away from Nineveh as a person could go. When Jonah booked passage on the tiny boat heading south, he was clearly determined to avoid God's northward call.

We all know the story of this reluctant prophet. We know that instead of angrily crushing the disobedient Jonah, God gently prepared a great fish: a submarine, programed to take him north. Jonah might refuse to serve God. But God wasn't ready to abandon His servant.

I've known a number of Christians who torment themselves with the thought that when young, or later in life, they rejected God's call to missions or some other "full-time service." Lost in regret about what might have been, these dear brothers and sisters live in the shadow of God's imagined anger or of supposed contemptuous dismissal from His best.

Jonah is a healthy corrective. We see in Jonah that God doesn't give up on His servants. As He acted to move Jonah into the center of His will despite the prophet's reluctance, He is still capable of guiding each of us to the place where we can serve Him best. We can believe with rejoicing that God wants and intends us to serve Him now—just where we are.

A past choice of yours may have shaped your future. But it has no more deprived you of your chance to serve God than Jonah's flight deprived him of his chance to serve.

That's one of the exciting things about this little Old Testament book. It might well be called the Gospel of the Second Chance. God never gives up on us. There is always an open door, and the wonderful invitation to serve.

SELF-CONCEPT. How do you view yourself? Do you feel strong and talented? Or do you feel weak and inadequate? If your feelings about yourself are positive, you've got what psychologists call a "good self-image." If they're negative, you're saddled with a "poor self-image."

What's important about our self-concept is that we tend to act in harmony with how we see ourselves. If we feel good about ourselves and our abilities, we're likely to move ahead confidently, willing to take on new challenges. If we're gripped by feelings of inadequacy, we may *want* to do well but will fear to try.

Spiritually, each approach to life is booby-trapped. The person with a good self-image may move out and act, but rely on his own abilities rather than on God. Yet Jesus reminds us that in the spiritual realm, "apart from me you can do nothing" (John 15:5). The person with a poor self-image, who fears to try, forgets the great truth that "I can do everything through him who gives me strength" (Phil. 4:13).

What's important for the Christian? We are to build new self-concepts that are in harmony with who God says we are. Paraphrasing, J. B. Phillips renders 1 Peter 1:22, 23 "you are not mere mortals now, for the live, permanent word of God has given you his own indestructible heredity." In Christ, God lifts us beyond our old selves, to make possible a vibrant new life in which Jesus Himself enables us to be and do good. When we learn to see ourselves as God says we are, we find the courage to live by faith. We neither try on our own, nor hold back from fear. Instead we step out boldly to meet life's challenges, relying on the empowering presence of our God and the wonderful truth that we are no longer mere mortals. We are new creations, reshaped by God's wonderful saving power.

SELF-RIGHTEOUSNESS. You remember the story of the two men at prayer. One was a Pharisee, zealously religious. He glanced contemptuously at his fellow worshiper, and then reminded God of all the religious duties he performed. The other man, well known for his failings, would not even look up to heaven but simply cried out for mercy. Jesus concluded the story by saying, "I tell you that this man, rather than the other, went home justified before God" (Luke 18:14).

But why did Jesus tell this story? He told it for the benefit of listeners "who were confident of their own righteousness and looked down on everybody else" (18:9). This phrase gives us the world's best description of self-righteousness: confident of one's own righteousness; looking down on everyone else. The story also shows us the danger of self-righteousness. Self-righteousness cuts us off from God's mercy, and cuts us off from other people as well.

There's only one cure for self-righteousness. It's to agree with God's announcement that "all have sinned and fallen short," and to cause us to approach God for mercy rather than carry a list of personal accomplishments. It's to look around at other human beings and realize that we are like them, not better than them, and are in no position to judge. → JUDGING When we abandon our self-righteousness, there is hope of personal relationships with God, and of healthy relationships with other human beings as well.

SELFISHNESS. We've probably all heard the Christian prescription for JOY: **J**esus first, **O**thers second, **Y**ourself last. But we may not be convinced. Particularly if Mom or Dad have insisted we stay at home to take care of them instead of stepping out to build a family and life of our own. Or if, whenever we express a need or desire, someone pounces on us and says, "Now don't be selfish!" It can happen to children. To teens. And to adults. We can be so conditioned by the "others first" syndrome that anything we want to do just for our own enjoyment or enrichment somehow seems wrong.

Jesus doesn't seem to look at life that way. In fact, self-love is understood to be something quite valid and right. When Jesus quoted the Old Testament call to love your neighbor He also quoted the Old Testament standard:

love others "as you love yourself." Not "more than" or "instead of," but "as" yourself. We can paraphrase by suggesting that Jesus expects us to want the very best for ourselves, and calls on us to want the very best for others as well.

There are two important things this tells us about selfishness. First, never let someone use the word to manipulate you, or make you feel guilty for caring about yourself. And second, be very clear about what really is the best for you.

It's this second idea that is the shocker. In the Book of Philippians Paul urges believers to "do nothing out of selfish ambition" but to "consider others better than yourselves. Each of you should look not only to your own interests, but also to the interests of others" (2:3, 4). Then he goes on to describe Jesus' attitude. He was willing, though He was God, to "make himself nothing, taking the very nature of a servant, being made in human likeness." He was willing to humble Himself and even accept death on the cross. *Because of this,* "God exalted him to the highest place" and decreed that He is Lord, before whom "every knee should bow" (2:5–11). Through humble, selfless giving of Himself Jesus was exalted to the highest place. It was by serving others that Jesus received what was the best for Him.

This is the surprising concept of humility and serving that infuses Scripture. Surrendering our interests to meet the needs of others is actually in our best interests! It is by serving that we too are exalted to the higher places in the coming, endless kingdom of God.

Strange, isn't it. If we are *foolishly* selfish, and act ambitiously to win the first places in our momentary present, we lose out on our ultimate good. If we are *wisely* selfish, we follow Jesus' example and consider the needs of others. We act in their interest, knowing that loving concern today wins us a full weight of eternal glory.

SENSITIVITY. One psychologist recently observed, "Blessed are the Insensitive Slobs." What he meant was, how good it would be if we couldn't be hurt. How many marriages would then hold together, and how many parents and children would find anger and pain gone away. If we were insensitive, how much easier it would be to do the right thing, never worrying about the possibility of rejection or ridicule from others.

Of course, God has a better idea. As usual. His approach is to cause us to become increasingly tender. With that tenderness, He provides us with His own matchless willingness to forgive. We are all sure to hurt and to be hurt. But when we forgive, and accept forgiveness, we make the wonderful discovery that it is the healing and not the absence of hurts that binds us closer to others, and to God.

SENTIMENTALITY.

Don't make snap judgments. For instance, don't mistake the tears that flow so easily when someone tells a tragic story, or when a TV drama unfolds, as evidence that a person is warm and caring. Surprisingly, there is a reverse correlation between the ability to feel directly in life, and the way a person responds to cheap sentiment. Too-quick tears may not be evidence of a warm and compassionate character at all. They may actually be a warning that the person lives on the superficial edge of life, unready for any committed kind of caring that can last through months and years and decades of shared life.

SEX.

Sex is one of God's finer inventions. He designed us with the capacity to enjoy every sensation and every thrill. Then He reassured us in Scripture that intercourse is a gift: one He intends to enrich our lives.

Of course, we may not use the gift wisely. All too often we want to unwrap the package hastily, before its time. Or we fail to read the directions that tell us how the present is to be assembled. It's likely that most Christians don't even grasp the purpose of sex. Certainly the world around us is heaped with distorted ideas and tarnished lives.

So let's sort through common notions about sex, to better understand this gift of God's. We want to handle sex with care, so it will enrich us rather than bring heartbreak.

The common notion that sex is natural, and therefore right. This is the popular Playboy view. Like hunger and thirst, sex is simply a physical thing: a need. In a way, this view makes sex something like a ham sandwich or a Coke. When you're hungry, you eat. When you're thirsty, you drink. When you're sexually excited, you find someone and jump into bed.

There's no doubt that the sex drive is powerful. In fact, Paul points out that satisfaction of sexual needs is one of the benefits of marriage, and that in marriage each partner belongs to the other, so neither is to withhold his or her body (1 Cor. 7:1–5). But the argument that, because the drive exists and is "natural," promiscuous sex is justified, just won't wash.

For one thing, there's a difference between our "natural" desire for food and water and our "natural" desire for sex. You can't survive without food and water. Try going without sex for months or even years, and you make the stunning discovery that chastity won't kill you! So sex hardly belongs on the same list with needs that our nature, as living beings, demands must be fulfilled.

There's another problem with the "it's natural" argument. It is used to justify specific sexual practices, not just the rightness of sex itself. Yet every society regulates all natural functions. It's "natural" to eat. But no one believes for a minute that this justifies walking into a restaurant, grabbing food off someone's plate, and walking out. In the same way, no society has ever held that because sex is "natural" you can have sex with anyone, any time, any place.

So to believe that sex is natural is certainly correct. But to conclude that "naturalness" justifies any specific sexual practices is foolish indeed.

The common notion that sex is an expression of love, and therefore love makes it right. This is the most common view, and has captured the allegiance of many

Christians. Sex is *the* way to show love. It's a short step from this conviction to the belief that "since we love each other" premarital sex is both good and right.

But this view has a number of problems. For instance, what do we mean when we say "love"? Everyone knows that "I love you" can mean "I'm excited by your presence and want you," or can mean "I care about you as a person and want the best for you." If we mean the first, we're using "love" as a synonym for sexual desire, and that never makes anything right. Of course, if we mean the second, it's hard to see how we'd engage in extramarital sex. Everyone knows that sex outside of marriage *might* lead to hurt. If that "I love you" really means I care for you as a person and want only your best, it won't lead to sex, because we won't risk harming a person we care deeply about.

Actually, there's a deeper problem most of us have never noticed. The basic notion, that having sex is how you show love, is wrong! Think about that for a moment. You rush home from vacation, and find Mom and Dad waiting in the front yard. You're so glad to see them again! You give each a big hug: "I've missed you so much," you say. "I really love you!" And no one ever dreams that your love for Mom and Dad is a call to sex.

You see, there are many people each of us loves, and we show that love in many ways. There's shared laughter, long conversations, hugs when we meet, helping, listening, giving support. And no one imagines loving those who are closest to us needs to find expression in sex.

Somehow it takes something more than "love" to make sex the right and good and beneficial gift God intends it to be.

The uncommon notion that sex is the sign and seal of commitment. This is the meaning of sex we find in the Bible. Sex has its meaning and offers its fullest potential only in the unique context of commitment.

We do have a natural desire for sex. And sexual experiences are associated with feelings of love. But the heart and soul of sex's meaning for mankind is found in its power to give ultimate expression to our complete, total commitment to another person. Sexual intercourse, expressing as it does full exposure of ourselves to another and the physical joining of two as one, affirms and reaffirms commitment.

This is why marriage is the only context in which sex can be good or right. God has planned that a man and a woman should one day commit themselves before Him and others → **MARRIAGE** to face life together as one, till death do them part. In the context of marriage sex takes on a sacramental character, meeting physical needs, expressing love, but more than that, reaffirming oneness. Sex within marriage is intended to say that, in every way, I fully trust myself to you, to be yours even as you are mine.

The tragedy of modern society and of the Christian misunderstanding of sex is that this deep meaning of intercourse has been lost, and the wonder of its potential for fulfillment misplaced. Sex as merely natural is an animal function, and can never sustain joy. Sex as expression of affection is superficial, and can never meet our deepest needs. But sex as the sign and seal of life-long commitment can become richer, fuller, and deeper as the years go by, bonding ever closer two whose lives in every sense are becoming one.

SEX EDUCATION. Someone has suggested there are six or seven approaches to sex education in our society. (1) Provide none: kids will learn when they get married. (2) Provide opportunities for frank discussion, clearly linking sexual questions with religion and morality. (3) Count on the gutter to do the job, along with R- and X-rated movies. (4) Blitz people with blunt biological data, and provide birth-control aids to kids who will try it anyway. (5) Separate the sexes in adolescence, and keep both busy with school work and sports. This approach was adopted in the '60s in Australia, and seemed to work well. (6) Help kids to grow up in situations rich in love and caring, so they "catch" the fact that meaningful sex is found in the context of relationships, and you can ignore "classes." (7) Encourage free access to books and paper-

backs on sex, and let young people figure it out for themselves.

The problem seems to be that, whatever theory a person is drawn to, it's abundantly clear in our promiscuous, sensual society, that young people need help in dealing with the many issues raised by budding sexuality. Recognition of the need has led many school systems to institute sex-education classes, some required, and others offered as electives. Nearly every effort by the schools has stimulated strong reaction from parents and others in the community who object to sex education in the schools.

The causes of controversy. The underlying reason for conflict over sex education in the schools is simple. The educators tend to see the whole thing as a public or emotional health issue, and want to design courses from this perspective. The objectors look at sex education not as a health issue but as a moral issue. It's fine to have information on anatomy and birth control and venereal diseases and to discuss different ethical standards. But many are convinced that any information provided must be linked with clear moral commitment to traditional values.

The insistence of conservatives in the community that any sex education be linked with religious and moral values raises a problem for the schools. We live in a pluralistic society. So *whose* moral code is to be taught? One influential sex-education text observes: "The minute a school tries to establish a code about masturbation, for example, or premarital sex, petting and necking, dating, and other such subjects, it places itself in a precarious position."

Usually the school attempts to teach sex education without referring to religious values or morality. But it is impossible to discuss sex in a value-free setting. Talking about sex as an experience, *without* linkage to morality, is itself a humanistic and relativistic position.

Court challenges to sex-education courses haven't been helpful for concerned parent groups. The courts have consistently ruled that sex education is a public health and not a morality issue. They have ruled that sex-education classes can be made compulsory. And they have ruled that sex-education classes do *not* interfere with the free exercise of religion. Whatever a parent who objects may think, the courts have agreed in general with the Maryland judge who stated that the sex-education courses required by state law for all students should be seen as "quite simply a public health measure."

At the same time, public outcry in many communities has often led to compromise. Sex-education courses have not been abandoned, but have been made voluntary. In today's social climate, in which Christian schools are increasingly popular and public school attendance is dropping, school boards are particularly sensitive about offending significant blocks in the community. → **CHRISTIAN SCHOOLS**

Sex education in your school.   What might a Christian do if he or she finds a child is assigned to a sex-education class? A first step certainly should be to talk with the child about what is being taught, and how the subject matter is handled. It's also appropriate to look at the text or texts used, and to talk with the teacher about his or her approach in class. It's possible that the approach is blatantly humanistic. But it is also possible that the teacher is sensitive to moral and values issues, and teaches in a positive, helpful way.

If, after this exploration, you feel a deep concern, there are several options you might consider.

• You might use the class as an opportunity to stimulate discussion with your child. If home is the best place for sex education, talking together about issues raised in school might be God's provision for you and your family.

• You might withdraw your child from the public schools and enroll him or her in a private or Christian school.

• You might encourage discussion groups at your church to deal with the issues raised in school.

• If other parents share your concern, you might meet together to raise the issue with the teacher and the school administration. This approach may not lead to cancellation of the classes, but it may have an impact on making attendance voluntary or lead to including units on moral and religious implications.

● You might determine to run for the school board where you can have an influence on the shaping of policy.
→ CENSORSHIP

Sex education in the home and church. The controversy over sex education in the schools does at least help us focus on the initial concern. Kids need help as they mature to understand and deal with their own sexuality. If we object to the schools providing courses, we should be willing to face up to our own responsibility as parents and/or church leaders. Are there guidelines to help us with sex education? Surely.

● As children evidence curiosity, answer their questions simply and without embarrassment. There are Christian books on this subject written specifically for children and teens that you can have in your home.

● Don't hesitate to show affection physically in the home. Hugging and kissing—your kids and spouse—can help to communicate the warmth and caring that are always to be associated with home, family, and sex.

● Keep communication lines open, so your kids can talk about their questions and feelings as they move to dating age. → COMMUNICATING The best time to talk through the questions children have is when they experience the problems that raise those questions.

Most curriculums for youth groups and Sunday school classes from Christian publishers these days have studies on sex and dating questions. But basic values and attitudes toward sex are most likely to be shaped, for good or bad, in the home.

SHAME. Tolstoy captures the meaning of shame in *Anna Karenina* as he describes the misery of Dmitri Karamazov at having to take off his socks:

> They were very dirty . . . and now everyone could see it. And what was worse he disliked his feet. All his life he had

thought both his big toes hideous. He particularly loathed the coarse, flat, corked nail on the right one, and now they would all see it. Feeling intolerably ashamed. . . .

Shame is different from guilt. Guilt is linked with specific acts of wrongdoing, which we know deserve punishment. Shame is linked with self-exposure. Suddenly that which has been hidden deep within us—some terrible inadequacy or failure—is threatened with exposure, and we are flooded with fear that others will reject or abandon us.

In some cultures guilt, as a feeling that we deserve punishment for violating a law or moral principle, is of little importance. In such cultures shame usually is very important: being exposed before others and shown a failure or inadequacy motivates behavior. Not an inner moral code, but maintaining the respect and admiration of the community is important.

Both guilt and shame are explored in the Bible, but from different perspectives. Guilt focuses on reality: on actual responsibility for acts that merit punishment. → GUILT AND GUILT FEELINGS Shame focuses on appearances: on exposure to the ridicule of a community that may judge wrongly. Hebrews tells us that Jesus "endured the cross, scorning its shame" (12:2). He knew that the contempt and ridicule heaped on Him by hostile onlookers would be turned back on them by the glory of His resurrection. The community had misjudged Jesus, and ultimately they would be exposed as the ones who were wrong.

The New Testament picks up this tension between reality as God sees it and as human beings see it, and three times states a wonderful promise: whoever trusts in God "will never be put to shame" (Rom. 9:33; 10:11; 1 Peter 2:6). When God strips away the final veils, the universe itself will bear witness that anchoring our lives in Jesus was no mistake. However those around may ridicule us today, it is the emptiness of *their* beliefs that will ultimately be exposed.

There are at least three ways we can apply what the Bible says about shame:

(1) We can confidently choose to respond to Jesus

rather than to the opinions of the people around us. John's Gospel speaks of foolish individuals who held back from making a full commitment to Jesus because "they loved praise from men more than praise from God" (12:43). When the day of unveiling comes, it is those who held back who will be exposed and ashamed.

(2) We can begin to share our inner selves with others. We are imperfect now, yes. But our imperfections will not drive either God or our brothers and sisters from us. Instead we know that God is at work, reshaping our personalities to become more like Jesus. We need not be ashamed, because when we unveil, what is discovered is the fact that God *is* at work. → BECOMING

(3) We can look forward with excitement to that great day when we are perfected. Then our faith in Jesus will be shown to be the most significant thing in the universe. In that day we will look at ourselves and discover the full freedom that comes with the realization that we never, ever again, will have any cause for shame.

SHYNESS. Shyness is a social disease.

We all know what it feels like. But it's helpful to review the symptoms. ● We feel uncomfortable meeting new people and making new friends. ● We may be depressed and feel lonely. ● We find it hard to express our opinions to others. ● We tend to draw back, and others do not see our strengths. ● We may appear snobbish or unfriendly. ● We are extremely self-conscious and preoccupied with our own responses and reactions.

How does a person overcome shyness? When Lee joined our Bible class she was so shy that she said not one word for six months. Then, gradually, in the small group of four or five that met daily at noon where we worked, she began to make hesitant contributions. After two years, she had found the freedom to talk not only with us, but also to share her faith with co-workers. What worked the cure of Lee's painful case of shyness?

● She found a smaller group of just a few Christians where she could be accepted, without being pressured to participate or change. → ACCEPTANCE

● She was not urged to be different. We waited until she felt comfortable with us, and took her first hesitant steps to reach out.

● She found her initiatives were met with loving affirmation and approval. And she grew.

It took two years. But that's what the family of God is for. To accept and love and welcome individuals where they are, without pressuring them. This cure is found in the body of Christ when we are living as the loving community God intends us to be. → **CHURCH** In fact, bonding to the body is the cure for all our social diseases: all the inner hurts and fears that keep us from reaching out to grow.

There are some steps a shy person can take on his or her own. → **FRIENDSHIP** But God calls the rest of us to gather around and help the shy among us feel a part of God's vital transforming community of love.

SIN. It's relatively easy to deal with the topic of sin theologically. Massive volumes have been written on sin; a subject theologians call *hamartiology*. Summarized, the main themes are:

● Sin's character. Two groups of Old Testament and New Testament words describe sin as (a) falling short, or (b) rebelling. Inability to live up to what we acknowledge to be good is one aspect of sin: unwillingness to choose the good and thus actively choosing what we know to be wrong is another.

● Sin's impact. We might note three things here. (a) Acts of sin are violations of God's or human standards and bring us a burden of guilt. We are responsible for our choices and deserve to be punished. → **GUILT** (b) The "sin nature" refers to the twisting of human motivations and will, so that every person descended from the first pair has had warped personalities. Our inner unresponsiveness to God is matched by a pull toward wrong-doing, so that without God's help we struggle unsuccessfully to do right even when we want to. (c) Injustice and oppression represent sin institutionalized. It is not only the individual who is twisted away from goodness; it is also man in society.

Guilty, driven by a passion for sin, and living in a world warped to oppress some and exalt others, we all are too familiar with the impact of sin.

While theologians find it easy to deal with sin theoretically, they find it no easier than the rest of us to deal with it personally. We all look around us at society, seeing the wars, the crime, the discrimination, and the economic brutality, and we hurt for our fellow human beings. We all struggle against that pull toward what we know is wrong, and then are burdened with the guilt that comes when we fall short or rebel. The good news for us does not come in dissecting sin, to master its anatomy, but in the discovery that God doesn't intend us to dwell on (or in!) sin. Once we've faced the fact that we all suffer from the disease, God wants us to turn to Him for the cure.

So the greatest Bible words associated with sin aren't terms like "rebellion" or "falling short" or "guilt." The greatest words the Bible associates with sin are words like "confession" and "forgiveness" and "new birth" and "salvation." These great Bible words assure us that in Christ God provides remission of guilt, power to choose against the pull of inner sin, and ultimately cleansing from the very presence of sin within our personality.

Sin is serious. But God doesn't intend us to dwell on sin, or to wallow in guilt, or to sink into hopelessness. God wants us to dwell on Him and the victory He offers us over humanity's curse. Because of Jesus, it's no longer sin that deserves our concentration.

So if a sense of sin is gnawing at your vitals, turn instead to meditate on: ● Confession ● Becoming ● Forgetting ● Eternal Life ● Acceptance.

SINGLENESS. For some it seems the real "fate worse than death." But attitudes—and our experiences—seem to be changing. For instance, in 1975 40.3% of the women 20–24 remained single, and 13.8% of those between 25–29. For men the figures were 59.9% and 22.3%. Add to these who have never been married an increasing number of widowed and divorced, and a significant number of Americans are living single lives.

It's hard, of course, when parents and others insist we *ought* to be married. It's even harder when we feel a little guilty or perhaps ashamed of not fitting in with what our society used to expect.

Actually, before a person makes up his or her mind, it's worth listing the attractions of each state. Many people find that there are advantages in being single that marriage can't seem to match. A search of the literature on singleness suggests that these are the primary things that attract people to one state or the other.

ATTRACTIONS OF . . .

marriage	*singleness*
• desire for a family	• career opportunities
• approval of parents	• sense of self-sufficiency
• example of peers	• freedom and mobility
• avoidance of loneliness	• social freedom
• physical relationship	• freedom to focus on
• security, status	personal development,
• emotional attachment/love	interests
• need to leave home	• expanding friendships,
• fear of independence	freedom from being
	"trapped"

There are advantages and disadvantages to each state. But the primary advantage perceived by most is that the single individual has a flexibility and potential for making personal choices denied those who live within the necessary restrictions of marriage.

Biblically. In Old Testament times the society and economy were structured around families, and marriage was expected. But looking into the New Testament, Paul gives a word of testimony for singleness. "Now to the unmarried and the widows I say: It is good for them to stay unmarried, as I am" (1 Cor. 7:8). Later Paul explains. When a person is married he or she is, rightly, concerned with spouse and family. "His interests are divided." But a single person is free to consider only the Lord: his or her "aim is to be devoted to the Lord in both body and spirit"

(1 Cor. 7:32–35). The freedom that is emphasized over and over in the attractions of singleness is seen by Paul as an important freedom indeed. The single can shape his or her own life, giving undivided devotion to the Lord.

While Paul does not develop this thought in Corinthians, it's also clear that the Christian single sacrifices less than a non-Christian in choosing a single life. A non-Christian may be sacrificing intimacy and family: a Christian is a member of the family of God, and can find in brothers and sisters the acceptance, intimacy, and support denied outside the body of Christ. → CHURCH We can be close to others, love and support and serve them, without the links provided by marriage.

There is, of course, the issue of sex. In our society singleness does not mean sexually inactive. But for Christians who realize that God's one context for intercourse is marriage, singleness raises the issue of celibacy. → CELIBACY Paul's advice in this area is valuable. He commends singleness. But points out that if "they cannot control themselves [sexually], they should marry, for it is better to marry than to burn with passion" (1 Cor. 7:9).

Paul's conclusion is one we must reach too. Our place in life is a matter of gift. Some are given the gift by God of living a meaningful, fulfilling single life. Some are given the gift by God of living a meaningful, fulfilling married life. Neither condition is "right" for everyone, or even "better" for everyone. Your own gift, whether to live as a single or as a married person, makes that state God's best for you.

SLEEPLESSNESS.

The eyelids droop, the head nods. And then you jerk awake. "Sorry. It's just that I couldn't get to sleep last night."

Sound familiar? If you're a poor sleeper, wake up often at night, have trouble getting to sleep, or don't log more than six hours of snooze, you may be all too familiar with the nodding head and need to apologize. But what can you do about it?

Normal sleep. We human beings operate on a sleep/

459

wake cycle calling for us to be active about two-thirds of the time, and to sleep the other third. But the amount of sleep an individual needs varies. Eight hours might not be normal for you now—and almost certainly won't be as you age and your sleep needs change.

Individual differences are so great that some persons seem quite comfortable with just three or four hours of sleep, while others can't make it with less than ten. So no one else can say with certainty what is the right amount of sleep for you.

There's another factor too. Sleep has been found to have four stages, ranging from light to very deep slumber. Children seem to slip easily into the deepest, most restful stage. Older persons may drift in and out of the three lighter sleep stages, and never reach the fourth. For most of us, the deep sleep stage comes early in a night's rest, usually within the first hour and a half or two hours. Again, because of individual differences, there's no set standard for "normal" or "right" sleep.

Sleeplessness. If you are plagued with poor sleep, though, what are the most likely causes? And what can you do about it?

Research on sleep shows how complex that answer can be. Some kinds of sleep problems have a physical cause. Your muscles cramp, or the pain of arthritis jerks you to wakefulness. Anxiety and depression are also linked with sleep problems. Or crises can break a normal sleep pattern that may not return after the crisis is resolved.

In some cases, doctors prescribe pills. Many others simply buy over-the-counter sleep aids. But pills do not cure insomnia. When used over a long period of time, they can even lead to drug dependency. A better approach is to adopt a sleep strategy, designed to restructure your approach to rest. Here are elements of the strategy that experts suggest:

• Exercise daily. Brisk walks in the afternoon are better than vigorous calisthenics at bedtime.

• Avoid big meals near bedtime. You sleep best on an under-stuffed stomach.

● Resist daytime naps. Take that walk instead, and reserve night for sleeping.

● Avoid coffee, soft drinks, and other stimulants in the evening.

● Sleep in a cool rather than warm, dry room.

● Build a bedtime routine, which you begin to follow an hour or so before bed. Build in activities that call for little physical or mental involvement.

The spiritual dimension. Sleep experts also call on us to "try to blank out the day's worries, and forget about tomorrow's." It is here the Christian has a great advantage.

David helps us see why. Psalm 3 tells of David's feelings when his son Absalom rebelled. Many of David's people followed Absalom. David was forced to flee Jerusalem to preserve his life, with only a few faithful supporters. On that road he was forced to listen to the taunts of those who took the rebellion as evidence that God Himself had forsaken the shepherd king.

That night, in the darkness, on the silent plains beyond Jerusalem, David stood alone. He was deeply hurt by the faithlessness of his people. He knew that his life was in danger, for he was pursued by his own army. Standing there, David's thoughts turned to God. He remembered all that God had been to him—shield, encourager, glory, and hope. In simple trust David prayed, and then, his psalm records.

> I lie down and sleep;
> I wake again, because the LORD sustains me.
> I will not fear the tens of thousands
> drawn up against me on every side.

It is never easy to "blank out the day's worries and forget about tomorrow's." But with our thoughts as David's fixed on the Lord, and our anxieties placed in His hands, we can sleep.

SMALL GROUPS. The term is a little deceptive. We're all part of "small groups." A family is a "small group.'' A Sunday school class, or a church board or committee is a "small group" too. But the term seems to have a special meaning for most Christians. A "small group" is a special gathering of just a few Christians for sharing, or Bible study, or prayer: a getting together with others that is somehow focused on spiritual and personal growth.

Kinds of "small groups." The behavioral science literature as well as church history is full of information on small groups and their functions. Small groups are often used in counseling: they've been found to have great impact for everything from rehabilitation of juvenile delinquents to marriage counseling to weight loss. Somehow the sense of support and the confrontation that marks small, face-to-face gatherings, helps persons face their own behavior and make steps toward change.

Church history suggests that small face-to-face gatherings of Christians also have unusual transforming power. Small groups were an integral aspect of the Wesleyan revival in England. The earliest meetings of the church were in homes, not massive church assembly halls. Probably for the first two hundred years of the Christian era nearly all church meetings were in "small groups." Great revivals in our own country grew out of cottage prayer meetings. Much modern evangelism takes place in living rooms and around restaurant tables, as "small groups" meet to study and share, and non-Christians are drawn to meet Christ.

At the same time, Christians gather in small groups with different focuses. Sometimes groups meet for the specific purpose of praying. Other groups meet to study the Bible, sometimes with a teacher, and sometimes using self-study material. There are sharing groups, in which members focus on their own experiences and needs and encourage each other to continued growth. Some small groups focus on specific problems: getting along as singles, raising young children, living with an alcoholic spouse or a teen who lives for drugs.

Each of these kinds of groups can offer significant

support and help. But there does seem to be a common format for the most important kind of Christian "small group" gathering: a group that focuses on stimulating spiritual growth and personal discipleship.

Small group format. What happens in one of these "basic" small group meetings? Here's a common pattern.

The members arrive and spend the first half hour or so chatting, catching up on what's been happening since they were together last week. There are probably eight to a dozen people there, although in time the group is likely to expand rapidly.

Then the group turns to the Bible. Each has studied a common passage during the week. Now each shares what he or she has seen in the passage, focusing on how this particular word from God touches daily life. How has each person tried to respond to what God is saying? What new discoveries and obedience have resulted?

The group time concludes with prayer. Personal needs and concerns are shared. Answers to earlier prayers are reported. Individuals are encouraged and exhorted to reach out to others as God leads, and every need and individual mentioned is prayed for by the group.

The meeting probably takes from one and one half to two hours, although members may stay on to talk and share. The close bonds that form, and the common commitment to follow Jesus, are powerful stimulants to personal discipleship and growth.

Keys to effective small groups. Sometimes Christians have unfortunate experiences with small groups. They get together. But nothing much seems to happen. Finally the group simply drags to a stop, or it drags on as another empty religious activity. What helps to keep small groups dynamic?

• Take time to build relationships. Sharing is important, for each person needs to feel he or she belongs, and is loved. Often when groups start, a simple sharing question will be used to launch each gathering. "What have you done in the last year you feel was a great success?"

"When are you most likely to be afraid of what other people will think?" As time goes on the group members begin to feel they know each other in significant ways, and that they themselves are also known—and accepted.

● Look at Scripture for personal guidance. Small groups are not the place to learn about doctrine. Small groups should look into Scripture for God's marching orders: to hear what He is saying to us as His people, and to learn how to obey. For this kind of study, it's best if each person studies a common Bible passage, asks God to help him or her understand and apply the Word, and then shares with the group what he or she has learned. This kind of study can be guided by study materials, or simply by three set questions applied to every passage: "What do I learn from this passage about God?" "What do I discover here that helps me understand how God wants me to live?" "How can I put what I find into practice this week?"

● Share personal crises and concerns for group prayer. The answers that God gives to prayers offered by the group often stimulate praise, and a growing conviction that God is real and present.

Small groups, meeting with such a simple format, continue to enrich the lives of believers, and draw others to Jesus. In the simplicity of shared faith, we can be God's servants and help each other grow.

SMILE. Experimenters made a fascinating discovery. When a person giving a test smiles at the person taking it, test scores are higher. So give your friends a big smile. Everyone can use a lift these days.

SOFT DRINKS. Miglions of Americans have given up cigarettes, dropped fatty foods, and cut down on alcohol. All for the sake of health. Others have turned to bean sprouts and "natural" tomatoes. And the big question is, Do we have to give up soft drinks too?

Heavy cola drinkers have been probed and tested, and now it can be told. The cola guzzler is ● more likely to feel jittery sometimes (18% more likely), ● more likely to have sleep problems (16% more likely), and ● more likely to report frequent mood changes (19% more likely). On the other hand, heavy cola drinkers are *not* prone to headaches or nail biting.

What does it boil down to? Inconclusive. So I compromise. I stick to diet Pepsi or diet Dr. Pepper, to cut out the sugar. And keep on enjoying the simple pleasure of pop.

SPIRITUAL GIFTS.

We all have questions about them. But there is one basic reality that each of us needs to grasp—and to delight in. *Every* Christian is given special enablement by the Holy Spirit, which makes it possible for him or her to minister to others (1 Cor. 12:7). This means that you and I are spiritually significant persons. We are needed. We each can contribute to the well-being of others and to the health of the body of Christ.

Whatever theological debate sidetracks us when we deal with spiritual gifts, we need to return to the most significant issue. What does the Bible's good news about *my* spiritual gift tell me about God's plan for *my* life?

The theological debates. Few these days question the importance of spiritual gifts. But there are questions about them.

● Does the Bible list them all? First Corinthians 12 and Romans 12 each list a number of spiritual gifts—such as faith, a message of wisdom, prophecy, etc. Some take these as an exhaustive listing of gifts: these are all the spiritual gifts there are. Others note that the Old Testament speaks of the Spirit enabling even the workers whose artistry enriched the Tabernacle (Exod. 31:1–11) and are not so sure. They take the lists as representative, and believe that *any* way in which a person can encourage or help others expresses the Spirit's gifting and enablement.

● Are they all for today? A number of the gifts listed in 1 Corinthians are unusual: gifts of healing, miraculous powers, ability to speak in different tongues, etc. Many Christians believe that these unusual gifts were expressed in New Testament times, but were intended to be temporary, until the canon of Scriptures was complete. They note that other New Testament letters do not talk about the miraculous, and that the exercise of these gifts has little testimony in later church history. Other Christians believe that the expression of the miraculous is a sign of a healthy church: that when believers are living in tune with Christ these gifts emerge. → SPIRITUALITY → "TONGUES"

Questions like these are important. But not as important as remaining open to brothers and sisters whose conclusions are different from ours. And not as important as remaining open to the ministry of the Holy Spirit, who is free to work as He wills, despite our interpretations.

My spiritual gifts. We can and should study the books of brothers and sisters who explore the theological questions. But we can never forget that the Bible's teaching about spiritual gifts is meant first of all to encourage us, and to give focus to our lives. Moving into the realm of Christian experience, we find a number of important questions that deserve answers.

● Who has a spiritual gift? As noted earlier, gifts are enablements given by God's Spirit, to equip us for service. They are given "to each one" for "the common good" (1 Cor. 12:7). *You* have a spiritual gift.

● How do I discover my spiritual gift? Not by reading the New Testament lists and deciding which gift you'd like. Spiritual gifts are given for "different kinds of service" (1 Cor. 12:5). We discover gifts by loving and serving others. As we reach out to encourage, to help and support and pray, God begins to use us in ways for which we have been gifted. We do not discover our gift and then serve. We begin to serve, and our gifts emerge.

● What kinds of service are linked with gifts? Each New Testament passage in which spiritual gifts are dealt with (1 Cor. 12; Rom. 12; Eph. 4) is in a context that emphasizes close and loving personal relationships with other believers. Gifts are primarily interpersonal. Any context in which we build relationships with others and seek to serve them is a context for the operation of spiritual gifts. The context can be a Sunday school class. But the institutional setting (a church agency or program) is not necessary. The context can just as well be a kitchen, a small group in a home, a chat on a telephone. The necessary context is simply one of caring and serving others, giving what you have to give to enrich another's life.

● How will I know my spiritual gift? Your gift emerges as you come to know and serve others. There will then be three clues. (1) You'll find satisfaction in serving in a particular way. (2) You'll see evidence that God is using you in others' lives. (3) You'll find that others in the body of Christ sense how God uses you, and affirm your contribution. When you discover how God uses you, then you'll be able to focus your efforts on ministering in that way.

SPIRITUALITY.

How do we know we're close to God? In Greek times an epileptic fit was taken to be an indication of the divine presence. No wonder converted pagans in Corinth were so impressed by the gift of tongues: they looked on these ecstatic utterances as proof of special spirituality (1 Cor. 12). In Colossae another idea took root. Spirituality was found in strict religious practices, and an ascetic self-denial that involved "harsh treatment of the body" (Col. 2:16–23). It wasn't the emotional but the grim that was thought to mark a man who lives close to the Lord.

These early notions were wrong, and our New Testament letters correct them. But through history believers have persisted in wandering away from Scripture, to look for spirituality in mysticism, self-discipline, emotionalism, zeal, or in following carefully constructed lists of dos and don'ts. These practices may have comforted some individuals. But they didn't bring them closer to the Lord, and they do not fit the Bible's picture of spirituality.

Which leads to the really important question for us. What is true spirituality? How is it expressed? How can you and I live close to our Lord?

To answer these questions Paul begins in Colossians by establishing an important point. Spirituality is not "otherworldly." Jesus, the Creator, stepped into the physical world and lived His godly life in the physical body, ultimately winning our freedom from sin through a real death in this real world. All those practices that call on us to deny the physical in the name of spirituality just don't fit the way God, in Jesus' incarnation, has set for us. In chapter 3 Paul tells the believers to reject anger and rage and malice and lying and such, so that in relationships with others they can "clothe yourselves with compassion, kindness, humility, gentleness and patience" (v. 12). It is in living out these qualities in our daily life . . . forgiving and loving, and working toward unity within the family of God . . . that we discover true spirituality.

In 1 Corinthians Paul encourages believers to honor every manifestation of the Spirit (ch. 12), but to recognize that God's "most excellent way" is simply to live love. "Love is patient," Paul says, describing the truly spiritual person, "love is kind. It does not envy, it does not boast, it is not proud. It is not rude, it is not self-seeking, it is not easily angered, it keeps no record of wrongs. Love does not delight in evil but rejoices with the truth. It always protects, always trusts, always hopes, always perseveres" (13:4–6).

This testimony of Scripture is so clear it is a wonder we have not all understood. The Spirit, Galatians says, produces qualities in human beings like love, joy, peace, longsuffering, patience, goodness, self-control. One whose life is lived in touch with the Spirit of God will express these qualities in his or her relationships with others.

STEPPARENTS. These days when families are reconstituted, it is often the result of divorce rather than the death of one or both previous partners. Age at first marriage is the early or mid-twenties; remarriage for both men and women is apt to come about thirty-five. The new family, rather than having the typical two children, is likely to have four. Even in the best of circumstances, there is going to be stress in the reconstituted home. While one study showed that about 24% of adults had excellent relationships with their stepchildren, and 38% good relationships, a significant 38% confessed to poor relationships. Understanding that there will be tensions and stress for both children and the stepparents, what guidelines offer direction in this increasingly common situation?

• Give first priority to the marriage. Unity and harmony between husband and wife is vital if healthy relationships with the children are to develop. Each adult needs assurance of the support and commitment of the other.

• Concentrate on good parenting skills, and open communication lines. → PARENTING → COMMUNICATING There are emotional strains on every member of the reconstituted family. Talking about feelings in an accepting atmosphere is a necessary part of learning to live together as a family.

• Don't expect instant liking—either way. It often takes years for children to respond warmly to a stepparent. Stepparents may find themselves disliking, or at least often annoyed by, their stepchildren. Growing to know each other, to understand and to care, is something that you should expect will take time.

• Guard against divide and conquer tactics. The reconstituted family is particularly vulnerable. You may feel guilt already about bringing a "stranger" between you and your children, and find yourself taking sides with them to compensate. You may have different ideas about discipline than your new spouse. It's important that the adults work out ways to deal with the issue when it emerges. You'll also need to work out ways to help a child—or spouse—with feelings of jealousy. It will be important to find time and ways to help each person realize he or she is loved, and still important.

In general, if the two adults work together on their own relationship and communicate freely about the children, they can cope with emerging problems and can build a strong new home. However, if a stepparent begins to feel angry or tense whenever with the children or when talking about them, it's a sign that outside counseling and help may be important. → COUNSELING

469

The Bible has little to say about stepparents. Basic principles of how Christians live together in acceptance, forgiveness, and hope, will help us find God's best in reconstituted homes.

STOP SMOKING. We all know everyone should. The link between smoking and heart disease, lung cancer, and other ills is firmly established. That passage in 1 Corinthians about taking care of the body because it's the temple of God's Spirit undoubtedly applies. So why don't people simply stop?

They don't stop because it's hard to stop. Even when a person knows he should, and asks God's help.

It may be that some expect too much from prayer. God never intended us to ask Him to take responsibility for our choices. And despite the fact that nine out of ten of our nation's 54 million smokers say they want to stop, most still cling desperately to cigarettes.

A number of stop-smoking programs exist to help individuals quit. Most use a group approach. The groups meet regularly, members talk about why they have smoked, and why they want to quit. Behavior modification techniques are often used. Members keep a record to discover when they are most likely to light up, and try to avoid those situations. The American Cancer Society runs more than 1,500 of these groups each year, and the Seventh-day Adventists operate a "cold turkey" five-day plan. Commercial groups have been formed and clinics use different kinds of therapy designed to make smoking unpleasant. Follow-up studies of the nonprofit groups show they are generally successful in the short run. But by the end of a year, three of four graduates are puffing away again.

If you're a smoker, and convinced you should stop, you can. Even if you haven't had enough will-power to do it on your own, there is effective help available. You don't need prayer, asking God to make you stop. You simply need to act on what you believe is right, join a stop-smoking group, and begin the process of weaning yourself from the weed.

STRESS. The concept of stress was introduced only in the 1930s. Hans Selye, the Canadian who coined the term, insists that the bad image stress has isn't entirely deserved. He speaks of a good kind of stress; something that makes people come alive. He points to studies that show that top business executives thrive on levels of stress once thought only to cause heart attacks or force early retirement. So stress is perhaps more complicated than we thought. And perhaps not so bad.

What causes stress? A number of inventories have been developed to identify experiences that bring stress. The inventories rank life events, giving points from most stressful to least stressful. Looking at such a list, it's easy to see why some of us never seem able to escape from stress.

RANK	EVENT	STRESS POINTS
1	Death of spouse	100
2	Divorce	73
3	Marital separation	65
4	Jail term	63
5	Death of family member	63
6	Injury or illness	53
7	Marriage	50
8	Fired from work	47
9	Marital reconciliation	45
10	Retirement	45
11	Change in health/family member	44
12	Pregnancy	40
13	Sex difficulties	39
14	Gain of new family member	39
15	Business readjustment	39
16	Change in financial state	38
17	Death of close friend	37
18	Change to different kind of work	36
19	Change in number of arguments with spouse	35
20	Mortgage over $10,000	31
21	Foreclosure of mortgage or loan	30
22	Change in work responsibilities	29
23	Son or daughter leaving home	29
24	Trouble with in-laws	29
25	Outstanding personal achievement	28
26	Wife begins or stops work	26

27	Begin or end school	26
28	Change in living conditions	25
29	Revision of personal habits	24
30	Trouble with boss	23
31	Change in work hours/conditions	20
32	Change in residence	20
33	Change in schools	20
34	Change in recreation	19
35	Change in church activities	19
36	Change in social activities	18
37	Mortgage or loan/less than $10,000	17
38	Change in sleep habits	16
39	Change in number of family get togethers	15
40	Change in eating habits	15

Inventories like this are fascinating. But they have one weakness. They fail to take individual differences into account. Some people seem better able to live with stress than others. Race-horse types are able to transform the energy stress creates into zest. Others may be crushed by the same experiences, and thrown into depression or anxiety. The issue isn't so much what causes stress as how we respond to it.

Reactions to stress. The anatomy of stress is beautifully illustrated in a well-known incident reported in the Gospels. Jesus and His followers arrive at Bethany, the home of Mary, Martha, and their brother Lazarus. The two women are excited. Martha rushes into the kitchen, arranges the table, gets dinner going and thinks, "Now, is there anything I've forgotten?" Energetic and thoughtful, Martha bustles about, eager to provide the best for Jesus.

But her sister Mary slips away from the work, and sits listening to Jesus. Finally Martha can't stand it any longer. She bursts into the little group in the living room. In her frustration she accuses Jesus of not caring about her, and blames Mary because "my sister has left me to do the work by myself." It seems to Martha that her efforts aren't appreciated, and that Mary is to blame for the stress Martha feels.

We know Jesus' response. He quiets her: "Martha, Martha, you are worried and upset about many things, but

only one thing is needed. Mary has chosen what is better"
(Luke 10:40, 41).

What do we learn from this story about stress and how to deal successfully with it?

● The signs of stress are anxiety and agitation. There's an inner feeling of turmoil; of being pulled in different directions.

● The symptoms of stress include a tendency to feel sorry for ourselves and unappreciated. There is also a tendency to blame others for making us feel as we do. →
EMOTIONS

● The solution to stress is found in reevaluating the situation. Circumstances may not change. But how we look at them can. Mary had looked at Jesus' visit as an opportunity to be with Him and to learn. Martha had looked at it as an occasion for putting on a special dinner. It was Martha's evaluation of the situation that led to her stress.

When we find ourselves experiencing the signs and demonstrating the symptoms of stress, how do we go about reevaluating? (1) We remember that God is in full control of our lives. He has not forgotten us, and He does care. (2) We take time out, like Mary, to listen to Jesus. The Bible contains hundreds of promises that offer us support. (3) We consciously turn the situation over to Jesus. The Book of Hebrews calls this act of trust "entering into his rest." Psalm 46:10 invites us to "Be still and know that I am God." We are to cease striving. Committing ourselves in this way to God we discover the resources that enable us to live with stress rather than be crushed by it.

The benefits of stress. Stress translated into anxiety will be destructive in any life. But stress—that state of heightened awareness that comes when life forces us to our toes—can be a very positive thing indeed. All too often life sags into a comfortable, dull pattern. Changes, even painful changes, remind us that life is more than routine. There are challenges to face, and God is stretching us that we might grow. When this kind of stretching experience comes, we may discover that stress awakens us from slumber to the realization that life holds more for us than we've imagined. In this way stress can add zest and excitement to our life.

When we know that God Himself accompanies us into each new and stretching experience, stress may offer even more. It may offer us the opportunity to experience Jesus' presence in more wonderful ways than we have known.

SUBMISSIVENESS. Yes, it's there in the Bible. Christians are taught to submit: to government, to spiritual leaders, wives to husbands, and all to one another. The idea is resented by some these days, particularly when it is misunderstood. To those who imagine some silent, demeaning bondage, we can only say that this is man's idea of submission, not God's.

What is the meaning of submission? The most common word means "be responsive to." Rather than resisting another person with whom we are in relationship, we are to be open to him, flexible, persuadable. The other New Testament word, seldom used, means to "fall in rank with." It is a call to reserve the order and standards of contemporary society rather than to push the Christian's charter deed to liberty and equality to radical extremes.

Encouragement to live submissively in the relationships in which men and women find themselves is based on a vital concept. Every station in life is important: every role—whether that of master or of slave—provides its own opportunities for a person to serve others. To serve well, we must fit into our role as society defines it. We use our freedom to choose to serve well, rather than as an excuse to flee responsibilities.

There is another special dimension of New Testament teaching that is absent from the views of the world. Submission is no "over/under" kind of thing in the body of Christ. Instead, while we act appropriately to our station, we do so knowing that we are all equal in the family of God—brothers and sisters, alike the children of one Father. Because of this, submission is a mutual thing.

Whatever our role, we are to be responsive to *each other* (cf. Eph. 5:21).

For Christians, submission is not a threatening word, and the concept demeans no individual. Submission is God's gentle reminder that we live in a world of ordered relationships, and are to use our freedom to demonstrate to all that relationship with God produces goodness among every rank. To those whose role would give them what men mistake as authority, "submission" is God's loving reminder that we are to be responsive to one another, and never to tyrannize brothers or sisters in the family of God.

SUCCESS. Everyone has noticed that "success" in our society is usually measured by size and dollars. Psychologists, more sophisticated, observe that success means different things to different persons. An artist may not measure the bottom line the same way a businessman would. But we can't help realizing that even in religion, size and dollars count. How big is your church? What's your budget? How much for missions? How many converts or new members this year?

I don't imagine we'll ever get away from such notions until Jesus comes, we appear before Him, and hear Him commend: "Well done, good and faithful servant" (Matt. 25:21, 23). Perhaps then we'll realize that to God, success isn't measured in results, but in faithfulness.

SUFFERING. The very existence of suffering in a universe shaped by a loving, all-powerful God, has always troubled thinking people. Browning put the problem this way:

> Wherefore should any evil hap to man—
> From ache of flesh to agony of soul—
> Since God's All-mercy mates All-potency?
> Nay, why permits He evil to Himself—
> Man's sin, accounted such? Suppose a world
> Purged of all pain, with fit inhabitant—
> Man pure of evil in thought, word, and deed—
> Were it not well? Then, wherefore otherwise?

In the abstract, there is no answer to the problem. We can observe that suffering and evil are related to human sin. We can continue to believe that God is able to transmute suffering into the believer's good. But there are no pat, easy answers as to why God chose to permit His creation to be warped out of its original state.

We also have to observe in wonder that permitting human suffering was no easy thing for God. In Christ God entered our world to suffer with us and for us. He suffered in an ultimate way we may not even be able to understand in eternity. For now, we can only trust that God, whose wisdom is beyond our own, understands the necessity that we cannot.

When we suffer. Most of us are less than tormented by the philosophical issue of suffering on the grand, universal scale. But each of us will face personal suffering. Then the tormenting questions *do* come. Why? What have I done? Is God punishing me? Is there anything I can do to find release?

Jesus made it clear that we human beings will suffer (cf. John 15:18–27). Romans 8:17 suggests we must. So Peter calls us to look at our reaction when suffering comes: "Do not be surprised," he says, "at the painful trial you are suffering" (1 Peter 4:12).

Perhaps the most helpful passage in Scripture on suffering is also found in Peter's first letter. There he reminds us that God is watching over us: He guards us as we continue to do good (1 Peter 3:8–12). But what if the unexpected comes, and "you should suffer for what is right"? Peter makes the startling statement that "you are blessed" (3:14). He then goes on to show us how to respond when suffering comes for which we are not to blame. [There is, of course, suffering that comes when we willfully choose to sin. This suffering is corrective, but it is not "blessing."] What is Peter's prescription?

● Do not be terrified (3:14). Suffering is not a sign that life is out of control.

● Set apart Christ as Lord (3:15). Remember that Jesus is still in control, and trust Him as Lord.

● Maintain a positive outlook (3:15). Others will be amazed, but you can explain the basis of your hope: not the circumstances, but the conviction that Jesus, who loves you, is still at work.

● Keep a clear conscience (3:16). Don't panic into doing wrong, but continue your commitment to good behavior.

Peter then goes on to point up a reassuring truth. He explains how we can be confident that suffering leads to blessing. He turns our attention to Jesus (3:18), and reminds us that He who did only good was the One who suffered on the cross—not the evil men who betrayed and condemned Him. But His suffering was not purposeless: through it Jesus brought us to God, and then went into heaven, and is now at "God's right hand—with angels, authorities and powers in submission to him" (3:22). Jesus' suffering was intended to lead to good for others, and to His own glorification.

Peter's encouragement to us is clear. We may not understand how, but we can be sure that when we suffer God intends to use our experience to enrich others, and to bless us.

SUICIDE PREVENTION.   Suicide has been given a number of definitions. It's been identified simply as self-inflicted death. But more significantly, it's been called "saying enough." And "the most tragic decision of a man who found nobody to hold out a hand to him."

There are a number of myths about suicide that need to be examined before we can think about suicide prevention.

MYTH	FACT
People who talk suicide don't do it.	Eight of ten suicides give definite warnings of their intentions.
Suicide happens without warning.	Suicidal persons give many clues and warnings.

Suicidal persons are intent on dying.	Most are undecided, and will "gamble," leaving it to others to save them. Most tell someone how they are feeling.
Once suicidal, always suicidal.	Suicidal intentions change over time.
Improvement in attitude means the danger of suicide has passed.	Most suicides take place within three months of the beginning of "improvement."
Suicide is more likely in some special group (like the rich, or the poor).	Suicide is represented in all levels of society.
Suicide runs in families.	Suicide is an individual response.
All suicidal persons are mentally ill.	Suicidal persons are extremely unhappy, but not necessarily mentally ill.

Clues. All verbal indications of an intention to kill one-self should be taken seriously. Dejected or angry asides, such as "I'd be better off dead," or "I won't be around much longer for you to put up with," should never be ignored. A person contemplating suicide may give away valued possessions—a stereo system—or make outright gifts of cash. Withdrawal, refusal to eat, or serious depression are also clues to possible suicide. It's not always possible to say that such a person is actually close to a suicide attempt. But it is possible to say that such a person does need help. The common irritated response, "He just wants attention," is not really true. But the fact that such a person should be given attention is true.

Helping. The basic approach to suicide prevention is befriending. This may be done by a family member or acquaintance who recognizes the special need of an individual. It can even be done through a Crisis Center that a potential suicide can call. A suicide prevention movement in England, called Samaritans, has had a significant impact on reducing the suicide rate. One in 200 of the British population called on Samaritans in 1977, and two thirds of individuals contacted in a random poll who had been to Samaritans said they had been helped.

The staff is made up of volunteers who are given some training in listening and helping. The people who call do so when particularly lonely or in despair, and a number who call are considering suicide at that moment. Simply talking with the Samaritans' volunteer—often for hours—helps a number of individuals through the immediate crisis. Samaritans often establish longer term relationships, which extend over months.

Professional help and counseling is undoubtedly necessary for many who consider suicide. But hundreds of others simply need to be befriended. For more information on how such a program works one can read *Answers to Suicide,* published by The Samaritans (Constable & Co. Ltd., London, 1978).

The thirty-year experience of Samaritans suggests that a similar network here, stimulated by the same Christian concern that initiated the British movement, is something believers might consider.

Specific principles to guide you if a friend or loved one seems suicidal are:

• Make a pact. Promise that you will be available to talk any time the person feels on the edge. Have the other person promise that he or she *will* call.

• Talk about suicide plans. Point out difficulties— pain, harm that might be done to others—as different plans are suggested. This often causes a person to reconsider.

• Do things with the person to help him or her deal with depression. Go to a ball game, take up jogging together, visit friends, discuss books, etc.

• Remain sensitive, showing empathy (but not pity) when the person hurts, and joy when he or she experiences little victories.

• Keep on loving. Unconditional, committed caring for as long as it takes provides a sense of security and of significance that those who have lost hope desperately need.

A Christian perspective. There is no doubt: suicide is self-murder, and surely not something that an individual can choose in the will of God. → EUTHANASIA More to the point, suicide comes when there is a loss of hope. We can befriend hurting individuals and help them over their crisis. But the ultimate solution is a life-given focus and purpose by Jesus Christ, and thus enriched with hope. Christians, like non-Christians, can lose sight of life's meaning. But restoration to Christian fellowship and a return to the One who is the ground of hope is the final answer for all. → HOPE

SUNDAY KEEPING. When one of our church "pillars" closes the shade, as some still do, so no one outside will see the family reading the Sunday papers, I imagine he's unaware of the roots of Sabbatarianism. No, the roots aren't in the Old Testament. They're sunk much more shallowly, in the 1500s.

Of course, most of us think of Sunday practices as going back to Scripture. The commandment to keep the Sabbath holy was understood by the Jews to mean avoid work, dress well, and so eat and drink as to make the Sabbath a delight. The first Christians modified these customs, meeting on the first rather than seventh day in honor of the Lord's resurrection. But aside from gathering for worship and fellowship, no New Testament passages suggest special Sunday rules (cf. Col. 2:16; Rom. 14:5, 6).

It took our British forebears and the Reformation to make Sunday-keeping an issue. By 1560 the Protestant reformers had concluded that Sunday was in some sense Sabbath, and that to keep it holy required abandoning all work and recreation. Queen Elizabeth I and James I found Sunday keeping was becoming a political as well as religious issue. Finally James was forced to issue a Declaration of Sports, listing permitted and forbidden Sunday recreation. No bear or bullbaiting, plays or bowling, but archery and morris dancing were all right . . . if done after the afternoon vespers service.

In the 1850s the Religious Tract Society informed the middle classes, who had decorous Sunday habits, that the sure way to distinguish the righteous from the unrighteous was to observe their Sunday amusements. The lower classes, of course, were the wicked. So it's not surprising that when Parliament passed a bill in 1855 restricting Sunday pub hours, the working classes rioted. Karl Marx, in London at the time, was so excited that he wrote an article announcing that the English revolution had begun!

The Sunday question is no longer an issue in Britain, of course. Most people there are simply pagan. The notion that their forefathers might have fought and argued, and that political parties' fortunes would have turned on something like Sunday-keeping practices, would—if known—undoubtedly be greeted with stunned disbelief. And then probably with a superior smile.

Oh. The church. What can one expect of *them?*

I'm sure no one can draw the conclusion that British Sabbatarianism is the cause of the loss of the church's influence there today. But the historic controversy there surely accomplished little but to cloud the gospel. As Paul says in the passage in which he gives us freedom to follow our own conscience in such matters, "the kingdom of God is not a matter of eating and drinking, but of righteousness, peace and joy in the Holy Spirit" (14:17).

How should you keep Sunday? In whatever way honors the Lord, and offers the release and enjoyment intended for a day set aside for rest and worship. → **LEISURE**

SURVIVALISM. You can hear the "crack" of rifle fire on the range and the grunts as boxes of dehydrated food are lifted into the back room. You may be invited over to look at the dugout shelter, replete with stores of water and oxygen, Geiger counters, walkie-talkies, and battery-powered AM/FM sets, although it's not too likely. Your neighbors don't really want you to know. There's only room for the family there, and those guns Mom and Dad and kids are practicing with are to make sure that, when the disaster comes, you won't break in and take their food. Try it, and they'll blow you away. They're survivalists.

As you can tell by now, survivalists are sure that some nuclear or other catastrophe is sure to strike humanity. They are determined to be ready. They will live through the days of hunger and terror, and seed the new civilization that may grow up afterward. They have also faced the painful fact that others around them will not be ready: that survival will require them to turn away the starving rabble who did not prepare.

What can we say about survivalism? Certainly the Bible is clear, and history adds its vivid testimony, that no society is secure. Preparing for difficult times isn't foolishness.

But there is something tragic about survivalism. These are people who are terrified by the savagery they sense in others. They are convinced that man's inhumanity to man means that a civilization shattering disaster must come. Looking ahead, the men and women who are preparing for that day have decided that, in the world beyond holocaust, they must adopt the same savage stance. They are prepared to kill other survivors, whom they believe will be enemies. How tragic. Driven to drastic preparations by their certainty that hostility between nations must bring disaster, they have themselves consciously chosen to be hostile to any whom the atomic fury spares.

God has a very different survival plan. Sin will drive the race to wars and terrors and to a great culminating conflict. But then Jesus will return. Then human beings who have shown over and over again that they have chosen Jesus' way of love will have goodness at last.

When Jesus comes we will not just survive.

Then we will *live!*

TEACHING. We think of it as a classroom kind of thing. Teachers, who know, pass on information to students, who do not. When the students know the information too, they have learned.

It's a different kind of thing in the Bible. "Teaching" has a different focus and dynamic. For instance, Titus 2 tells us to "teach what is in accord with sound doctrine." The thrust is not communication of the doctrine, which is known, but encouragement of a lifestyle in harmony with it. So the "teacher" comes alongside the learner, sharing life with him or her. The Titus 2 verbs that describe the teaching ministry are "bid," "explain what is good," "train," "urge," "show yourselves in all respects a model," "declare," "exhort," and "reprove."

Paul helps us understand even more clearly in 1 Timothy. He insists that sound doctrine be communicated, and explains that "the goal of this command is love, which comes from a pure heart and a good conscience and a sincere faith" (1:5).

Certainly we need to know the great truths and doctrines of our faith. But the ministry of teaching is far more than telling. It is walking alongside others to model, encourage, train, and guide them into a life that glorifies God.

TELEVISION WATCHING. In 1972 the U.S. Surgeon General reported in congressional hearings that "the causal relationships between televised violence and antisocial behavior is sufficient to warrant appropriate and remedial action." Ten years later Congress is still having hearings. The 1982 hearings featured Dr. David Pearl of the National Institute of Mental Health, who said: "We have come to a unanimous conclusion that there is a causal relationship between television violence and real-life violence." Another expert witness expressed his conviction that violence on TV may be responsible for 25% to 50% of all real-life violence in American society. The more realistic the portrayal of violence, the more likely it is to stimulate real-life violence, whether the violent person is the "good guy" or the "bad guy."

Based on our Congress' record of courageous action, it's unlikely any reduction in the level of TV violence will be initiated in Washington. This leaves you and me with the task of regulating our own TV watching—and that of our children. One friend of mine, who operates a garbage disposal company in Colorado, resolved the problem in his home once and for all. He treated his TV like garbage, and disposed of it. Most of us won't take such a radical step. We'll continue to be among the 98% of American families that have a TV. For us, the issue of taking control of our own TV viewing is vital.

Good and bad. One encouraging note has come from the research of Dr. David Lowe, of the UCLA School of Medicine. He reports that "television's effects are of two basic and very simple kinds, beneficial and harmful—or in the down-to-earth language most of us use to assess everything from breakfast foods to schools for our children, *good* and *bad*." While violence viewing adults maintain a more aggressive mood, pro-social and educational program viewers were less anxious and showed less antisocial behavior.

The impact of TV on children has been the subject of much more intense study. Heavy TV viewing by preschoolers decreases imaginative play and hinders vocabulary development. High IQ kids who watch lots of TV don't read as well as those with the same IQ who watch less. Children aged 6 through 10 benefit both from good books and good TV, though each medium calls for different kinds of thinking. In general, it is important to help children choose beneficial programs that reflect positive values and encourage learning, and to help children limit their TV viewing so growth can be balanced.

How much TV is too much for children? A good general guideline is: if TV viewing is crowding out growing-up experiences, such as reading and being read to, homework, chores, playing alone or with others and talking with the family, or getting a good night's sleep, it's too much. A good way to draw the line is to set a time limit: X number of half-hours per day. Then go through a

TV guide with your children and help them select the shows they want to watch within the time allotment.

There's one problem. When you begin to establish and maintain standards for your kids, you really need to establish some of the same disciplines for yourself. Setting your own time limits, and selecting programs for something other than mere entertainment value, is something you may want to consider for your own benefit as well as for the kids. → COMMERCIALS → PARENTING

TEMPTATION. Somehow we've gotten the peculiar idea that temptations are terrible things. Certainly struggling against temptation isn't on anyone's list of fun things to do. But temptations aren't really *bad*.

Remember Adam and Eve. God placed this special tree in Eden and told the first pair not to eat its fruit. Why? It wasn't a trap, if that's what you've been taught. God wasn't hiding in nearby bushes, waiting to pounce when one or the other succumbed. Actually, the tree was important for another reason. You see, God determined that we human beings would be special. Alone in all creation, we would be created in His own image. Like God, these new living beings would be able to love, to think, to create, to relate . . . and to choose.

That's the significance of the tree. To be like God, humanity must have the chance to choose between good and evil.

Adam and Eve must have been tempted many times as they strolled hand in hand in the garden. The fruit seemed good for food and looked tasty. They often must have exercised their ability to choose, and turned away. Finally, picking a moment when the pair was separated, Satan confused Eve. She used her freedom to choose wrongly.

But the tree that was the occasion for the Fall was a good gift, not a trap. It was an opportunity to choose the right and become stronger, as well as an opportunity to choose the wrong and grow weak.

How then are we to view our temptations? As fearful things, forcing a struggle we are sure to lose, under the scrutiny of a God determined to catch us out? Or as a fresh opportunity to choose good; a fresh occasion for the joy that follows when we overcome through the strengthening love of God. Temptations are serious. But they are not *bad*. When we choose the right, we discover they are God's good gifts to us, which strengthen us rather than destroy.

The anatomy of temptation. James protects us from the notion that temptations are evils, brought on us by God. He explains that "each one is tempted when, by his own evil desire, he is dragged away and enticed" (1:14). Our problem isn't in the circumstances, but in ourselves. Temptation is sin's inner reaction to situations, pulling us toward a wrong rather than a right response. "God cannot be tempted by evil," James explains, "nor does he tempt anyone" (1:13). The pull we feel toward the wrong, that if we so choose will become an act of sin, is not from God. Ever. God gives us only "good and perfect" gifts (1:17).

Paul and the writer of the letter to the Hebrews both talk about gifts God has given us for times of temptation. God always gives us a way of escape (1 Cor. 10:13), and God always gives us sympathetic understanding and help (Heb. 4:15, 16). Jesus experienced temptation without ever choosing sin. He who became a human being understands our weaknesses. When we turn to Him, He provides "grace to help in time of need."

Temptation is experienced, then, when a situation offers us a choice between good and bad, and when something within pulls us toward the bad. God does not condemn us for our inclinations. He knows how weak we are. And He promises us help, that we might choose the good.

Overcoming temptation. Jesus' own experience with temptation, reported in the Gospels of Matthew and Luke, provides us a model for dealing with our temptations. Matthew 4 and Luke 4 both portray Jesus turning to Scripture for specific guidance, and then determining to do what the Word of God says.

Jesus' use of Scripture was far from magical. He simply recalled guiding principles, and chose to act on them. Thus we return to the basic issue in all temptation: the will of man, and the will of God. God tells us what is good. We are given the wonderful privilege of choosing to listen to His voice, and to obey.

We are never to ask God for temptations (cf. Matt. 6:13). As Jesus pointed out, situations that involve temptation to sin are sure to come (Matt. 18:7). They arise aplenty in our twisted world. But when such situations do come, and we feel temptation's pull, we need not cower in terror. Instead we can recognize the inner source of our feelings, and exercise that freedom God has renewed for us in Christ. When temptations come, we can choose to do what is good.

TIME. We all have vastly different amounts of money. But everyone has exactly the same amount of time. You and I can't be good stewards of cash we don't have. But we can be good stewards of our time.

TITHING. It's a grand old tradition. And a not unreasonable guideline. But it's an Old Testament regulation never repeated in the New Testament epistles. For New Testament principles, see → **GIVING**

TOLERANCE. Tolerance? Too often today it means being indifferent about evil. God help us never to be tolerant of sin. But intolerance isn't right either, particularly when intolerance focuses not on wrongs but on persons. And we Christians do love to claim the right to condemn.

God is intolerant of evil but tolerant of sinners. He knows they have to come close enough to Him to discover His forgiveness and love and isn't at all eager to drive them away.

It's not easy. But we're called to walk the divine tightrope. We too must find ways to resist sin . . . and welcome the sinners to whom we are to offer Jesus' kind of love.

"TONGUES."   In many churches it's a scare word. In others, it's the very touchstone of spiritual life. Hundreds of congregations have split over "tongues," and thousands of individuals have been torn by doubt and uncertainty. "Tongues" is undoubtedly one of those theological and emotional questions that merits the descriptive adjective, "divisive."

What are "tongues"?   The New Testament Book of Acts reports that on the day the Spirit came to unite the disciples into the church, the body of Christ, visitors in Jerusalem heard the believers speaking in their own languages. Luke says they "began to speak in other tongues" (Acts 2:4). The same term is used when Cornelius, the first Gentile convert, responded to Peter's message by praising God and "speaking in tongues" (Acts 10:46). While the gift of tongues is not mentioned in the other New Testament epistles, Paul has much to say about it in 1 Corinthians. He says that he himself has and exercises the gift, but takes pains to correct Corinthian misunderstandings and abuses. There seems no question that the experiences described in Acts and Corinthians are not quite the same: both are called "tongues," but in early Acts the listeners heard their own language. In later Acts and Corinthians, the tongues seem to have been unintelligible except to those with the related gift of interpreting.

Why the modern emphasis on "tongues"?   Many Christians have been concerned at times when the church of Jesus seems powerless. At such times, believers have searched the Scriptures to discover some key to the lost dynamic. One group came to the conclusion that the church had lost its vision of the power available through the person of the Holy Spirit. The Spirit's power glows on the pages of Acts and in the history of the early church. That power, if claimed by faith, should be available to God's people today. The lost dynamic, these believers concluded, was the expectation that God's Spirit would again bring explosive power to the people of God, if only the people of God would once again take the supernatural seriously.

Out of this conviction, a theology of the Spirit was developed, with fresh insights and understandings. Part of that theology was the conviction that Christians could take a step beyond faith in Jesus, to experience a baptism by the Spirit, and that that baptism would be evidenced by speaking in tongues.

In the decades since this movement began a number of branchings have taken place. Not all Charismatics [the name often identified with speaking in tongues, but meaning simply those who emphasize the Spirit's empowering gifts] have the same view of the role of tongues. But in general they hold the common belief that, even if tongues are not for all, the gift *is* operative today, and that there is a special relationship with the Spirit available to believers that is not known by all Christians.

Why the conflict?   The conflict that has often developed between Charismatics and noncharismatics has two roots. One is theological. Each group is convinced its understanding is biblical, and that the other group distorts Scripture by its interpretation. Because Truth is important to each group, this dispute over doctrine is serious. →
DOCTRINAL DISPUTES

The other cause of conflict is emotional. Convinced Charismatics are often enthusiasts: they want other Christians to experience what they believe is their own richer experience. Sometimes immature Charismatics have urged their views in divisive ways—and immature noncharismatics have struck back. Congregations have been polarized by the emotional dynamics of attack and defense as well as by doctrinal differences. To many noncharismatic pastors and lay leaders, tongues-speaking brethren represent a real threat, so they are rejected with fear.

The first issue in any such conflict is not who is right and who is wrong. None of us has a complete understanding of Truth, as the Bible reminds us (1 Cor. 8:1–3). But there is one Truth that is so basic it cannot be overlooked. People who belong to Jesus, whatever their differences, are brothers and sisters in the family of God. The one overwhelming obligation we owe others in the family

489

is love (Rom. 13:8–14). We can differ with one another. But we cannot reject or scorn one another. Having been an elder in a congregation in which about two-thirds were noncharismatics, and another third did speak in tongues, I can say with assurance that when we commit ourselves to love, this difference need not divide.

How to maintain unity. Our foundational commitment to one another is based on the fact that God accepts an individual into His family through faith in Jesus Christ. We can never reject such a brother or sister, or refuse to love him or her. So we share differences, and seek honestly to understand each other's views. But we also grant each other freedom to be responsible to Jesus, who is Lord, for our convictions. In our relationship we learn to stress those great areas in which we agree—the deity of Jesus, the gospel of life through Him, the authority of the Word, the empowering of the Spirit, and our shared concern that we each learn to be better disciples, more obedient to our common Lord.

The differences we have will be real. But we can live with differences. We cannot live close to Jesus if we disobey His commandment to love (John 13:33, 34). → **CONFLICT AND RESOLUTION**

TOUCHING. Sometimes there's no other way to show love.

TRADITION. There's nothing wrong with tradition. Until we mistake it for the voice of God.

TRUST. The secret of building trust relationships is to be trustworthy.

TRUTH. Robert Louis Stevenson describes the young hero of *Kidnapped* as sitting on a winding stone stair without a candle, and being told he is to sleep in the room at the top. The youngster stumbles upward in the pitch dark, his hand against the rough-hewn wall. As he comes to the upper landing, about to step through the promised

but unseen door, a flash of lightning illumines empty
space. The uncle, fearful of the boy's claim on the estate,
intended him to be dashed to death on hidden rocks at the
base of the unfinished stair.

The scene Stevenson describes helps us understand
the meaning of the biblical term, Truth. In both Testaments, its underlying meaning stresses a "correspondence
with reality." Like the flash of lightning, the Word of God
as Truth unveils the hidden realities of the dark world
through which we stumble. Through the Word we come to
know that which we could never have discovered on our
own.

The Bible also links our freedom to God's Truth.
"Knowing the truth," means letting Jesus' words guide us
away from the dangers always lurking on the edges of our
lives, to show us our next, safe step. Walking in that light,
we discover that we are free indeed: free from all that
hurts, and free to experience all that helps. When we live
the Truth, we become disciples of our Lord.

† † †

UNCOMPROMISING. It's one thing to have an
uncompromising commitment to doing good. And quite
another to take an uncompromising attitude in our relationships with others. The one wins respect, the other
loses it. The one is a virtue, the other a vice. The one helps
to overcome weakness, the other is a weakness. The one
builds character, the other destroys closeness. The one
expresses our values, the other our pride. The one demonstrates love for God, the other a lack of love for our
brothers and sisters. The one shows our determination to
overcome human weaknesses, and the other shows our
determination to ignore them. It takes grace to maintain an
uncompromising commitment to good. It takes even more
grace to remain open, sensitive, and responsive to loved
ones and friends.

UNDERSTANDING YOUR BIBLE. The Bible is a book of revelation: a message from God delivered in human language. It's intended to be understood. It's intended to give you and me guidance. While the Bible is rich and complex, it is *not* difficult to interpret. The Bible is God's Word to common men, not His puzzle to be unraveled only by theologians.

How then do you and I go about understanding the Bible so we experience His guidance? Here are the simple steps you can take to building your understanding of the Bible.

Get a good modern version. There are many translations and paraphrases of the Bible in English. Paraphrases (like *Living Letters* or the *Good News* version) are attempts to capture the sense of the original. Translations are more careful attempts to render the original words. Paraphrases may be interesting but involve too much interpretation to be used as a basic study text. Probably the best current version for accuracy and readability is the New International Version (niv). This paragraphed, readable translation is a text you can trust as your basic study Bible.

Get an inexpensive Bible Handbook. There are many kinds of literature in the Bible. Its 66 books are written against the background of changing historical settings. A good Bible handbook will give you an overview of every paragraph in every book of the Bible, and help you understand the setting and theme of each book. This kind of information is very important if we are to understand what God is saying to you and me today—and what may not apply directly to us. I'm partial to the *Word Bible Handbook,* published in 1982, because it gives paragraph by paragraph orientation. And because I wrote it.

Read to understand, and then listen. Before we can apply a particular Bible teaching to our life, we need to understand what God is saying. Too often Christians take a verse out of context and treat it as God's guidance to them. Understanding the Bible isn't a magical process, such as pointing at a verse and then acting on it. Understanding the Bible calls for us to master the who, what, when, where, and why of what a Scripture passage states, and *then* to see how it relates to us.

Most of Scripture is written in ordered patterns of thought. The simplest and best method to build understanding is to read a paragraph carefully, and then jot down in a sentence or two what it teaches. When we have a number of sentences summarizing a sequence of paragraphs, we're able to trace the thought [argument] of a chapter or section. We can then go back and look at specific verses, to understand them in their context. (A good Bible handbook will do that job of summarizing argument for you.)

To "listen" to the Bible means to consciously go beyond the first step in study. The first step asks, "What does this paragraph or verse mean?" Going beyond asks, "What does this paragraph or verse mean *for me?*" We are searching now for insights that will help us better understand our own experiences, feelings, decisions, and relationships, as well as help us better understand who God is.

Read ready to obey.   Many images in the Bible make it clear that we are to respond to what we read. Scripture, the psalmist says, is a light to our path. The picture is of an individual walking through the night, holding a glowing lamp that shows just enough for him to take each next step. As we study the Bible and apply what we learn to ourselves, God shows us how to take our next steps. When we understand this character of Scripture, and realize that the Holy Spirit is with us, to use God's Word to show us our next step, we understand the importance of obedience. It is only as we act on what God shows us in Scripture that we experience the benefit of God's Word in our lives.

Read with regularity.   To understand our Bibles we need to read them regularly. As we spend time daily in God's Word, learning to recognize God's thoughts and values, and listening daily to His guidance for our next steps, we are gradually reshaped and transformed. The Bible is not simply a book to turn to in crisis. It is a book on which to build our whole lives. You and I can come to the Word with a great sense of joy. In Scripture we will meet God. Through Scripture we will grow. In living by Scripture, our lives will be transformed and enriched.

Yes, the Bible is a book that *you* can understand.

UNFORGIVABLE SIN. I've talked with several people tormented by the fear that they might have committed the "unforgivable sin." The phrase, of course, comes from a single incident repeated in three of the Gospels, defined in each as blasphemy against the Holy Spirit. But the fear doesn't arise from the passages. In fact, no one I've spoken with who has this fear has even tried to understand the passage. I remember one young woman who somehow got my Arizona phone number, and called me regularly from Canada. A talk would reduce her fear momentarily, but in a day or so she'd call again. So if you're plagued with anxiety and doubt that just won't go away, and you wonder if you've committed that "unpardonable sin," perhaps the first thing to ask yourself is whether you've talked with a Christian counselor, and tried to gain insight into possible roots of your anxiety. → ANXIETY → COUNSELING

The reason you need to look elsewhere is, as someone has observed, if you're worried that you've committed the unpardonable sin, you can't have.

The incident that stimulated Jesus' remark (cf. Matt. 12; Mark 3; Luke 12) was a vicious attack on Jesus by Pharisees. They observed the great miracles He performed in the power of the Holy Spirit. But completely rejecting Jesus' claim to be Lord and promised Messiah (cf. Matt. 12:1–14, 15–21), these hardened enemies tried to explain Jesus' miracles as works done by demonic rather than divine power. Jesus' statement offers forgiveness for "every sin and blasphemy," but states that "the blasphemy against the Spirit will not be forgiven" (12:31, 32). Jesus' point is that anyone so hardened against God that he refuses to recognize the Son even when attested by God's Spirit, and calls His truth a lie, *cannot* be forgiven. Such a person rejects the gospel offer.

This is why worry about committing the "unforgivable sin" is evidence that it has *not* been committed. The anxious *do* believe the gospel: they simply cannot bring themselves to believe that God will accept *them*. The angry Pharisees who hated Jesus would not acknowledge Him at all, but bitterly accused Him of operating in Satan's power rather than the Spirit's power. These men were not worried they might not be forgiven; they were furious that anyone would suggest they required forgiveness, especially a forgiveness offered by Jesus!

There are, no doubt, some today who also angrily reject every suggestion that the gospel might be true. They will not be forgiven as long as their attitude persists. But for every person who hears of Jesus' love, and wonders fearfully if the promise of forgiveness might be for him, the promise of God is clear: whosoever will, may come.
→ BELIEVING IN

UNITY. The biblical images are powerful, the teaching direct. We are linked to one another as cells of a single body, as branches growing out of one vine, as bricks mortared lovingly by the divine builder into a single temple. All this is made possible because Jesus has destroyed old barriers of hostility, to make different cultures one so there is "one body and one Spirit—just as you were called to one hope when you were called—one Lord, one faith, one baptism; one God and Father of all, who is over all and through all and in all" (Eph. 4:4, 5).

This unity exists and is to be experienced: we are to "make every effort to keep the unity of the Spirit." We are to serve one another so that we can all be built up, "until we all reach unity in the faith and in the knowledge of the Son of God and become mature" (4:3, 13).

Just how our unity is to be expressed has been a matter of much debate. → ECUMENICAL MOVEMENT But the fact that unity is our heritage in Christ is clearly taught throughout the Word. In fact, unity was a major thrust of

Jesus' last recorded prayer. About to leave the disciples, He prayed in Gethsemane that believers might "be one as we [Father/Son] are one" (John 17:11, 21–23). There is little you or I can do about universal "unity." But we have everything to do with our own experience of unity and the observable, local expression of oneness that lets the world around us know that Jesus is real and living and vital, and still able to save (17:20–23).

UNSAVED LOVED ONES. For many of us, unsaved family and friends cause continual concern. We are not sure just how to pray for them. We're even more uncertain about how we can communicate our faith effectively. What biblical principles can guide us?

"You and your house." Paul told a Philippian jailer, "believe in the Lord Jesus, and you will be saved." Then he added, "and your household" (Acts 16:31). Some Christians have fastened on this statement, believing it expresses God's commitment to bring the family members of believers to salvation. Others understand Paul to simply state the universality of the gospel offer, and note that the next verse reports that Paul went to tell the Good News about Jesus to the jailer and "all the others in his house." It is also important to note that "household" in New Testament times did not mean only "family," but included slaves, servants, and employees.

Yet it is clear that members of believers' families do have a unique opportunity to come to know God. As guardians of a believing spouse, they even serve the Lord (1 Cor. 7:14). God has shown a special goodness to family members by placing a believer among them to show and share the gospel.

Praying for family. Prayer has sometimes seemed to pose a problem for concerned believers. They want to pray with faith and not fear, but don't know how confident they can be that their loved ones will be saved. This hesitation comes at least in part from misunderstanding so-called "conditions" for answered prayer. → **PRAYER** The wonderful truth is that our confidence in prayer is not in whether we "do it right," but in the God to whom we bring our requests. We know that God shares our concern for our loved ones: we are invited to pray, and told that God "wants all men to be saved and to come to a knowledge of the truth" (1 Tim. 2:4). Praying for our loved ones is never out of the will of God. We can pray in fullest confidence that our request is in harmony with God's own desire.

Witnessing to family.   It's often hardest to witness to parents, spouses, and children. Even when our relationship is ideal, telling about Jesus and our new experience with Him may create doubt, ridicule, or even resentment. It's not always like this, of course. But all too often it seems that intimacy creates its own barriers. In such cases, aggressive witnessing may do more harm than good.

This thought is behind Peter's instruction to wives in his first letter: "Wives, in the same way be submissive to your husbands so that, if any of them do not believe the word, they may be won over without talk by the behavior of their wives, when they see the purity and reverence of your lives" (3:1, 2). We can communicate the gospel better at times without words, by showing love and responsiveness that win a partner over. → SUBMISSIVENESS

The stress here and in other New Testament passages helps us realize that all evangelism → EVANGELISM is a gentle, loving kind of thing. Even in the face of open opposition, "the Lord's servant must not quarrel; instead, he must be kind to everyone, able to teach, not resentful. Those who oppose him he must gently instruct, in the hope that God will grant them repentance leading to a knowledge of the truth" (2 Tim. 2:24, 25).

What might we suggest as specific guidelines for witnessing to unsaved loved ones?

● Pray regularly for them, that God's Spirit will open their hearts to the gospel. Pray with confidence, knowing that God loves your loved ones even more than you do.

● Pay attention to the quality of your relationship with your loved ones. Seek to be an even better husband, wife, parent, or child than before. Let your own life be a testimony to the fact that Jesus enriches relationships. Be a living advertisement for the faith you want another to accept.

● Talk naturally about your faith and experiences, without pressuring your loved one to make a commitment. It is important to protect a loved one's sense of freedom to make his or her own choice, without coercion.

● Form a fellowship with others who have unsaved loved ones, to pray together and encourage one another.

● Set no goals or expectations related to time. God may work and faith may come quickly. Or your quiet, faithful loving and sharing may continue for years before response comes.

● Encourage yourself with passages like Hebrews 10:35, 36. "Do not throw away your confidence; it will be richly rewarded. You need to persevere so that when you have done the will of God, you will receive what he has promised."

† † †

VALUES. We all evaluate, looking at things and choices to rank them bad, good, better, or best. But something is only *a* value to me if it is important enough for me to act on.

VEGETARIANISM. For tens of thousands of Americans, vegetarianism is the way to go. Low cholesterol. Less heart disease. Health! The motive may be religious, it may be economic, or health related. Whatever the motive, thousands move into—and out of—a vegetarian lifestyle each year.

Vegetarian diets. There are three basic types of vegetarianism. ● The strict diet rules out everything of animal origin. Eggs, milk, and cheese are out, as is ice cream. ● The lacto vegetarian diet permits milk and dairy products. But still no meat, poultry, fish, or eggs. ● The ovo-lacto vegetarian diet adds milk and eggs to the basic fruit and vegetable regime.

Health. Two major advantages of the vegetarian diet seem to be the reduction of cholesterol and saturated fats, related to heart disease, and the addition of fibre, believed by some to reduce the danger of colon cancers. The vegetarian does need to take special care in planning his diet to include sources of all the necessary amino acids. This can be done, and books available in all health-food stores explain how. However, strict vegetarians will be deficient in certain essential vitamins, such as B^{12}, and in elements such as calcium and iron, and should take supplements.

Cost. In general, vegetarian diets provide essential nutrients less expensively than regular diets. For instance, 20 grams of protein in dry beans costs only 10 cents; in peanut butter, 17 cents. The same 20 grams of protein in porterhouse steak would cost 79 cents, or in lamb chops, 91 cents. Surprisingly, vegetarian meals can be delicious, and main dishes prepared in great variety. A glance at a vegetarian cookbook will quickly convince the doubter that going vegetarian does not mean giving up tasty food.

Vegetarianism and the Bible. References to vegetarianism in the Bible are few, but fascinating. Genesis 9:3 makes it clear that in the Garden of Eden and in the centuries or millenniums before the Flood, all human beings were vegetarian. Isaiah 65:25 suggests that when Jesus establishes His kingdom, even carnivores will become vegetarian: "The wolf and the lamb will feed together, and the lion will eat straw like the ox. . . . They will neither harm nor destroy in all my holy mountain." It seems unmistakable that in an unfallen world no living being would feed on another.

At the same time, Scripture never imposes vegetarianism, or even suggests that it is a spiritually superior way of life. Romans 14:2 states that adopting vegetarianism as a religious duty is an expression of weak faith, but adds "the man who eats everything must not look down on him who does not, and the man who does not eat everything must not condemn the man who does." We simply are not to judge one another on such issues that must rest on personal conviction. Paul goes even further in 1 Timothy. Warning against "deceiving spirits and things taught by demons" he includes: "They forbid people to marry and order them to abstain from certain foods, which God created to be received with thanksgiving by those who believe and know the truth. For everything God created is good, and nothing is to be rejected if it is received with thanksgiving, because it is consecrated by the word of God and prayer" (4:1–5).

What can we conclude? Simply that believers are free to be either vegetarians or meat eaters. No one is to be "ordered" to choose one way or the other. In this as in so many things, we have been invited by God to use the liberty that is ours as children of God.

VICE. Drawing up juicy lists of vices and glowing compilations of virtues was a popular pastime for Greek Stoics. The Jews seem to have taken up the same pastime in the centuries between the writing of our two testaments. In fact, some think that Jesus may have been quoting from a popular list of vices when He strung together the catalog found in Mark 7:21ff.: "evil thoughts, sexual immorality, theft, murder, adultery, greed, malice, deceit, lewdness, envy, slander, arrogance, and folly." Only one thing. Jesus did something unusual. To the Pharisees who were obsessed with externals, these things were themselves the evil. But Jesus explained to the confused disciples that vices originate "from within, out of the heart of man." God's solution to human vice is not to identify and decry them. God comes with His transforming gospel to change the hearts from which the vices flow. When Jesus comes, out of the same heart, renewed by Jesus' love, will flow every virtue and every good.

VISIONS. How much reliance should be placed on our own or others' visions? Probably not much. The trouble with visions is that it's difficult to tell which come from our subconscious, which from underdone asparagus, and which from God. Actually, the Lord has solved the problem for us. If we want information from Him, it's laid out for us in Scripture. We can trust the Bible. Visions? We can never be sure. → **PROPHECY**

VITAMINS. Vitamins are chemical compounds necessary for life and well-being. In the past, and in underdeveloped countries today, serious vitamin deficiencies cause a number of diseases. The average diet in the United States and Canada, even though some forms of cooking and preserving lower vitamin levels, provides sufficient vitamin intake. Because most vitamins are water-soluble, extra vitamins typically pass through the system. They are not stored in the body, and seldom become concentrated to a toxic, or harmful, degree. Should we take vitamins then? If our doctor prescribes them. But probably most of the vitamins taken in our country are more helpful to the companies that sell them than to the people who take them.

† † †

WAITING. In our "I want it *now*" society, waiting is hard. Particularly when TV proclaims that every problem can be resolved in 30 or 60 minutes. It's hard for us when we realize that most things in life have no quick solution: many of our years will be spent looking for something we hope to have, but do not have now.

God, however, seems to have a marvelous capacity for waiting. He waits patiently for us to respond to Him. He walks beside us as we stumble toward godliness, and no one senses anger or impatience, but only overflowing grace.

The psalmist David knew the importance of trusting God for the timing in things. In Psalm 37 David encourages us to trust the Lord and do good, then to "be still before the LORD and wait patiently for him" (v. 7). We're not to fret at the successes of evil: in God's own "little while" the "wicked will be no more" and "the meek will inherit the land and enjoy great peace" (vv. 10, 11). God's timing may not be ours. And God's sense of timing hasn't been shaped by television. So let's relax. "Wait for the LORD and keep his way," David teaches us. It is up to God when we will experience the promise, "He will exalt you to possess the land" (v. 34).

WAR. It's Memorial Day, 1982, as I write this. On the TV a pregnant Argentine woman follows the body of her Ensign husband, while his father shakes his fist for the camera, vowing vengeance on Great Britain. The scene is quickly replaced by shots of a funeral in England. There is a montage of victory headlines and interviews in which the man and woman on the street promise in traditional British fashion that England will carry on.

There may be necessary wars. But there are no just wars. Good men may come to the conviction that they have to fight, but fighting is never good. God will work despite war, for He is able even to turn injustice to the believer's benefit. But God hates war as He does all sin. For His people to glory in battle is nothing less than evil. James makes it clear. "What causes fights and quarrels among you? Don't they come from your desires that battle within you? You want something but don't get it. You kill and covet, but cannot have what you want. You quarrel and fight" (4:1–2). We can never be justified in the suffering we cause the widows and the orphans or the men who die. Some wars may be necessary. But very few. And none are just. → PACIFISM

WEAKNESS. Weaknesses are only a problem when we try to hide them from ourselves or others. At least, that's the point of view taken by the apostle Paul, who discovered the great benefit God intends weaknesses to confer. Paul talks about his experience in 2 Corinthians 12, reporting that the Lord explained to him, "'My grace is sufficient for you, for my power is made perfect in

weakness. Therefore I will boast all the more gladly
about my weaknesses, so that Christ's power may rest on
me. That is why, for Christ's sake, I delight in weaknesses,
in insults, in hardships, in persecutions, in difficulties. For
when I am weak, then I am strong" (12:9, 10).

How foolish it is to pretend about our weaknesses and
struggle on alone. We can admit them and learn to rely on
Jesus' own perfecting power.

WIDOWS.   Are most widows like the cartoon character "Momma," nagging and complaining and worried
about their children? Or are they more like the widows
postulated in the 1961 book *Growing Old:* busy, happy,
socially active, and looking back on the past without too
much longing? How individuals respond will of course
differ. But neither stereotype is statistically true.

What studies seem to show is that most widows live
on limited incomes. About 90% do not live with married
children. They prefer to live alone and are uncomfortable
about intruding on the lives of their loved ones. Most feel
happier alone: they have a sense of independence and the
feeling of being in a place that is their own.

Widowhood brings particular stresses. There may be
money worries. Old friendship patterns, usually linked to
couples, seldom survive. Some widows choose social isolation. But most are able in time to reach out and build new
circles of friends. The feeling of being a "fifth wheel" is
likely to persist until the new social patterns are developed.

The New Testament prescribed a pattern for the lives
of widows living in biblical times, which reflected that
culture. A widow lived with the extended family, remarried, or devoted herself to ministry as a member of a
"widow's ministry corps" (cf. 1 Tim. 5:3–16). Today
too we need to appreciate the many gifts that widows can
bring to the body of believers, as well as meet the need of
women alone to be important, and a part. → **RETIREMENT**
→ **SINGLENESS**

WIFE BEATING.   Whether it's called conjugal
crime or domestic violence, assaults by husbands on their

wives have become increasingly visible since the mid '70s. Before that, most battered women maintained an embarrassed silence, or they quietly divorced abusive husbands. Many women, trapped in brutal marriages by fear or lack of finances, had no one to turn to even if they had dared to complain.

Today the problem is more in the open, and many stereotypes have been shattered. We've discovered that it's not just the poor and uneducated who are batterers. Wife beating is a middle- and upper-class phenomenon as well.

But why do men beat their wives, and why do wives take such mistreatment? Typically, wife-beaters feel they were not sufficiently loved in childhood. They are often described as angry, resentful, suspicious, competitive, moody, or tense. Jealousy, alcoholism, and frustration, often associated with unemployment, are contributing factors. It's clear that wife-beaters are themselves in desperate need of help, even though many appear respectable outside the home.

What about the wives? Weak or dependent women, who react to violence by trying harder to please, are the most likely targets of repeated beatings.

Guidelines. If you are a battered wife, what options might be open to you? Here are the three most likely, with suggestions from others of what to do.

(1) You might resign yourself to your situation, and determine to endure. If you do, you'll need support. Find someone with whom you can share your experiences; someone who will listen and care. For insight you might check out the public library and read some of the many books now available.

(2) You might want to keep the marriage but realize your husband needs help to change. Here too having a person to talk things through with is important. But you also must face the fact that unless your husband wants help and is willing to seek it, there's little you can do to change him.

(3) You might be convinced you have to leave for

your own safety and for your children. Today one of the best groups to contact for help is a local chapter of the National Organization for Women (NOW). Legal aid offices may also offer help, as might your Family Court. Library research can help uncover a number of sources of aid. If you do become convinced you must leave, don't do it on the spur of the moment. Research first and plan where you'll go and what you'll do.

Biblical.   Many victims of wife beating are troubled by a sense of personal guilt. They feel that somehow they are to blame for their husband's actions. It is important for them to realize that no fault justifies violence and abuse. →
GUILT AND GUILT FEELINGS

Other wives are motivated to stay in an abusive marriage because of their conviction that divorce is never right. This attitude toward marriage is commendable. But when Jesus gave the rationale for the Old Testament's institution of divorce, He said that God permits divorce "because your hearts were hard" (Matt. 19:8). Jesus meant that God, knowing how sin warps human relationships, was fully aware that some marriages would be harmful rather than healing. Marriages are never to be lightly dissolved. But divorce *is* a biblically justified option. → DIVORCE AND REMARRIAGE

Actually, there are actions a battered wife can take that are short of divorce. Separation is legally and biblically recognized, and leaves the door open for reconciliation. It is even possible that leaving may jolt a husband into counseling, and be a step toward saving the marriage. However, if a wife does leave it's important that she stay away until the husband has actually appeared for several therapy sessions with a qualified counselor. Otherwise her return will encourage re-establishing the old pattern.

What if you are family or friends, and you know of battered wives? What can you do? Certainly be ready to listen and give warm support. Probably also research sources of help available in your community. But in it all, friends need to respect the integrity of the wife and resist telling her what she should do. Like each of us, battered wives must find personal guidance and direction from the Lord, seeking His wisdom to deal with this tragedy in their lives.

WILLS. Everyone needs to make a will, for a simple reason. If you don't leave a will, state law will determine how your estate is divided. It might not be distributed as you wish. Good wills can also avoid much tax liability. Having a lawyer work on yours is likely to mean savings in the end.

What things are important when drawing up your will? List all your assets and possessions. If you have young children, set up a guardianship in case both parents die. Select an executor, who will see that your possessions are distributed as you intend. Because state laws differ, if you move you'll probably want to check whether your will needs to be redrawn.

Probably, like me, you expect the Lord to come before you die. He may. But He may not. So making out a will is simply good stewardship.

WOMEN IN THE CHURCH. Women preachers? Women elders? Women deacons? Women teaching men in Sunday school? Only a few these days answer with that resounding No! we would have heard just a handful of decades ago. We're much more aware these days that women are persons with significance and gifts and callings. If it were not for two or three biblical passages that lead some to hesitate, just about everyone would probably have joined the chorus of those shouting an enthusiastic—or demanding—Yes. So what about women in the church, and especially in church leadership? While closely linked with other women's issues, this one is distinct and special. → FEMININE AND MASCULINE → FEMINISM → HEAD OF THE HOUSE → SUBMISSIVENESS

General attitude toward women. In the ancient world women were often considered inferior, and the male invariably exercised leadership and legal responsibility. The Old Testament uniquely made a place for women in worship: a place that later Judaism denied them. The church brought revolutionary change, opening worship to women in new ways and inviting unexpected participation. Peter understood Pentecost as the arrival of the day of the Spirit, when "your sons and your daughters will prophesy" (Acts 2:17). Women like Priscilla are acknowledged by Paul as "my fellow worker in Christ" (Rom. 16:3). Galatians asserts that the old social distinctions that existed between Jew and Greek, slave and free, and male and female, are swallowed up in a oneness that comes through personal relationship with Jesus Christ (Gal. 3:26–28). Spiritual gifts enabling ministry are extended to all, and when the community gathers women are expected to pray and prophesy—but with covered heads (1 Cor. 11:5). Anyone sensitive to the attitude toward women in every significant culture in New Testament times, must be stunned by the open door through which women were invited within the church. The Christian community has not kept those doors open, any more than Judaism maintained the stance of the Old Testament Scriptures. But testimony to the significance of women burns bright on the pages of our New Testament.

Limitations on women's role. While regarding women as full participants in the life of the congregation, many today see a limitation when it comes to church office. They note that none of the Twelve were women, and that 1 Timothy 2 and 3 seem to restrict the office of elder/bishop/presbyter [carrying responsibility for spiritual oversight] to men. This would involve positions calling for authoritative teaching or exercise of discipline over the whole local body of men and women.

The office of deacon [taking the lead in ministry to meet physical needs within or outside the fellowship] is unquestionably open to women, as Phoebe (Rom. 16:1) is identified as a deacon of the church of Cenchrea.

Those who believe Scripture teaches this kind of limitation will often vary in their application. In some traditions the paid "preacher" is not an elder responsible for spiritual oversight, and women are accepted in professional ministry. To others it seems this role is denied. To some teaching a Bible class on Sunday or in homes is not viewed as "authoritative teaching," a phrase taken to mean the judgment of the leaders of a congregation given on a matter in dispute that calls for an interpretation of Scripture.

Others reject this particular understanding of those passages dealing with women and leadership. Texts have been dismissed as reflecting of Paul's male bias, condemned as inconsistent, or explained away as expressing guidelines appropriate to first-century culture, but not appropriate in our culture where women are better understood and more highly valued. Others who take the Scriptures seriously and honor the Word of God have advanced careful arguments that suggest that 1 Corinthians 11:2–16; 14:33–35; 1 Timothy 2:8–15 and 3:1–13 are not as restrictive as they have been understood.

The debate and the scholarship it has stimulated seem to focus on one area and to raise a number of questions of application.

(1) If there are restrictions on women's role, those restrictions clearly are limited to the elder [overseer] ministry.

(2) The application of this limitation is not clear, and many gray areas exist. It would seem clear by this interpretation that women would not be elected elders, but . . .

- What about paid minister?
- What about teacher of a mixed Bible class?
- What about chairman of a church board or committee?
- Etc.

Two critical issues. Each local congregation or fellowship of churches must work through its own understanding of the biblical passages. There are dozens of books now in Christian bookstores that examine and argue the passages. In doing so, however, there are two critical issues that must be considered within the framework of one's convictions.

• Women *are* spiritually gifted members of the body of Christ. Each woman, like each man, is to be developed as a ministering person, to make her own vital contribution on which the spiritual health and well-being of the Christian community depends. We have not broken the bonds of our own cultural perception of women in the church, nor affirmed them as the Scriptures do. Whatever our conclusions on the leadership question, we need the contribution women can make—and have been denied the opportunity to make.

• We must maintain our balance in a very difficult area. If we should conclude that the elder role is not open to women (even if we conclude all other roles are), it will seem to be discrimination. It's not enough to point out that there are many men who are not elders: women will be excluded because they are women. Inferiority will be implied, even though this may not be the case at all. On the other hand, our sensitivity to the legitimate concerns of women and our commitment to the equality of persons may lead us to reject or slant our interpretation of relevant biblical passages. Somehow we must deny inferiority, affirm full personhood, remain true to Scripture, and seek actively to equip all women and all men for ministering works (Eph. 4:16).

WORK.   Values are changing, and the word "work" no longer has that sterling ring that once echoed in the old days of the "Protestant work ethic." The change is reflected in a late '70s survey by the University of Michigan, which reported that more than one in four American workers (27%) "felt so ashamed of the quality of the products they were producing that they would not want to buy them themselves." The recession of the early '80s may have halted or reversed the trend. But more emphasis is given to "humanizing" work than to building healthy attitudes toward work.

What is "humanizing" work? Basically the phrase has come to indicate that a job should be designed so that it (1) does not damage, degrade, or consistently bore the worker; (2) will be interesting and satisfying; (3) will utilize the skills the worker has and provide opportunities to acquire new skills; (4) will leave unimpaired the worker's ability to function as spouse, parent, citizen, and friend; and (5) will pay a wage that enables the worker to live a "comfortable life." These are, of course, fine goals. They do help us realize that any employer is responsible to an employee for more than his or her wages. But in focusing on job conditions, we take our attention away from the meaning of work and from our own attitudes toward our work.

Work as a ministry. This is one of the first considerations from a Christian point of view. Every job (even slavery in New Testament days) provided an opportunity to serve others in some way. The person on the assembly line in Detroit isn't just building cars: he or she is serving the buyer by providing safe transportation. The job may be boring. But viewed as ministry, it is lifted beyond meaningless repetition. Garbage collecting, even when upgraded by the label "sanitation engineer," is hardly an occupation that "utilizes the skills the worker has and provides opportunities to acquire new skills." But no one who has suffered through a collector's strike can doubt that this work is essential; a ministry to individuals and the whole community. Work understood as ministry is sanctified, and doing our jobs well becomes a significant way of serving Jesus Christ (Eph. 6:7).

Work as source of autonomy and responsibility. The New Testament is very clear that all who are able are to work for their own living, rather than remain idle and live off others (2 Thess. 3:6–13). From the beginning God provided work as a vital gift, enabling each person to maintain the respect won only by accepting responsibility for himself as an autonomous rather than dependent person (cf. Gen. 2:15). Even the meanest job that enables us to gain this type of self respect and to be responsible, has great worth and value to us.

Work as a means for gaining riches. This theme has

historically been associated with the Protestant work ethic. It reflects the notion that God will bless with material riches those who do good. But that idea is not reflected in the New Testament. Instead, Ephesians 4:28 presents work as both "useful" (e.g., a ministry) and as a way to earn money "that he may have something to share with those in need." In fact, Timothy is warned that "people who want to get rich fall into temptation and a trap" (1 Tim. 6:6–10). To view work primarily as a way of getting rich, rather than as a means to (1) minister, (2) win autonomy, and (3) be able to help others who are in need, is to distort the nature and the glory of work from a call to responsible servanthood to an invitation to selfishness.

Perhaps that's what is so troubling about the talk of work in the world around us, and the work values that research shows have captured our younger generations. Do I evaluate my work merely in terms of what it offers me? Or do I evaluate my work in terms of what it enables me to do for others?

God's perspective seems clear.

Work is ministry.

Work gives you and me opportunities to serve.

WORSHIP. In the broadest sense, worship is every appropriate response we make to God. In the most common biblical sense, and the most exciting, worship is talking or singing to God, simply telling Him how wonderful He is. → **PRAISE**

YES. For people who can't say "No," "Yes" is a terrifying word. They feel a tremendous pressure to agree; to go along with the crowd. They fear the loss or withdrawal of love. Or they feel an anguished uncertainty: self-doubt keeps them from expressing what they believe or feel.

The picture may seem overdrawn, but for too many trapped in bondage to "Yes" it is all too familiar.

It probably doesn't help to tell such people that it's better to be wrong than to surrender responsibility for ourselves to others. But it is. We Christians are each responsible to a single master, Christ, who alone is Lord. Under Him we have been given the freedom to "be fully convinced" in our own mind, and then to act on our convictions (cf. Rom. 14:5–8).

"Yes" and "No" are the symbol of our responsibility and of our freedom. Let's not surrender our right to choose to anyone. → DECISION MAKING

YOUTH. Youth isn't, as some have suggested, "wasted on the young." The older I grow, the more I discover that however the body sags and the knee joints pain, I'm still young and fresh inside. What a prospect! Time and eternity to grow wiser while staying young.

† † †

ZEAL. Zeal is something like sincerity: both make good qualities, but poor excuses. Believing sincerely can never make what a person believes true, and acting zealously can never make what we do right. That was the fault, according to the Old Testament and New Testament, of the Jewish leaders. They had a "zeal for God" but it was "not according to knowledge" (Rom. 10:2; Gal. 1:14; cf. Prov. 19:2). It's good for you and me to be zealous in our faith. But zeal is never a good excuse for rushing in insensitively to overwhelm others. God appreciates our zeal. But He commands us to temper it with love.

ZEST. The word never appears in the Bible. But it captures the excitement that is our heritage as Jesus' people. We meet each day with zest and enthusiasm, for it holds a fresh experience of Jesus. We greet each challenge with zest and enthusiasm, for it provides a fresh opportunity to experience Jesus' power.

Living close to Jesus, may you know the zest of a life lived in His presence and power.

ZOOS.   My *Enclyclopedia Britanica* says simply that a zoo is a place where wild animals are exhibited in captivity.

Zoos aren't a new invention. They are suggested by Egyptian tomb pictures from 2500 B.C. And the Chinese emperor Wen Wang, about 1100 B.C., kept a 1500-acre zoo he called the Garden of Intelligence.

I suppose that zoos are a good place to take boys and girls to impress them with the wonder of God's creation. But I'm glad that God doesn't operate with a zoo mentality.

God doesn't capture us in our wild state and immediately thrust us into zoos to be protected and cared for. His church isn't a zoological garden, with bars and moats constructed of dos and dont's, or even of convictions. When God captures our hearts, He turns us back to live in the wilds of human society. Why should He set up barriers? God doesn't want to protect the world from us. And because Jesus is with us, we don't need to retreat behind bars to protect ourselves from them.